The Westminster Handbook to Women in American Religious History

Editors
SUSAN HILL LINDLEY
ELEANOR J. STEBNER

Westminster John Knox Press
LOUISVILLE • LONDON

Book design by Sharon Adams
Cover design by Eric Walljasper, Minneapolis, MN
Cover photos: Margaret Fuller, Elizabeth Caddy Stanton, Lucretia Mott, and Sojourner Truth courtesy of GettyImages/Hulton Archive

First edition

Published by Westminster John Knox Press
Louisville, Kentucky

This book is printed on acid-free paper that meets the American National Standards Institute Z39.48 standard. ♾

PRINTED IN THE UNITED STATES OF AMERICA

08 09 10 11 12 13 14 15 16 — 10 9 8 7 6 5 4 3 2 1

Library of Congress Cataloging-in-Publication Data is on file
at the Library of Congress, Washington, DC.

The Westminster Handbook to Women in American Religious History

Dedicated to
Susan Hill Lindley (1945–2005)
who never stopped believing in the
transformative good of women's religious history

Contents

Preface

Toward the end of 2000 Donald K. McKim, editor for academic and reference works for Westminster John Knox Press, asked Susan Hill Lindley if she would consider coediting a dictionary devoted to women and religion in North America. Lindley was an excellent choice on his part. A respected scholar and beloved teacher, Lindley had started teaching at St. Olaf College in 1976, two years after she had received her doctorate from Duke University. As the first full-time female faculty member in the religion department, Lindley was widely published on topics such as the social gospel, feminist theology, and women's religious history. Her book, *"You Have Stept Out of Your Place": A History of Women and Religion in America* (1996), was the first narrative one-volume text published on women and religion in the United States. Lindley, however, was not only a dedicated professor and academic, she was also active in her own religious community, the Episcopal Church in the U.S.A., on local and national levels.

Lindley decided to go ahead with the project—she considered it to be her last major professional contribution to her discipline—even though she could not find a coeditor with whom to work. The goal of the reference work was to provide an accessible (and affordable) one-volume book for scholars, religious leaders, students, and the general public. She knew that other solid sources existed on this topic (some of which are listed as our standard sources). She also knew that the *Encyclopedia of Women and Religion in North America* (ed. Rosemary Skinner Keller et al.) was in process. The proposed Westminster book therefore needed to offer something of distinction. In Lindley's original conception, it was to be unique in at least three ways: (1) while the entries would be mostly biographical, they would highlight not only well-known women but also lesser-known women, many of the latter being renowned only within their particular communities; (2) the entries would emphasize practitioners and leaders (the "faithful") within their various religious communities and would not stress scholars of religion or theologians; and (3) women's organizations and some specific events would be included, but not movements or broader topics since such are discussed quite well in other sources. It goes almost without saying that the book needed to be ecumenical and interreligious so as to more accurately reflect the assorted religious commitments of women.

In order to undertake a project of such scope, Lindley needed financial funding for the project and also experts and advisors to help her identify its content and parameters. She applied for (and received) a generous grant from the Louisville Institute, and she established an advisory board comprising experts who represented various fields of women and religion. The initial advisors were Mary Farrell Bednarowski, Anthea D. Butler, Donald W. Dayton, Sharon Mahood, Barbara E. Reed, Jeannette Rodriguez, Shuly Rubin Schwartz, and myself. A meeting was held in the fall of 2001 in Northfield, Minnesota, and the advisors confirmed the direction of Lindley's vision and decided upon such mundane items as length and style of entries. We decided to include living or contemporary women, but only if they were firsts, founders, or unusually prominent in their fields, or if they were members of underrepresented groups. We also decided to include artists and women in popular culture, if they had a known public religious identity. While the initial advisors generated a preliminary list of entries and direction for the project, the board did not provide the kind of support and exchange of ideas for which Lindley had hoped. Still, Lindley persisted in the project. Specific religious bodies were consulted as a way to identify important entries (and potential authors), and advice was obtained from other consultants, such as Anne Patrick. A second meeting was held with advisors in November 2004 in San Antonio at the American Academy of Religion, which focused mostly on identifying potential contributors to the dictionary.

Lindley intended to finish the project within a few years, but illness interfered with her goals. In 1993 Lindley was first diagnosed with breast cancer. She lived "cancer-free" until late 2001, at which point her cancer metastasized to the lungs. Numerous rounds of chemotherapy kept her going, but such treatments created periods of tremendous fatigue and illness. By the fall of 2004 Lindley asked me if I would complete the book if she was unable to do so herself. I agreed, saying, "Don't worry. Of course I'll take care of it." (Lindley and I had met in 1999 as members of the advisory board for the *Encyclopedia of Women and Religion in North America*, and we had become fast friends.) Even when Lindley asked me to continue the work, I had assumed that she would live into her sixties or even her seventies; perhaps naively, I held on to the notion that she would have untold years to enjoy her life with family and friends and more projects. I simply couldn't imagine the world without her kindness, her commitment to justice, or her scholarship. Her death at the end of 2005 is still mourned by many. Ironically, Lindley did end up with a coeditor on this reference work, even though we would have wished it otherwise.

Many words of thanks need to be expressed. Capable and energetic research assistants were of tremendous aid to both of us. (Special thanks to my research assistants, Daniel Kline and Andrew Bingham, with extra help from Natalie Wing.) Grant money from the Louisville Institute, with extra financial support from the SFU Woodsworth Endowment, enabled this work to proceed until completion. Unwavering encouragement from Don McKim and skilled administrative backing from Dilu Nicholas, both from WJKP, were a lifeline. But the final words of thanks must be extended to the competent and committed authors who have contributed to this resource. A project such as this depends upon seemingly endless conversations and correspondence, and an overall spirit of collaboration. Our hope is that this work may be a worthy offering to the present-day public and to future readers and researchers.

Eleanor J. Stebner
Simon Fraser University

Contributors

Barbara Adle is a doctoral student at Emmanuel College, Toronto School of Theology, in the field of theology and ethics.

Christopher J. Anderson is Methodist librarian and coordinator of special collections at Drew University in Madison, New Jersey.

Dianne Ashton is professor of religion and director of American studies at Rowan University.

Mary Christine Athans, BVM, is professor emerita at the Saint Paul Seminary School of Divinity of the University of St. Thomas, Minnesota.

Craig D. Atwood is the John Comenius visiting professor of Moravian studies at Wake Forest University School of Divinity and theologian-in-residence at Home Moravian Church in Winston-Salem, North Carolina.

Irene Baros-Johnson grew up in New York City, is a graduate of Hunter College and Drew Theological Seminary, and lives in Halifax, Nova Scotia.

Sandra Beardsall is professor of church history and ecumenics at St. Andrew's College in Saskatoon, Saskatchewan, and an ordained minister in the United Church of Canada.

Mary Farrell Bednarowski is professor emerita of religious studies, United Theological Seminary of the Twin Cities.

Lila Corwin Berman is assistant professor of history and religious studies and the Mal and Lea Bank Early Career Professor in Jewish studies at Penn State in University Park, Pennsylvania.

Edith Blumhofer is professor in the history department at Wheaton College in Wheaton, Illinois, where she also directs the Institute for the Study of American Evangelicals.

Catherine Bowler is a doctoral student in American religious history at Duke University in Durham, North Carolina.

Linda B. Brebner is a retired Presbyterian minister (ordained 1965), who served in local congregations, on synod and general assembly staffs of the denomination, and as a professor of theology and ethics in an ecumenical seminary in Lima, Peru.

Sarah Bruer is a diaconal minister in the United Church of Canada and pastors the Rundle Memorial United Church in Banff, Alberta.

Barbara Coeyman is a fellowshiped parish minister in the Unitarian Universalist Association and serves on the boards of the UU Historical Society and the UU Women's Heritage Society.

Oscar Cole-Arnal is professor of church history at the Waterloo Lutheran Seminary and Wilfred Laurier University in Waterloo, Ontario.

Colleen Carpenter Cullinan is assistant professor of theology at the College of St. Catherine in St. Paul, Minnesota.

Mary Sudman Donovan is adjunct professor of history at Hunter College, City University of New York.

Veronica M. Dunne, RNDM, is coordinator of doctor of ministry studies at St. Stephen's College in Edmonton, Alberta.

Keith Durso is a freelance copy editor and writer living in Lawrenceville, Georgia.

Pamela R. Durso is associate executive director of the Baptist History and Heritage Society in Atlanta, Georgia.

Deborah Skolnick Einhorn is a doctoral candidate in the department of Near Eastern and Judaic studies at Brandeis University in Waltham, Massachusetts.

Maria Erling is associate professor of church history and mission at the Lutheran Theological Seminary in Gettysburg, Pennsylvania.

Barbara Fears is a doctoral student in Christian education and congregational studies at Garrett-Evangelical Theological Seminary in Evanston, Illinois, and is affiliated with the United Church of Christ.

Trudy Flynn is program director at Congregation Etz Chayim in Winnipeg, Manitoba.

Matthew Francis is coordinator for youth and young adult ministry for the Orthodox Church in America's Archdiocese of Canada.

Joan S. Friedman is visiting assistant professor of history and religious studies at the College of Wooster in Ohio.

Judith Gibbard is a graduate student in history at the University of Victoria in British Columbia.

Carolyn De Swarte Gifford is a research associate in gender studies at Northwestern University in Evanston, Illinois.

David J. Goa is director of the Chester Ronning Centre for the Study of Religion and Public Life, Augustana campus, University of Alberta, in Camrose, Alberta.

Rebekah Goodyear is an editor at Synaxis Press, a Canadian Orthodox publishing house.

Louise Graves is executive director of the Institute for International Theological Education (Winnipeg) and a minister in the United Church of Canada.

Elaine Guillemin taught at Ryerson University in Toronto, Ontario.

Joan R. Gundersen is founding professor of history emerita at California State University, San Marcos, and a research scholar at the University of Pittsburgh.

Ann M. Harrington, BVM, is professor of history and director of Asian studies at Loyola University Chicago.

Jane Harris is professor of religion at Hendrix College in Conway, Arkansas.

Robynne Rogers Healey is associate professor of history and chair of the department of history, political, and international studies at Trinity Western University in Langley, British Columbia.

Mary J. Henold is assistant professor of American history at Roanoke College in Salem, Virginia.

Elizabeth Hinson-Hasty is associate professor of theology at Bellarmine University in Louisville, Kentucky, and writes on faith and public life, and social gospel theology.

Ephrem Hollermann, OSB, is associate professor of theology and holds the Koch Chair in Catholic Thought and Culture at the College of Saint Benedict/Saint John's University, St. Joseph, Minnesota.

Lydia Huffman Hoyle is associate professor of church history and Baptist heritage at Campbell University Divinity School in Buies Creek, North Carolina.

Loretta Long Hunnicutt is associate professor of history and director of graduate studies in history at Pepperdine University in Malibu, California.

Nancy J. Hynes, OSB, is professor emerita at the College of Saint Benedict/Saint John's University in Minnesota.

Stan Ingersol is director of the Nazarene Archives in Kansas City, Missouri.

Lynn Japinga is associate professor of religion at Hope College (Holland, Michigan), teaching American religious history and feminist theology, and is an authority on the Reformed Church in America.

Emily Alice Katz completed her doctorate in modern Jewish studies at the Graduate School of the Jewish Theological Seminary and wrote her dissertation on Israel in American Jewish culture in the postwar period.

Karen M. Kennelly is coordinator of the History of Women Religious and a past member of the congregational leadership team of the Sisters of St. Joseph of Carondelet (CSJ).

Shira Kohn is a doctoral candidate in Hebrew and Judaic studies and history at New York University.

Sheryl A. Kujawa-Holbrook holds the Suzanne R. Hiatt Chair in Feminist Pastoral Theology at the Episcopal Divinity School, Cambridge, Massachusetts.

L. DeAne Lagerquist is professor of religion at St. Olaf College in Northfield, Minnesota, and past executive director of the Lutheran Academy of Scholars.

Alan Ka Lun Lai is pastor of the Mount Olivet Lutheran Church in North Vancouver, British Columbia, and publishes in the area of multicultural teaching and learning.

Janet Moore Lindman is associate professor of history and coordinator of women's studies at Rowan University in Glassboro, New Jersey.

Barbara J. MacHaffie is professor of history and religion at Marietta College in Marietta, Ohio.

Susan Marie Maloney, SNJM, teaches at the University of Redlands in California and is a consultant to UNANIMA International, a nongovernmental organization accredited at the United Nations.

Margaret McManus is assistant professor of U.S. religious history at American Baptist Seminary of the West and the Graduate Theological Union in Berkeley, California.

Mandy E. McMichael is a doctoral student at Duke University specializing in American religious history.

Judith Metz, SC, is archivist and historian for the Sisters of Charity of Cincinnati and adjunct instructor at the College of Mount St. Joseph.

Sandra Yocum Mize is the chair of religious studies at the University of Dayton.

Kendal P. Mobley is pastor of Enon Baptist Church in Salisbury, North Carolina.

Pamela S. Nadell is professor of history and director of the Jewish studies program at American University in Washington, DC.

Lynn S. Neal is assistant professor of religion at Wake Forest University, Winston-Salem, North Carolina.

Mary Jane O'Donnell teaches in the religious studies department at California State University, Northridge.

Anne E. Patrick, SNJM, is William H. Laird Professor of Religion and the Liberal Arts at Carleton College in Northfield, Minnesota, and a former president of the Catholic Theological Society of America.

Lisa J. M. Poirier is assistant professor and director of graduate studies in the department of comparative religion at Miami University in Ohio.

Priscilla Pope-Levison is professor of theology and assistant professor of women's studies at Seattle Pacific University.

Barbara E. Reed is professor of religion and Asian studies at St. Olaf College in Northfield, Minnesota, and focuses her research on women in Chinese Buddhism.

Valerie Rempel is associate professor of history and theology at the Mennonite Brethren Biblical Seminary in Fresno, California.

Susan B. Ridgely is an assistant professor of religious studies, University of Wisconsin–Oshkosh.

Annie Russell is university registrar at Willamette University and a doctoral candidate in history at the Graduate Theological Union; her dissertation examines the history of the Society of the Companions of the Holy Cross.

Scott D. Seay is assistant professor of church history at Christian Theological Seminary in Indianapolis, Indiana.

Graeme Sharrock teaches humanities and is writing a dissertation at the University of Chicago Divinity School on the visions and writings of Ellen White.

Janet Silman is a writer, educator, and minister of the United Church of Canada; of English, Cree, and Scottish ancestry; and former codirector of the Dr. Jessie Saulteaux Resource Centre near Beausejour, Manitoba.

Angela D. Sims is an associate professor of Christian ethics and Black Church studies at Saint Paul School of Theology in Kansas City, Missouri.

Michael A. Singer is a doctoral candidate in Hebrew Bible and ancient Near East at Brandeis University in Waltham, Massachusetts.

Beth Spaulding is a United Church of Christ minister serving as a chaplain at the Germaine Lawrence School for Girls in Arlington, Massachusetts, and a doctoral student in liturgy and American religious history at the Boston University School of Theology.

Eleanor J. Stebner holds the J. S. Woodsworth Chair in the Humanities at Simon Fraser University in Burnaby, British Columbia.

Andrew H. Stern is assistant professor of history at Southern Catholic College in Dawsonville, Georgia.

Tracy J. Trothen is associate professor of theology and ethics, and head of theological studies at Queen's University in Kingston, Ontario.

Amy Black Voorhees is a doctoral student at the University of California, Santa Barbara.

Randi Walker is associate professor of church history at Pacific School of Religion in Berkeley, California.

Laceye Warner teaches evangelism and Methodist studies as an assistant professor at Duke Divinity School in Durham, North Carolina.

Ellen Whelan, OSF, is a historian and author of *The Sisters' Story: Saint Marys Hospital—Mayo Clinic, 1889 to 1939* (2002) and *1939 to 1980* (2007).

Marilyn Färdig Whiteley is an independent scholar living in Guelph, Ontario, and specializing in the study of Canadian Methodist women.

Karen-Marie Woods is a research assistant for the Social Planning and Research Council of British Columbia and a teaching assistant at Simon Fraser University in Burnaby, British Columbia.

Beverly Zink-Sawyer is professor of preaching and worship at Union Theological Seminary and the Presbyterian School of Christian Education in Richmond, Virginia.

Abbreviations for Standard Sources

ANB — Garraty, John A., and Mark C. Carnes, ed. *American National Biography*. New York and Oxford: Oxford University Press, 1999.

ANBO — *American National Biography Online*. New York and Oxford: American Council of Learned Societies and Oxford University Press, 2005–.

ANBs — Betz, Paul, and Mark C. Carnes, ed. *American National Biography: Supplement* 1. New York and Oxford: Oxford University Press, 2002.

BWA — Hine, Darlene Clark, ed. *Black Women in America: An Historical Encyclopedia*, 2 vols. Brooklyn, NY: Carlson Publishing, Inc., 1993.

BWA2 — Hine, Darlene Clark, ed. *Black Women in America*, 3 vols., 2nd ed. New York: Oxford University Press, 2005.

BWARC — Hine, Darlene Clark, ed. *Black Women in America: Religion and Community*. New York: Facts on File, Inc., 1997.

DARB — Bowden, Henry Warner. *Dictionary of American Religious Biography*, 2nd ed. Westport, CT: Greenwood Press, 1993.

DCB — *Dictionary of Canadian Biography*. Toronto: University of Toronto Press, 1966– [online].

DUUB — Hughes, Peter, ed. *Dictionary of Unitarian and Universalist Biography*. Portland, OR. Unitarian Universalist Historical Society, 1999–2007 [online].

EACH — Glazier, Michael, and Thomas J. Shelley, ed. *Encyclopedia of American Catholic History*. Collegeville, MN: Liturgical Press, 1997.

EAWR — Benowitz, June Melby. *Encyclopedia of American Women and Religion*. Santa Barbara, CA; Denver, CO; and Oxford: ABC-CLIO, 1998.

EE — Balmer, Randall. *Encyclopedia of Evangelicalism*. Louisville, KY: Westminster John Knox Press, 2002.

ES-CM — Foster, Douglas A., et al, ed. *Encyclopedia of the Stone-Campbell Movement*. Grand Rapids: Wm. B. Eerdmans Publishing Co., 2004.

HDB — Brackney, William H., ed. *Historical Dictionary of the Baptists*. Lanham, MD, and

London: Scarecrow Press, 1999.

JWA Hyman, Paula, and Deborah Dash Moore, ed. *Jewish Women in America: An Historical Encyclopedia*. New York: Routledge, 1997.

NaAW Bataille, Gretchen M., ed. *Native American Women: A Biographical Dictionary*. New York and London: Garland, 1993.

NBAW Smith, Jessie Carney, ed. *Notable Black American Women*, 3 vols. Detroit and London: Gale Research, 2002.

NCE Carson, Thomas, and Joan Cerrito, ed. *New Catholic Encyclopedia*, 2nd ed. Farmington Hills, MI: Gayle, 2003.

NoAW James, Edward T., Janet Wilson James, and Paul S. Boyer, ed. *Notable American Women, 1607–1950: A Biographical Dictionary*, 3 vols. Cambridge, MA: Belknap Press of Harvard University Press, 1971.

NoAWC Ware, Susan, and Stacy Braukman, ed. *Notable American Women, Completing the 20th Century*. Cambridge, MA: Harvard University Press, 2004.

NoAWMP Sicherman, Barbara, and Carol Hurd Green, ed. *Notable American Women, The Modern Period: A Biographical Dictionary*. Cambridge, MA: Belknap Press of Harvard University Press, 1980.

NoHAW Telgen, Diane, and Jim Kamp, ed. *Notable Hispanic American Women*, 1st ed. Florence, KY: Gale Research, 1993.

RLA Melton, J. Gordon, ed. *Religious Leaders of America*. Detroit: Gale, 1991.

ROWUS Dehay, Elinor Tong. *Religious Orders of Women in the United States*. Hammond, IN: W. B. Conkey, 1930.

UU Robinson, David. *The Unitarians and the Universalists*. Part 2, *A Biographical Dictionary of Unitarian and Universalist Leaders*. Westport, CT: Greenwood Press, 1985.

UUWM Champ, Catherine M. *Universalist and Unitarian Women Ministers*. Universalist Historical Society, 1975.

WBC Schultz, Rima Lunin, and Adele Hast. *Women Building Chicago, 1790–1990: A Biographical Dictionary*. Bloomington and Indianapolis: Indiana University Press, 2001.

A–Z Entries

ACHTUS (Academy of Catholic Hispanic Theologians of the United States) (1988). Hispanic theological association. ACHTUS is a scholarly association that promotes theological research and reflection from the point of view of American Hispanics. Theologian *Maria Pilar Aquino served as the first woman president of ACHTUS in 1993. Prominent women members of the organization include *Ada Maria Isasi-Diaz, Daisy Machado, and Jeannette Rodriguez. ACHTUS provides networking resources for Hispanic theologians and holds an annual colloquium of scholarly papers and discussions. Since 1993 it has published a quarterly journal, *The Journal of Hispanic/Latino Theology*. ACHTUS honors both an individual (with the Virgilio Eliziondo Award) and an organization (with the ACHTUS Award) each year for contributions to theology and advancing the goals of the organization.

María Pilar Aquino, Daisy L. Machado, and Jeanette Rodríguez, *A Reader in Latina Feminist Theology* (2002).

COLLEEN CARPENTER CULLINAN

Ackerman, Paula Herskovitz (1893–1989). Jewish spiritual leader. In 1919, when religious school teacher Paula Herskovitz wed Rabbi William Ackerman, she embarked on her first career as the rabbi's wife. That took her in 1924 to Meridian, Mississippi, and the Reform Temple Beth-El. William Ackerman became its rabbi while Paula Ackerman taught Sabbath school, advised the sisterhood, and occasionally stood in his stead in the pulpit. When her husband died suddenly in 1950, the temple's leaders pleaded with Ackerman to carry on as their religious leader until they could hire another. Despite opposition from the Reform Temple's national leaders, Ackerman became the temple's unordained rabbi, a role she held until 1953. This second career led her to champion ordaining women rabbis.

EAWR; JWA; Pamela S. Nadell, *Women Who Would Be Rabbis* (1998).

PAMELA S. NADELL

Adams, Hannah (1755–1831). Historian of religion. Born into a Massachusetts family of modest means, Hannah Adams was largely self-educated. In her early adulthood she attempted to support herself as a full-time writer, perhaps the first woman in the U.S. to do so. Her early works earned her the respect of the New England elite, but her liberal religious views drew her into the emerging Unitarian Controversy (1805–25). She attempted to clarify her views in an eclectic collection of essays on key figures in the history of Christian theology. Two later works focused on the topic of Jewish history and theology. These works were aimed at theological liberals, who were interested in the relationship between first-century Judaism and emergent Christianity. Although she was never able fully to support herself by writing alone, her contemporaries regarded Adams as an able historian of religion.

ANB; DARB; NoAW; Hannah Adams, *A Memoir of Miss Hannah Adams* (1832), *Letters on the Gospels* (1824), *History of the Jews* (1812), *The Truth and Excellence of the Christian Religion* (1804), *Summary History of New England* (1799), *An Alphabetical Compendium of the Various Sects* (1784).

SCOTT D. SEAY

Addams, Laura Jane (1860–1935). Social reformer, humanitarian, peace activist. Jane Addams grew up in Cedarville, Illinois. Her mother died when Addams was two, but Addams was close to her father. She graduated from Rockford Female Seminary (later Rockford College) in 1881. Her life was in flux for the next eight years: Her father died; she started—and dropped out of—medical school; she had back surgery and wrestled with other illnesses; she traveled extensively in Europe where she finally visited Toynbee Hall, a settlement house in London. Here she found her calling. She and *Ellen Gates Starr opened Hull House in Chicago in 1889. Addams and others lived at the house, which was located near several different immigrant communities. Hull House offered a variety of classes, a day-care center, a place for unions to meet, bathing facilities, and many other services. Addams emphasized the gifts of each immigrant group and encouraged them to celebrate their heritage. She tried to avoid paternalism and condescension. Addams was widely praised for her social reform work. She was also a pacifist, however, and was vilified during and after World War I for her efforts to find alternative solutions to armed conflict. She organized and served as president of the Women's International League for Peace and Freedom. In 1931 she received the Nobel Peace Prize. Although Addams became less vocal about her beliefs as she aged, her humanitarianism was based on her understanding of Christianity as a force for social change.

ANB; DARB; EE; NoAW; WBC; Jean Bethke Elshtain, *Jane Addams and the Dream of American Democracy* (2002); Allen F. Davis, *American Heroine* (1973); Jane Addams, *Peace and Bread in Time of War* (1915), *Twenty Years at Hull House* (1910), *Democracy and Social Ethics* (1902).

LYNN JAPINGA

Adler, Margot (1947–). Wiccan, journalist, writer. Born in Little Rock, Arkansas, Margot Adler became a Gardnerian Priestess in 1973. In 1979 she wrote *Drawing Down the Moon*, which served as the first systematic examination of nature religions in the U.S. Currently in its second printing, the book remains one of the most popular books on neo-paganism, and is often a first point of contact for potential members to find information on the movement. Adler's 1988 handfasting was the first pagan wedding covered in the *New York Times* society pages. She is a frequent lecturer on neo-paganism. In 1997 she published her memoirs, *Heretic's Heart: A Journey through Spirit and Revolution*. She hosts a weekly show, *Justice Talking*, on U.S. National Public Radio.

EAWR; RLA; Margot Adler, *Encyclopedia of Occultism and Parapsychology*, ed. J Gordon Melton, vol. 1 (2001); "Margot Adler, NPR Biography," www.npr.org.

SUSAN B. RIDGELY

Aglow International (1967–). A nondenominational Christian evangelical women's organization. Aglow is active in 166 countries. Its central focus is on prayer and outreach through small-group studies, various support groups, prison ministries, conferences, retreats, and a variety of local ministries. Worldwide conferences are held biannually in the U.S. Aglow's mission is threefold: to restore and mobilize women, to promote gender reconciliation, and to expand awareness of global issues from a biblical perspective. In addition to leadership development among women, Aglow is concerned especially with mission to Muslim people and support for Israel. The organization began as an outgrowth of the Full Gospel Business Men's Fellowship International. Four women began meeting for prayer and fellowship in Seattle, Washington, in 1967. They organized as the Full Gospel Women's Fellowship, and in 1972 they incorporated as Women's Aglow Fellowship International. It is now the largest independent evangelical women's organization in the world. Aglow's belief statement affirms the full presence and validity of all the gifts of the Holy Spirit. The emphasis on the work of the Holy Spirit encourages local chapters to adapt their meetings to the particular cultural patterns and needs of their various locales. Regional boards oversee the various local chapters and leaders. A nine-member board of directors governs the international organization. Its headquarters is in Seattle, Washington.

Marie R. Griffith, *God's Daughters: Evangelical Women and the Power of Submission* (1997).

VALERIE REMPEL

Aikenhead, Elizabeth Hannah Dimsdale (ca. 1863–1945). Methodist evangelist. Elizabeth Dimsdale was born in a village on the shores of Lake Simcoe to a Methodist family, but at about age 20, she moved for the sake of her health to the Muskoka region of what is now Ontario. She taught and also held religious services because there was no church in the area. Her preaching met with such success that in 1885 the Toronto Conference of the Methodist Church appointed her conference evangelist. For six years she traveled extensively, conducting evangelistic services. Although several other women, including her younger sister Gertrude, became "lady evangelists," Elizabeth Dimsdale was the pioneer and the most prominent. In 1891 she married James Robert Aikenhead, an ordained Methodist minister. She assisted in his ministerial labors and accepted invitations to lecture and to preach for many decades, as long as her health permitted.

Marilyn Whitely [sic], "Elizabeth Dimsdale Aikenhead: 'Lady Evangelist,'" *Touchstone: Heritage and Theology in a New Age*, 7, no. 1 (January 1989).

MARILYN FÄRDIG WHITELEY

Alden, Isabella Macdonald (1841–1930). Writer and educator. Isabella Macdonald was born to Isaac and Myra Spofford Macdonald and raised in upstate New York. She married a minister, Gustavus Rossenberg Alden, and they had one son, Raymond. Alden wrote fiction for children as well as adults. Her book, *Four Girls at Chautauqua* (1876), was credited for raising the popularity of the cultural programs of the newly founded Chautauqua Institution. She was a frequent contributor to religious periodicals and an editor for the *Pansy* and for the Presbyterian *Primary Quarterly*. She lectured at primary Sunday school conventions and was involved (from its inception) with the training program for Sunday school teachers at Chautauqua. She was also a staff writer for the *Christian Endeavor World*.

NoAW; J. B. Dobkin, "Isabella Alden (Pansy)," in *American Writers for Children before 1900*, ed. Glenn E. Estes (1985); "Alden, Isabella Macdonald (1841–1930)," in *Liberty's Women*, ed. Robert McHenry (1980); Isabella M. Alden, *Memories of Yesterdays* (1931); Jesse Lyman Hulbert, *The Story of Chautauqua* (1921).

VALERIE REMPEL

Alkhateeb, Sharifa (1946–2004). Muslim activist, writer, educator. Sharifa Alkhateeb was born in Philadelphia of a Yemeni father and a Czech mother. She founded the North American Council for Muslim Women (NACMW) in 1992. The NACMW is a forum for Muslim women to address specifically women's issues, such as domestic violence. Alkhateeb was also active in expanding American knowledge of Islam through her work with the Muslim Education Council. She chaired the Muslim caucus at the United Nations Fourth World Conference on Women (Beijing, 1995).

"A Tribute to Sharifa Alkhateeb: Carrying the Mantle," *Hawwa* 3, no. 1 (2005); Nimat Hafez Barazangi, "The Legacy of a Remarkable Muslim Woman," *The Middle East Women's Studies Review* (March 2004); Hibba Abugideiri, "The Renewed Woman of American Islam: Shifting Lenses toward 'Gender Jihad?'" *Muslim World* 91 (Spring 2001).

BARBARA E. REED

Allebach, Annie J. (1874–1918). First woman ordained by the General Conference Mennonite Church. Annie

Allebach was born to Jacob and Sarah Markley Allebach. She became a teacher and then a principal of East Orange (New Jersey) Collegiate School. She was active in the suffragist movement while studying at Columbia and New York universities and connected with Trinity Parish. As a worker employed by the parish she founded an employment bureau, kindergarten, and a commercial school, and began a church paper, the *Intercession Messenger*. She was a vice president of the International Purity League, president of the New York University Philosophical Society, and a founder of the Institute of Business Engineers. A lifelong Mennonite, she became in 1911 the first woman ordained by the General Conference Mennonite Church. She began serving as pastor of the Sunnyside Reformed Church (Long Island) in 1916, where she remained until her death.

Mary Lou Cummings, "Ordained into Ministry: Annie J. Allebach (1874–1918)," in *Full Circle: Stories of Mennonite Women*, ed. Mary Lou Cummings (1978); "Sketch of Miss Annie J. Allebach," *The Mennonite* (19 January 1911).

VALERIE REMPEL

Allen, Sarah Bass (1764–1849). Methodist laywoman and wife of renowned Methodist leader. Sarah Bass was born into a slave family from the Isle of Wight in Virginia. At eight years of age Bass was moved to Philadelphia, where she would later marry and assist Richard Allen, founder and first bishop of the African Methodist Episcopal (AME) Church. Sara Bass Allen was socially active in the Underground Railroad. Her interest in Christian service motivated her to help raise funds toward the formation of the missionary society of the AME Church. Allen was also concerned for the well-being and respectability of early traveling ministers. Together with a network of friends, Allen provided nourishing meals and repaired worn clothing to assist with the appearance of itinerant preachers. Allen raised six children. She is entombed, alongside her husband, at Mother Bethel AME Church in Philadelphia.

Jean Miller Schmidt, *Grace Sufficient: A History of Women in American Methodism* (1999); Daniel A. Payne, *History of the African Methodist Episcopal Church* (1969).

CHRISTOPHER J. ANDERSON

Allione, Tsultrim (1947–). Author, teacher, and founder of Tara Mandala Buddhist center. Tsultrim Allione was one of the first Western women ordained as a Tibetan Buddhist nun. She was ordained by H. H. Karmapa, the leader of the Kagyu lineage, in 1970 in Bodhgaya, India. After more than three years living as a nun, studying the Tibetan language and Buddhist meditation, she gave up her status as a nun, married, and had children. In 1993 she founded Tara Mandala retreat center in southwestern Colorado. In her writings and teachings she has explored the feminine aspects of Tibetan spirituality, the idea of motherhood as a spiritual path, and the role of emotions.

Tsultrim Allione, *Women of Wisdom* (2000); Sandy Boucher, *Turning the Wheel: American Women Creating the New Buddhism* (1988).

BARBARA E. REED

Alpha Epsilon Phi Sorority (1909–). Jewish sorority. Founded at Barnard College by seven Jewish women, Alpha Epsilon Phi offered a social outlet for female Jewish students in the university setting. Several Jewish women had applied for admission in established houses, but were denied membership due to their Jewish heritage. However, by joining Alpha Epsilon Phi, its members gained entry and, in some cases, acceptance into the larger campus culture through participation in social events and philanthropic projects. The sorority saw itself as representing the best that Jewish women had to offer and therefore demanded the utmost of its members in their scholarship, campus participation, dress, and etiquette. The sorority provided an environment to form friendships with other women and, on numerous occasions, led them to meeting eligible men from the Jewish fraternity system. Chapters of the organization were later opened at numerous universities throughout the U.S. and Canada. The sorority currently boasts over 40 active chapters and a membership of more than 50,000.

JWA; Marianne Sanua, *Going Greek: Jewish College Fraternities in the United States* (2003); Jack Anson and Robert Marchesani Jr., eds., *Baird's Manual of American College Fraternities* (1991).

SHIRA M. KOHN

American Female Moral Reform Society (AFMRS) (1834–ca. 1870s). Organization to prevent and eliminate prostitution. Inspired by calls for moral reform by missionary John McDowall, the AFMRS formed with the intention of being a distinctively women's organization. Begun as the New York Female Moral Reform Society, it soon changed its name and expanded to include 445 auxiliaries. Its periodical, the *Advocate of Moral Reform,* emphasized that the full responsibility for prostitution belonged to the men who seduced women. The *Advocate* sought to educate and warn young women and children in order to prevent their victimization and to encourage purity. Some argue that the origins of the feminist movement in the U.S. can be traced to such societies.

Daniel S. Wright, *The First of Causes to Our Sex* (2006); Mary P. Ryan, "The Power of Women's Networks: A Case Study in Female Moral Reform in Antebellum America," *Feminist Studies* 5, no. 1 (Spring 1979).

LYDIA HUFFMAN HOYLE

Ames, Jessie Daniel (1883–1972). Women's suffrage and antilynching activist. Jessie Daniel was ambivalent toward the church of her parents, the Methodist Episcopal Church, South, despite her mother's activity as a devoted volunteer visiting among the sick. Daniel graduated from Southwestern University in 1902 and married Roger Post Ames in 1905, a friend of her father's and a military physician 13 years her senior. Because of his service in Central America, the couple lived separately for most of their nine-year marriage. After his death, Ames organized a county suffrage association in 1916. Her effort led to Texas becoming the first southern state to ratify the 19th Amendment. Ames was involved in numerous political organizations, but focused her attention on racial injustice. She founded the *Association of Southern Women for the Prevention of Lynching (ASWPL) in 1930. With substantial support from southern Methodist women and the *YWCA, the ASWPL challenged the rationalizations for mob violence against African American males by working to abolish the stereotype of white women's vulnerability and their need for protection. With a decrease in the number of lynchings, the ASWPL dissolved in 1942, eventually contributing to Ames's reluctant retirement.

ANB; NoAWMP; Jacquelyn Dowd Hall, *Revolt against Chivalry,* rev. ed. (1993) [1979].

LACEYE C. WARNER

AMIT (Americans for Israel and Torah) (1925–). Zionist organization. Originally named Mizrachi Women's Organization of America, its founder, Bessie Gotsfeld, reshaped the women's auxiliaries of a men's religious Zionist society (Mizrachi) into an independent women's agency. In 1933 and 1938 AMIT opened schools in Jerusalem and Tel Aviv. From 1943 to 1947 it organized three communal villages to care for hundreds of orphaned children who had been raised in religious homes and who had fled Nazi Europe. From 1955 through 1991 AMIT established additional villages for Ethiopian Jewish refugees. Since the 1980s AMIT has become a leader in public religious education, and in 1996 it won the Religious Education Prize of Israel's Ministry for Education. Today it maintains 34 educational and child-care facilities in Israel. Following the assassination of Prime Minister Yitzhak Rabin, AMIT developed a prize-winning curriculum to teach tolerance. Today it is the largest Zionist organization in the U.S., with 80,000 members in 475 chapters.

JWA

DIANNE ASHTON

Anderson, Phyllis B. (1943–). Lutheran pastor and first woman to head an Evangelical Lutheran Church in America (ELCA) seminary. Born in Baltimore, Phyllis Anderson graduated from California State University in Sacramento, California, and earned theological degrees at Wartburg Theological Seminary in Dubuque, Iowa, and Aquinas Institute of Theology in St. Louis, Missouri. Anderson served as the ELCA's first director for theological studies and later became the first director of the Institute for Ecumenical and Theological Studies in Seattle. She became president of Pacific Lutheran Theological Seminary in Berkeley, California, in 2005.

ELCA News Service, 8 November 2004.

LINDA B. BREBNER

Andrews, Barbara Louise (1935–78). Lutheran pastor. In 1970 Barbara Andrews became the first woman ordained by the American Lutheran Church (ALC). She already had worked in campus ministry and earned a master's of divinity degree in anticipation of medical chaplaincy. She served parishes in Minnesota and Michigan and was a chaplain for Lutheran Social Service of Michigan before her early death.

EAWR; L. DeAne Lagerquist, *The Lutherans* (1999); Gloria E. Bengston, ed., *Lutheran Women in Ordained Ministry* (1995).

L. DEANE LAGERQUIST

Angelou, Maya (1928–). Writer, actress, educator, and social justice activist. Maya Angelou's first autobiographical book, *I Know Why the Caged Bird Sings* (1969), and the five that followed it document her experiences as a black woman in 20th-century America. She writes prolifically in a variety of genres and has been active in numerous social justice movements. In 1981 she was appointed a lifetime professor at Wake Forest University. Her life and thought have been shaped most profoundly by the African American Methodist and Baptist traditions, and by the civil rights movement. Her poem "On the Pulse of Morning," written for the 1993 inauguration of President Bill Clinton, evokes a sense of human unity with all its diversity. Her poem "Amazing Peace," read for the 2005 National Christmas Tree Lighting and Pageant of Peace ceremony, calls on all people, regardless of their religion, race, or culture to claim a common humanity and evoke peace. Angelou has become a powerful and unique voice of hope within the U.S. and throughout the world.

Lucinda Moore, "A Conversation with Maya Angelou at 75," *Smithsonian Magazine* (1 April 2003) [online]; Archive, "Maya Angelou (1928–)," *Poetry Foundation* [online].

SARAH BRUER

Anthony, Susan B. (1820–1906). Suffragist and social reformer. Both Susan B. Anthony and her friend and coactivist, *Elizabeth Cady Stanton, worked in abolition efforts and in their joint leadership of the dissident National

Woman Suffrage Association (NWSA). Founded in 1869 the NWSA challenged the 15th Amendment's exclusion of women from the vote. Anthony became the aggressive organizer and populist leader in the NWSA, stretching her suffragist values into the broader arena of women's rights in the home, the school, and the workplace. Her outspoken integrity within and outside the suffragist movement included a broad, liberal, and pluralist religiosity extending from her Quaker heritage to her membership in the Unitarian community. Anthony embodied a piety that was suspicious of hard-line dogma and geared toward action and just social change.

ANB; Geoffrey C. Ward et al., *Not for Ourselves Alone* (1999); Judith E. Harper, *Susan B. Anthony* (1998).

OSCAR COLE-ARNAL

Aquino, Maria Pilar (1956–). Catholic theologian. Born in Mexico to a family of migrant farm workers who became active in César Chávez's United Farm Workers movement, Aquino learned as a child the deep connection between Catholicism and working toward social justice. She earned her doctorate at the Pontifical University of Salamanca (Spain). She is professor of theology at the University of San Diego and also serves as associate director of the Center for the Study of Latino/a Catholicism. She was a cofounder and the first female president of *ACHTUS (Academy of Catholic Hispanic Theologians of the U.S.). Aquino has published widely in both Spanish and English on systematic theology, Latina and Latin American feminist liberation theologies, and Christian social ethics. She is a passionate teacher and active mentor for younger Latina scholars.

Orlando O. Espin and Miguel H. Diaz, *From the Heart of Our People* (1999); Maria Pilar Aquino, *Our Cry for Life* (1993).

COLLEEN CARPENTER CULLINAN

Armstrong, Annie Walker (1850–1938). Baptist churchwoman. Annie Armstrong was first corresponding secretary of the Woman's Missionary Union (WMU), auxiliary to the Southern Baptist Convention. Armstrong never married, and she gave indefatigable energy to missions. She was president of the Woman's Baptist Home Mission Society of Maryland (1882–1906) and corresponding secretary and editor-in-chief of the Maryland Baptist Mission Rooms (1886–1906). She helped found the WMU in 1888 and served as its corresponding secretary from 1888 until 1906, but refused a salary. She created the denomination's first mailing lists, made pioneering efforts to collect field information and statistics, produced and distributed missionary literature, gathered resources for missionaries, traveled thousands of miles, worked across racial lines, and initiated numerous home mission ventures. She resigned when it became clear that the WMU would fund a training school for missionary women at the Southern Baptist Theological Seminary, despite her objections. The WMU renamed its annual home missions offering in her honor in 1934.

EAWR; EE; HDB; Keith Harper, ed., *Rescue the Perishing: Selected Correspondence of Annie Armstrong* (2004); Catherine Allen, *Laborers Together with God* (1987); Bobbie Sorrill, *Annie Armstrong* (1984).

KENDAL P. MOBLEY

Armstrong, Hannah Maria Norris (1842–1919). Baptist missionary. Hannah Maria Norris joined the Baptist church in her home community of Canso, Nova Scotia, at age 23. After receiving a normal school education, she herself taught. She volunteered to the Foreign Mission Board of the Maritime Baptist Churches as a missionary but was turned down because there were no funds to support her. Advised to appeal to her "sisters," in 10 weeks during the summer of 1870 she formed 33 women's missionary aid societies across the region. She was quickly commissioned a missionary by the Baptist Convention and in September 1870 departed to work among the Karens in Burma (present-day Myanmar). There she married the Reverend William F. Armstrong in 1874. The following year they moved to India, returning to Burma in 1884, where they remained until William died in 1918.

DCB; Gerald Anderson, ed., *Biographical Dictionary of Christian Missions* (1998).

MARILYN FÄRDIG WHITELEY

Ashbridge, Elizabeth Sampson Sullivan (1713–55). Quaker minister. Born in Cheshire, England, Elizabeth Sampson was married at the age of 14 and consequently estranged from her family. After the untimely death of her husband and a stay with relatives in Ireland, she set sail for America in 1732. In New York she met and married a schoolteacher, and by 1738 the couple had both become Quakers. Following her second husband's death in 1741 she was commissioned by the Quakers in Goshen, Pennsylvania, as a traveling preacher. She married a wealthy landowner, Aaron Ashbridge, in 1746. Between 1753 and 1755 she undertook missionary work in England and Ireland, where she died of an illness that she developed during her Atlantic crossing two years before.

ANB; EAWR; Cristine Levenduski, *Peculiar Power* (1996).

SCOTT D. SEAY

Association of Southern Women for the Prevention of Lynching (ASWPL) (1930–41). Reform organization. Under the leadership of *Jessie Daniel Ames, a group of 26 white women from seven southeastern states convened in Atlanta at the invitation of the Commission on Interracial Cooperation. They drafted a statement, with 12 women accepting responsibility to educate personally against the acceptance of lynching as a protection to white women. Ames, adopting practices similar to those employed almost 20 years earlier by *Ida Bell Wells-Barnett, conducted on-the-scene investigations and discovered disparity between the facts and the reports of lynchings published by the white press. By challenging the link between racial violence and sexual attitudes, Ames and the ASWPL hoped to contribute to a new gender and racial order. Ames, however, did not partner with black women reformers, and this resulted in nominal black participation within the ASWPL. They argued that white people were more effective social reformers than black people. The ASWPL was also criticized for its refusal to endorse federal antilynching legislation. While protesting lynching, the ASWPL supported social barriers between blacks and whites.

EAWR; Alan Brinkley, "Jessie Daniel Amers," in *Invisible Giants*, ed. Mark C. Carnes (2002); Philip Dray, *At The Hands of Persons Unknown: The Lynching of Black America* (2002); Lynne Olson, *Freedom's Daughters* (2001); William F. Pinar, *The Gender of Racial Politics and Violence in America* (2001); Carolyn DeVore Yandle, *A Delicate Crusade: The Association of Southern Women for the Prevention of Lynching* (1969); Association of Southern Women for the Prevention of Lynching, *Southern Women Look at Lynching* (1937).

ANGELA D. SIMS

Austin, Ann (17th century). Quaker preacher and missionary. Little is known about Ann Austin, except that she was a frequent companion of *Mary Fisher (ca. 1632–98). She probably accompanied Fisher on her missionary journeys in Barbados, New England, and the Far East between 1655 and 1662. The two women were the first Quakers to land in Boston, but they were soon deported. Austin may have settled among the

South Carolina Quakers in the early 1680s.

Rufus M. Jones et al., *The Quakers in the American Colonies* (1911).

SCOTT D. SEAY

Avery, Martha Moore (1851–1929). Roman Catholic lecturer and lay evangelist. Raised in an established New England family, Martha Moore worked as a milliner in Ellsworth, Maine, before marrying Millard Avery. In 1888 Avery and her daughter, Katherine, moved to Boston, where Avery joined the Socialist Labor Party. She climbed rapidly through its ranks and became known as a gifted public speaker. When her daughter joined a convent, Avery, disillusioned with socialism, investigated Catholicism. At the age of 53 she joined the Roman Catholic Church. She and David Goldstein founded the lay evangelism organization, the Catholic Truth Guild, in 1917. They held meetings during the summer throughout the Northeast, giving lectures and answering questions about Catholicism. Avery was known for her citywide lectures, frequent newspaper editorials, and tireless work to benefit Boston Catholicism.

ANB; NoAW; Martha Moore Avery and David Goldstein, *Campaigning for Christ* (1924), *Bolshevism: Its Cure* (1919), and *Socialism: The Nation of Fatherless Children* (1911); Martha Moore Avery, *Woman: Her Quality, Her Environment, Her Possibility* (1901).

PRISCILLA POPE-LEVISON

Aylestock, Addie (1909–98). Methodist minister. Addie Aylestock was ordained in the British Methodist Episcopal (BME) Church, the first black woman ordained in Canada. Born near Waterloo, Ontario, Aylestock moved to Toronto at the beginning of the Great Depression, where she worked as a domestic and then as a dressmaker. She decided to study at the Toronto Bible College, in part because she wanted to become a missionary in Liberia. Raised in the predominantly white Methodist Church, which became part of the United Church of Canada in 1925, Aylestock joined the BME Church in Toronto. (The BME Church was formed in 1856 by Canadian members of the U.S.-based African Methodist Episcopal Church.) Aylestock was consecrated a deaconess in 1944 and graduated from the Toronto Bible College in 1945. The church sent Aylestock to Africville, a black community in Halifax, Nova Scotia. She also worked as a deaconess in Montreal, Toronto, and Owen Sound, Ontario. In 1950 the BME Conference superintendent wrote a resolution calling for the ordination of women, because he believed that Aylestock was doing what male ministers were doing. The 1951 conference passed the resolution, and Aylestock was ordained. She served as pastor in North Buxton, St. Catherines, Fort Erie, and Niagara, and received numerous honors for her lifework before her death.

Rella Braithwaite, *Some Black Women: Profiles of Black Women in Canada* (1993); Dione Brand, ed., *No Burden to Carry: Narratives of Black Working Women in Ontario* (1991); *Older, Stronger, Wiser* [video] (1989).

ELEANOR J. STEBNER

Ayres, Anne ("Sister Anne") (1816–96). First Episcopal sister and founder of the Sisterhood of the Holy Communion. Born in London, Anne Ayres moved to New York City with her parents in 1836. In 1845 Ayres heard a sermon, "Jephtha's Vow," by William Augustus Muhlenberg; discerned a call to the religious life; and was formally consecrated a "sister of the Holy Communion" in a private ceremony. Sister Anne sought a vocation when there were no existing sisterhoods in the Episcopal Church and thus became the first Episcopal sister. Under the leadership of Muhlenberg and Ayres, an order was founded in 1852, which embarked on a variety of ministries including teaching, social work, nursing, and hospital administration. They also staffed a facility for the rural poor, orphans, homeless, and handicapped on Long Island.

ANB; EAWR; NoAW; Sheryl A. Kujawa-Holbrook, *Freedom Is a Dream* (2002); Boone Porter Jr., *Sister Anne, Pioneer in Women's Work* (1960); Anne Ayres, *Evangelical Sisterhoods* (1867).

SHERYL A. KUJAWA-HOLBROOK

Babcock, Clara Celestia Hale (1850–1924). Pioneer preacher. The daughter of a Methodist minister, Clara Babcock joined the Stone-Campbell movement around 1875. For over a decade she lectured for the *Woman's Christian Temperance Union and engaged in itinerant evangelism throughout the Midwest, while also raising six children. The congregation in Erie, Illinois, ordained her in 1888, making her the first woman in the movement to be ordained as a congregational pastor. For the next 36 years she engaged in pastoral ministry in Illinois, Iowa, and North Dakota. Her obituary claims that she baptized over 1,500 people during her ministry. In part because of her example, at least 15 other women were ordained as pastors in the movement by 1915. Her early ministry caused a storm of controversy during 1892 and 1893, and forced the first substantive discussion of women's ordination in the tradition that would become the Christian Church (Disciples of Christ).

ES-CM; Nathaniel Haynes, *History of the Disciples of Christ in Illinois* (1915).

SCOTT D. SEAY

Bagby, Anne Luther (1859–1942). Southern Baptist missionary. Anne Bagby helped organize the first Woman's Missionary Union (1880) in Texas and shortly thereafter was appointed with her husband, William Buck Bagby, as a missionary to Brazil. She served for 61 years. She helped establish churches and associations, did evangelistic work with women, organized the first Woman's Missionary Union (1889), and trained indigenous leadership. She took over a school for girls in Sao Paulo (1901) and made it a leading Southern Baptist school. She bore three daughters and six sons, but one son died in infancy, another in early childhood, and a third drowned at the age of 24; a fourth son abandoned Galveston Medical College at the age of 25 and was never seen again. Her remaining children became missionaries in Brazil and Argentina.

EAWR; Daniel B. Lancaster, *The Bagbys of Brazil* (1999); Helen Bagby Harrison, *The Bagbys of Brazil* (1954); Papers, the Texas Collection, Baylor University.

KENDAL P. MOBLEY

Bailey, Alice Anne La Trobe-Bateman Evans (1880–1949). Theosophist and founder of Arcane School. Born in England, Alice La Trobe-Bateman lived on her grandfather's estate and was raised in the Anglican tradition. After attending finishing school in London, she worked for the *YWCA (Young Women's Christian Association) (1899–1907), preaching evangelistic sermons to British troops in Ireland and India. In 1907 she married Walter Evans and they moved to the U.S. Divorced in 1919 Evans worked in California while studying theosophy ("divine wisdom"), an eclectic movement emphasizing the spiritual essence of all reality. She joined the Theosophical Society in 1917 and in 1921 married Foster Bailey, the society's national secretary. In 1922 she published *Initiation: Human and Solar*, the first of 19 books. In 1923 Bailey founded the Arcane School, which is dedicated to teaching people the science of the soul.

ANB; EAWR; RLA; Alice A. Bailey, *The Unfinished Tradition* (1951).

KEITH DURSO

Bailey, Hannah Clark Johnston (1839–1923). Quaker pacifist, suffragist, reformer, and temperance leader. Born in New York state, Hannah Bailey was an active social reformer throughout her life. She championed suffrage and served as the president of the Maine Woman Suffrage Association from 1891 to 1899. She was also a tireless peace activist. In 1887 Bailey became the superintendent of the department of peace and international arbitration of the *Woman's Christian Temperance Union (WCTU), an office she held until 1916. Throughout her term the department circulated extensive peace education literature, including two magazines she edited herself; she traveled globally promoting peace, and her leadership led to the establishment of a WCTU department of peace and international arbitration in 26 states and 14 countries. In the militaristic years before World War I Bailey was instrumental in the WCTU maintaining its pacifist stance.

ANBO; H. J. Bailey, *Reminiscences of a Christian Life* (1885); Papers, Swarthmore College Peace Collection.

ROBYNNE ROGERS HEALEY

Baker, Ella (1903–86). Civil rights leader. Ella Josephine Baker was raised in a poor Baptist family in Littleton, Virginia. In 1918 she entered Shaw Boarding School and later Shaw University in Raleigh, North Carolina. Graduating as valedictorian in 1927 Baker moved to New York City in hopes of doing graduate work in sociology. The Depression prevented her from doing so and therefore, during the 1930s, she worked for the Workers' Education Project and the Works Progress Administration. In 1938 she joined the staff of the National Association for the Advancement of Colored People (NAACP). She resigned from the NAACP in 1953 to become executive secretary of In Friendship, a coalition aimed at raising funds for the emerging civil rights struggle in the South. She joined the staff of the Southern Christian Leadership Conference (SCLC) in 1958, but was frustrated by the chauvinism of its clerical leadership. Baker left the SCLC in 1960 to help found the Student Non-violent Coordinating Committee. In 1964 she helped form the Mississippi Freedom Democratic Party, and from 1962 to 1967 she worked for the Southern Conference Education Fund. Failing health curtailed her activism in the 1970s and 1980s, but she served as a role model and symbol for a number of civil rights groups. Baker is remembered for her insistence on interdependence, equality, and nonhierarchical sharing of power.

ANB; BWA; NBAW; NoAWC; Barbara Ransby, *Ella Baker and the Black Freedom Movement* (2003); Joanne Grant, *Ella Baker: Freedom Bound* (1998).

SCOTT D. SEAY

Bakker Messner, Tammy Faye LaValley (1942–2007). Televangelist. Born in International Falls, Minnesota, into a strict Pentecostal family, Tammy Faye LaValley attended North Central College, the Assemblies of God school in Minneapolis, but left in 1961 to marry Jim Bakker. Becoming itinerant evangelists, the couple specialized in children's ministries until 1966 when they joined Pat Robertson's Christian Broadcasting Network. In 1974 the Bakkers began hosting *The PTL Club*, which became one of the highest-rated religious television shows. There Tammy Faye Bakker stretched the rules of Pentecostalism by wearing makeup and jewelry. By the late 1980s problems stemming from their opulent lifestyle, marital infidelity, and financial irregularities caused their ministry to crumble. Jim Bakker was convicted to a lengthy prison term. Tammy Faye Bakker divorced and remarried. In her final years she appeared on television shows and in 2003 published her best-selling book, *I Will Survive . . . and You Will Too.*

EAWR; EE.

JUDITH METZ, SC

Balch, Emily Greene (1867–1961). Pacifist and social activist. Born in Boston, Emily Balch was one of the first graduates of Bryn Mawr College and an early settlement house worker. She joined the Wellesley College faculty in 1896, where she taught economics and sociology for more than 20 years. She served on state commissions on immigration and industrial education, and participated in the women's suffrage movement. The outbreak of World War I convinced Balch, however, that her focus should be on eradicating war. She spent her sabbatical time during the war engaged in extensive pacifist work, which included active attendance at the 1915 International Congress of Women at the Hague. She was dismissed from the Wellesley faculty in 1918 as a result of these activities. She cofounded the Women's International League of Peace and Freedom with *Jane Addams in 1919, became a Quaker in 1921, and devoted the remainder of her life to world peace. Balch was awarded the Nobel Peace Prize in 1946, the first Quaker to be so honored.

ANB; NoAWMP; Patricia Ann Palmieri, *In Adamless Eden: The Community of Women Faculty at Wellesley* (1995); Mercedes Randall, *Improper Bostonian: Emily Greene Balch* (1964); Papers, Swarthmore College Peace Collection.

ANNIE RUSSELL

Barnard, Hannah Jenkins (ca. 1754–1825). Quaker preacher. Born to Baptist parents in Massachusetts, Hannah Jenkins received no formal education. She became a Quaker in 1772 and married Peter Barnard eight years later. They relocated to Hudson, New York. Throughout the 1790s Barnard was a representative to the New York Yearly Meeting, did missionary work in western Connecticut, and was an emissary to the Friends' meetings in Scotland, Ireland, and England. Shocked by her theological rationalism, the London Yearly Meeting charged her with heresy and censured her in 1800. Her own meeting conducted a similar heresy trial upon her return and silenced her as a minister in 1802. Her standing as a minister was never restored, even though theological views similar to hers were eventually adopted by the Hicksite Quakers in the 1820s.

ANB; NoAW; Thomas Foster, *A Narrative of the Proceedings. . . in the Case of Hannah Barnard* (1804); Hannah Barnard, *An Appeal to the Society of Friends* (1801).

SCOTT D. SEAY

Barr, Amelia Edith Huddleston (1831–1919). Author. Amelia Huddleston was born in Lancashire, England, to a Quaker mother and Methodist minister father. She married Robert Barr in 1850, and they immigrated to the U.S. in 1853, eventually settling in Texas. After the 1867 death of her husband and all three of their sons (three other children having died previously), Barr moved with her three surviving daughters to New York City, where she wrote full-time for the rest of her life. She published 80 books. Barr accepted reincarnation as a human being's progression from original sin to celestial perfection; she believed in the moral influence of mystical visions; and she affirmed that past errors could always be remedied. Readers prized her stories for their wholesome plots.

ANB; EAWR; NoAW; RLA; *Dictionary of Literary Biography;* Amelia E. Barr, *All the Days of My Life* (1913); Papers, the Center for American History, University of Texas at Austin.

SANDRA L. BEARDSALL

Barrett, Janie Aurora Porter (1865–1948). Educator. Janie Porter was educated alongside the children of the family where her mother, a former slave, worked as a housekeeper. She graduated from Hampton Institute and became a teacher. In 1889 she married Harris Barrett, a bookkeeper at Hampton. She began teaching neighborhood children informally in her home, and in 1890 she established the Locust Street Social Settlement. The following year the Barretts built a home for its activities on their property. In 1908 she helped to found the Virginia State Federation of Colored Women's Clubs and served as its first president. Barrett was concerned for African American girls who had served time in prison, and through the federation she founded what became the Virginia Industrial School for Colored Girls in 1915. She became its superintendent, and following her death it was renamed the Janie Porter Barrett School for Girls.

BWARC; NBAW; NoAW.

MARILYN FÄRDIG WHITELEY

Barrett, Kate Harwood Waller (1858–1925). Advocate for unwed mothers. Kate Waller was raised and educated in Virginia. She married an Episcopal priest, Robert Barrett, and they moved to Kentucky where they offered pastoral care to prostitutes. Barrett received her MD at the Women's Medical College of Georgia in 1892, while her husband was dean of the St. Luke's Cathedral in Atlanta. The following year, despite public disapproval, Barrett opened a home for unwed mothers with a gift from millionaire evangelist Charles Crittenton. In 1895 the National Florence Crittendon Mission was established, with Charles Crittendon as president and Barrett as vice president and general superintendent of over 50 homes across the country. Barrett became national president of the organization in 1909. Under her leadership, the Florence Crittenden homes gradually gave up the cause of converting prostitutes and focused efforts on unwed mothers and the care of their infants.

EAWR; NoAW; Katherine Aiken, *Harnessing the Power of Motherhood: The National Florence Crittendon Mission* (1998); Kate Waller Barrett, *Some Practical Suggestions on the Conduct of a Rescue Home* (1974) [1903]; Otto Wilson with Robert South Barrett, *Fifty Years' Work with Girls* (1974) [1933]; Emma O. Lundberg, *Unto the Least of These* (1947); Bridgette Zerfas, "Barrett, Kate Harwood Waller," www.learningtogive.org/papers.

SHERYL A. KUJAWA-HOLBROOK

Barry, Leonora Marie Kearney (1849–1930). Labor organizer, suffragist, temperance worker. Leonora Kearney was born in Ireland and came to the U.S. with her parents in the 1850s. In the 1880s she was an organizer for the Knights of Labor. Her labor activism rose out of her experience as a widowed mill worker and parent. Pennsylvania's first factory inspection act of 1889 was a direct result of her outrage over working conditions. In 1890 Barry remarried and left union organizing because of her belief that women should not work outside the home except in cases of economic necessity. She then spoke for the Catholic Total Abstinence Union of America and, after her husband's death in 1916, lectured on the Chautauqua circuit.

ANB; EACH; NoAW; Betsy Kepes, "Leonora Barry: First Voice for Working Women," *Labor's Heritage* 12 (Winter–Spring 2003); Deirdre M. Moloney, *American Catholic Lay Groups and Transatlantic Social Reform in the Progressive Era* (2002).

ANNIE RUSSELL

Bateham, Josephine Abiah Penfield Cushman (1829–1901). Social reformer. Josephine Penfield married her first husband in 1848, and they became missionaries in Haiti, where her husband died after 11 months of service. She returned to the U.S. in 1849 and married Michael Bateham, founder and editor of the *Ohio Cultivator*, in 1850. As editor of the ladies' department for the *Cultivator*, Bateham discussed domestic issues, woman's rights, education, peace, and temperance. In 1853 she was the president of the temperance society for the women of Ohio. After the Civil War, Bateham helped organize the Ohio chapter of the *Woman's Christian Temperance Union (WCTU). From 1884 to 1896 she served as superintendent of the national WCTU's department for the suppression of Sabbath desecration. She worked through the WCTU in 1888 on behalf of the National Sunday Rest bill, which would have prohibited work on Sunday.

NoAW; RLA; Nancy Hardesty, *Women Called to Witness* (1984).

KEITH DURSO

Bayer, Adèle Parmentier (1814–92). Roman Catholic social worker. Born in Belgium, Adèle Parmentier moved to New York City with her family in 1824. After the death of her father she and her family devoted much of their income to religious causes and to social ministries. She married Edward Bayer in 1839, and three years later they purchased land in southeastern Tennessee where they established the Vineland or Bayer's Settlement, a colony for 17 German, French, and Italian Catholic families. The colony eventually failed, and the land was given away or sold in 1897. Bayer devoted herself to ministering to seamen in Brooklyn, Bedloe Island, and Staten Island. Her fluency in German, Italian, Spanish, English, and French helped her in this ministry. During the Civil War, she helped sailors at the Brooklyn Naval Yard (BNY). Concerned about the sailors' religious life, Bayer was involved in having a priest appointed to the BNY. In 1888 she was instrumental in having Father Charles H. Parks appointed as the first Catholic chaplain of the U.S. Navy.

ANB; NoAW; *Catholic Encyclopedia*, www.newadvent.org/cathen.

KEITH DURSO

Beall, Myrtle D. Monville (1896–1979). Pentecostal leader. Myrtle Monville was raised in a Roman Catholic home but converted to Methodism upon her marriage. In the 1930s, while living in Detroit, she experienced baptism of the Holy Spirit. She then began her own Sunday school and eventually opened the Bethesda Missionary Temple. In 1939 God revealed to Beall his plans for her to "build an armory" from which "soldiers" would be equipped for the Christian battlefield. The size of her church increased from 350 to 3,000 seats. In the 1940s Beall began live broadcasts from the Bethesda Missionary Temple. Bethesda also became the center of the Latter Rain Movement. In 1949 participation in this movement precipitated a split with the Assemblies of God denomination.

EE; Edith L. Blumhofer, *Restoring the Faith: The Assemblies of God, Pentecostalism, and American Culture* (1993); Bethesda Christian Church, www.bethesdachristian.org.

JUDITH L. GIBBARD

Beasley, Mathilda Taylor (ca. 1832–1903). Franciscan sister and founder of first African American convent in Georgia. Married sometime in the 1850s to a freed, wealthy black man in Savannah, Mathilda Beasley clandestinely taught black children. After her husband died in 1878 she donated her inherited land to the Roman Catholic Church to establish the St. Francis Home for Colored Orphans, the first orphanage for African American girls, and went to England, where she became a *Franciscan sister. She later returned to Georgia and started the Third Order of St. Francis, the first community of black nuns in Georgia. Receiving no assistance from the Franciscan Order, the community eventually disbanded. Beasley lived the rest of her life in a small house in Savannah, sewing and doing charitable works.

BWA; NCE; Cyprian Davis, *History of Black Catholics in the United States* (1990);

Georgia Women of Achievement, www.gawomen.org/honorees/beasleym.htm.
KEITH DURSO

Bedell, Harriet M. (1875–1969). Episcopal deaconess and missionary. Harriett Bedell attended the New York Training School for Deaconesses and was set apart as a deaconess in 1922, after she had worked as a missionary among the Cheyenne in Oklahoma and as a teacher and nurse in Alaska, 40 miles south of the Arctic Circle. In 1932 she learned about the plight of the Seminoles in Florida and used her own salary to reopen a mission among the Mikasuki Indians. Although forced to officially retire at the age of sixty-three, she continued her ministry of health care, education, and economic empowerment until 1960. The Diocese of Southwest Florida celebrates Harriet Bedell Day on January 8, the anniversary of her death.

Sheryl A. Kujawa-Holbrook, *Freedom Is a Dream* (2002); William and Ellen Hartley, *A Woman Set Apart* (1963); Harriet Bedell, "Among the Indians of Oklahoma," *The Spirit of Missions* 85 (April 1910).
SHERYL A. KUJAWA-HOLBROOK

Beecher, Catharine Esther (1800–1878). Author and educator. Eldest daughter of prominent clergyman Lyman Beecher, Catharine Beecher was born in East Hampton, New York, and raised in Connecticut. When her fiancé, Alexander Fisher, died at sea in 1822, possibly without the conversion experience that would assure his salvation, Beecher turned her energies to women's education. She and her sister, Mary, founded the Hartford Female Seminary in 1823 to offer young women a rigorous education, as well as training in teaching and domestic science. After moving to Cincinnati with her father in 1832 she opened the Western Female Institute. Beecher promoted her ideas on educational reform, including the need for female education and teachers and an emphasis on moral and religious education, through several publications: *Suggestions Respecting Improvements in Education* (1829), *A Treatise on Domestic Economy* (1841), and *The Duty of American Women to Their Country* (1845). When the Western Female Institute closed in 1837 Beecher traveled and lectured for decades on behalf of women teachers and schools on the frontier. The 1822 crisis of her fiancé's death also set Beecher on a lifetime of theological questioning and writing. She ultimately rejected her father's Calvinism and the concept of original sin and developed her own admittedly Pelagian theological system, emphasizing free will and the importance of Christian nurture and education. (Refer to her *Common Sense Applied to Religion* [1857] and *Religious Training of Children in the School, the Family, and the Church* [1864].) Beecher saw the place of women as distinctive and crucial in shaping the future of the U.S. through their roles as mothers and teachers, and she spent her life trying to enhance support and respect for female contributions.

ANB; EE; NoAW; Katherine Kish Sklar, *Catharine Beecher* (1973); Lyman Beecher Stowe, *Saints, Sinners, and Beechers* (1934).
BEVERLY ZINK-SAWYER

Bender, Elizabeth Horsch (1895–1988). Scholar, editor, and translator. Elizabeth Horsh was born to John and Christine Funck Horsch in Elkhart, Indiana. She received a BA from Goshen College (Indiana) and an MA in German literature from the University of Minnesota. She married Harold S. Bender, a Mennonite writer and theologian, and served as primary editor for his books and articles. They had two daughters. A skilled linguist, Bender translated works from Dutch, French, Spanish, Latin, and German into German and English. She is noted for her translation of the *Mennonitisches Lexikon* that became the core of the four-volume *Mennonite Encyclopedia* (1955–59). She was an editor for the *Mennonite Quarterly Review* (1927–85) and was on the faculty of Goshen College. Her scholarly interests focused on Mennonites in German and American literature.

The Mennonite Encyclopedia, vol. 5, ed. Cornelius J. Dyck and Dennis D. Marten (1990); Elaine Sommers Rich, *Mennonite Women: A Story of God's Faithfulness* (1983).

VALERIE REMPEL

Benedictine Sisters (ca. 547–). Roman Catholic uncloistered women's branch of the Order of Saint Benedict. Women began following the *Rule of Saint Benedict* in sixth-century Italy. Until the middle of the 19th century, Benedictine women were enclosed (cloistered) within a monastery unit, devoted to prayer, work, and community living, and without external works of charity. These cloistered women were typically called nuns. In 1852 three nuns from an 11th-century monastery in Eichstätt, Bavaria, immigrated to St. Marys, Pennsylvania, under the leadership of Mother *Benedicta Riepp. So began the evolution of a new form of Benedictine life in North America. The process of transplanting the female tradition of Benedictine life from Europe necessitated some fundamental innovations. Among the changes were a modified form of enclosure (thus the designation "sister" instead of "nun"), an adapted schedule for the praying of the Divine Office, the incorporation of external works, and the custom of members living in branch houses away from the main monastery. Twenty years later, Benedictine nuns from Maria-Rickenbach (Niederrickenbach) in Switzerland immigrated to Maryville, Missouri, under the leadership of Mother Anselma Felber. Within the next 15 years, additional groups of Swiss Benedictines emigrated from Sarnen and Mecthal. Today the legacy of these pioneer sisters is represented in four major North American federations, numbering approximately 3,000 members in 54 monasteries located in the U.S., Canada, Mexico, the Bahamas, Puerto Rico, Japan, and Taiwan. The sisters of the Bavarian and Swiss traditions profess vows of stability, fidelity to monastic life, and obedience in a way of life characterized by prayer, work, and communal interaction. They are widely engaged in ministries of education and health care, pastoral and spiritual ministries, social justice work, research and writing, the arts, and liturgical renewal.

EACH; Bennett D. Hill, ed., *Encyclopedia of Monasticism*, 2 vols. (2000); Richard P. McBrien, ed., *The HarperCollins Encyclopedia of Catholicism* (1995).

EPHREM (RITA) HOLLERMANN, OSB

Benedictsson, Margaret Jonsdottir (1866–1956). Suffragist and newspaper editor. Born in northwest Iceland, Margaret Jonsdottir immigrated to North Dakota in 1887 and then to Winnipeg, Manitoba. She was a founder of First Unitarian Church of Winnipeg in 1891, and she married poet Sigfus Benedictsson in 1892. After her first suffrage speech in 1893 she joined the *Woman's Christian Temperance Union. In 1898 she began editing a newspaper, *Freyja* (meaning woman or goddess), the only women's suffrage paper then published in Canada. *Freyja* was published for 12 years. She was the founding president of the First Icelandic Suffrage Association in 1908. Benedictsson separated from her husband in 1910 and moved to Seattle, Washington, in 1913 with her children.

Harry Gutkin and Mildred Gutkin, "'Give Us Our Due!' How Manitoba Women Won the Vote," *Manitoba History* 32 (Autumn 1996) [online]; Evelyne Hloenski, *Margaret Jonsdottir Benedictsson* (1991); Sigrid Johnson, "The Icelandic Women in Manitoba and the Struggle for Women's Suffrage," *Lögberg-Heimskringla* (June 1981).

IRENE BAROS-JOHNSON

Bennett, Anne McGrew (1903–86). Religious educator and author. Anne McGrew was born in Nebraska to Scots-Irish homesteaders. Raised in the Christian Church (Disciples of Christ), the church was always a central part of her life. Upon completing high school, McGrew taught in a country school and received a degree in elementary education from the University of Nebraska in 1928. She married John C. Bennett, a professor of theology and ethics, in 1931, and received a MA in religious education in 1932. They moved back and forth between California and New York, while her husband taught at various seminaries. Bennett renewed her involvement in the church later in life, after she became a Congregationalist. She participated in numerous committees and organizations, and addressed issues of peace, justice, and women's rights. Bennett received an honorary doctorate of humane letters from the Starr King School for the Ministry in 1983.

Mary E. Hunt, ed., *From Woman-pain to Woman-vision* (1989); Papers, Graduate Theological Union (Berkeley).

BETH SPAULDING

Bennett, Isabel ("Belle") Harris (1852–1922). Methodist churchwoman and social reform advocate. In 1884, at Lake Chautauqua, New York, Belle Bennett received "baptism of the Spirit." Recognizing an urgent need for training women missionaries, she conferred with *Lucy Rider Meyer in 1887. Bennett presented the idea of establishing a missionary training school for women to the Woman's Board for Foreign Missions, Methodist Episcopal Church, South (MECS), in 1889 and was promptly appointed as their agent for the project. From these efforts Scarritt Bible and Training School was established in Kansas City in 1892. Bennett served as president of the MECS Woman's Home Missionary Society (1896–1910) and its successor, the Woman's Missionary Council (1910–22). With Bennett's leadership the MECS's first settlement house opened in Nashville in 1901. She helped to establish as many as 40 Wesley Community and Bethlehem Houses, the latter for work among African Americans. These efforts coincided with Bennett's petition to General Conference, MECS, for the office of deaconess, which was recognized in 1902. Bennett, among others, launched the campaign for women's laity rights in 1910, following the denomination's amalgamation of missionary work that resulted in the loss of autonomy for women's missionary organizations. Although women were granted laity rights in 1918 and Bennett was elected as the Kentucky Annual Conference's first female delegate to General Conference in 1922, she was too ill to attend and died that summer.

ANB; EAWR; EE; NoAW; Jean Miller Schmidt, *Grace Sufficient: A History of Women in American Methodism* (1999); Mrs. R. W. MacDonell, *Belle Harris Bennett* (1928).

LACEYE C. WARNER

Best, Marion (1932–). Canadian church and global ecumenical leader. Born in New Westminster, British Columbia, Marion Best found her spiritual home in the United Church of Canada (UCC). After a decade of hospital nursing she moved into the field of lay education at the Naramata Center (1977–87). Her gracious manner and consummate leadership abilities were soon recognized. In 1987 Best was elected president of the British Columbia Conference of the UCC. In 1988 she chaired the national denominational committee that resolved the historic issue of ordaining gays and lesbians. She was elected moderator of the UCC in 1994. A leader in global ecumenism Best began to serve on the central and executive committees of the World Council of Churches in 1991 and later was elected its vice moderator, a position she held from 1998 to 2006.

Marion Best, *What in the World Is Happening to Ecumenism?* (2001); Michael Riordon, *The First Stone: Homosexuality and the United Church* (1990).

JANET SILMAN

Bethune, Mary McLeod (1875–1955). Educator and public servant. Born of ex-slaves on a rice and cotton farm in South Carolina, Mary McLeod was the 15th of 17 children. Convinced that education was the key to improving the lives of African Americans, she took advantage of every opportunity. Her faith, organizational skills, and persistence won her the support that allowed her dream to become a reality. In 1898 she married Albertus Bethune, and they had one child. In 1904 she founded the Daytona (Florida) Literary and Industrial School for Training Negro Girls. In 1923 her school became coeducational and was renamed the Bethune-Cookman Institute. She served as president from 1923 to 1942 and again from 1946 to 1947. She also became involved in such issues as women's suffrage and African Americans' right to vote. By the 1920s she was well known in leadership roles in civil rights and women's organizations. U.S. presidents, from Calvin Coolidge to Harry Truman, appointed her to government positions. She was appointed as Franklin Roosevelt's special advisor on minority affairs (1935–44), for example, and as director of the Division of Negro Affairs of the National Youth Administration (1936–44). She formed the Federal Council on Negro Affairs, known as Roosevelt's "Black Cabinet." Bethune was a key figure in national conferences on education, child welfare, and home ownership, as well as in the black women's club movement. Besides her involvement in business ventures, she wrote articles and contributed chapters to several books. She is regarded as one of the most influential African American leaders in U.S. history.

ANB; BWA; EE; NBAW; Rackman Holt, *Mary McLeod Bethune* (1964); Beverly Johnson-Miller, "Mary McLeod Bethune." Christian Educators of the 20th Century, www.talbot.edu/ce20.

JUDITH METZ, SC

Bible Study Fellowship (BSF International) (1958–). Educational program. The program grew out of a small Bible study class begun in 1952 and was led by Audrey Wetherell Johnson (1907–84), a former missionary to China. Its headquarters were first established in Oakland, California, in 1958 and moved to San Antonio, Texas, in 1981. Aided by the administrative skills of Alverda Hertzler (1900–91), BSF International developed into a strongly centralized organization offering classes for women, men, and children, and young, single adults. Johnson's lesson plans and study notes served as the basis for what is now a seven-year rotation of study featuring Romans, Matthew, the Life of Moses, John, History of Israel and the Minor Prophets, Acts of the Apostles, and Genesis. It provides a highly structured course of Bible study featuring lectures, discussion groups, study notes, and daily questions for individual study. The program relies on a core of highly trained volunteers who lead classes and small discussion groups. Lesson materials are available to students only, but are provided without cost. BSF International is active in over 30 countries.

A. Wetherell Johnson, *Created for Commitment: The Remarkable Story of the Founder of the Bible Study Fellowship* (1982).

VALERIE REMPEL

Billings, Mary Charlotte Ward Grannis Webster (1824–1904). Author, missionary, first ordained woman Universalist minister in Texas. Mary Charlotte Ward was born to an Episcopal family in Litchfield, Connecticut, and converted to Universalism in her teens. She first married (1845–66) Hartford silk merchant Frederick Granniss. They enjoyed European travel and a beautiful home. Being childless, she devoted herself to writing stories, poems, hymns, and travelogues. She published widely, as in the *Ladies Repository*. Her stories expressed her theology, since public preaching was not widely available to women. Next she married Universalist minister Charles Webster (1869–77). As lay preacher, she transitioned toward public ministry. Finally, she married James Billings (1885–98), first Texas Universalist missionary. Based in Hico, they established the Texas Universalist Convention, which ordained her in 1892. Universalism in Texas significantly declined after her death.

DUUB; UUWM; E. R. Hanson, *Our Woman Workers* (1884).

BARBARA COEYMAN

Blackwell, Antoinette Louisa Brown (1825–1921). Clergywoman and suffragist. Born into a devout Congregational family in Henrietta, New York, Antoinette Brown sensed a call to a religious vocation from a young age. She attended Oberlin Collegiate Institute in Ohio, receiving a literary diploma in 1847, and returned the following fall to study theology and pursue ordained ministry. Despite opposition from family, friends, and the Oberlin faculty, Brown completed a course in theology and was invited to serve as pastor of a small Congregational church in South Butler, New York. The congregation voted to ordain her on 15 September 1853, making her the first woman in the U.S. to be ordained as a minister. She left the church in 1854 in response to theological differences with the congregation and her increasing popularity as a speaker for the woman's rights movement. Later in life she became a minister in the Unitarian Church. One of the first women admitted to the American Association for the Advancement of Science and a founding member of the Association for the Advancement of Women, she published 10 books covering subjects such as metaphysics, gender, philosophy, and theology, as well as a novel and a book of poetry. With her husband, Samuel Blackwell, she raised five daughters. One of those daughters took her to vote in 1920 in the first national election open to women.

ANB; DARB; EAWR; NoAW; RLA; UU; Beverly Zink-Sawyer, *From Preachers to Suffragists* (2003); Elizabeth Cazden, *Antoinette Brown Blackwell* (1983); Papers, Schlesinger Library, Radcliffe Institute, Harvard University.

BEVERLY ZINK-SAWYER

Blavatsky, Helena Petrovna (1831–91). Occultist, writer, cofounder of the Theosophical Society. Born in Russia to a military father and literary mother, Helena Blavatsky traveled widely in Europe, Egypt, and Russia after running away from an early marriage. She arrived in New York in 1873 and in 1875 founded with Colonel Henry Steel Olcott the Theosophical Society, a religio-scientific occultist movement that incorporated Eastern teachings. Blavatsky claimed as her inspiration the teachings of ascended masters or mahatmas. By 1883 the society headquarters was established in Adyar, India. She died in London, where she had gone in 1887 to found the Blavatsky Lodge of Theosophy, edit the magazine *Lucifer*, and complete one of her best-known publications, *The Secret Doctrine* (1889). A controversial figure, Blavatsky has been assessed as both a creative and charismatic leader and as an imposter.

ANB; DARB; EAWR: NoAW; RLA; Sylvia Cranston, *H. P. B.: The Extraordinary Life and Influence of Helena Blavatsky* (1993); Helena P. Blavatsky, *Isis Unveiled* (1877).

MARY FARRELL BEDNAROWSKI

Bliss, Anna Elvira (1843–1925). Missionary and educator. The daughter of a Congregational minister, Anna Bliss was born in Jericho, Vermont. Upon her father's retirement from the ministry, the family moved to western Massachusetts. Bliss graduated from Mount Holyoke College in 1862. Joining *Abbie Park Ferguson, another Mount Holyoke alumnus, Bliss left for Cape Town, South Africa, in 1873 to found a seminary for girls; Huguenot Seminary was opened in 1874. The school grew over the years, with Bliss assuming more administrative responsibilities. As the gold rush in the late 1880s brought more settlers into the area, Ferguson went on to found Huguenot College, while the seminary became the Huguenot Girls High School, with Bliss as president. Bliss became the president of Huguenot College when Ferguson retired in 1910. The Huguenot network of schools produced the first well-educated women in South Africa.

NoAW; George P. Ferguson, *The Builders of Huguenot* (1927).

BETH SPAULDING

Bloomer, Amelia Jenks (1818–94). Editor, temperance reformer, and suffragist. Born in Homer, New York, Amelia Jenks taught school and worked as a governess until her 1840 marriage to Dexter Bloomer, an attorney, reformer, and editor. After their move to his home in Seneca Falls, Bloomer wrote on social, moral, and political subjects for the Seneca County *Courier*, as well as for a local temperance journal. In 1849 she started her own paper, the *Lily*, to address temperance and other reforms, especially woman's rights, making her the first U.S. woman to own, operate, and edit a newspaper for women. Her paper advocated the Turkish pantaloons style of dress worn by some women through the 1850s, earning them the nickname "bloomers." The Bloomers, who adopted two children, moved to Council Bluffs, Iowa, in 1855. Bloomer sold the *Lily* before their move, but continued to write and lecture on behalf of women's suffrage. An Episcopalian, Bloomer rejected scriptural arguments used to oppose women's rights.

ANB; NoAW; Dexter C. Bloomer, *Life and Writings of Amelia Bloomer* (1895).

BEVERLY ZINK-SAWYER

Bonney Rambaut, Mary Lucinda (1816–1900). Educator and advocate for Native American rights. Born in New York and educated at the Troy Female Academy (1833–35), Bonney became a Baptist while teaching in South Carolina in 1842. She opened the Chestnut Street Female Academy in Philadelphia, Pennsylvania (later the Ogontz School for Young Ladies), where she was senior principal from 1850 to 1888. In 1880 she and Amelia S. Quinton established what ultimately became the Women's National Indian Association to lobby for Native American rights and support missionary outreach and education. Bonney paid the bills initially, served briefly as president (1881–84), and gave the organization her lifelong, energetic support. Her 1888 marriage to Thomas Rambaut, a Baptist minister, ended with his death in 1890.

ANB; EAWR; NoAW; RLA; Frances E. Willard and Mary A. Livermore, ed., *A Woman of the Century* (1893).

KENDAL P. MOBLEY

Bonnin, Gertrude Simmons (Zitkala-Sa) (1876–1938). Writer and activist. Gertrude Simmons (Yankton Nakota) attended White's Manual Labor Institute (Wabash, Indiana), the Santee Normal Training School, and Earlham College. She taught briefly at the Carlisle Indian Industrial School, where she created her literary nom de plume, Zitkala-Sa (Red Bird). In 1901 she published *Old Indian Legends*, a retelling of Iktomi (trickster) stories. In 1902 she married Raymond Talesfase Bonnin (Yankton). They moved to Utah and became opponents of peyote religion. Bonnin joined the Society of American Indians (SAI), gave birth to a son, and collaborated with William Hanson on *The Sun Dance Opera*. In 1916 the Bonnins moved to Washington, DC. She edited the SAI's *American Indian Magazine* and continued her activism against peyote and for Native citizenship. In 1926 the Bonnins founded the National Congress of American Indians; as president she advised the influential 1928 Merriam Commission. She is buried in Arlington Cemetery.

ANB; NaAW; NoAW; Zitkala-Sa, *Dreams and Thunder*, ed. P. Jane Hafen (2001); Margaret A. Lukens, "The American Story of Zitkala-Sa," in *In Her Own Voice*, ed. Sherry Lee Linkon (1997); Doreen Rappaport, *The Flight of Red Bird* (1997).

LISA J. POIRIER

Boole, Ella Alexander (1858–1952). Temperance leader. Ella Boole and her husband William Hilliker Boole, a prominent Methodist clergyman and Prohibition lecturer, ministered to alcoholics in Brooklyn, New York. Elected corresponding secretary of the Brooklyn *Woman's Christian Temperance Union (WCTU) in 1886 Boole promoted other social causes, such as child labor reform, woman's suffrage, and international peace. A gifted speaker and organizer, Boole served as president of the New York State WCTU (1898–1903; 1909–26), vice president (1914) and president of the National WCTU (1925–33), and head of the World WCTU (1931–47). As president of the national WCTU, she lobbied to have alcohol removed from military installations, Native American reservations, and government buildings. Boole served as secretary of the Woman's Board of Home Missions (1903–09) and as an ordained deaconess of the Presbyterian Church. In 1920 she ran unsuccessfully for the U.S. Senate as the Prohibition candidate.

ANB; NoAWMP; RLA.

KEITH DURSO

Booth, Evangeline Cory (1865–1950) and **Maud Ballington Booth** (1865–1948). Salvation Army leaders. Evangeline Booth was the daughter of William Booth and Catherine Mumford Booth, founders of the Salvation Army. By pen and example, Catherine Booth was a defender of the right of women to preach and lead. As a teenager Evangeline Booth preached and distributed literature in the slums of London. She quickly developed a reputation as a mediator and inspirational leader and was given command of the army in London. In 1896 she was sent to the U.S. to settle a dispute between her brother, Ballington, and her father over the latter's autocratic rule of the American army. Ballington and his wife, Maud (born Maud Elizabeth Charlesworth), had done much as commanders to build up the organization in the U.S. Maud, in particular, gained supporters among New York's social and political elite and was admired for her day-care centers for working women and her shelters for the homeless. The Ballington Booths both resigned their commands, but Evangeline Booth succeeded in holding the organization together. She was then called in 1896 to head the army in Canada, and in 1904 she began a 30-year career as leader in the U.S. The army flourished, expanding its program to include disaster relief, homes for young working women, and a myriad of other social services. Evangeline Booth developed a network of wealthy sympathizers and was able to hand over a financially stable organization when she returned to London to become general, an office she held from 1934 to 1939. Maud Ballington Booth became cofounder of the Volunteers of America and became especially involved in prison reform.

ANB; DARB; EAWR; EE; NoAW; RLA; John F. McMahon, *The Volunteers of America* (1972); Sigmund A. Lavine, *Evangeline Booth, Daughter of Salvation* (1970); Susan F. Welty, *Look Up and Hope!* (1961); Philip Whitwell Wilson, *General Evangeline Booth of the Salvation Army* (1948); Veronica Constantine, "Booth, Maud Ballington," www.learningtogive.org/papers.

BARBARA J. MACHAFFIE

Bourgeoys, Marguerite (1620–1700). Founder of the Congregation of Notre Dame. Marguerite Bourgeoys was born into a middle-class family in Troyes, France. When she was 20, she entered the external congregation of the cloistered *Sisters of Notre Dame, directed by the sister of Paul de Chomedy de Maisonneuve, governor of Ville-Marie (Montreal). At the age of 33 Bourgeoys was invited to go to Montreal to begin the education of women and children of the colony. She and her sisters lived with the immigrant women, helped them to adapt, and provided free instruction to them and to the French and native children. She soon became known as the "mother of the colony." Bourgeoys's congregation was one of the first noncloistered communities of women, meaning that they were able to move freely among the poor and disadvantaged. She was canonized in 1982.

DCB; Patricia Simpson, *Marguerite Bourgeoys and Montreal* (1997).

ELAINE GUILLEMIN

Bowen, Louise deKoven (1859–1953). Episcopal reformer, philanthropist, and suffragist. Although Louise deKoven Bowen experienced frustration with the limited role of women in the Episcopal Church, her early church work with male youths set her reform agenda in motion. A colleague of *Jane Addams and lifelong financial supporter and active leader at Hull House, Bowen used her wealth and influence there (and in numerous other organizations) to improve the welfare of women and children in Chicago and Illinois. Throughout her long career, she developed powerful social and bipartisan political networks. Bowen was a pioneer in the effort to establish a juvenile court system in Chicago, which led to the formation of the Juvenile Protective Association. She was one of the first reformers in Chicago to recognize the needs of African Americans. During World War I she was the only woman appointed to the Illinois Council of Defense. She continued her philanthropic, political, and reform work until the mid-20th century.

ANB; NoAWMP; WBC; Sheryl A. Kujawa-Holbrook, *Freedom Is a Dream* (2002); Eleanor J. Stebner, *The Women of Hull House* (1997); Louise DeKoven Bowen, *Growing Up with a City* (1926).

SHERYL A. KUJAWA-HOLBROOK

Bowles, Eva del Vakia (1875–1943). *YWCA executive. Eva Bowles was appointed secretary of the Harlem branch of the New York City YWCA in 1905. After becoming secretary of the Committee on Colored Work for the National Board of the YWCA, she trod a fine line between the black branches and the administrative control exercised over them by the white central associations. She argued for gradual growth of the black program, while denouncing any establishment of a permanent "colored" department. As coordinator of the Committee on Colored Work in the 1920s, she worked toward interracial integration. She regarded the dissolution of the committee in 1931 as a victory for her efforts toward full integration of the YWCA.

ANBO; BWA; BWARC; EAWR; NBAW; NoAW; RLA; Linda Gordon, "Black and White Visions of Welfare: Women's Welfare Activism, 1890–1945," *Journal of American History* 78, no. 2 (September 1991).

ANNIE RUSSELL

Bowman, Bertha ("Sister Thea") (1937–90). Educator and evangelist.

Born in Yazoo City, Mississippi, to a physician father and a schoolteacher mother, Bertha Bowman attended a school staffed by *Franciscan Sisters of Perpetual Adoration. At age nine she asked her parents' permission to leave her Methodist church and become a Roman Catholic. At 15 she joined the Franciscan Sisters of Perpetual Adoration, an all-white community, and took the name Sister Thea. Believing in the power of black sacred songs, she used her beautiful voice and dynamic personality to communicate her African American heritage. She combined singing, gospel preaching, prayer, and storytelling in presentations across the country, breaking down racial and cultural barriers while communicating that "we are all beautiful children of God." Diagnosed with bone cancer in 1984, she continued to work from a wheelchair; she was determined to live fully until she died.

BWA; BWARC; *United States Catholic Catechism for Adults* (2006).

JUDITH METZ, SC

Boyd, Mary (1937–). Roman Catholic activist. Mary Boyd was the first woman Catholic Diocesan Director of Social Action in Canada (1972–94), serving in the Charlottetown, Prince Edward Island, diocese. Earlier she performed lay missionary work in Africa and marched for civil rights in Selma, Alabama. Holding a bachelor's degree in history and a master's degree in sociology, she concentrated her later work on the conscientizing methodology of Brazilian liberationist Paulo Freire. This emphasis led to her book, *From the Grass Roots* (1987), which adapted Freire's work to the Canadian scene, and her workshops on activist pedagogy in Australia. She has received various awards and written articles on social justice. Her faith prompts her to remain involved in social justice activities that, most recently, led her to protest the U.S. invasion of Iraq.

"P.E.I. Legens," *Charlottetown Guardian*, July 2001; Zonta Club of Charlottetown, *Making History: A Celebration of Prince Edward Island Women* (2000); Christopher Lind and Joe Mihevc, eds., *Coalitions for Justice: The Story of Canada's Interchurch Coalitions* (1994).

OSCAR COLE-ARNAL

Bradstreet, Anne Dudley (ca. 1612–72). Puritan poet. Born in Northampton, England, Anne Bradstreet immigrated to the Massachusetts Bay Colony in 1630 with her new husband, Puritan minister Simon Bradstreet. She moved among the most cultured persons of New England society. Although she initially despaired of being able to do so, she bore and raised eight children. In her early poetry Bradstreet imitated the formal style of her male literary contemporaries. Nevertheless she was dissatisfied with her work *The Tenth Muse* (1650), and never again wrote imitative poetry. Instead, she wrote affectively about her experiences as a wife and mother, reflecting her deep Puritan piety. Much of her work was probably lost when her Andover home burned in 1666. Her *Several Poems Compiled with Great Variety of Wit and Learning* appeared posthumously in 1678, and it included many poems to her children. Her influence on later poets is a matter of considerable debate, but she is widely regarded as America's first important woman poet.

ANB; NoAW; Ann Stanford, *Anne Bradstreet: The Worldly Puritan* (1974); Anne Bradstreet, *The Works of Anne Bradstreet*, ed. Robert Hensley (1967).

SCOTT D. SEAY

Brahma Kumaris (1936–). Hindu organization. The Brahma Kumaris World Spiritual Organization started in Hyderbad (now in Pakistan) when its founder, Dada Lekhraj (1876–1969), had visions about the nature of the soul and God. Women have played a central role in the organization. In 1937 Dada Lekhraj appointed a managing committee of eight young women. In 1952 he sent some women from his community to spread its teachings throughout India. Although their teachings are best understood as a reform movement within Hinduism, they have sought recognition as a religion separate from Hinduism in recent years. Their teachings are from the Raja Yoga tradition of Hinduism. Followers are encouraged to practice meditation, vegetarianism, and devotion. Full-time participants, men and women, lead celibate lives. Brahma Kumaris centers in the U.S. and Canada offer free courses in meditation, books, and spiritual counseling.

John Walliss, *The Brahma Kumaris as a "Reflexive Tradition"* (2002).

BARBARA E. REED

Brayton, Patience Greene (1733–94). Quaker minister and abolitionist. Born in Rhode Island, Patience Brayton was one of numerous women who believed they were called by God to sustain and expand the Quaker community through preaching. Her ministry took her beyond New England to the southern colonies, and in 1783 to Philadelphia, England, and Ireland. While in England she supported Quaker women seeking their own London Yearly Meeting. Her journals reflect her experiences as a traveling female minister who suffered from bouts of self-doubt, physical ailments, and homesickness, but who also rejoiced in seeing God working through her. Brayton carried out her ministry while married to Massachusetts abolitionist Preserved Brayton. They had three children, one of whom died while she was traveling. Poor health restricted her ministry to the eastern New England meetings toward the end of her life.

Patience Brayton, *A Short Account of the Life and Religious Labours of Patience Brayton* (1801).

BARBARA J. MACHAFFIE

Breckinridge, Madeline McDowell (1872–1920). Reformer and suffragist. From a prominent Kentucky family, educated at elite women's schools and the University of Kentucky, Madeline McDowell married Desha Breckinridge, editor of the *Lexington Herald*, in 1898. Her husband and sister-in-law (social worker Sophonisba Breckinridge) encouraged her reform interests. She led her women's group at Grace Episcopal Church (Lexington) to found a settlement home near Proctor, Kentucky. An advocate in the fight against tuberculosis, Breckinridge lost part of her leg to the disease. Later reform work convinced her that the success of reform agendas depended on women's suffrage. A leader in both state and national suffrage associations, she coordinated efforts for Kentucky's ratification of the 19th Amendment shortly before dying of a stroke.

ANB; NoAW; Sophonisba P. Breckinridge, *Madeline McDowell Breckinridge* (1921).

JOAN R. GUNDERSEN

Bridgman, Eliza Jane Gillet (1805–71). Missionary educator. Episcopalian Eliza Gillett aspired to become a missionary but delayed her wish for 17 years while she supported her widowed mother as a New York City girls' school principal. She arrived in China in 1845 as America's first single female missionary, but married Elijah Bridgman within two months and became a Congregationalist missionary with the American Board of Commissioners for Foreign Missions. She adopted two Chinese girls in Shanghai and started the city's first girls' school. After her husband's death in 1861 and a two-year stay in the U.S., Bridgman returned to China. She settled in Peking and opened the capital's first Protestant educational institution, the Bridgman School, which educated a large number of China's women leaders. She died in Shanghai, where she had started another Chinese girls' school.

ANB; NoAW; R. Pierce Beaver, *American Protestant Women in World Mission*, rev. ed. (1980) [1968]; E. G. Bridgman, *Daughters of China* (1853).

JANE HARRIS

Brigden, Beatrice (1888–1977). Social reformer. Beatrice Brigden grew up on a homestead in Manitoba, where J. S. Woodsworth, Methodist minister and social activist, became a strong influence in her life. She graduated from Brandon College and, after studying vocal expression at the Toronto Conservatory, worked in factories to understand the situation of the workers. In 1913 she began training to do social purity work on behalf of the Methodist Church and subsequently spent the next six years lecturing on sex education and social problems across Canada. She became frustrated with the Methodist Church and left it to become part of the Brandon Labor Church, where she served as a leader from 1920 until 1928. She continued working until her death for such causes as socialism, women's rights, and pacifism.

Eleanor J. Stebner, "More Than Maternal Feminists and Good Samaritans: Women and the Social Gospel in Canada," in *Gender and the Social Gospel*, ed. Wendy Deichmann Edwards and Carolyn DeSwarte Gifford (2003); Beatrice Brigden, "One Woman's Campaign for Social Purity and Social Reform," in *The Social Gospel in Canada*, ed. Richard Allen (1975).

MARILYN FÄRDIG WHITELEY

Brooks, Nona Lovell (1861–1945). New Thought teacher, healer, and cofounder of Divine Science. As a persistently ill young woman in Denver, Nona Brooks experienced healing through a student of *Emma Curtis Hopkins and consequently discovered her own healing powers. In 1889 Brooks and her sister met San Francisco healer *Malinda Elliott Cramer; Cramer was willing to collaborate with the sisters and lend her own term, Divine Science, to the movement they started. By 1925 Divine Science had centers in several U.S. cities, and Brooks was engaged in administration, teaching, healing, and lecture tours, spending extended time in Australia and Chicago. She served on the Colorado State Prison Board for many years and was president of the Divine Science College in Denver from 1938 until 1943.

ANB; EAWR; RLA; Hazel Deane, *Powerful Is the Light: The Story of Nona Brooks* (1945); Nona L. Brooks, *Short Lessons in Divine Science* (1928).

MARY FARRELL BEDNAROWSKI

Broughton, Virginia (1856–1934). Teacher, missionary, writer, and speaker. Virginia Broughton was born a free black in Tennessee. In 1875 she graduated with a collegiate degree from Fisk University. She taught in the public school system for 12 years before becoming a full-time missionary. Broughton established 57 Bible Bands, a black women's organization for the daily study of the Bible. These bands were seen by some to undermine the authority of men in the church by allowing women to interpret the Bible. While elevating the importance of women's God-given role as mothers, Broughton nonetheless argued that God approved of women functioning within the public sphere. She also served for over 20 years as the recording secretary of the newly formed Woman's National Baptist Convention.

NBAW; Evelyn Brooks Higginbotham, *Righteous Discontent* (1993); Virginia Broughton, *Twenty Years' Experience of a Missionary* (1907).

JUDITH L. GIBBARD

Brown, Catharine (ca. 1800–1823). Educator, intercultural mediator. In 1817 Catherine Brown enrolled at the Brainerd School in Chattanooga, Tennessee. A year later, she became the first Cherokee person to be baptized by the American Board of Commissioners for Foreign Missions, a group of Congregationalists and Presbyterians dedicated to Christian missions to Native peoples. While she was dedicated to Christianity and developed strong relationships with the women teachers at Brainerd, she demonstrated a powerful blend of Cherokee religious symbols with Christian doctrine. In 1820 she founded a school for Cherokee girls at Creek Path, Alabama, where she taught for nine months before returning to Brainerd. She returned home to nurse her brother through a fatal illness, but contracted tuberculosis herself. Her parents brought her to traditional healers and European American physicians, but she died of the disease.

NaAW; Theda Perdue, *Sifters: Native American Women's Lives* (2001); Rufus Anderson, *Memoir of Catharine Brown* (1825).

LISA J. POIRIER

Brown, Charlotte Eugenia Hawkins (1883–1961). African American educator and activist. Born in North Carolina, Charlotte Hawkins's family moved to Cambridge, Massachusetts, in 1888. Alice Freeman Palmer sponsored her education at the State Normal School in Salem. Hawkins took charge of an American Missionary Association (AMA) school in Sedalia, North Carolina, in 1901. The AMA withdrew support after the first year, but Hawkins persevered, opening the Alice Freeman Palmer Institute in 1902. The institute became one of the nation's leading African American preparatory schools, and she remained its innovative and charismatic leader until 1952. Hawkins's brief marriage to Edward Sumner Brown (1911–15) ended in divorce. Her strategy for racial uplift demanded cultural refinement and social justice.

ANB; BWA; NBAW; NoAWMP; Constance H. Marteena, *The Lengthening Shadow of a Woman* (1977); Charlotte Hawkins Brown, *The Correct Thing to Do, to Say, to Wear* (1941), *Mammy: An Appeal to the Heart of the South* (1919).

KENDAL P. MOBLEY

Brown, Hallie Quinn (1850–1949). Educator, civil rights activist, church leader. Hallie Brown was born to former slaves in Pittsburgh, Pennsylvania. At the age of 14 her family moved to Ontario, Canada, to start a farming business. The family later returned to the U.S., where Brown attended Wilberforce College (later renamed Wilberforce University) in Ohio. Brown worked for a variety of public and private educational institutions, including Allen University, Tuskegee Institute, and Wilberforce University. Brown was an advocate for racial justice and served in leadership for the *National Association of Colored Women. She was also a suffragist and worked for the voting rights of African American women. Brown supported the Republican Party and addressed its national convention in 1924. Active in the African Methodist Episcopal Church, Brown campaigned for the inclusion of women as representatives to the General Conference.

BWA; BWARC; NoAW; Hallie Q. Brown, *Homespun Heroines and Other Women of Distinction* (1926).

CHRISTOPHER J. ANDERSON

Brown, Marie Burgess (1880–1971). Assemblies of God pastor. Marie Burgess spent her early years in Eau Claire, Wisconsin. An Episcopalian, she moved with her family to Zion, Ilinois, a community established by the healing evangelist John Alexander Dowie. Drawn to evangelism, Burgess preached in various missions. In 1906 she embraced Pentecostalism, and in 1907, on the advice of Pentecostal evangelist Charles Parham, she opened a storefront Pentecostal mission in midtown Manhattan. In 1909 Burgess married Robert Brown, an Irish immigrant Methodist preacher whom she had converted to Pentecostalism. In 1916 the Browns brought their congregation into the newly formed Assemblies of God. They purchased a large Baptist church in midtown Manhattan in 1921 and named it Glad Tidings Tabernacle. The Browns broadcast their services and shared the preaching responsibilities. Their congregation was noted within the church for its support for foreign missions. As the founding pastor of a congregation that served as a hub for Pentecostals in the Northeast, Marie Brown was the pastor of Glad Tidings Tabernacle for 64 years.

Gordon P. Gardiner, *Out of Zion, Into All the World* (1990); Stanley M. Burgess et al., eds., *Dictionary of Pentecostal and Charismatic Movements* (1988); Edith L. Blumhofer, "Marie Burgess Brown," *Paraclete* (Summer 1987).

EDITH BLUMHOFER

Brown, Olympia (1835–1926). First American woman ordained by denominational authority, suffragist. Olympia Brown was born in Michigan to Universalist parents from Vermont. Her family supported abolition and female education. She graduated from Antioch College in 1860, during Unitarian Horace Mann's presidency. Influenced by *Antoinette Brown (Blackwell), she graduated from St. Lawrence University and was ordained in 1863 by the Lawrence Association, Malone, New York. Brown was minister in Weymouth Landing, Massachusetts, from 1864 to 1870. In 1867 she spent four months promoting suffrage in Kansas. In 1870 she served the Universalist church in Bridgeport, Connecticut. She married John Henry Willis in 1873 (she kept her surname), and they had two children. The Universalist congregation of Racine, Wisconsin, flourished under her 1876–85 ministry. Brown left parish ministry in 1887 to work for women's rights in Wisconsin and the National Woman Suffrage Association. She demonstrated before the White House when she was in her 80s and lived to cast a vote.

ANB; DUUB; EAWR; NoAW; RLA; UU; UUWM; Dorothy Emerson, ed., *Standing Before Us* (2000); Stephen Kendrick, *A Faith People Make* (1988); E. R. Hanson, *Our Woman Workers* (1884).

BARBARA COEYMAN

Brownson, Josephine Van Dyke (1880–1942). Roman Catholic author and teacher. Josephine Brownson wrote 11 books (some of which became the standard for catechists) and founded 75 centers for religious instruction. In 1916 she organized the Catholic Instruction League (CIL) for Catholic children attending public schools in Detroit, for which she developed the religious curriculum. After teaching in public schools for many years, Brownson resigned in 1930 to devote her time to the CIL. In 1933 she received the papal decoration *Pro Ecclesia et Pontifice*, and the University of Detroit awarded her an LLD. In 1939 the University of Notre Dame awarded her the Laetare Medal, and she was named a member of the American Social Service Mission to Venezuela.

NCE; NoAW; Mary L. Putrow, "Josephine Van Dyke Brownson: Conviction, Commitment, Wit and Wisdom," www.aodonline.org; Josephine Van Dyke Brownson, *Living Forever* (1928), *To the Heart of a Child* (1918).

KEITH DURSO

Bryant, Anita (1940–). Singer and activist. Born in Oklahoma, Anita Bryant began singing in her father's church at age two. She used her singing talents to garner a record contract at age 17, to become Miss Oklahoma 1959, to entertain troops in Vietnam, and to work alongside Billy Graham. Her popularity, gained in part as a spokeswoman for

Florida orange juice, was evidenced by the more than one million Americans who bought her 1972 autobiography. In 1977 she led the Save Our Children crusade against gay rights in Florida, which served as a model for other antigay rights groups around the country. Her political activism severely damaged her career and contributed to the demise of her marriage.

EE; Dudley Clendinen, "Anita Bryant, b. 1940, Singer and Crusader," *St. Petersburg Times* 28 (November 1999); Michael Lienesch, *Redeeming America: Piety and Politics in the New Christian Right* (1993).

SUSAN B. RIDGELY

Buffalo Bird Woman (ca. 1839–1932). Medicine woman and Hidatsa autobiographer. Buffalo Bird Woman was a member of the Hidatsa tribe in North Dakota. Originally named Good Way, her father renamed her Buffalo Bird Woman to protect her from illness. Because she was a descendant of chiefs on both sides of her family, she was well educated on the ways and beliefs of her people. She recounted her life and the life of her people to Gilbert Wilson, an anthropologist and Presbyterian minister, who recorded her story in *Buffalo Bird Woman's Garden* (1917) and *Waheenee: An Indian Girl's Story Told by Herself* (1921). These writings contain personal accounts of the life of a Plains Indian woman, such as the contribution of the Hidatsa women to architecture, economics, agriculture, child rearing, and art.

EAWR; NaAW; RLA; Gilbert Livingstone Wilson, *Buffalo Bird Woman's Garden* (1917) [online].

KEITH DURSO

Burleigh, Celia (1826–75). First woman ordained Unitarian minister. Celia Burleigh was born in Cazenovia, New York. After a brief career in Cincinnati as an editor, she divorced her first husband and moved to New York City in 1850. She supported herself by writing, composing music, and teaching. A second marriage in the early 1850s also failed. By 1862 she was living in Troy, New York, and serving as secretary to Emma Willard. She married William Henry Burleigh in 1865 and moved with him to Brooklyn, Connecticut, where they both joined the Unitarian Society. Burleigh emerged as a leader in women's suffrage conventions in New York, Cleveland, and Detroit. Following her husband's death in 1871, she became the first woman ordained in the Unitarian Church.

DUUB; EAWR; UUWM; Catherine F. Hitchings, "Universalist and Unitarian Women Ministers," *Journal of the Universalist Historical Society* 10 (1975).

SCOTT D. SEAY

Burns, Lucy (1879–1966). Suffragist and women's rights activist. Born in Brooklyn, New York, and educated at Vassar and Yale, Burns moved to Germany in 1906 to continue her studies. After several years at the University of Berlin and the University of Bonn, she traveled to England and enrolled at Oxford. She became active in the Women's Social and Political Union there, and met Alice Paul, with whom she later founded the Congressional Union for Woman Suffrage in the U.S. Burns was arrested for the first time in England for her militant activities; she was to become the most jailed suffragist in the U.S. She was often assaulted during demonstrations, was force-fed during hunger strikes, and may have been tortured. She retired from direct action politics once women won the vote.

EACH; NoAWMP; Eleanor Clift, *Founding Sisters and the Nineteenth Amendment* (2003); Doris Weatherford, *A History of the American Suffragist Movement* (1998); Linda G. Ford, *Iron-Jawed Angels* (1991) [HBO film of the same name, 2004].

COLLEEN CARPENTER CULLINAN

Burroughs, Nannie Helen (1879–1961). Reformer, teacher, civil rights activist, and religious leader. Nannie Burroughs was born in Orange County, Virginia. As a high school graduate and black woman, she found it difficult to find work appropriate to her skills. She moved to Louisville, Kentucky, in 1900 to accept a position as secretary to the Foreign Mission Board of the National Baptist Convention (NBC). In the same year she attended the annual meeting of the organization and delivered a memorable speech, "How the Sisters Are Hindered from Helping." She was elected secretary of the newly formed Woman's Convention (WC) of the NBC, a position she held from 1900 to 1948. She was then elected president, a position she held until her death. The WC opened the National Training School for Women and Girls in 1909, reflecting Burroughs's commitment to the education of black women. Believing that adherence to a clean life, body, and home would aid in the advancement and independence of black women, the three Bs of Bible, bath, and broom were stressed. Burroughs lectured against discrimination, lynching, and segregation. She supported women's suffrage and, when the 19th Amendment was ratified, mobilized black women to vote.

ANB; BWA; BWARC; DARB; EAWR; HDB; NoAWMP; NBAW; Karen Ann Johnson, *Uplifting the Women and the Race* (2000); Opal V. Easter, *Nannie Helen Burroughs* (1995); Evelyn Brooks Higginbotham, *Righteous Discontent: The Women's Movement in the Black Baptist Church* (1993).

JUDITH L. GIBBARD

Burry, Stella Annie (1897–1991). Teacher, deaconess, social activist. Stella Burry's childhood dream was to become a deaconess, and she explored that aspiration while working as a Methodist schoolteacher during her teen years. When Burry received a marriage proposal in 1922, she seriously considered it, but since a woman could not marry and become a deaconess, she decided to pursue deaconess training. Her ministry began in Toronto at Woodbine Heights United Church and Carlton Street United Church. Burry returned to Newfoundland in 1938 to found the United Church Community Service Centre (now Stella Burry Community Services), where she worked tirelessly to eradicate poverty. Burry's advocacy against injustice continued through volunteer work during her retirement years. She was officially honored as St. John's Citizen of the Year in 1967. It has been said that every village in Newfoundland benefited from Burry's ministry.

Joseph C. Burke, *No Ordinary Woman* (2000); Dean Salter, *The First Book of Saints* (1988); Stella's Circle, www.stellaburry.ca.

SARAH BRUER

Butler, Mother Marie Joseph (1860–1940). Founder of Marymount College. Born in Ireland, Johanna Butler received a public and a parochial education. She became Sister Marie Joseph six months after entering the Congregation of the Sacred Heart of Mary at Béziers, France, in 1879. That same year she began teaching in Oporto, Portugal, where she took her first vows in 1880. She became the superior of the Braga (Portugal) convent and school in 1893. Ten years later she moved to Long Island, New York, to further the order's work. She opened the Marymount School in 1908, and the school officially became a college in 1918. She was elected as mother general of the Congregation of the Sacred Heart of Mary in 1926 and became a U.S. citizen in 1927.

ANB; EAWR; NCE; NoAW; RLA; J. Kenneth Leahy, *As the Eagle: The Spiritual Writing of Mother Butler* (1991).

KEITH DURSO

Butler, Selena Sloan (1872–1964). Educator and community leader. Born in

Thomasville, Georgia, Selena Sloan Butler's career aimed at providing education for young children and promoting interracial cooperation. After early education provided by missionaries, she attended Atlanta Baptist Female Seminary (now Spelman College). She married Henry Butler in 1893. In 1911, when she could not find a teacher for the young children in her community, she opened a kindergarten in her own home. Later she formed a parent-teacher association to promote learning among all black elementary students. This evolved into the National Congress of Colored Parents and Teachers (founded in 1926). She was a delegate to the founding convention of the *National Association of Colored Women, joined the *Association of Southern Women for the Prevention of Lynching, and attended the First Congregational Church of Atlanta.

BWARC; NBAW; NoAWMP; the Congress, *History of the Georgia Congress of Colored Parents and Teachers* (1970).

LORETTA LONG HUNNICUTT

Cabot, Laurie (1933–). Wiccan high priestess, founder of the Witches' League for Public Awareness. Laurie Cabot has claimed that she is descended from witches and that she has had psychic powers since she was six years old. At 16 she learned Druidic/Celtic witchcraft. Cabot privately taught witchcraft as a science during the 1960s and then publicly during the 1970s in Massachusetts's Wellesley High School's Adult Education program, at Salem State College, and at the Cambridge Center for Adult Education. In 1977 she received the Paul Revere Patriot's Award for her work with dyslexic children. Governor Michael Dukakis informally bestowed on her the title "Official Witch of Salem." In 1986 Cabot founded the Witches' League for Public Awareness to educate the public about witches and witchcraft, and in 1988 she founded the Council of Isis Community.

EAWR; RLA; Rosemary Ellen Guiley, *The Encyclopedia of Witches and Witchcraft*, 2nd ed. (1999) [1989].

KEITH DURSO

Cabrini, Frances Xavier (Maria Francesca) (1850–1917). Founder of the Missionary Sisters of the Sacred Heart of Jesus and first American citizen to be canonized a saint. Born in Lombardy, Italy, Francesca Cabrini was refused entrance into two religious communities due to delicate health. In 1880 her local bishop encouraged her to establish a new congregation devoted to the education of girls in Codogno, Italy. Nine years later she and five of the congregation's members immigrated to New York in answer to Archbishop Michael Corrigan's appeal to have them work with Italian immigrants. In 1892 Cabrini opened her first hospital in New York. During the next 27 years she established numerous hospitals, schools, orphanages, and convents throughout the U.S. and the Americas, as well as in France, Spain, and England. In 1901 she became an American citizen. By the time of her death, the Missionary Sisters numbered approximately 3,000 members. Today the congregation, based in New York, serves on six continents and in 16 countries throughout the world.

NCE; EACH; Mary Louise Sullivan, *Mother Cabrini: Italian Immigrant of the Century* (1992).

EPHREM (RITA) HOLLERMANN, OSB

Cady, Harriet Emilie (1848–1941). Homeopathic physician and author. After a brief teaching career, H. Emilie Cady became one of the first female physicians in the U.S. By the late 1880s she was a homeopathic physician in New York City, interested in connections between medicine and religious healing and beginning to see her work as a metaphysical ministry. A booklet she wrote (ca. 1888) about the Christ within caught the attention of Charles and *Myrtle Fillmore, the founders of Unity. In 1892 she began a longtime commitment to writing for *Unity* magazine while she continued her medical practice. During 1894 and 1895 Cady wrote 12 lessons for *Unity*, eventually published as *Lessons in Truth* (1896), which remains to this day one of Unity's best-known textbooks.

EAWR; RLA; E. Emilie Cady, *Complete Works of H. Emilie Cady* (2004) [1995]; Charles S. Braden, *Spirits in Rebellion: The Rise and Development of New Thought* (1987) [1967].

MARY FARRELL BEDNAROWSKI

Caesar, Shirley (1938–). Gospel singer, minister, and evangelist. Shirley Caesar began her public singing ministry when she was eight years old. At age 10 she began singing with the Caesar Sisters, and later she sang with the Charity Singers. She began singing with Albertina Walker and the Caravans in 1958. In 1961 she became an evangelist. Caesar's 1972 recording of "Put Your Hand in the Hand of the Man from Galilee" made her the first African American woman gospel singer to win a Grammy Award. She received the Dove Award in 1982 and the Stellar Award in 1987. Caesar has pastored two churches and has been the presiding bishop with the Mount Calvary Holy Churches of America. She is also active in social ministries through the Shirley Caesar Outreach Ministries, which she founded.

BWA; EAWR; NBAW; RLA; Sherry Sherrod DuPree, ed., *Biographical Dictionary of African-American, Holiness-Pentecostals* (1989).

KEITH DURSO

Cagle, Mary Lee Wasson Harris (1864–1955). Church of the Nazarene minister and evangelist. Born on a farm in Alabama, Mary Lee Wasson experienced a religious conversion at age 15. She also sensed a call to ministry, but her family adamantly quelled her enthusiasm. She married an evangelist, Robert Lee Harris, and assisted him with evangelistic meetings. When on his deathbed with tuberculosis, Harris founded a denomination, the New Testament Church of Christ. Harris took up her husband's work and was largely responsible for the group's subsequent growth. She was an effective evangelist and new church organizer. In 1908 her denomination merged with the Church of the Nazarene. For over 40 years, she and her second husband, Henry C. Cagle, held evangelistic meetings and organized churches together and separately from Tennessee to Wyoming.

Rebels in the Pulpit, prod. Wendy Bruce (2003); Robert Stanley Ingersol, "Burden of Dissent: Mary Lee Cagle and the Southern Holiness Movement" (PhD diss., Duke University, 1989); Mary Lee Cagle, *The Life and Work of Mary Lee Cagle* (1928).

PRISCILLA POPE-LEVISON

Cameron, Donaldina Mackenzie (1869–1968). Missionary and social reformer. Born on a sheep ranch in New Zealand, Donaldina Cameron was raised in California in a devoutly Presbyterian family. When she was 16 years old, a family friend persuaded her to spend a year assisting at the Presbyterian Mission House in San Francisco's Chinatown. The house rescued Chinese girls and women from abuse, slavery, and prostitution. Cameron stayed at the house as a worker. She became its superintendent in 1900 and stayed until her retirement in 1934. Famous for her role in the protection and education of nearly 3,000 girls, Chinese women honored her as their Lo Mo ("old mother"), and she was credited with weakening the Chinese female slave trade by the 1920s. Cameron House (as it was renamed) became a center of social service ministry in the 1930s.

ANB; NoAWMP; Mildred Crowl Martin, *Chinatown's Angry Angel* (1977); Lorna E. Logan, *Ventures in Mission: The Cameron House Story* (1976).

BEVERLY ZINK-SAWYER

Campbell, Selina Bakewell (1802–97). Leader in the Stone-Campbell movement. Born in Litchfield, England, Selina Bakewell immigrated with her family to Wellsburg, (West) Virginia, in 1804. Around 1820 she began attending Wellsburg Church of Christ, then under the leadership of Alexander Campbell. After Campbell's first wife died, Bakewell married him in 1828 and became a stepmother to his five daughters. She bore and raised six more children and maintained the Campbell mansion at Bethany. Because her husband was away frequently, she also maintained his business affairs; she answered correspondence, oversaw the publication of his *Millennial Harbinger*, and managed his finances. She was a vigorous advocate for education and assisted significantly with the founding of Bethany College in 1847. After her husband died in 1866, Campbell emerged as an important leader in her own right. Over the next 30 years, she published more than a hundred articles and a lengthy memoir of her husband.

ES-CM; Loretta M. Long, *The Life of Selena Campbell* (2001).

SCOTT D. SEAY

Campbell Williams, Lucie Eddie (1885–1963). Educator and composer. Lucie Campbell grew up in Memphis, Tennessee. Endowed with abundant natural gifts and unrelenting determination, she graduated from high school as valedictorian at age 14 and began a distinguished career in public education (1899–1954). She earned degrees from Rust College (1927) and Tennessee Agricultural and Industrial State University (1951). A self-taught musician, she was a pioneering gospel music composer whose beloved hymns created an enduring legacy. As musical director for the National Baptist Convention's Sunday School and Baptist Young People's Union Congress from 1916 to 1962, she exerted enormous influence on African American sacred music. A dedicated churchwoman and a popular inspirational speaker, her imperious and uncompromising personality occasionally enmeshed her in power struggles with male church leaders. At age 75, she married Rev. C. R. Williams.

BWA; NBAW; Bernice Johnson Reagon, *We'll Understand It Better By and By* (1992); William M. Washington, ed., *Miss Lucie Speaks* (1971).

KENDAL P. MOBLEY

Canadian Girls in Training (CGIT) (1915–). Ecumenical Christian girls' movement. CGIT was founded by the YMCA and *YWCA of Canada, Sunday school associations, and the Anglican, Baptist, Presbyterian, and Methodist churches. It was a Canadian alternative to U.S. organizations, such as Girl Guides. Four elements of the CGIT purpose—to cherish health, seek truth, know God, and serve others—inform the movement's work. Its motto is based on Luke 2:52. CGIT seeks to empower girls between the ages of 12 and 17, and to develop their leadership capacities in the context of relationship. A broad Christian emphasis is maintained. Girls wear the CGIT uniform, consisting of a navy and white middy blouse. They usually meet once a week and engage in various activities, including music, games, Bible study, drama, banquets, parties, bike hikes, camping, and worship. They also participate in summer camps and rallies. Overall, the CGIT aims to provide girls with a solid foundation for life.

Elissa Katharine How, *"To Build Our Lives on a Sure and Strong Foundation": Religion and Gender as Exemplified by the Executive Leadership of the CGIT* (MA thesis, Queen's University, 1994); Molly Hewitt, *Sixty Years of CGIT* (1975).

TRACY J. TROTHEN

Cannon, Harriet Starr (1823–96). Founder of the first sisterhood approved by the Episcopal Church. Born in Charleston, Harriet Cannon moved to Bridgeport, Connecticut, after her parents' death from yellow fever in 1824. She entered the Episcopal Sisterhood of the Holy Communion in 1851 and nursed at St. Luke's Hospital in New York City. Yearning for a more monastic form of religious life, Cannon and several other sisters were asked to leave the order. Under the direction of the diocesan bishop, the sisters became the Community of Saint Mary, the first religious order constituted by an Anglican bishop since the dissolution, and Cannon was elected first superior. The Community of Saint Mary ran homes for children and prostitutes, and founded girls' schools in New York, Tennessee, and Wisconsin.

EAWR; NoAW; Morgan Dix, *Harriet Starr Cannon: First Mother Superior of the Sisterhood of St. Mary* (1896).

SHERYL A. KUJAWA-HOLBROOK

Cannon, Katie Geneva (1950–). Presbyterian clergywoman and womanist theologian. Katie Geneva Cannon was the first African American woman ordained in the United Presbyterian Church in the U.S.A., the first African American woman to earn a PhD (1983) from Union Theological Seminary (New York City), and an early voice in womanist ethics. Born and raised in Kannapolis, North Carolina, during the era of Jim Crow, Cannon found in womanism the means to challenge and to overcome oppressive racist, classist, and sexist social structures. Her essays in *Katie's Canon* (1995) lay out womanist norms of moral wisdom and social action. Cannon draws upon African American women's experiences and the work of African American women literary figures as sources of moral wisdom. Her writing and leadership in both church and academy chart a course for action that breaks cycles of oppression for people of color in the U.S. and around the world.

Davidson College, News Archives, 20 January 2005; Katie Cannon, *Katie's Canon* (1995).

ELIZABETH HINSON-HASTY

Carcaño, Minerva (1954–). First Hispanic woman bishop in the United Methodist Church. Born in Edinburg, Texas, Carcaño was ordained an elder in 1980. In 2004 she was elected bishop by the church's Western Jurisdiction and assigned to the Desert Southwest Annual Conference. During her career, Carcaño has led churches across the country and has lectured extensively. She has been involved in ecumenical programs, including as a delegate to the 1998 World Council of Churches Assembly in Zimbabwe and as a member of the church's General Commission on Christian Unity and Interreligious Concerns. She has also advocated for immigrants' rights. In 2005 she joined a group of bishops voicing support for a movement aimed at overturning the church's disapproval of homosexual practice.

United Methodist Directory (2007); Patricia J. Thompson, *Courageous Past—Bold Future: The Journey toward Full Clergy Rights for Women in the United Methodist Church* (2006).

ANDREW H. STERN

Carder, Muriel Spurgeon (1922–). Educator, missionary, and chaplain. Muriel Spurgeon was the first female missionary candidate to receive a BD from McMaster University and to be ordained by the Baptist Convention of Ontario and Quebec, in 1947. She received an STM from Union Theological Seminary (New York City) in 1958 and a ThD from the Toronto School of Theology in 1969. From 1947 to 1976 she taught theology and New Testament at Andha Christian Theological College in South India while translating Christian texts into Telegu. She met and married W. Gordon Carder in 1951, while in India, and they have two children. After watching the churches of North India negotiate for 40 years, Carder attended the 1970 union ceremony forming the Church of North India; she considers this the proudest day of her life. She and her family returned to Canada in 1976. Carder then worked as a chaplain with the developmentally challenged, the most satisfying and challenging work of her career. She received certification as a Clinical Pastoral Education supervisor in 1984.

"Baptist Woman Honoured as 2007 Katherine Hockin Award Recipient," Canadian Churches' Forum for Global Ministries, www.ccforum.ca/news.shtml #katherinehockin.

BARBARA ADLE

Carmelite Sisters (1452–). Roman Catholic women's congregation. Although evidence suggests that women followed the Carmelite Rule as early as the 13th century, the previously male order (which developed from the growth in the number of lay hermits around Mount Carmel in Palestine in the latter part of 12th century) was formally opened to women by papal bull upon the founding of the Convent of Our Lady of the Angeles in Florence, Italy, in 1452. The great reformation of the Carmelites came in 1562 with Teresa of Avila and John of the Cross who sought to take the order back to its eremitical roots of rigorous asceticism. Both the original order, now known as the Carmelite Nuns of the Ancient Observance (OCarm), and the new order, known as the Discalced (OCD) (which means unshod, a reference to their rigorously contemplative lifestyle), continue to this day. There are convents representing both orders in the U.S. and Canada. In 1790 the OCD established a convent in Port Tobacco, Maryland, the first Roman Catholic convent in the U.S. In 1930 the OCarm established their first convent in the U.S. in Allentown, Pennsylvania, which was followed by three others. There are currently 64 Carmelite convents in the U.S.

NCE; ROWUS; Mary Jo Weaver, *Cloister and Community: Life within a Carmelite Monastery* (2002); Darryl V. Caterine, *Conservative Catholicism and the Carmelites: Identity, Ethnicity, and Tradition in the Modern Church* (2001); George C. Steward Jr., *Marvels of Charity: History of American Sisters and Nuns* (1994).

MARY JANE O'DONNELL

Carr, Anne Elizabeth (1934–2008). Feminist theologian. A native of Chicago, Anne Elizabeth Carr graduated from Mundelein College in 1956 and joined the *Sisters of Charity of the Blessed Virgin Mary in 1958. She earned degrees in theology from Marquette University (MA 1962) and the University of Chicago Divinity School (MA 1969, PhD 1971). She taught at Mundelein College (1963–66, 1971–73) and Indiana University (1973–75) prior to becoming the first woman with a permanent faculty appointment to the University of Chicago Divinity School, where she taught Christian theology (1975–2003). In 1984 Carr was among 24 Catholic sisters whose endorsement of a statement on "pluralism and abortion," published in the *New York Times* during the vice-presidential campaign of Geraldine Ferraro, led to tensions with the Vatican. Her feminist study of Christian symbols and practices, *Transforming Grace* (1988), was translated into several languages. She also published books on Karl Rahner and Thomas Merton. She extended her influence through many articles, coedited volumes, and lectures; visiting professorships at Harvard Divinity School, Boston College, and Trinity College (Dublin); and her editorial work for *Concilium*, *Horizons*, and the *Journal of Religion*. In 1997 the Catholic Theological Society of America recognized Carr for her "distinguished service and achievement in theology."

Trevor Jensen, "Anne Carr: 1934–2008," *Chicago Tribune* (Feb. 15, 2008); "John Courtney Murray Award—1997," *Proceedings of the Catholic Theological Society of America* 52 (1997); Anne E. Patrick, *Liberating Conscience* (1996); Papers, Women and Leadership Archives, Gannon Center, Loyola University Chicago.

ANNE E. PATRICK, SNJM

Carter, Sybil (1842–1908). Deaconess and missionary. Born in New Orleans and forced to be self-supporting after her father's death in the Civil War, Sybil Carter went to Utah as a teacher for the New West Education Commission. She became a spokesperson for their work, and in 1884 Carter was set apart as a deaconess in the Episcopal Church. She became a special agent for the church's missionary society. She toured missions in Japan and China between 1880 and 1890. On her return she organized efforts to teach Belgian lacemaking to Indian women so that they could be self-sufficient while being taught white culture. Carter marketed the lace around the world. She died from a stroke while traveling in Connecticut.

Sandra Boyd, "Sybil Carter, Pauline Colby, and the Indian Lace Makers," *The Episcopal Women's History Project Newsletter* (Winter 1991); Episcopal Deaconess Project Files, Archives of the Episcopal Church.

JOAN R. GUNDERSEN

Cary, Mary Ann Shadd (1823–93). Teacher, newspaper editor, civil rights advocate, lawyer. A historical plaque located at the First Baptist Church in Chatham, Ontario, states that Mary Ann Shadd Cary was a "teacher and anti-slavery crusader" who promoted the full racial integration of black people into North American society. Born a free black in Delaware, Shadd Cary arrived in Canada West (Ontario) following the U.S. Fugitive Slave Act of 1850. She returned to the U.S. in 1863, where she worked as an enlistment officer for the Union Army and then as a schoolteacher. She became the first black woman to study law at Howard University, receiving her LLB in 1883, and worked as a lawyer until her death. Influenced by her abolitionist parents, Quaker schoolteachers, and 19th-century Christian idealism, Shadd Cary upheld education as central to black people achieving full equality. She opened a school in Windsor in 1852, supported in part by the American Missionary Society, and founded the *Provincial Freeman* in 1853, an antislavery newspaper. She supported racial integration, temperance, and women's rights.

ANB; BWA; DCB; NoAW; Rinaldo Walcott, "'Who Is She and What Is She to You?' Mary Ann Shadd Cary and the (Im)possibility of Black/Canadian Studies," *Atlantis* 24 (Spring 2000); Jane Rhodes, *Mary Ann Shadd Cary* (1998); Shirley J. Yee, "Finding a Place: Mary Ann Shadd Cary and the Dilemmas of Black Migration to Canada, 1850–1870," *Frontiers* 18 (1997); Sylvia Sweeney, *Breaking the Ice: The Mary Ann Shadd Story* [video] (1997).

ELEANOR J. STEBNER

Case, Adelaide Teague (1887–1948). First woman elected to a theological faculty in an Episcopal or Anglican seminary. Born in St. Louis, Missouri, Adelaide Teague Case was raised in New York City and always considered herself to be a native New Yorker. Her religious faith followed a conventional pattern until a conversion experience after college. A devout Anglo-Catholic, Case received her PhD in religious education at Teachers College, Columbia University, in 1924. Her work focused on progressive religious education, faith development, peace education, the Bible, and social ethics. Case also served on many denominational committees. She was an educational consultant for the woman's auxiliary and vice president of the Episcopal Peace Fellowship. After a long professional career at Columbia University, she was appointed to the rank of full professor at Episcopal Theological School, Cambridge, Massachusetts, in 1941.

ANB; NoAW; Sheryl Kujawa-Holbrook, "Adelaide Teague Case," Christian Educators of the 20th Century Project, www.biola.edu.

SHERYL A. KUJAWA-HOLBROOK

Case, Eliza Barnes (1796–1887). Methodist missionary. When she was about 30 years old, Eliza Barnes moved from her home in Massachusetts to what is now southern Ontario to work among the Indians. Traveling from mission to mission, she taught and organized the Indian women into Dorcas societies so that the moccasins, straw hats, gloves, and brooms they produced could be sold in city bazaars to support projects of the women's choosing. She also made trips to the U.S. to speak, raise funds, and arrange for translations. She was especially noted for her preaching ability. In 1833 she married Methodist missionary William Case, who did not approve of women preaching, so in subsequent years she no longer preached. She continued to instruct Indian women in housekeeping, work that she maintained even after her husband's death in 1855.

Elizabeth Gillan Muir, *Petticoats in the Pulpit* (1991).

MARILYN FÄRDIG WHITELEY

Casgrain, Thérèse Forget (1896–1981). Feminist, suffragist, political leader, social activist, and Canadian senator. Thérèse Forget, born into upper-class French Canadian society, received the standard convent education given to young Catholic women. After her marriage to lawyer-politician Pierre Casgrain in 1916, Thérèse Casgrain embarked on an activist whirlwind that kept her at the front of Quebec public life until her death. A suffragist from the founding of the provincial suffrage committee, Casgrain shepherded the struggle for women's votes in Quebec until its success in 1940, in spite of massive opposition from her own church. Her feminism drove her into labor and civil rights issues. Although never elected to public office, she led the Quebec socialist party (the Co-operative Commonwealth Federation) after World War II. Her career culminated with her appointment to the Canadian Senate.

Micheline Dumont et al., *Quebec Women* (1987); Isabel Bassett, *The Parlour Rebellion* (1975).

OSCAR COLE-ARNAL

Caspary, Anita M. (1915–). Leader of progressive Roman Catholic women religious. A 1937 graduate of Immaculate Heart College in Los Angeles, Anita Caspary joined the sisters of the *Immaculate Heart of Mary (IHM), receiving the name Sister Mary Humiliata. After earning a Stanford University PhD, she became dean (1950–57) and president (1957–63) of the Immaculate Heart College. Elected superior of the California IHMs, she oversaw renewal efforts from 1963 to 1969, and reclaimed her original name in 1968. When conflicts developed with the local cardinal, James F. McIntyre, over reforms such as teacher preparation, dress, and prayer schedules, the Vatican authorities sided with McIntyre. Rather than dismantle their reforms, Caspary and 300 others left canonical religious life to form the *Immaculate Heart Community. Caspary served as its president from 1969 to 1973.

Anita M. Caspary, IHM, *Witness to Integrity: The Crisis of the Immaculate Heart Community of California* (2003).

ANNE E. PATRICK, SNJM

Castillo, Ana (1953–). Poet and novelist. Born to a working-class family in Chicago, Ana Castillo began her involvement in the Chicano movement in her late teens and became a prominent protest poet and novelist. She has published collections of poems, including *Women Are Not Roses* (1984) and *My Father Was a Toltec* (1988), which use both English and Spanish to examine Chicana and indigenous Mexican women's experiences. In 1986 she published her first novel, the award-winning *The Mixquiahuala Letters*. In 1993 she released *So Far from God*. The novel was revolutionary in its use of New Mexican Spanish, code switching, and the telenovela format. Castillo inspired other Chicana writers to incorporate their traditions and their native language in their work.

James R. Giles, ed., *Dictionary of Literary Biography* (2000); Elsa Saeta, "A MELUS Interview: Ana Castillo," *MELUS* 22 no. 3 (Fall 1997).

SUSAN B. RIDGELY

Catholic Network for Women's Equality (CNWE) (1981–). Feminist-focused support and advocacy organization. Begun as an advocacy group for women's ordination known as Canadian Catholics for Women's Ordination (CCWO), the movement's name was changed in 1988 to Catholic Network for Women's Equality (CNWE). The name change reflected the members' evolving understanding of their mission within the interconnected structural oppressions of women in society and particularly in the Roman Catholic Church. The women and men of CNWE seek to live their baptismal vocation as a discipleship community of equals, and work so that the experiences and voices of marginalized persons, particularly women, are central to genuine ecclesial renewal and decision making. They seek a renewed priesthood within a transformed church, with the full participation of women in all aspects of the life and public ministry of that church. Presently the CNWE has members in every Canadian province and is linked with Women's Ordination Worldwide (WOW) and *Women-Church. CNWE sponsors an annual conference, publishes a newsletter three times per year, hosts an e-mail list, and maintains a Web site.

CNWE, www.cnwe.org.

VERONICA M. DUNNE, RNDM

Catholic Women's League (CWL) of Canada (1920–). Spiritual formation and social reform organization for laywomen. Initially organized in England in 1906, the Canadian movement began in Montreal in 1920 under the direction of Belle Guerin, its first national president. By the end of the 1920s the league emerged in every major city from Halifax to Victoria. In order to combat religious indifference in urban Canada, the Toronto league inspired the birth of the Sisters of Service in 1922 and took the new order under its wing. Until World War II the league expanded and consolidated its gains. With the Depression it turned to relief work, especially the provisioning of drought sufferers in Saskatchewan. Even before the war, the organization formed international links with the Vatican and other European Catholic women's leagues. During the war years the league collected care packages for soldiers and raised money to assist in the care of orphans in war-torn countries. In the ensuing decades the league has pursued its initial mandate, all the while adapting it to the spirit of Vatican II.

CWL, www.cwl.ca.

OSCAR COLE-ARNAL

Chapin, Augusta Jane (1836–1905). Universalist minister and educator. Born in Lakeville, New York, Augusta Chapin matured in Vevey, Michigan. Already a teacher, she was refused admission to the University of Michigan as a woman, but later earned an MA there. She attended Olivet College, studied at Lombard University, and received a call to preach. Ordained in Lansing, she was settled in Portland, Michigan, for three years and served several other short pastorates. Chapin was a charter member of Sorosis and a founding member of the American Woman Suffrage Association. As the first woman on the Universalist General Convention Council in 1870, she proposed gender-neutral wording for ministerial accreditation and aided formation of the Woman's Centennary Association. She was a director and speaker at the 1893 World Congress of Religions. On the initial executive committee of the Association for the Advancement of Women, Chapin reflected on women in ministry at its first meeting. She was on the revising committee of *Elizabeth Cady Stanton's *Woman's Bible*. Lombard University awarded Chapin an honorary MA (1868) and an honorary DD (1893). Chapin lectured at Lombard University (1886–97) and offered University of Chicago extension courses (1892–97). She later led tours of Europe.

NoAW; UUWM.

IRENE BAROS-JOHNSON

Chapman, Maria Weston (1806–85). Abolitionist. Maria Chapman became involved in the antislavery movement during the 1830s and helped organize the Boston Female Anti-Slavery Society (ASS) in 1832. From 1835 to 1858 she managed the annual Antislavery Fairs, an organization for raising funds for the American ASS. She began the Subscription Anniversary in 1858, a successful fund-raising venture for abolitionism. From 1835 to 1865 Chapman served various tenures on the committees of the Massachusetts ASS, the New England ASS, and the American ASS; she edited the *Liberty Bell*, an abolitionist magazine, and served as acting editor of the *Liberator* (during the editor's absences and illnesses). Chapman also worked for women's rights in Massachusetts. She was an influential member of the Boston Circle, an abolitionist group advocating the immediate end to slavery and working for complete civil rights for African Americans and women. The group attempted to achieve its goals through moral suasion, such as publications, speeches, and nonresistance. Chapman also advocated using "come-outerism," the disassociation with slaveholders, and after the beginning of the Civil War she supported using force to end slavery.

ANB; DUUB; NoAW; RLA; Jane H. Pease and William H. Pease, *Bound with Them in Chains* (1972).

KEITH DURSO

Chappell, Winifred Leola (1879–1951). Social reformer and deaconess. Winifred Chappell was born in Iowa, the daughter of a Methodist Episcopal preacher who in 1895 enrolled in Garrett Biblical Institute in Evanston, Illinois. Chappell attended Northwestern University in 1899, where she was shaped by a philosophical predisposition to social science as a tool for building an ideal society. Chappell identified this ideal society with the reign of God on earth, which she hoped could be achieved through social reform shaped by Christian ideals. In 1906 Chappell entered the Chicago Training School (CTS) and in 1908 was consecrated a deaconess in the Rock River Annual Conference. After graduation she served as a teacher and assistant principal at CTS for 15 years. Following World War I Chappell pursued a master's degree in sociology at Columbia University in New York City. She edited the *Social Service Bulletin* (currently *Social Questions Bulletin*, published in Washington, DC). Strongly committed to social reform, Chappell worked alongside Harry Ward at the Methodist Federation for Social Service.

Miriam Crist, "Winifred Chappell: 'Everybody on the Left Knew Her,'" *Radical Religion* 5, no. 1 (1980).

LACEYE C. WARNER

Chemberlin, Peggy ("Peg") Bean (1949–). Ecumenical leader. Peggy Bean was one of four children born to Charles and Donna Bean. A graduate of the University of Wisconsin (1973) and United Theological Seminary (1982), Chemberlin was ordained in the Moravian Church in America (Northern Province) in 1982. She worked as a campus minister at St. Cloud University (1982–88), the director of Minnesota Food Share Program (1988–95), and the executive director of the Minnesota Council of Churches (1995–present). In November 2007 she was named president-elect of the National Council of the Churches of Christ in the U.S.A. (NCC), and is to assume office in November 2008. Chemberlin will be the first Minnesotan to serve as NCC president. She is committed to working for social justice and building bridges across institutional, cultural, and religious differences. She has one daughter.

NCC Biography, www.ncccusa.org.

ELEANOR J. STEBNER

Cheung, Victoria (1897–1966). Pioneer Chinese Canadian female physician and Presbyterian/United Church of Canada missionary. Victoria Cheung was born to Chinese immigrant parents in Victoria, British Columbia, and received part of her education at Victoria's Oriental Mission Home. The Presbyterian Women's Missionary Society (WMS) funded Cheung's Toronto medical school education and, after her 1922 graduation, appointed her to Kongmoon's Marion Barclay Hospital for Women, part of the South China mission. Cheung negotiated deftly the challenges of a nation in turmoil, including setting up her own clinic when overseas mission funding was curtailed during the war years. She severed her relationship with the WMS in 1952 in order to continue her medical practice in the new Communist republic, where she remained until her death.

Donna Sinclair, "Victoria Cheung," *Touchstone: Heritage and Theology in a New Age* 11, no. 3 (September 1993).

SANDRA L. BEARDSALL

Chidvilasananda, Swami (Gurumayi) (1954–). Head guru of Siddha Yoga in the U.S. Swami Chidvilasananda became the head guru of the Siddha Yoga organization in the U.S. in 1985. Siddha Yoga Dham of America was established in the U.S. by Swami Muktananda (1908–82) in 1974 as a branch of his Shree Gurudev Siddha Peeth in Ganeshpuri, India. The teachings of chanting, meditation, and service were influenced by the traditions of Kashmiri Shaivism. The primary ashram is in South Fallsburg, New York. Their female guru, Chidvilasananda, was born as Malti Shetty to followers of Swami Muktananda in Bombay. Siddha Yoga followers believe that the spiritual power of the founding guru Swami Muktananda was transferred to Chidvilasananda in rituals. Chidvilasanada and her organization emphasize both knowledge (*jnana*) and devotion to the guru (bhakti). The transmission of shakti energy from the guru to the disciple is considered necessary to attain the spiritual goal.

Karen Pechilis, ed., *The Graceful Guru* (2004).

BARBARA E. REED

Child, Lydia Maria Francis (1802–80). Author and abolitionist. Lydia Francis received an important part of her education from her brother, a Unitarian minister in Watertown, Massachusetts. She briefly ran a private school until her novels brought her distinction. She went on to edit the first children's magazine in the U.S. and wrote popular domestic advice books. In 1828 she married David Child and settled in Boston. David Child only erratically supported the couple, and Lydia Child was forced to depend on her writing for income. She adopted her husband's passion for abolition and in 1833 incensed her public by writing *An Appeal in Favor of That Class of Americans Called Africans*. One of the first Americans to speak out against slavery, Child also wrote in support of black suffrage and education, as well as land redistribution. She promoted Native American rights, religious tolerance, and women's rights, although she did not join an organization dedicated to suffrage. Despite damage to her literary career, Child never abandoned her reform convictions.

ANB; DUUB; NoAW; UU; Lori Kenschaft, *Lydia Maria Child* (2002); Carolyn L. Karcher, *The First Woman in the Republic: A Cultural Biography of Lydia Maria Child* (1994).

BARBARA J. MACHAFFIE

Chinese Women's Associations (ca. 1913). Cultural and social support organizations. The earliest Chinese women's associations began with the San Francisco Chinese Women's Self-Reliance Association (Lumei Zhongguo Nujie Zili Hui), with its emphasis on Chinese nationalism and women's equality. In 1916 the Chinese *YWCA began functioning in San Francisco. Although not always religious, most early Chinese women's associations met either at kinship halls (with their traditional Chinese religious environments) or at Chinese churches.

Judy Yung, *Unbound Feet: A Social History of Chinese Women in San Francisco* (1995).

BARBARA E. REED

Ching, Julia (1934–2001). Asian religion scholar and human rights advocate. Author of more than 15 books, Julia Ching was University Professor (a rank of highest honor) at the University of Toronto for over 20 years. Her life encompassed much more than Toronto or the academy, however. She lived on three continents and spoke half a dozen languages. As a child she experienced cultural violence and familial displacement resulting from revolution in China and refugee status in Hong Kong. An *Ursuline religious sister for almost two decades, she received a master's degree from the Catholic University of America. After leaving the order, she pursued a doctorate at the Australian National University. She arrived at the University of Toronto in 1978, after teaching stints at Columbia and Yale. In addition to being a scholar in Neoconfucianism, she was a bridge builder between Christianity and Chinese religions. She coauthored a 1989 book on this topic with Roman Catholic theologian Hans Küng. She was an outspoken advocate of human rights and a frequent commentator on China in the Canadian news media. She married Willard G. Oxtoby (1933–2003) in Toronto, with whom she also professionally collaborated. Ching struggled numerous times with cancer. In her spiritual autobiography, *Butterfly Healing*, she explored the topics of illness and health, life and death.

Rick Guisso, *Studies in Religion/Sciences Religieuse* 31, no. 1 (2002); Willard G. Oxtoby, *Journal of the History of Ideas* 62 (2001); Julia Ching, *The Butterfly Healing: A Life between East and West* (1998).

ELEANOR J. STEBNER

Chodron, Ane Pema (1936–). Writer and leader in the Tibetan Buddhist tradition. Ane Pema Chodron was born Deirdre Blomfield-Brown in New York City. She became a Buddhist nun in the Tibetan tradition in 1974 and received full *bhikkhuni* ordination in the Chinese lineage of Buddhism in 1981.

Her primary guru was the Tibetan teacher Chogyam Trungpa, with whom she studied until his death in 1987. In 1984 she became the director of the Buddhist monastery called Gampo Abbey in Cape Breton, Nova Scotia, which she runs according to directions given to her by Chogyam Trungpa.

Sandy Boucher, *Turning the Wheel: American Women Creating the New Buddhism* (1988); Gampo Abbey, www.gampoabbey.org.

BARBARA E. REED

Chona, Maria (1846–1936). Papago religious leader. Born in the Spanish territory of Upper Pimeria (now in southwestern Arizona), Maria Chona grew up during a time of transformation for her people, the Papago or Tohona O'odham. As a young woman in a family of medicine men, she sought to join her father and husband in the cultivation of visions, song writing, and other expressions of religious leadership. Her efforts were suppressed initially by the male-dominant Papago culture. But when her husband took a second wife, she defied her tribe's traditions by leaving him and practicing her own form of medicine. Her autobiography, *Papago Woman*, is the first recorded by a Southwestern Indian woman and reveals a feminist perspective on Papago culture. Chona eventually learned to heal babies and became an elder in her tribe.

Sharon Malinowski and George H. J. Abrams, eds., *Notable Native Americans* (1995); Ruth Underhill and Maria Chona, *Papago Woman* (1985) [1936].

LORETTA LONG HUNNICUTT

Christ, Carol P. (1945–). Leader in goddess thealogy movement and educator. Carol Christ received a PhD in religious studies from Yale University in 1974. She considers her time at Yale as the birthing of her passion for reimagining religious symbolism and calling forth the wisdom and power of the feminine. Christ strives to uphold the importance of women's experience in religious understanding. She finds that the threefold image of the goddess empowers women to claim the strength of their creativity, nurturance, and wisdom. Christ believes that the goddess offers women a means to resist the patriarchy of traditional Western theology. She finds in process philosophy, especially in the works of Charles Hartshorne, a similar thread offering a vision of hope and joy embodied in the divine. In 1987 Christ left academia and moved to Greece, where she continues to teach, write, and share her vision of the feminine in religion.

Carol P. Christ, in *Transforming the Faiths of Our Fathers*, ed. Ann Braude (2004); Ariadne Institute, www.goddessariadne.org.

BARBARA ADLE

Christie, Katharine Harriet (1913–75). Deaconess and educator. Having graduated from Victoria University (Toronto), Harriet Christie's career in leadership began with the Student Christian Movement, *Young Women's Christian Association, and *Canadian Girls in Training. Following a year of study in England, Christie began her work at the United Church Training School in 1948. Beyond her work with students, Christie coordinated the school's national building campaign, which led to her appointment as principal for 16 years. Her career continued as coordinator of the United Church of Canada's department of Christian development. Beyond the church, Christie served on two federal committees regarding the status of women. A tribute to Christie's leadership was evidenced in her being in 1974 the first woman nominated for moderator of the United Church of Canada.

Catherine McKeen, "Harriet Christie: The People-Maker Lady," *Touchstone: Heritage and Theology in a New Age* 8, no. 2 (1990);

Gwyn Griffith, "Remembering Harriet," *Tapestry* (Winter 2006); Association of Professional Church Workers, "The Newsletter: Historical Issue" (1988).

SARAH BRUER

Church, Mary Ann Hayden (1807–77). Universalist preacher. Mary Ann Church was the first Universalist woman preacher in Canada. Although never ordained, in the 1830s she organized a congregation in Merrickville, Upper Canada (now Ontario), where she had moved with her husband, Basil Rorison Church, a physician. In 1838 the *Universalist Register*, the registry of Universalist preachers in North America, listed her as the only female preacher on a list of over 400. Scholar Phillip Hewett suggested that she was perhaps the first woman preacher in Canada. While she may have been the first woman preacher to have sole charge of a congregation, there were some Quaker and Methodist women ministers in Upper Canada who predated her. Nonetheless, her contribution to the Universalist Church in Canada is notable.

Dorothy Boroush, ed., *Notable Universalist and Unitarian Women*, 7th ed. (2000); Phillip Hewett, *Unitarians in Canada* (1978).

ROBYNNE ROGERS HEALEY

Church Women United (CWU) (1941–). Christian ecumenical organization. Church Women United was founded by the meeting of three interdenominational Protestant women's groups to form the United Council of Church Women (UCCW). In 1950 the UCCW joined with other interdenominational groups to form the National Council of the Churches of Christ in the U.S.A. (NCCC). The UCCW was renamed the general department of United Church Women (UCW). In 1966 the group became autonomous. The name was changed to Church Women United to encourage Protestant, Roman Catholic, Eastern Orthodox, and other women to join. The mission statement of CWU is to serve as a "racially, culturally, theologically inclusive Christian women's movement, celebrating unity in diversity and working for a world of peace and justice." Throughout its history, and through various name changes, the CWU has fought for the inclusion of women into church administration and policymaking. Beginning in the 1960s members became active in work to combat racism. The CWU distinguished itself from the mainstream liberal women's movement by including African American women in positions of leadership. In addition, as advocates for women and children, the CWU involved itself in broader social issues, including the right to shelter, food, health care, education, and work. It has a commitment to justice, peace, and human rights.

James F. Findlay Jr., *Church People in the Struggle: The National Council of Churches and the Black Freedom Movement* (1993); EAWR; Virginia Brereton, "United and Slighted: Women as Subordinated Insiders," in *Between the Times*, ed. William R. Hutchinson (1989); Margaret Shannon, *Just Because: The Story of the National Movement of Church Women United in the U.S.A.* (1977).

JUDITH L. GIBBARD

Cisneros, Rosa Judith (1938–81). Lawyer and author. Rosa Cisneros was a lay leader in the Episcopal diocese of El Salvador. Active in humanitarian causes dedicated to women and indigenous people, she received frequent death threats as the director of a family planning project under the auspices of the Salvadoran Demographic Association. She was assassinated in 1981 while leaving for work in the morning. At the time of her death, Cisneros was the legal director of CREDHO, an Episcopal program designed to assist the rural poor through seven agricultural cooperatives in El Salvador. She received the John

Nevin Sayre Award of the Episcopal Peace Fellowship posthumously in 1985. An Episcopal parish and a home for abused and abandoned girls in the diocese of Honduras are named after her.

"Episcopalian Killed in El Salvador," *Episcopal News Service*, Press Release #81227; Coleta Mills, "Feminist Lawyer Murdered," *Planned Parenthood Federation* (13 April 1990).

SHERYL A. KUJAWA-HOLBROOK

Clarke, Mary Frances (1802–87). Founder and superior general of the *Sisters of Charity of the Blessed Virgin Mary (BVM). Mary Clarke's Catholic and Quaker heritage led her to form a living and praying community with four other women in 1831 and to open Miss Clarke's Seminary in Dublin in 1832. The women moved to Philadelphia to teach Irish immigrants the next year. Irish priest Terence James Donaghoe assisted them in formalizing the founding of the BVMs. Bishop Mathias Loras of Dubuque invited the women to the Iowa Territory. With 14 additional women, they arrived in Dubuque in 1843. They taught and expanded their schools into Illinois, Kansas, Missouri, Wisconsin, and California under Clarke's quiet, spiritual leadership. Clarke served as superior general from 1833 until her death.

ANB; EACH; NCE; Ann M. Harrington, *Creating Community: Mary Frances Clarke and Her Companions* (2004); Kathryn Lawlor, ed., *Your Affectionate: Commentary on Mary Frances Clarke's Writings* (2003); Jane Coogan, *The Price of Our Heritage*, 2 vols. (1975, 1978).

ANN M. HARRINGTON, BVM

Clarke, Maura (1931–80). Catholic woman religious and mission worker. Maura Clarke, a generous and dedicated *Maryknoll sister, served the poor of Nicaragua for 20 years. In 1980 she moved to war-torn El Salvador, despite escalating violence and the military's open hostility toward church workers. Four months later, Clarke was traveling in the company of *Ita Ford, *Dorothy Kazel, and *Jean Donovan when all four were arrested, assaulted, and assassinated by El Salvadoran national guardsmen at the command of officials in the El Salvadoran army.

Judith M. Noone, *The Same Fate as the Poor* (1995); Gail Pellett, dir., *Justice and the Generals* [DVD] (2002).

MARY J. HENOLD

CLOUT (Christian Lesbians OUT) (1990–). Collective of Christian lesbians. At a time when few Christian lesbians were candid about their sexual orientation in the churches, Cathy Ann Beaty, Carter Heyward, and Melanie Morrison took action. Through their initiative, 10 Christian lesbians gathered in New York City in 1990 to discuss an interdenominational vision toward lesbians coming out in the church. This meeting resulted in the development of CLOUT, which self-identifies as a "sisterhood of female-identified, same-gender-loving mujeristas, womanists, and feminists from all Christian backgrounds" (CLOUT Web site). Rooted in Jesus' commitment to justice, CLOUT seeks to empower lesbians, encourage inclusive faith communities, network with similar organizations, and normalize conversations about sexuality. CLOUT's members address these goals in their hosting of national gatherings, publishing of a quarterly newsletter, and connecting with like-minded organizations.

CLOUT, www.cloutsisters.org.

SARAH BRUER

Coffey, Lillian Brooks ("Mother Coffey") (1891–1964). Christian denominational leader. From an early age, Lillian Coffey was a protégée of Bishop C. H. Mason, founder of the Church of

God in Christ (COGIC). After spending several years traveling and establishing local churches, she was appointed financial director of COGIC in 1927. In 1934 Coffey was appointed as assistant general mother of COGIC, the second-highest position available to a woman. Coffey brought the women's board of COGIC into relationships with other African American women's groups, particularly the *National Council of Negro Women. An outgrowth of Coffey's work was her friendship with *Mary McLeod Bethune. Mother Coffey was the national supervisor of the women's board of COGIC from 1942 until her death. Her tenure was marked by expansion of women's service in the church, the establishment of an annual national church convention for women, and a platform of engagement in society that mirrored the rise of the civil rights movement. After Mason's death in 1961, Coffey was considered a candidate to succeed him.

Anthea D. Butler, *Women in the Church of God in Christ* (2007); Evelyn Brooks Higgenbotham, *Righteous Discontent: The Women's Movement in the Black Baptist Church* (1993).

ANNIE RUSSELL

Coffin, Emma Cook (1854–1951). Quaker minister and evangelist. Emma Coffin was part of the Gurneyite (evangelical) tradition of Quakerism. She and her husband, Charles Coffin, were the first couple in the Western Yearly Meeting to have a pastor officiate their 1876 wedding, a break from traditional Quaker style. Recorded as a minister in 1888, Coffin pastored across the country and was a popular evangelist. In the 1900s Coffin became discouraged that women pastors were aging and young women were not being encouraged to develop in ministry. She found it paradoxical that, given the long Quaker tradition of equality, female leadership in society at large and in other denominations was expanding while it was contracting among Gurneyites.

Mary Van Vleck Garman, "Quaker Women in North America," in *Encyclopedia of Women and Religion in North America*, ed. Rosemary Keller and Rosemary Ruether (2006); Obituary, *The American Friend* (8 November 1951).

ROBYNNE ROGERS HEALEY

Cohen, Nina Morais (1855–1918). Writer, teacher, community leader. Born in Philadelphia, Nina Morais married at the age of 30, after helping raise her younger siblings. Her husband, Emanuel Cohen, became a successful insurance lawyer in Minneapolis. As a leader in the women's suffrage movement, Cohen was an organizer and charter member of the Woman's City Club, and was a writer, teacher, and public speaker on literary and political issues. She and her husband enjoyed prominent roles in the Jewish and non-Jewish communities. At the 1893 Congress of Religions in Chicago she was present at the founding of the *National Council of Jewish Women. At home she organized a local council section, serving as president from 1894 to 1907. She hosted Saturday study sessions in her home for 13 years, as a way to encourage members to study the Bible, Jewish literature, and history.

JWA.

JUDITH METZ, SC

Coleman, Alice Blanchard Merriam (1858–1936). Baptist leader. Before becoming a Baptist in 1886 Alice Merriam served as one of the Women's Home Missionary Association's (Congregational) board managers. She married George Coleman in 1891 and helped him direct the Ford Hall Forum, America's oldest free public lecture series, and plan the Sagamore Sociological Conferences (1907–10). Coleman was president of the Woman's American Baptist Home

Mission Society (WABHMS) in Boston (1890–1909). When the WABHMS merged with the Woman's Baptist Home Mission Society (Chicago) in 1909 she became its first vice president. She was a founder and the first president of the Council of Women for Home Missions (an interdenominational organization), and a trustee of Spelman Seminary (Atlanta), Hartshorn Memorial College (Richmond), Atlanta University, and Gordon College (Boston).

ANB; NoAW; Margaret Tustin O'Harra, "An Appreciation of Mrs. George W. Coleman," *Watchman-Examiner* (19 July 1928); Mrs. Orrin R. Judd, "Mrs. George W. Coleman," *Watchman-Examiner* (21 July 1921).

KEITH DURSO

Collson, Mary Edith (1870–1952). Born near Humbolt, Iowa, into a poverty-stricken rationalist family, Mary Collson taught four years before attaining a State University of Iowa economics degree. Her study at Meadville was supported by her minister, Marian Murdock, teacher *Eleanor Gordon, and Iowa Sisterhood ministers' mentor *Mary Safford. She was then encouraged to serve the Unitarian church at Ida Grove, Iowa. Adopting a social gospel theology she became a juvenile court parole officer at Hull House. In Boston she organized for the National Women's Trade Union League and studied to be a Christian Science practitioner in 1904. She flourished as the first reader in Evansville, Indiana, despite national paternalism and negativity; still, she resigned from Eddyism in 1914. She then organized in New York City for the Women's Political Union and the Socialist Party's women's committee marches. Reinstated as a Christian Science practitioner, she offered patients her own mystical transcendentalist wisdom until 1928. She again ceased membership in 1932.

Cynthia Grant Tucker, *Healer in Harm's Way: A Clergywoman in Christian Science* (1995) [1984], *Prophetic Sisterhood: Liberal Women Ministers of the Frontier* (1990).

IRENE BAROS-JOHNSON

Comstock, Elizabeth Leslie Rous Wright (1815–91). Minister and reformer. Born in England, Elizabeth Rous was educated and taught at Quaker schools. She immigrated to Canada in 1839 and met and married John T. Comstock, a wealthy Quaker. They moved to Michigan and were active members of the Quaker community. Allied with the Gurneyite Friends, the most evangelical of Quakers, she became a Public Friend. Comstock and her husband aided runaway slaves during the Civil War. She gained a national reputation for her work in prison reform and advocated change in the areas of poverty, welfare, and temperance. In the 1870s she moved to Kansas with the Exodusters (former slaves who migrated west in hope of attaining better lives) and served as secretary of the state's Freedmen's Relief Association, where she worked with *Laura Smith Haviland.

ANB; EAWR; NoAW; Catherine Hare, ed., *Life and Letters of Elizabeth Leslie Comstock* (1895).

JANET MOORE LINDMAN

Conant, Hannah (1809–65). Baptist religious writer and linguist. Fluent in German, Hannah Conant had a working knowledge of the Oriental languages, Greek, Hebrew, French, and Latin. She translated G. F. A. Strauss's *Lea, or the Baptism in Jordan* (1844), Augustus Neander's *Scriptural Expositions of the First Epistle of John, the Epistle of Paul to the Philippians, and the Epistle of James* (1859), H. F. Uhden's *The New England Theocracy: A History of the Congregationalists in New England to the Revivals of 1740* (1859), and several of Gustav Meritz's children's stories. Along with her husband, Thomas Jefferson Conant, she translated and revised Gesenius's *Hebrew Grammar*.

She authored *The Earnest Man* (1856), a bibliography of the Baptist missionary Adoniram Judson, and *The English Bible: History of the Translation of the Holy Scriptures into the English Tongue* (1856).

NoAW; Maud Wilkinson, "Baptist Women of the Nineteenth Century," in *A Century of Baptist Achievement*, ed. A. H. Newman (1901).

KEITH DURSO

Concerned Women for America (CWA) (1979–). Conservative women's public policy organization. In 1979 *Beverly Ratcliffe LaHaye founded a grassroots organization called Concerned Women for America. LaHaye's impetus for forming the organization was her reaction to a televised interview with feminist Betty Friedan, founder of the National Organization of Women (NOW). LaHaye was concerned that secular humanism was undermining what she considered to be traditional family values and was offended by the notion that Friedan spoke for all women in the U.S. LaHaye founded CWA as a counter-organization to NOW. CWA members organized initially against NOW and against feminism in general. LaHaye (and other CWA members) believed that a woman's God-ordained role was as the helpmate and servant to men. In the 1980s CWA members opposed the Equal Rights Amendment and prayed for its defeat. Members have also organized against equal pay for work of equal value, feminism, pornography, abortions, gay rights, and secular humanism. They have supported their understanding of biblical values, government-supported religious schools, as well as prayer in public schools. In the early 1980s, 10 years after the organization was founded, there were CWA chapters in all 50 states. In 2005 the organization claimed a membership of over 500,000.

EAWR; EE; Randall Balmer, *Mine Eyes Have Seen the Glory* (2000); Stephen Bates, *Battleground: One Mother's Crusade, the Religious Right, and the Struggle for Control of Our Classrooms* (1993).

JUDITH L. GIBBARD

Connelly, Cornelia Augusta Peacock (1809–79). Educator and founder of the Society of the Holy Child Jesus (SHCJ) in England. Born in Philadelphia, in 1831 Cornelia Peacock married Pierce Connelly, an Episcopalian rector. They had five children. Both converted to Roman Catholicism in 1836. Connelly later acquiesced to a Vatican-approved permanent marital separation so that her husband could be ordained as a Catholic priest. In 1845 Connelly herself took a permanent vow of chastity. Her spirituality, personality, and devotion to children attracted ecclesiastical authorities, and they invited her to begin the SHCJ. A woman of extraordinary talent, she simultaneously fulfilled her roles as mother and Catholic sister. With her children in English schools, she started schools for the poor and illiterate working girls. In 1847 Connelly's husband embarked on a violent public attack against her. He renounced his priestly vows, took their children, and sought to restore his conjugal rights through court action. Amid public scandal, Connelly suffered, yet continued to increase the influence of the new order. Her strong character, subordinated for years, clashed with church authorities, and they suppressed her original rule. After her death, the Holy See restored her original constitution. Her canonization process commenced in 1959.

ANB; EACH; NCE; NoAW; ROWUS.

SUSAN MARIE MALONEY, SNJM

Converse, Florence (1871–1967). Author, poet, and settlement worker. Born in New Orleans, Florence Converse received her education at Wellesley College and lived in New England for most of her adult life. Although her family was Unitarian, she became a devout Anglo-Catholic as a young woman and was a leader in the College Settlements Association. A voluminous writer and poet, she also served on the editorial staffs of the *Churchman* and the *Atlantic Monthly* and wrote for numerous other publications. Known for her contemplative spirituality, Converse wrote *The House of Prayer* for children, a work considered among the best of its kind. She ceased writing after the 1961 death of her longtime companion, *Vida Scudder. Both Converse and Scudder were active in social justice causes and were members of the *Society of the Companions of the Holy Cross.

Vida Scudder, *On Journey* (1937).

SHERYL A. KUJAWA-HOLBROOK

Cook, Charity Wright (1745–1822). Quaker preacher. Charity Wright received no formal education, but was influenced by numerous Quaker woman preachers during her childhood. An accusation in 1760 of sexual impropriety against her resulted in her estrangement from the Quakers for eight years. Nonetheless, in 1762 she married a Quaker, Isaac Cook, and they had 11 children. By 1772 the earlier controversy had died down and the Bush Run Meeting commissioned her to be a preacher. During the Revolutionary War, Cook traveled throughout the South advocating pacifism. Beginning in 1797 she toured Quaker meetings throughout Europe. She returned to the U.S. in 1802, and she and her husband established Quaker meetings throughout Ohio and Indiana.

Algie I. Newlin, *Charity Cook* (1981).

SCOTT D. SEAY

Cook, Gladys Evelyn Taylor (Topah-hde-win, Wakan-mani-win) (1929–). Dakota elder, counselor, and advocate. Born on Sioux Valley First Nation, Manitoba, Gladys Cook was given powerful traditional names, "help in four directions" and "woman who walks with the Great Spirit." In Indian residential school from age four to 16, her culture was suppressed and she was sexually abused. In her adult journey of recovery and reclaiming Dakota ways, Cook became a leader in the Anglican Church and forerunner for many Aboriginal community services. From 1978 until her retirement in 1996, she coordinated the National Native Alcohol and Drug Abuse Program in Portage la Prairie, Manitoba. Providing decades of spiritual guidance for incarcerated women and youth, Cook has also educated Canadians about Native Christianity and residential school abuse.

Joyce Carlson and Alf Dumont, eds., *Bridges in Spirituality* (1997); John Bird, "The Shining Spirit of Gladys Cook," *This Country Canada* 9 (1996); *Topahdewin: The Gladys Cook Story* [video] (2005).

JANET SILMAN

Cooper, Anna Julia Haywood (ca. 1859–1964). Episcopal educator, advocate, and scholar. Born in Raleigh, North Carolina, to an enslaved woman and a white man (presumably her mother's master), Anna Julia Haywood was an academically gifted child and received a scholarship to attend St. Augustine Normal School and Collegiate Institute, a school founded by Episcopalians to educate African American teachers and clergy. There she began her membership in the Episcopal Church. After forcing her way into a Greek class for male theology students, Haywood later married the instructor, George A. C. Cooper, the second African American ordained to the Episcopal priesthood in North Carolina. After her husband's death in 1879, Cooper earned a bachelor's and master's degree in mathematics from Oberlin College and continued her teaching career. She became principal of the only African American high school in Washington, DC, in 1901, but was denied reappointment in 1906 because she refused to lower her educational standards. Cooper emphasized the importance of education to the future of African Americans and was critical of the lack of support they received from the church. An advocate for African American women, Cooper assisted in organizing the Colored Women's League and the Colored Settlement House in Washington, DC. She wrote and spoke on issues of race and gender and took an active role in national and international organizations. At the age of 55 she adopted the five children of her nephew. Cooper became in 1925 the fourth African American woman to complete a PhD, granted from the University of Paris-Sorbonne. From 1930 to 1942 she served as president of Frelinghuysen University.

ANB; BWA; NBAW; NoAWMP; Sheryl A. Kujawa-Holbrook, *Freedom Is a Dream* (2002); Charles Lemert and Esme Bhan, eds., *The Voice of Anna Julia Cooper* (1998); Leona C. Gabel, *From Slavery to the Sorbonne and Beyond* (1982); Anna Julia Cooper, *A Voice from the South* (1892).

SHERYL A. KUJAWA-HOLBROOK

Cooper, Sarah Brown Ingersoll (1835–96). Educator and civic activist. Sarah Ingersoll was born in upstate New York and educated at the coeducational Cazenovia Seminary. When she was 20 years old she was employed as governess for the governor of Georgia and taught a Bible class for slaves on the plantation. She married in 1855. In 1869 Cooper's family moved to San Francisco where she taught a popular Bible class; wrote extensively about women, children, and education; and opened free kindergartens. In 1881 Cooper gained public support with her feisty and eloquent self-defense against heresy charges brought against her by the Presbyterian Church. (She had denied the doctrine of infant damnation and everlasting punishment.) In 1891 she founded the Golden Gate Kindergarten Free Normal Training School, the first U.S. organization to train kindergarten teachers. Cooper's model inspired the establishment of hundreds of free kindergartens across the country.

ANBO; NoAW; Papers, Cornell University Library.

ROBYNNE ROGERS HEALEY

Coppin, Fanny Jackson (1837–1913). Educator, community leader, activist. Fanny Jackson Coppin's lifelong commitment to education was evoked by an early experience of divine urging, "Speak to the people that they go forward." Born a slave in Washington, DC, and freed at a young age, Fanny Jackson initiated her formal education in the 1850s by hiring a tutor with funds earned as a domestic servant. She graduated from Oberlin College in 1865 with an outstanding reputation for teaching. She is best known for her brilliant and visionary leadership of the Institute for Colored Youth in Philadelphia from 1869 to 1902. Utilizing her exceptional gifts Jackson made bold innovations in black education, while also providing activist leadership in the Philadelphia African American community. She held elected positions in the *National Association of Colored Women and the Women's Home and Foreign Missionary Society of the African Methodist Episcopal (AME) Church. She married AME minister Levi Coppin in 1881, and worked to establish women's mission services after his election as bishop for South Africa in 1900.

BWA; NoAW; Linda M. Perkins, *Fanny Jackson Coppin and the Institute for Colored Youth* (1987); Fanny Jackson Coppin, *Reminiscences of School Life, and Hints on Teaching* (1913).

MARGARET MCMANUS

Cortez, Luisa ("Mama Luisa") (unknown). Leader of the women's lodges of the Filipino Federation of

America. Luisa Cortez, known by fellow Filipinas as Mama Luisa, was the leader of the women's lodges of the Filipino Federation of America based in Stockton, California. She was a follower of Lorenzo de los Reyes, the spiritual leader of the federation founded by Hilario Camino Moncado. (Moncado was understood to be the reincarnation of the Filipino saint/martyr Jose Rizal, who was executed by the Spaniards in the Philippines in 1896 and viewed as the reincarnation of Christ within folk Catholicism.) Little biographical information exists on Cortez, but she was an active leader of the lodges in the 1920s and 1930s.

Steffi San Buenaventura, "Filipino Folk Spirituality and Immigration: From Mutual Aid to Religion," in *New Spiritual Homes: Religion and Asian Americans*, ed. David K. Yoo (1999).

BARBARA E. REED

Cox, Cordelia (1901–97). Lutheran agency executive. Brought up in a southern Lutheran parsonage, Cordelia Cox was teaching social work when she heard of Lutheran involvement in resettling Europeans displaced by World War II. As director of Lutheran Resettlement Services, a division of the Lutheran Council in America, Cox coordinated resettlement of over 57,000 persons, oversaw work in Europe, negotiated with U.S. sponsors, and contributed to development of government policies for refugee resettlement. Cox also provided direct services to newly arrived immigrants. She later directed the Lutheran Welfare Council of New York (1957–61). Beyond the church, she consulted with the Council of Social Work Education and the U.S. Department for Health, Education, and Welfare, and volunteered at the United Nations. When she was in her 70s, she went to Western Samoa with the Peace Corps.

L. DeAne Lagerquist, *The Lutherans* (1999); Oral History Collection of the Archives of Cooperative Lutheranism, Evangelical Lutheran Church in America Archives.

L. DEANE LAGERQUIST

Cramer, Malinda Elliott (1844–1906). Founder of Divine Science. Malinda Elliott Cramer turned in midlife to meditation and prayer and experienced progressive healing from her infirmities. She studied under *Emma Curtis Hopkins, and then offered her own course in Divine Science and began *Harmony* magazine. In 1892 she created the International Divine Science Association and in 1898 cofounded the Colorado College of Divine Science. Her work continued in the New Thought movement.

EAWR; RLA; Divine Science School, www.divinescience.com.

GRAEME SHARROCK

Crandall, Prudence (1803–90). Educator and abolitionist. Prudence Crandall's Quaker family moved to Canterbury, Connecticut, in 1810. Encouraged by town leaders, she opened an academy for local girls in 1831. Trouble began when the daughter of an affluent black farmer applied for admission and local residents withdrew their children from the school in protest. Crandall reopened the school as a teacher training institution for young black women and attracted pupils from Philadelphia, Boston, and New York. Locals harassed the school and helped pass a state law prohibiting the education of nonresident blacks. Crandall was arrested and tried three times for violating this law; the last trial ended in her favor. A cause célèbre among abolitionists, she later married, moved west to farm, and opened a school. She spoke out until her death on temperance, women's rights, pacifism, and spiritualism.

ANB; NoAW; Susan Strane, *A Whole-Souled Woman* (1990); Philip S. Foner and

Josephine F. Pacheco, *Three Who Dared* (1984).

JANET MOORE LINDMAN

Crane, Caroline Julia Bartlett (1858–1935). Minister and reformer. Born in Hudson, Wisconsin, Caroline Bartlett received a BA (1879) and an MA (1882) from Carthage College. She taught school and staffed newspapers before ministering at the Unitarian church at Sioux Falls, Dakota Territory (1886–89). Ordained in 1889 she served at Kalamazoo, Michigan, until 1898, when she built a nonsectarian People's church. She married Augustus Crane in 1896. Influenced by the Salvation Army, Crane addressed civic needs such as kindergarten, women's fitness, vocational training, and music, and established an African American literary group. She lobbied for meat inspection, founded the Woman's Civic Improvement League, and organized the Charity Organizations Board. Crane belonged to the American Civic Association, National Municipal League, National Tuberculosis Association, and was on the board of the League to Enforce Peace. She was also active in the National Woman Suffrage Association.

DUUB; NoAW; UUWM; Dorothy May Emerson, ed., *Standing Before Us* (2000); Cynthia Grant Tucker, *Prophetic Sisterhood* (1990); Papers, Western Michigan University Library.

IRENE BAROS-JOHNSON

Crank, Sarah McCoy (1863–1948). Itinerant evangelist. Born in Illinois into a large farming family, Sadie McCoy became a schoolteacher at the age of 16. Upon joining the Stone-Campbell movement in the mid-1880s, she was appointed to be its Sunday school evangelist for the state. The congregation in Marceline, Illinois, ordained her in 1892, making her the second woman in the movement ordained for preaching ministry. In that same year she married James Rawser Crank, another well-known evangelist in the movement. Together they formed a ministry team and led revivals and established new churches throughout western Illinois and southwest Missouri. After her husband died in 1940 Crank continued her evangelistic work for another eight years. Her obituary credits her with organizing 50 churches and baptizing at least 7,000 people.

ES-CM; Earl Sechler, *Sadie McCoy Crank* (1950).

SCOTT D. SEAY

Cratty, Mabel (1868–1928). Social worker and *YWCA leader. Born and raised in rural Ohio, Mabel Cratty graduated from Ohio Wesleyan University in 1890. A deeply pious Methodist, she began her career as a Latin instructor and principal of Delaware High School. In 1902 she joined the YWCA (Young Women's Christian Association) in Ohio. She quickly ascended in its ranks, and by 1906 she became general secretary of the newly formed national board. She succeeded *Grace Hoadley Dodge as president in 1914, a position that she held until her death. The dramatic growth of the YWCA continued under her leadership: the number of local associations and membership tripled; almost 200 staff were added; and the annual budget ballooned to $2 million. An advocate of the social gospel, Cratty's irenic spirit helped bridge the gap between modernists and fundamentalists in the YWCA.

ANB; NoAW; Marion Robinson, *Eight Women of the YWCA* (1966).

SCOTT D. SEAY

Crawford, Florence Louise ("Mother Crawford") (1872–1936). Founder of the Apostolic Faith Movement in Portland, Oregon. Florence Crawford was a native of Oregon. She was a sickly child who was reared without formal religion. In 1890 she married a building contractor, Frank Mortimer Crawford. They lived in Los Angeles. The mother of two children, Crawford visited the Azusa Street Mission in 1906 where she professed sanctification, Spirit baptism, and healing. Crawford embraced strict legalism and parted from her husband, who did not share her religious zeal. Crawford became a leader in the Azusa Street Mission, and in 1908 she returned to Oregon and established the Apostolic Faith Church. For the next 30 years, Mother Crawford preached; evangelized; trained young people for ministry; published tracts, books, and a monthly paper; and presided as general overseer over a Pentecostal association that developed separately from (and in tension with) other Pentecostal groups. Crawford never had more than several thousand followers, but her outspoken views, published materials, and vigorous evangelism made her a force with which to reckon.

EAWR; EE; RLA; Stanley M. Burgess et al., eds., *Dictionary of Pentecostal and Charismatic Movements* (1988); Apostolic Faith Church, *A Historical Account of the Apostolic Faith* (1965); Raymond Robert Crawford, *The Light of Life Brought Triumph*, 2nd ed. (1955) [1936].

EDITH BLUMHOFER

Crawford, Isabel Alice Hartley (1865–1961). Baptist missionary. Isabel Crawford lived in Ontario, Manitoba, and North Dakota before attending the Baptist Missionary Training School in Chicago. In 1893 the Woman's American Baptist Home Mission Society appointed her a missionary among the Kiowa Indians of Oklahoma. She served at Elk Creek and then at Saddle Mountain. Deaf as a result of illness, she learned Indian sign language, which enabled her to communicate with Indians of many tribes. She encouraged the Saddle Mountain congregation to decide whether to allow their own deacons to serve communion. This action prompted severe criticism of Crawford and led to her resignation in 1906. Following 13 years on the mission field she did deputation work on behalf of missions for the next 23 years, traveling from coast to coast.

HDB; Isabel Crawford, *Kiowa* (1998) [1915], *Joyful Journey: Highlights on the High Way* (1951).

MARILYN FÄRDIG WHITELEY

Crosby, Frances ("Fanny") Jane (1820–1915). Hymn writer. Fanny Crosby became blind as an infant after her parents received bad medical advice. Her grandmother helped her memorize poetry and the Bible, and took her on nature walks where she provided detailed descriptions of all the things Crosby could not see. Crosby began attending the New York Institute for the Blind in 1835, and taught there from 1847 to 1858. She married Alexander Van Alstyne in 1858. They had one child who died in infancy, and the two eventually separated. Crosby had written poetry since she was a student, and she became a very successful hymn writer. She wrote between 6,000 and 9,000 hymns, many under pseudonyms. Some of these include "Jesus, Keep Me Near the Cross," "Praise Him, Praise Him," "Safe in the Arms of Jesus," "Rescue the Perishing," "Blessed Assurance," "All the Way My Savior Leads Me," "Draw Me Nearer," and "To God Be the Glory." Many of her hymns still appear in contemporary hymnbooks. She was a member of a Methodist church and worked in rescue missions and other religious organizations in New York City.

ANB; DARB; EAWR; EE; NoAW; RLA; Edith Blumhofer, *Her Heart Can See: The Life and Hymns of Fanny J. Crosby* (2005).

LYNN JAPINGA

Crucified Woman (1976–). Sculpture. Created by German Canadian artist

Almuth Lutkenhaus-Lackey (1930–96), the bronze sculpture depicts the naked body of a woman with arms outstretched. There is no cross, but her pose is cruciform. The sculpture generated great controversy when first exhibited at the Bloor Street United Church (Toronto) in 1979 during Lent and Eastertide. Some viewers were offended by the sculpture for theological and aesthetic reasons. Other viewers, for whom *Crucified Woman* symbolized a call for justice and solidarity with all women crucified through abuse and violence, were inspired and strengthened. Lutkenhaus-Lackey donated the sculpture to Emmanuel College, the United Church's college at the University of Toronto, in 1986. Hundreds of mourners gathered there the day after the massacre of 14 women in Montreal on December 6, 1989; the anniversary of the "Montreal Massacre" continues to be marked by memorial vigils at the foot of the sculpture. As theologian Doris Jean Dyke observed, "It draws the sorrows of women. It is a place where women know that their suffering is gathered up into the suffering of Christ."

Julia Clague, "The Christa: Symbolizing My Humanity and My Pain," *Feminist Theology* 14, no. 1 (2005); Doris Jean Dyke, *Crucified Woman* (1991).

TRACY J. TROTHEN

Curtiss, Harriette Augusta Brown (1856–1932). Metaphysical teacher and author. The well-educated daughter of Philadelphia parents, Harriette Brown gave up the life of a musician and actress, although she wrote a column for many years for the *Philadelphia Inquirer* called "The Batchelor Girl." After discovering her clairvoyant gifts, she married F. Homer Curtiss in 1907. As lifelong partners in teaching and writing, they founded the Order of Christian Mystics, an organization eventually replaced by the Universal Religious Foundation. The Curtisses' goal was to reconcile theosophical teachings with orthodox Christianity. The fruits of their esoteric and eclectic collaborations are seen in publications like the *Key to the Universe* (1915) and its sequel, the *Key of Destiny* (1919), books that influenced the poet H.D. (Hilda Doolittle) and that analyzed the numbers 1 through 22 from biblical and occult perspectives with an emphasis on esoteric Christianity.

EAWR; RLA.

MARY FARRELL BEDNAROWSKI

Cushing, Ellen Howard Winsor (1840–1915). Baptist missionary and educator. Ellen Winsor taught school in Boston, assisted former slaves in adjusting to their freedom, and served as the administrator of the Home for Little Wanderers. She and her husband, Josiah Nelson Cushing, served as missionaries in northeast Burma, working with the Shan tribe. Together they translated the Gospels into Shan and produced the first English-Shan dictionary and a Shan grammar book. Following several illnesses, the birth of a son, and periodic separations from her husband, Cushing and her son returned to the U.S. in 1880. In 1886 she became a field secretary for the Philadelphia Baptist Missionary Union and helped found (in 1892) and then direct the Baptist Training School for Christian Workers. After the death of her husband in 1905 Cushing returned to Burma to complete his translation projects.

HDB; Bill J. Leonard, ed., *Dictionary of Baptists in America* (1994).

PAMELA R. DURSO

Cushman, Vera Charlotte Scott (1876–1946). Social worker and leader in the *YWCA. Born into a religious Presbyterian family, Vera Scott served as president of the Christian Association, an affiliate of the YWCA (Young Women's Christian Association), while a student at Smith College. She married a wealthy New York businessman, James S. Cushman, enabling her to be active in and supportive of the national and international YWCA. Cushman served for three decades on the YWCA's national board and was vice president of the national YWCA for several terms (1906–36). During World War I she was the chairwoman of the War Work Council of the YWCA and supervised the work of the YWCA in the U.S. and Europe. Cushman was one of six women to receive the Distinguished Service Medal for her work during the war. After the war she traveled worldwide to promote the mission of the YWCA.

EAWR; NoAW; RLA.

KEITH DURSO

Dall, Caroline Healey (1822–1912). Lecturer and writer. A merchant's daughter with modern language education, Caroline Healey volunteered at Boston Sunday schools and, at the age of 18, co-ran a nursery for working women. She was an early supporter of the Reverend Theodore Parker. In 1841 she recorded recollections of *Margaret Fuller's unusual male-dominated "Conversations." For two years she was vice principal of a young ladies school in the Georgetown neighborhood of Washington, DC. In 1844 she married the Reverend Charles Dall. As the minister's wife, she helped raise funds for a new Toronto church, nurtured the Sunday school, dispersed American Anti-Slavery Society monies, and wrote for the periodical *Una*. After her husband's breakdown and departure for Calcutta missionary work, she supported two children by writing and lecturing on expanding women's education and employment. She was a founder of the American Social Science Association and preached from many pulpits.

ANB; DUUB; NoAW; Caroline Dall, *Alongside* (1900); Papers, Massachusetts Historical Society.

IRENE BAROS-JOHNSON

Daly, Mary (1928–). Philosopher, theorist, and theologian. A former Roman Catholic, Mary Daly's critique of patriarchy began with *The Church and the Second Sex* in 1968. It then spiraled out "beyond God the Father," the title of her 1973 book. Her six other books include the influential *Gyn/Ecology* (1978) and the ecofeminist *Amazon Grace* (2006). Daly earned three PhDs between 1954 and 1965 and was an associate professor of theology at Boston College from 1967 to 2000. Her contentious relationship with the academy included a well-publicized fight for tenure, which she ultimately won, and two dismissal suits filed by the college. She settled the second in 2000 and left her position. Some feminists have critiqued Daly for ethnocentrism, essentialism, promoting male gendercide, and shunning critique. Nevertheless, as a well-known radical and a self-described lesbian "quintessentialist," Daly has had a pivotal impact upon an entire generation of feminists. She is known for her creativity, wry humor, and passionate, dogged intelligence.

EAWR; Mary Daly, *Quintessence. . . Realizing the Archaic Future: A Radical Elemental Feminist Manifesto* (1998); *Outercourse: The Bedazzling Voyage* (1992); *Websters' First New Intergalactic Wickedary of the English Language*, with Jane Caputi and Sudie Rakusin (1987).

AMY BLACK VOORHEES

Darling, Caroline Louise (Sister Constance) (1846–78). Episcopal nun, one of the Memphis Martyrs. Constance Darling was born in Boston, Massachusetts. She joined the Episcopal Church in 1864 and made her profession as a Sister of Mary in 1871. Darling was sent to Memphis in 1873 as superior of the small group of nuns forming St. Mary's Cathedral School for Girls and a church home for orphans. In 1878, when yellow fever struck Memphis, Darling mobilized the order to nurse the ill and shelter the orphaned. She, along with three other Episcopal nuns and two priests, died while caring for the sick. They are memorialized in the Episcopal Church's Book of Lesser Feasts and Fasts. Their widely publicized deaths helped reconcile Episcopalians to the idea of religious orders.

Mary Hilary, *Ten Decades of Praise* (1965); Morgan Dix, *The Sisters of St. Mary at Memphis* (1879).

JOAN R. GUNDERSEN

Daughters of Charity (DOC) (1633–). Roman Catholic religious congregation. Founded in Paris, France, by Vincent de Paul (1581–1660) and Louise de Marillac (1591–1660) to care for the sick poor, the sisters' work soon expanded to include instruction of the young, care of foundlings, operation of hospitals and orphanages, and ministry to galley slaves, wounded soldiers, refugees, and the aged. Missions were founded throughout France and eventually around the world. The DOC in the U.S. trace their origin to *Elizabeth Bayley Seton's 1809 foundation of the *Sisters of Charity (SC) in Emmitsburg, Maryland. This community was modeled after the DOC and adapted their rule. Nearly 30 years after Seton's death, at the urging of their priest superiors, some American Sisters of Charity formed a union with the Daughters of Charity, becoming the American province centered at Emmitsburg. In 1910 a second U.S. province was established in St. Louis. An additional three provinces were founded in 1969 in Albany (New York), Evansville (Indiana), and Los Altos (California). The ministries of the Daughters of Charity continue to serve the most needy through work in education, health care, parishes, and social service agencies. Their national health system is recognized as one of the leaders in U.S. Catholic health care. There are approximately 27,000 Daughters of Charity worldwide.

EACH; NCE; ROWUS; Daniel Hannefin, *Daughters of the Church* (1989).

JUDITH METZ, SC

Davidson, Carrie Dreyfuss (1879–1953). Magazine founder and editor. Born in Brooklyn, Carrie Dreyfuss married a seminary professor, Israel Davidson. In 1918 she joined with other Conservative Jewish women to form a national organization, the United Synagogue of America's National Women's League. As a board member, in 1930 she singlehandedly founded the league's journal, *Outlook*, which she edited for almost 24 years. As editor and author of numerous articles on topics affecting all Jews, she was influential in forming the opinions of several generations of American Jewish women. A supporter of Zionism, Davidson served on steering committees for the prestigious *Menorah Journal*. In 1939 she wrote a memoir, *Out of Endless Yearnings*, recounting her husband's personal and academic life.

JWA; Karla Goldman, "Reform Judaism," *Encyclopedia of Women and Religion in North America*, vol. 2, ed. Rosemary Skinner Keller et al. (2006).

JUDITH METZ, SC

Davis, Addie (ca. 1921–2005). First ordained Southern Baptist woman. On August 9, 1964, Watts Street Baptist Church in Durham, North Carolina, ordained Addie Davis, making her the first Southern Baptist woman to be ordained to the ministry. She was pastor of First Baptist Church in Readsboro, Vermont, from 1964 to 1972, where the

Vermont State Baptist Convention named her Vermont's Pastor of the Year in 1971. She became Rhode Island's first Baptist woman pastor in 1972, when she became the pastor of the Second Baptist Church in East Providence, a position she held until 1982. She was the first woman elected to the Providence Baptist Theological Circle and the first woman to serve as the vice president of the East Providence Clergy Association.

Keith E. Durso and Pamela R. Durso, "'Cherish the Dream God Has Given You': The Story of Addie Davis," in *Courage and Hope*, ed. Pamela R. Durso and Keith E. Durso (2005); Addie Davis, "A Dream to Cherish," *Folio* (Autumn 1984).

KEITH DURSO

Davis, Alice Brown (1852–1935). Intercultural mediator and Seminole chief. Alice Brown Davis advocated on behalf of the Seminoles and taught them "white" ways. Educated by Presbyterian and Baptist missionaries, she was superintendent of Emahaka Mission Academy until forced to turn over the school to a government-appointed superintendent. She acted as interpreter for her people in legal courts and on missions to Mexico. She was appointed chief of the Seminoles in 1922 by President Warren Harding.

NoAW; *Encyclopedia of Oklahoma History and Culture* [online].

ELIZABETH HINSON-HASTY

Davis, Mary Fenn Robinson (1824–86). Spiritualist lecturer, reformer, and writer. A relatively well-educated native New Yorker, Mary Robinson was born to Baptist parents but later rejected religious authority. She emulated, however, her father's antialcohol activism and gave temperance lectures. Her first marriage to Samuel Love ended in divorce in 1854. In 1855 she met and married the Spiritualist medium Andrew Jackson Davis. In 1860 they founded a Spiritualist newspaper, *Herald of Progress*, which Davis edited and for which she wrote essays and poetry. Known for her oratorical gifts and dedication to women's rights, Davis wrote for other Spiritualist periodicals and worked with her husband for educational, economic, and marriage reform. Her marriage was ended by her husband's initiative when, in 1885, he declared that he no longer considered her his spiritual affinity.

ANB; NoAW; Ann D. Braude, *Radical Spirits* (1989).

MARY FARRELL BEDNAROWSKI

Dawson, Emma Churchill (1862–1957). Pioneer Salvation Army officer. Born in Portugal Cove, Newfoundland, Emma Churchill immigrated to Toronto, where she became part of the first group of 25 officers commissioned in the Salvation Army's new Canadian territory in 1883. In 1885 she married Charles Dawson, and they spent five months introducing Salvationist-style meetings in Newfoundland. Their successful work led to the Salvation Army's official decision to expand their efforts in the colony in 1886. The Salvation Army grew rapidly in Newfoundland and later spread into Labrador. While the Dawsons returned to Ontario, where they established prison ministries through Toronto's Prison Gate Home (which opened in 1890) and at the Guelph Reformatory, Emma Dawson is considered the founder of the Salvation Army in Newfoundland.

R. G. Moyles, *The Salvation Army in Newfoundland* (1997); Newfoundland and Labrador Heritage, www.heritage.nf.ca/society/salvation army.html.

SANDRA L. BEARDSALL

Day, Dorothy (1897–1980). Social activist, founder of the Catholic Worker Movement. Dorothy Day drew many young Americans into a movement of Catholic renewal between World Wars I and II. She believed that the church offered an alternative to capitalism and communism. She upheld the gospel tradition, papal social teaching, and the binding together of all people in the mystical body of Christ. Day devoted her life to the poor as a young girl in Chicago. In 1914 she entered the University of Illinois, where she joined the Socialist Party. Two years later she moved to New York City to write for socialist publications. Although militantly antireligious, she developed a curiosity about Christianity. After several disastrous relationships, she formed a common-law marriage with naturalist Forster Batterham. A daughter, Tamar, was born, and Day was overwhelmed by the love and joy she experienced. She left Batterham and was baptized into the Roman Catholic Church in 1927. Peter Maurin, an advocate of farming cooperatives, helped Day reconcile her faith and social justice. They started the *Catholic Worker* newspaper, which gave rise to the Catholic Worker Movement (CWM). At the heart of the CWM were hospitality houses for the poor. Day was also active in the antiwar and civil rights movements. She eventually became frustrated by the CWM's disregard for Catholic devotion.

ANB; DARB; EACH; EAWR; NCE; RLA; Dorothy Day, *The Long Loneliness* (1997); Jim Forest, *Love Is the Measure* (1994); Michael Ray Rhodes, dir., *Entertaining Angels* [video] (1996).

BARBARA J. MACHAFFIE

Dease, Teresa (1820–89). Founder and superior general of the Institute of the Blessed Virgin Mary (IVBM). The IVBM, known popularly as the *Sisters of Loretto (or Loreto), was created by Mary Ward of England. Born in Ireland, Ellen Dease took the name Teresa upon entering the Irish founding house of her order. Upon the request of Toronto's Catholic bishop, four Loretto sisters, including Sister Teresa, sailed to North America. In the midst of a cholera epidemic they founded the first North American Loretto house in Toronto. Other mission houses and schools were soon organized throughout Ontario. Mother Teresa herself traveled back to Ireland to raise money and recruits for her Canadian sisters. She exhibited the wise discernment so necessary for the founding of a religious order.

NCE; Marion Norman, "Making a Path by Walking," *CCHA Historical Studies* 65 (1999); *Life and Letters of Rev. Mother Teresa Dease* (1916).

OSCAR COLE-ARNAL

Delaney, Emma Bertha (1871–1922). Baptist missionary. After graduating from Spelman Seminary (now Spelman College), Emma Delaney completed missionary and nursing training. In 1902 the National Baptist Convention sent her to Malawi. She cofounded Providence Industrial Mission with Landon N. Cheek, the first African American missionary in Malawi. She taught at a school on the mission station and organized a women's society. Returning to the U.S. in 1906, Delaney encouraged African American Baptist women to support mission work in Africa. In 1912 she began work in Liberia, where she supervised the construction of Sụehn Industrial Mission and served as the first principal of Suehn Industrial Academy. Delaney returned to the U.S. in 1920 to raise money for the work in Liberia; while on furlough, she died of yellow fever.

BWA; BWARC; Gerald H. Anderson, ed., *Biographical Dictionary of Christian Missions* (1999); Willy Hardy Ashley, *Far from Home* (1987).

PAMELA R. DURSO

Delany, Annie Elizabeth (Bessie) (1891–1995), and **Sarah Louise**

Delany (Sadie) (1889–1999). Civil rights pioneers and Episcopal laywomen. Daughters of an African American bishop for the Protestant Episcopal Church, the sisters graduated from St. Augustine College (Raleigh) and moved to New York City in 1916. Sadie earned degrees from Pratt Institute and Columbia University. Her appointment as domestic science teacher at a Bronx high school in 1930 made her a racial pioneer. Bessie entered dental school at Columbia University. She was the second black woman dentist licensed in New York. They published a memoir, *Having Our Say*, which was a national bestseller. The book revealed much about the family and religious ties that sustained them. A book of sayings followed, and Sadie published a third work after Bessie died.

ANBO; BWA; NBAW; Sarah Louise Delany and Amy Hill Hearth, *On My Own at 107* (1998); Sarah L. Delany and A. Elizabeth Delany with Amy Hill Hearth, *Having Our Say* (1993); Lynne Littman, dir., *Having Our Say* [VHS] (1999); Papers, Library Archives, St. Augustine College.

JOAN R. GUNDERSEN

Delille, Henriette (1813–62). Educator and social worker. Born in New Orleans of a liaison between a free woman of color and a wealthy white businessman, Henriette Delille's education included training in the social graces and the arts. Rejecting the expectation that she would follow in her mother's footsteps, she was influenced by her Roman Catholic faith and the example of a French nun to become involved in outreach to the poor, the education of blacks, and the care of the sick. Despite opposition she and several friends formed a confraternity to formalize their work, but were prohibited from continuing because of the group's mixed racial composition. In 1842 Delille and two companions formed the African American *Sisters of the Holy Family. While continuing their earlier work, they cared for the elderly and orphans, using Delille's inheritance to subsidize their efforts. At the time of her death there were 12 Creole women of color in the order. The U.S. bishops endorsed her cause for sainthood in 1997, and the process of canonization has begun in Rome.

EACH; Dorothy Dawes and Charles Nolan, *Religious Pioneers* (2004); Cyprian Davis, *The History of Black Catholics in the United States* (1990).

JUDITH METZ, SC

Deloria, Ella Cara (1889–1971). Anthropologist and linguist. Born on the Yankton Sioux Reservation in South Dakota, Ella Deloria was given the Dakota name Anpetu Waste, "Beautiful Day." Traditional Sioux values and Christian values as expressed in the Episcopal Church were the focus of the Deloria family's life and work. After traveling throughout the West and visiting many American Indian schools and reservations, Deloria worked with anthropologist Franz Boas, first as a translator and later as a field researcher, on Dakota language and culture. Deloria gained national recognition as a scholar and a leading authority on the Sioux through her research, writing, and lectures. She directed the mission school at Standing Rock Reservation and was on the board of St. Mary's School for Indian Girls.

ANB; NaAW; NoAWMP; Sheryl A. Kujawa-Holbrook, *Freedom Is a Dream* (2002); Ella Cara Deloria, *Speaking of Indians* (1998) [1944], *Waterlily* (1984); Janette K. Murray, "Ella C. Deloria: A Biographical Sketch and Literary Analysis" (PhD diss., University of North Dakota, 1974).

SHERYL A. KUJAWA-HOLBROOK

Dempsey, Sister Mary Joseph (Julia Dempsey) (1856–1939). Nurse and hospital administrator. Born in Salamanca, New York, Julia Dempsey moved as a child to Rochester, Minnesota, and later entered the Rochester Franciscan congregation. Sister Joseph taught in congregational schools until 1889, when she was summoned to help staff Rochester's new Saint Mary's Hospital. The hospital's medical staff consisted of Dr. W. W. Mayo and his surgeon sons, Charles and William. Sister Joseph was Dr. William J. Mayo's legendary first surgical assistant for 25 years and, concurrently, hospital superintendent for almost 50 years. During this time the hospital underwent six major expansions, growing from 27 to 600 beds. In 1906 Sister Joseph opened Saint Mary's School of Nursing and in 1915 helped organize the Catholic Hospital Association of America.

NCE; NoAW; Ellen Whelan, *The Sisters' Story* (2003); Vern Bullough et al., *American Nursing: A Biographical Dictionary* (1988).

ELLEN WHELAN, OSF

Denis, Margaret Mary (1933–). Catholic educator and group facilitator. A pioneer in the 1960s Canadian catechetical renewal, Margaret Denis developed intuitive learning and group methodologies. She completed her doctoral thesis on intuitive learning, and she recognized this deep capacity especially among aboriginal peoples. Denis subsequently taught intuitive learning skills and process facilitation in Canada and internationally. Denis believes that process is not simply a way of proceeding, it is also a way of being; it is the ultimate empowerment of the person and group, an energetic expression of God's shared creativity; it is also an important tool for justice. Her work has helped numerous religious communities shift their dominant paradigms, choose alternative models for exercising leadership, and investigate the shadow sides of group life as a locus for transformation. She is the founder of Margaret Denis and Associates.

Margaret Denis, *The Beatitude People* (1973).

VERONICA M. DUNNE, RNDM

Denison, Ruth Elisabeth Schaefer (1922–). Western Theravada meditation teacher, founder of Dhamma Dena Desert Vipassana Center. Born in East Prussia, Ruth Schaefer immigrated to the U.S. after World War II and married Henry Denison. They both spent time in parts of Asia studying meditation. Denison found her primary teacher in Burma in the person of U Ba Khin who recognized her abilities and gave her permission to teach. An innovator of teaching methods, she introduced all-women retreats and the use of dance and movement. She taught at the Insight Meditation Society in Barre, Massachusetts, as well as at her own retreat center, the Dhamma Denna Desert Vipassana Center in Joshua Tree, California.

Sandy Boucher, *Dancing in the Dharma: The Life and Teachings of Ruth Denison* (2005); "Bowing to Life Deeply: An Interview with Ruth Denison," *Insight Magazine Archives* 8 (Spring 1997) [online].

BARBARA E. REED

Denton, Mary Florence (1857–1947). Missionary teacher. Descended from Massachusetts settlers, Mary Denton was born in a mining camp in California. She was educated in local schools and became a teacher in Pasadena, where she became acquainted with Congregational missionaries who told her about the Doshisha schools of Kyoto, Japan. These schools were founded by a Christianized Japanese man in cooperation with American missionaries, and included schools for both boys and girls. Denton volunteered for service with the American Board of Commissioners for Foreign Missions. She arrived in Japan in 1888; her association with the Doshisha was to continue for nearly 60 years. Denton taught English, the Bible, and Western-style cooking. Her fund-raising ability helped to increase the size and prestige of the university. Upon her death she was awarded the Order of the Sacred Treasure by the Japanese government.

NoAW; Frances Benton Clapp, *Mary Florence Denton and the Doshisha* (1955).

BETH SPAULDING

Dickey, Sarah Ann (1838–1904). Educator and ordained minister. Born near Dayton, Ohio, Sarah Ann Dickey had almost no schooling until she was 16 years old. She was determined to become a teacher, however, and obtained her certification at age 19. Dickey trusted visions and a voice she considered to be God's voice. She joined the Church of the United Brethren in Christ in 1858 and was ordained in 1896. In 1863 the church selected Dickey and two other teachers to open a freedmen's school in Vicksburg, Mississippi. Two years later she returned north to attend Mount Holyoke Female Seminary; she graduated in 1869. Dickey returned to Mississippi where she defied local hostility and threats from the Ku Klux Klan to lay the foundations for Mount Hermon Female Seminary, which opened in 1875. She remained committed to the work of the school until her death.

ANBO; NoAW; Helen Griffith, *Dauntless in Mississippi*, 2nd ed. (1966) [1965].

ROBYNNE ROGERS HEALEY

Dickinson, Frances (Mother Claire Joseph) (1755–1830). Cofounder of the first Roman Catholic convent in the U.S. Frances Dickinson was born in London, England, and joined the Order of Our Lady of Mount Carmel (*Carmelite) convent in Antwerp, Belgium, in 1772. She took the name Claire Joseph of the Sacred Heart of Jesus and her final vows in 1773. Along with *Ann Teresa Mathews (Bernardina Teresa Xavier of St. Joseph) and Mathews's two nieces, Dickinson immigrated to the U.S. in 1790. With Mathews, she founded the first Roman Catholic convent in the U.S., the Carmel Convent in Port Tobacco, Maryland. Dickinson assisted Mother Bernardina, the convent's first prioress. Dickinson became the convent's prioress in 1800, a position she held for 30 years. She and Ann Teresa Mathews are buried in the Bonnie Brae cemetery in Baltimore, Maryland.

EACH; EAWR; NoAW; Robert McHenry, *Famous American Women* (1983); Archives of the Carmelite Monastery, Towson, Maryland.

KEITH DURSO

Diffee, Agnes White (1889–1970). Pastor. Born Agnes White in Arkansas, she graduated from Oklahoma State Teachers College and taught school, but also conducted revivals in the summers. She was ordained in 1919 and was senior pastor of Little Rock First Church of the Nazarene from 1931 to 1949. Under her leadership, its membership grew to 1,163, with 1,000 in weekly attendance. Her husband, Roy, was her assistant. Diffee hosted a daily program on radio station KARK, and Sunday services were also broadcast, extending her influence so wide that Nazarenes were best known in Arkansas simply as "Sister Diffee's church." Typically she preached 98 sermons a year, made 700 pastoral visits, and was the only woman on the Little Rock Ministerial Alliance. Later she was a pastor in Pine Bluff and other locales. Her ministry continued in retirement. On the day she died, she visited patients in every Little Rock hospital who had requested her presence.

Tamara Walker, "Rev. Agnes White Diffee," and various undated newspaper clippings, in the Agnes Diffee Collection, Nazarene Archives; *Pine Bluff Commercial* (11 October 1958); *Arkansas Democrat* (24 September 1949); *Herald of Holiness* (22 November 1933).

STAN INGERSOL

Dilling Stokes, Elizabeth Kirkpatrick (1894–1966). Author and evangelist. Elizabeth Kirkpatrick attended the Episcopal Church throughout her childhood. She married Albert Dilling in 1918. After a trip to the Soviet Union in 1931 she began a lifelong crusade against both Communism and Jews. Her books during the 1930s warned of the Communist Party's desire to overthrow the U.S. By the 1940s, under the pseudonym "Reverend Frank Woodruff Johnson," her work became openly anti-Semitic. In 1940 she wrote and published the *Octopus*, which claimed that the Jews were conspiring to rob Gentiles of constitutional rights. In 1943, despite an indictment for subversive activity, Dilling openly claimed that America's true enemies were Jews, Negroes, and the New Deal. She married fellow anticommunist and anti-Semite Jeremiah Stokes in 1948. Fanatical in her beliefs, her widespread speaking engagements and written works contributed to the anti-Semitism of the 1930s and 1940s.

EAWR; Glen Jeansonne, *Women of the Far Right* (1996); Richard Gid Powers, *Not without Honor* (1995); Leo P. Ribuffo, *The Old Christian Right* (1983); Harry Thornton Moore, "The Lady Patriot's Book," *The New Republic* 85 (January 8, 1936).

SHERYL A. KUJAWA-HOLBROOK

Dix, Dorothea Lynde (1802–87). Advocate for the mentally ill. After a difficult childhood, Dorothea Dix ran away to live with her grandmother. She started a school for girls in Worcester, Massachusetts, in 1816 and a school in Boston in 1821. She resigned because she had tuberculosis and went to England to recover. In 1841 she taught a Sunday school class for women prisoners in East Cambridge, Massachusetts, where she realized that some incarcerated women were mentally ill and were housed in crowded, filthy conditions, often with no heat. She visited the prisons in Massachusetts to research the conditions for the mentally ill. She wrote an extensive report, which she submitted to the state legislature along with a request for money to build a hospital. She eventually traveled to most states in the eastern half of the U.S. and to many countries in Europe. Her efforts led to the founding of over 30 hospitals for the mentally ill. During the Civil War she volunteered as the superintendent of army nurses. She also wrote a number of books for children.

ANB; EAWR; NoAWMP; Thomas J. Brown, *Dorothea Dix* (1998); David Gollaher, *Voice for the Mad* (1995).

LYNN JAPINGA

Dodge, Grace Hoadley (1856–1914). Philanthropist. Born into a wealthy Presbyterian family in New York City, Grace Dodge received her education from private tutors. The preaching of Dwight L. Moody convinced her to commit to a lifetime of volunteer work and Christian philanthropy. In the 1880s and 1890s she consolidated 75 nascent labor unions into the Association of Working Girls' Societies. She also organized the Industrial Education Association (IEA), a group that promoted quality education for young men and women. By 1892 the IEA had merged with Columbia University to become its Teachers College, and Dodge served as the new school's treasurer until 1911. Dodge negotiated a merger between rival groups in 1905 and 1906 to form the national *YWCA (Young Women's Christian Association). She served as president of the national board until her death.

ANBO; NoAW; Marion Robinson, *Eight Women of the YWCA* (1966); Abbie Graham, *Grace H. Dodge* (1926).

SCOTT D. SEAY

Doherty, Catherine de Hueck (1896–1985). Founder of Madonna House and a lay apostolate that serves the poor in many countries. Catherine Kolyschkine was born in Russia. She had a Christian Orthodox formation, and a Roman Catholic formation from the Sisters of Sion school she attended after her father was posted to Alexandria, Egypt. She was received into the Roman Catholic Church in England in 1920. Kolyschkine's mother took her on expeditions to care for the poor in the various communities in which she lived. This experience—combined with her witnessing of two world wars, the Russian Revolution, and the Depression of the 1930s—moved her to work for social justice in the U.S. and Canada. She worked with *Dorothy Day, the founder of the Catholic Worker Movement, in establishing Friendship House in Harlem. In 1947 she moved with her second husband, Eddie Doherty, to Combermere, Ontario, and established the Madonna House of hospitality. Their work among the poor attracted many women and men, and she established a lay apostolate that requires a life of voluntary poverty, chastity dedicated to the love of Christ, and obedience to the director of the particular house in which one is serving. There are over 200 lay apostles and priests living in two dozen houses of hospitality around the world. They engage in works of mercy with the poor, have a common liturgical life influenced by both Roman Catholic and Orthodox traditions, and guide spiritual seekers through a contemplative discipline known as *poustinia*. Doherty was a prolific writer. Her book *Poustinia: Encountering God in Silence, Solitude and Prayer* (1975) is considered a 20th-century spiritual classic.

Mary Bazzett, *The Life of Catherine de Hueck Doherty* (1998).

DAVID J. GOA

Dominican Sisters (1206–). Roman Catholic religious congregation. Apostolic sisters of St. Dominic—vowed women who were not cloistered, but active in ministries of education, health care, and so on—grew out of the third order of St. Dominic, which consisted of laypeople who associated themselves with the order. St. Catherine of Siena (1347–80) is the most famous lay Dominican, essentially a Dominican sister before such congregations were officially formed and recognized. A Dominican province was founded in the U.S. in 1805 at St. Rose, Kentucky, and the first congregation of Dominican sisters began there in 1822 (the Dominican Sisters of St. Catharine). Nineteen more congregations were established across the U.S. during the remainder of the 19th century. Several more congregations began in the early part of the 20th century, with the *Maryknoll Sisters (founded in 1912 as the Foreign Mission Sisters of St. Dominic) being perhaps the best known. Study is one of the four pillars of Dominican life. The Sinsinawa (Wisconsin) Dominican Sisters were the first to open a college in 1904, St. Clara College (now Dominican University); the San Rafael Sisters opened the Dominican College of San Rafael (now the Dominican University of California) in 1917; and others followed. Over a dozen congregations of Dominican sisters have recently founded farms or Earth Spirituality Centers, which focus on a Dominican response to the ecological crisis. The most famous of these is Genesis Farm, founded by the Caldwell Dominican Sisters (New Jersey).

EACH; NCE; ROWUS; Sharon Therese Zayac, *Earth Spirituality* (2003).

COLLEEN CARPENTER CULLINAN

Donnelly, Catherine (1884–1983). Founder of the Sisters of Service (SOS). Catherine Donnelly was born in Alliston, Ontario. Her exposure to a mixed religious environment of Irish Protestants and Catholics contributed to the ecumenical spirit that permeated her congregation. Donnelly was an independent woman with a forthright manner when dealing with ecclesiastical and educational authorities. In 1922 she founded a congregation extremely modern in terms of ministry, residence, and habit. Initially placed under the authority of the *Sisters of St. Joseph, the SOS became independent in 1931. Donnelly, however, was neither elected superior general nor was she officially credited with its foundation. Her pioneering vision of providing Catholic education in western Canada resulted in the establishment of the first English-speaking Canadian congregation. Its missions, schools, hospitals, and social work, especially with immigrants, and its residences for women contributed significantly to Canadian history.

DCB; Jeanne R. Beck, *To Do and to Endure* (1997).

ELAINE GUILLEMIN

Donovan, Jean (1953–80). Lay Catholic mission worker. A vivacious woman, Jean Donovan surprised many when she moved to El Salvador in 1979 to work in a Catholic mission for refugees. She stayed in El Salvador despite escalating violence and the military's open hostility toward church workers. On 2 December 1980 Jean Donovan was traveling in the company of *Ita Ford, *Maura Clarke, and *Dorothy Kazel when all four were arrested, assaulted, and assassinated by El Salvadoran national guardsmen at the command of officials in the El Salvadoran army.

Ana Carrigan, *Salvadoran Witness* (1984); Ana Carrigan and Bernard Stone, dir., *Roses in December* [film] (1982).

MARY J. HENOLD

Doremus, Sarah Platt Haines (1802–77). Churchwoman. Sarah Doremus was a wealthy woman, the mother of nine children, and a member of the South Reformed Church in New York City. In 1834 David Abeel, missionary to China, encouraged her to organize a society to send single female missionaries to minister to Chinese women, but the major missionary board opposed the idea. In 1861 she organized the *Women's Union Missionary Society (WUMS) of America for Heathen Lands and served as its president until her death. This was the first society to send and support single female missionaries for women. She corresponded with missionaries and provided hospitality when they were on furlough. She also engaged in prison ministry and managed several evangelistic societies. She was a remarkable Protestant laywoman.

NoAW; Patricia R. Hill, *The World Their Household* (1985); R. Pierce Beaver, *American Protestant Women in World Mission*, rev. ed. (1980) [1968]; Helen Barrett Montgomery, *Western Women in Eastern Lands* (1910).

LYNN JAPINGA

Douglass, Sarah Mapps (1806–82). Educator and abolitionist. Born into an affluent black family in Philadelphia, Sarah Douglass attended a school founded by her mother, Grace Bustill Douglass, and James Forten. She served as a teacher and supervisor of the girls' department at the Institute for Colored Youth and taught until her retirement in 1877. A Quaker, she criticized the racism of the Friends. In 1833 she joined an interracial group of women to found the Philadelphia Female Anti-Slavery Society, where she served in many positions and became lifelong friends with the *Grimké sisters. She attended the Female Medical College of Philadelphia and lectured on women's health. After the Civil War, she served as an officer of the American Freedmen's Aid Commission.

ANB; BWA; NBAW; NoAW; Julie Winch, ed., *The Elite of Our People* (2000); Dorothy Sterling, ed., *We Are Your Sisters* (1984).

JANET MOORE LINDMAN

Dozier, Verna J. (1917–2006). Episcopal educator and expert on the ministry of the laity. Verna J. Dozier was born in Washington, DC, where her parents served as government employees. Dozier was an English teacher in the Washington, DC, school system from 1941 to 1975 and directed a prizewinning teacher-training program. An active lay leader, Dozier began a second career as a consultant on Bible study and the ministry of the laity after her retirement. She also served as adjunct faculty in New Testament at Virginia Theological Seminary and at the College of Preachers. She authored numerous works, including *The Authority of the Laity* (1982) and *The Calling of the Laity* (1988). She received honorary doctorates from Virginia Theological Seminary and the University of the South.

Marianne Arbogast, "Stumbling in the Dark," *The Witness* 80 (July/August 1977); Fredrica Harris Thompset, "Verna J. Dozier," Christian Educators of the 20th Century, www.talbot.edu/ce20.

SHERYL A. KUJAWA-HOLBROOK

Drexel, Katherine (1858–1955). Founder of the *Sisters of the Blessed Sacrament. Born in Philadelphia to a wealthy J. P. Morgan banker, Drexel inherited a family fortune of over $20 million and devoted her life in service to Native and African Americans. Despite sometimes fierce opposition to their work, Drexel and the members of her congregation, founded in 1891, established numerous schools on Indian reservations and in black neighborhoods. In 1915 they opened Xavier University in New Orleans, the only Catholic university for African Americans in the U.S. By the time of her death, Drexel had founded 49 convents and built 62 schools. Today the members of her congregation, based in Bensalem, Pennsylvania, serve in inner cities and rural areas in 14 states, and in Haiti and Guatemala. Drexel was canonized a saint in the year 2000.

EACH; NCE; Consoela Marie Duffy, *Katherine Drexel: A Biography* (1965).

EPHREM (RITA) HOLLERMANN, OSB

Dryer, Emeline ("Emma") (1835–1925). Religious educator and relief worker. Orphaned at a young age, Emma Dryer was raised by an aunt in New York. She had several educational positions, including one as dean of women and instructor in grammar and drawing at Illinois State Normal University (1864–70). After a serious bout of typhoid fever, she moved to Chicago and became associated with Dwight L. Moody. Moody encouraged her to begin a "Bible Work," which included a school for training women as Bible teachers and urban missionaries. Although this school eventually developed into the Moody Bible Institute, due to differences in vision regarding Moody's emphasis on training "gap men" (i.e., laymen who were to bridge the religious gap between ministers and laity), Dryer resigned from Moody's church in 1889. Her institute, the Bible Work of Chicago, became a department of the Chicago Bible Society, where she worked until her retirement in 1903.

EE; NoAW; WBC.

PRISCILLA POPE-LEVISON

Duchemin, Theresa Maxis (1810–92). First U.S.-born black Catholic sister educator. Theresa Duchemin's biracial mother and white British father never married, and she was raised in a black, French-speaking Catholic community. She was a highly educated woman caught between two distinct racial and cultural settings, and circumscribed by the anti-Catholic, racist, and sexist society of her times. Her creative, daring, and determined character to minister to the poor met with alternating approval and criticism from ecclesiastical authorities. She left her position as superior general of the Oblates of Baltimore in 1845 to establish with Father Louis Gillet the Sisters, Servants of the *Immaculate Heart of Mary (IHM) of Monroe, Michigan. The local bishop removed her as superior of this order. However, Bishop John Newmann invited her to Philadelphia to staff schools. This was the origin of the Scranton and Immaculata, Pennsylvania, branches of the IHM sisters. Amid great tension, church authorities forbade her to communicate with either congregation. She lived voluntarily with the Grey Nuns of Ottawa in the hope that her absence would unite the communities. After 17 years she returned to the Pennsylvania convent, where she lived until her death.

EACH; NBAW; NCE; ROWUS.

SUSAN MARIE MALONEY, SNJM

Duchesne, Rose Philippine (1769–1852). Roman Catholic missionary and educator. Born into a prosperous family in Grenoble, France, Duchesne joined the *Visitation Sisters in 1788. Swept up in the turmoil of the French Revolution, her convent closed and she returned home, but in 1804 she entered the newly formed Society of the Sacred Heart. In 1818 she was named superior of her congregation's first mission to the U.S. The sisters started a school in St. Charles, Missouri, and within 10 years it had opened a novitiate and established six schools and orphanages. For a brief time in 1841 Duchesne worked among the Native Americans, where she was known as "the woman who prays always." She died in St. Louis and was named a saint in the Roman Catholic Church on July 3, 1988.

ANB; DARB; EACH; NCE; NoAW; ROWUS; Louise Callan, *Philippine Duchesne* (1965).

JUDITH METZ, SC

Duck, Ruth Carolyn (1947–). Hymn text writer and theological educator. Raised as a conservative Christian, Ruth Duck was taught to believe that religion was a private matter between God and the individual believer. The ministry of Martin Luther King Jr., however, caused Duck to embrace social justice advocacy as fundamental to the Christian faith. Her hymns utilize inclusive language and uplift gender equality. Her commitment to eradicating "isms" in ministry is reflected in her hymns and philosophy toward teaching. She seeks to reconcile culture, practice, history, and theology. Duck is an ordained minister in the United Church of Christ and works as a professor of worship at Garrett-Evangelical Theological Seminary in Evanston, Illinois.

Dallas (Dee) A. Brauninger, *Antoinette Brown Women: Finding Voice* (December 2006), www.ucc.org/women/finding.html.

BARBARA A. FEARS

Dudley, Helena Stuart (1858–1932). Settlement worker, labor activist, and pacifist. Born in Nebraska, Helena Stuart Dudley attended the Massachusetts Institute of Technology and Bryn Mawr College to study biology. While at Bryn Mawr, she participated in the College Settlements Association. After college she left her teaching career to work in settlements full-time and eventually became the head of a new settlement house in Boston, Denison House. At Denison House, Dudley became active in the labor movement and was an organizer of the National Women's Trade Union League. She resigned as head resident of Denison House in 1912, concerned that her participation in organized labor would offend the settlement's contributors. She then pursued pacifist causes. She became an Episcopalian during the last 10 years of her life and was a member of the *Society of the Companions of the Holy Cross.

ANB; NoAW; Vida Scudder, *On Journey* (1937).

SHERYL A. KUJAWA-HOLBROOK

Dunbar, Helen Flanders (1902–59). Psychiatrist and leader in psychosomatic medicine. Born in Chicago to a mathematician and a genealogist, Helen Dunbar attended a series of private, largely experimental schools and graduated from Bryn Mawr College in 1923. Included among her four graduate degrees is a bachelor of divinity degree from Union Theological Seminary. Dunbar's interest in integrating religion and science led to the directorship of the Council for the Clinical Training of Theological Students. She held appointments in medicine and psychiatry at Columbia Presbyterian Hospital and the Vanderbilt Clinic in New York City, while teaching at Columbia University's College of Physicians and Surgeons. Her major contribution to the medical and psychiatric fields was her demonstration of the importance of emotional factors in the course of disease. Dunbar established the *Psychosomatic Medicine* journal and was instrumental in the founding of the American Psychosomatic Society.

NoAWMP; Constance M. McGovern, *American National Biography* (2000).

BETH SPAULDING

Duncan, Sara J. Hatcher (1869–?). Missionary society worker. Sarah Hatcher was born in Alabama, the daughter of a slave. Following her 1889 marriage to Robert H. Duncan, she lived for several years in Georgia, but then they returned to her native state. She was member of the African Methodist Episcopal Church. In 1896 southern and midwestern women who did not feel included in the denomination's existing missionary society organized their own Women's Home and Foreign Missionary Society. Duncan became the group's general superintendent in 1897 and its president in 1900. She spoke and wrote about the role of women in the church and started a missionary newspaper, *Missionary Searchlight*, in 1898. In 1906 she published a book entitled *Progressive Missions in the South: An Address with Illustrations and Sketches of Missionary Workers and Ministers and Bishops' Wives.*

BWARC; Jualynne E. Dodson, *Engendering Church: Women, Power, and the A.M.E. Church* (2002); Sara J. Duncan, *Progressive Missions in the South* (1906) [online with Documenting the American South (DocSouth), University of North Carolina at Chapel Hill.]

MARILYN FÄRDIG WHITELEY

Dunne, Sarah Theresa (Mother Mary Amadeus of the Heart of Jesus) (1846–1920). Catholic sister and missionary. Born in Ohio, Sarah Dunne joined the *Ursuline sisters in Toledo in 1862 and, despite being the youngest member of the community, was elected the superior in 1874. At the request of her bishop, Dunne traveled west with five other sisters in 1884 to establish missions and schools for Native Americans in Montana. Childhood friend and African American pioneer "Stagecoach Mary" (Mary Fields) joined her and worked at the convent. Beloved by the Cheyenne, Dunne became known as "Great Holy White Chief Woman." In 1905 Dunne moved to Alaska, founding schools and missions in the Yukon Delta and Valdez, where she gained a reputation as "Theresa of the Arctic."

EACH ("Ursulines"); EAWR; ROWUS; RLA ("Amadeus"); Suzanne H. Schrems, *Uncommon Women, Unmarked Trails* (2002); Robert Miller, *The Story of Stagecoach Mary Fields* (1995).

COLLEEN CARPENTER CULLINAN

Dunstan, Sylvia G. (1955–93). Hymn writer and minister. Sylvia

Dunstan studied theology at Emmanuel College in Toronto. Ordained in the United Church of Canada in 1980 she served as minister in two pastoral charges and as prison chaplain in Ontario. She was also involved in Christos Metropolitan Community Church in Toronto. Dunstan was raised by her grandparents and shaped by their love of singing and church. At age 19 she was introduced to Sister Miriam Therese Winter, who taught her to put Scripture into verse. Dunstan became an internationally recognized hymn writer. Many of her hymns appear in *Voices United*, the United Church hymnbook. Dunstan also published numerous prayers, litanies, and benedictions. Her writing reflects her commitment to reform tradition and encourage mission, justice, inclusion, and compassion.

Lynette Miller, "Sylvia G. Dunstan: A Priest Forever," *Touchstone: Heritage and Theology in a New Age* 15, no. 1 (January 1997); Sylvia Dunstan, *Where the Promise shines* (1995) and *In Search of Hope and Grace* (1991).

TRACY J. TROTHEN

Durocher, Eulalie ("Mother Marie-Rose") (1811–49). Founder of the *Sisters of the Holy Names of Jesus and Mary. Eulalie Durocher was born in Saint-Antoine-sur-Richelieu, Quebec. Educated by the Sisters of the Congregation of Notre Dame, she twice attempted to live the religious life herself, but was unsuccessful due to her poor health. She then lived and worked with her brother, a parish priest. She became a leader in the Legion of Mary and taught religion to the rural French-speaking children for whom formal education was almost nonexistent. At the invitation and under the guidance of Bishop Ignace Bourget, bishop of Montreal, she founded a congregation of teaching sisters in Longeuil, Quebec, in 1843. She embodied practical sense, deep faith, and concern for the poor. She was beatified in 1982.

DCB; M. Eulalia Teresa, *So Short a Day* (1954); Pierre Duchaussois, *Rose of Canada* (1934).

ELAINE GUILLEMIN

Duveneck, Josephine Whitney (1891–1978). Educator and Quaker. Born into privilege in Boston, Massachusetts, Josephine Whitney attended private school. In 1913 she married Frank Duveneck Jr. The couple moved to Palo Alto, California, and bought a ranch called Hidden Villa, which became a haven for displaced people, including European refugees and Japanese Americans. In 1945 the Duvenecks began an interracial summer camp to eradicate racial prejudice. The camp expanded into a community center offering environmental and multicultural education programs. In 1925 Duveneck helped found the Peninsula School to provide a child-centered education. The Duvenecks' lifelong interest in social justice led them to help establish many local organizations, including the Fair Play Committee, Friends Outside, and a chapter of the Sierra Club. Today, Hidden Villa is a nonprofit educational center for children and adults, and includes a hostel, organic farm, and nature trails.

Josephine Whitney Duveneck, *Life on Two Levels* (1978); Duveneck collection, Hoover Institution on War, Revolution, and Peace (Stanford).

JANET MOORE LINDMAN

Dyer, Mary (ca. 1605–60). Quaker martyr. Born and married in England, Mary Barrett Dyer immigrated to Massachusetts Bay in 1635. She was banished from Massachusetts after she sided with *Anne Hutchinson and Roger Williams. After helping build the colony in Newport, Rhode Island, Dyer and her husband returned to England in 1651, where she became a Quaker. Dyer returned to the colonies in 1656. Over the next three years she was imprisoned repeatedly for heresy. She was tried with fellow Quakers William Robinson and Marmaduke Stephenson in 1659; the two men were executed, but she was spared and banished. Upon returning to Boston in 1660 she was imprisoned and hanged. When he learned of her execution Charles II banned the execution of Quakers in Puritan New England.

ANB; DARB; EAWR; NoAW; Ruth Plimpton, *Mary Dyer* (1994); Carla Pestana, *Quakers and Baptists in Colonial Massachusetts* (1991); Jonathan Chu, *Neighbors, Friends, and Madmen* (1985).

SCOTT D. SEAY

Eastman, Annis Bertha Ford (1852–1910). Congregational minister and women's rights activist. Born in Peoria, Illinois, Annis Ford espoused women's rights from a young age. She studied education at Oberlin College, but was a self-taught theologian. She married in 1875. Eastman began preaching in 1889, and in 1891 she was the first woman in New York State ordained as a Congregational minister. Her eloquence and humor made her a popular speaker. In 1893 she spoke at the Congress of Women at the World's Columbian Exposition in Chicago, and defined herself as an "undenominational Christian." After 1900 she began to study contemporary philosophy and shifted toward Unitarianism. She was progressive in her attitudes; her children, Crystal Eastman and Max Eastman, attributed their progressive ideas to their mother.

ANBO; NoAW; Max Eastman, *Enjoyment of Living* (1948); Mary Kavanaugh Oldham, ed., *The Congress of Women* (1894); Sermons in the Crystal Eastman Papers at the Schlesinger Library, Harvard University.

ROBYNNE ROGERS HEALEY

Ebert, Anna (1901–97). Deaconess. Anna Ebert's career spanned much of the 20th century, and reflects its many changes in opportunities for women in general as well as changes within American Lutheranism. Ebert was consecrated a deaconess by the Philadelphia Motherhouse in 1927. She received a BS from Temple University three years later and worked as a nurse at Lankenau (Deaconess) Hospital in Philadelphia. Ebert's leadership in the Lutheran Church and the deaconess movement included serving as directing sister for more than three decades. Following the formation of the Lutheran Church in America (LCA), she served on the board for college education and church vocations. Ebert helped to organize the ecumenical Diakonia, an international federation of deaconess groups, in America. She was the first woman president of the World Federation of Diaconal Associations and Diaconal Communities.

Frederik S. Weiser, *Pioneers of God's Future* (1991); the Deaconess Community, Evangelical Lutheran Church in America, www.elca.org/deaconess.

L. DEANE LAGERQUIST

Eddy, Mary Baker (1821–1910). Metaphysical healer and founder of Christian Science. Mary Baker was born to Congregationalist parents whose contrasting pieties—her father's frighteningly stern Calvinism and her mother's appealing emphasis on a loving God—influenced her to conclude that experiences of sin, suffering, and evil emerged from an erroneous understanding of God. Until her mid-40s, Eddy suffered from physical and emotional illness, widowhood and poverty, inability to care for her son, and a failed second marriage. She tried without success alternative therapies like hydropathy, homeopathy, and mesmerism. In 1866 Eddy experienced healing from a physical injury while reading the Bible. She then embarked on articulating her emerging convictions that God is spirit, mind, truth and that "there is no reality in matter." She formulated a radical revision to Christian theology that included a healing method. Eventually, after she realized she would not find acceptance in established Protestantism, she founded a new church. The first of more than 50 versions of her major text, *Science and Health with Key to the Scriptures*, was published in 1875. After some trial and error with institutional structure, the Church of Christ, Scientist, was established in 1892. The Mother Church building in Boston was completed in 1894, and the *Christian Science Monitor* began publication in 1908. Mary Baker Eddy and the Christian Science healing method generated controversy in her lifetime and subsequently. Eddy herself has drawn both excessive adulation and denigration, but recent scholarship has produced increasingly sophisticated interpretations of her as a theological innovator and female religious leader.

ANB; DARB; EAWR; NoAW; RLA; Gillian Gill, *Mary Baker Eddy* (1998); Stephen Gottschalk, *The Emergence of Christian Science in American Religious Life* (1973); Robert Peel, *Mary Baker Eddy*, 3 vols. (1977, 1971, 1966); Mary Baker Eddy, *Prose Works Other Than Science and Health* (1925).

MARY FARRELL BEDNAROWSKI

Edmiston, Althea Brown (1874–1937). Lecturer and missionary. The child of former slaves who valued education and independence, Althea Brown graduated from Fisk University with a desire to work as a missionary in the Congo region of Africa where some of her ancestors had originated. The Presbyterian Church in the U.S. appointed Brown to their Luebo station in the Congo in 1902. She stayed for more than two decades, and married her coworker, Alonzo Edmiston. She often oversaw more than 100 students, and she authored the first dictionary of the Bushonga or Bukuba language. During visits to the U.S., Edmiston lectured to church groups on the need for missions in the Congo and was known for her eloquence and oratory skills.

NBAW; Julia Kellersberger, *A Life for the Congo* (1947); Hallie Paxson Winsborough, comp., *Glorious Living: Informal Sketches of Seven Women Missionaries of the Presbyterian Church, U.S.* (1937); Papers, Special Collections, Robert E. Woodruff Library, Emory University.

LORETTA LONG HUNNICUTT

Edwards, Sarah Pierpont (1710–58). Mystic and wife of Jonathan Edwards. Sarah Pierpont married her husband in 1727, and they raised 11 children. Widely admired for her beauty and pious dignity, she presided over a home that was a model of evangelical hospitality for more than 30 years. Her diary entries of 1738—during the height of the First Great Awakening—give a glimpse of a mystical piety that rivaled that of celebrated medieval women: sensuous experiences that raise the soul beyond the body to a direct encounter with God. Her husband's *Treatise Concerning Religious Affections* (1746) could be read as a defense of the piety that she displayed. She died in Philadelphia of dysentery, just six months after her husband's death.

ANB; NoAW; George Marsden, *Jonathan Edwards* (2003); Elizabeth D. Dodds, *Marriage to a Difficult Man* (1971); Sereno Dwight, ed., *The Works of Jonathan Edwards* (1830).

SCOTT D. SEAY

Eilberg, Amy (1954–). First female Conservative rabbi. Born to politically active Jewish parents in Philadelphia, Amy Eilberg developed an interest in Judaism during her adolescence. At Brandeis University, Eilberg majored in Jewish studies and learned about a new movement within Judaism: feminism. For the first time, she contemplated the idea of becoming a rabbi. The Reform movement had ordained its first female rabbi in 1972, but the Conservative movement, in which Eilberg felt most comfortable, admitted only men to its rabbinical program. Eilberg was not deterred. She enrolled at the Jewish Theological Seminary and studied alongside the men who were in rabbinical school. Shortly after the Conservative movement voted to allow women to become rabbis, Eilberg was ordained in 1985. She has done chaplaincy work.

EAWR; Pamela Nadell, *Women Who Would Be Rabbis* (1998).

LILA CORWIN BERMAN

Einstein, Hannah Bachman (1862–1929). Volunteer, social activist, and the first woman to hold a position on the board of the United Hebrew Charities. Hannah Bachman grew up in the German Jewish Reform community in New York City and married in 1881. She attended the prominent Temple Emanu-El, and the temple's emphasis on social justice inspired her. In 1897 Einstein became president of the temple's sisterhood organization, a position she held for 25 years. She eventually became the president of the New York Federation of Sisterhoods. After working with the poor as sisterhood president, Einstein began to recognize the limitations of volunteer and philanthropic work and started lobbying the New York legislature for widow's pensions. Einstein later headed the state-appointed committee that drafted the Child Welfare Law of 1915 and served as president of the New York State Association of Child Welfare Boards.

ANBO; JWA; NoAW.

KAREN-MARIE WOODS

Eisenstein, Judith Kaplan (1909–96). Composer, musicologist, teacher. Daughter of Rabbi Mordecai M. Kaplan, the founder of Reconstructionist Judaism, Judith Kaplan is perhaps best known as the first woman to receive a bat mitzvah in the U.S. in 1922. After studying music at the Juilliard School, Kaplan received degrees in music education from the Teacher's Institute of the Jewish Theological Seminary and Columbia University's Teacher's College. She married Ira Eisenstein, an assistant rabbi, in 1934. Her publications include popular songbooks for children, such as *Gateway to Jewish Song* (1937), and widely performed cantatas, such as *What Is Torah* (1943), with lyrics by her husband. Eisenstein received a PhD in 1966 from the School of Sacred Music of the Hebrew Union College–Jewish Institute of Religion.

JWA; Obituary, *New York Times* (15 February 1996); Judith K. Eisenstein, "Have Jews Today a Common Musical Language?" *The Reconstructionist* 16, no. 20 (9 February 1951); Oral History Interview, New York Public Library for the Performing Arts.

EMILY ALICE KATZ

Elaw, Zilpha (ca. 1790–1845). Holiness preacher. Zilpha Elaw was born to free parents near Philadelphia and spent much of her childhood in domestic service. She joined a Methodist Society (African Methodist Episcopal Church) in 1808. Two years later she married Joseph Elaw, and they moved to Burlington, New Jersey, in 1811. While attending her first camp meeting in 1817 Elaw experienced a second blessing of sanctification. Believing that her will was in harmony with God's will, she moved beyond the acceptable roles of exhorter and visitor to that of preacher. Following the death of her husband in 1823 Elaw eventually became an itinerant preacher and conducted missions to several slave states and in England. She maintained a strong sense of God's providential care and approval of her work, despite male opposition.

BWA; NBAW; Zilpha Elaw, "Memoirs," in *Sisters of the Spirit*, ed. William L. Andrews (1986).

BARBARA J. MACHAFFIE

Elizondo, Santos (1867–1941). Elder and church planter. Born in Chihuahua,

Mexico, Santos Elizondo joined the Church of the Nazarene during a visit to Los Angeles in 1905 and established a church in El Paso, Texas, in 1907. She started another church in Juarez, Mexico, and oversaw its work for 35 years; she managed a day school, women's society, orphanage, and medical clinic (where she served as midwife). With few resources, Elizondo creatively overcame Mexican hostility to Protestant church work and focused her energies on helping the underprivileged. Although repeatedly rejected in her role as a female minister by both the Mexican culture and her own coreligionists, she was ordained an elder in 1911. Representatives of the Mexican government and the Roman Catholic Church attended her funeral.

Rebecca Laird, *Ordained Women in the Church of the Nazarene* (1993); Amy Hinshaw, *Messengers of the Cross in Latin America* (1985).

LORETTA LONG HUNNICUTT

Elliott, Barbara Joan (1930–92). Deaconess and educator. Barbara Elliott grew up in southern Ontario. Elliott's working career began with an insurance company that transferred her to Alberta, where the arid prairie air eased her struggle with bronchiectasis. She returned to Ontario to attend the United Church Training School (1956–59). Her subsequent ministry with Calgary's Central United Church, Winnipeg's Harrow United Church, and the United Church of Canada's Saskatchewan Conference was characterized by her commitment to justice and inquisitiveness. These same attributes inspired Elliott's interest in feminist theology, which birthed the Saskatchewan Christian Feminist Network and a feminist professorship at St. Andrew's College (Saskatoon). Elliott's final project was a presentation on disabilities, offered just one week before her struggle with bronchiectasis finally claimed her life.

Charlotte Caron, ed., *Not All Violins* (1997); *The Unbeaten Path* 38 (1993); Association of Professional Church Workers, *The Newsletter: Historical Issue* (1988).

SARAH BRUER

Elster, Shulamith Reich (1939–). Educator. A trailblazer even in her teenage years, Shulamith Reich Elster helped found United Synagogue Youth, the groundbreaking Conservative Jewish youth group. Her father was a rabbi in the movement, and her mother was a Jewish educator in their hometown of Norfolk, Virginia. Elster received a bachelor's degree from New York University, a master's degree from Columbia University Teacher's College, and a doctorate from George Washington University. After moving to the greater Washington, DC, area, Elster climbed the ranks of her children's school, rising from volunteer to part-time counselor to assistant principal and ultimately to headmaster (1982). The Charles E. Smith Jewish Day School came to be considered a model community day school and Elster a model leader; she is often referred to as the dean of Jewish education. She has acted as professor, consultant, and executive director to a diverse group of Jewish educational institutions.

JWA.

DEBORAH SKOLNICK EINHORN

Emery sisters: Mary Abbot Emery Twing (1843–1901); **Margaret Theresa Emery** (1849–1925); **Julia Chester Emery** (1852–1922); **Helen Winthrop Emery** (1862–1924). Episcopalian church workers. The Emery sisters were responsible largely for the development of the woman's auxiliary of the Protestant Episcopal Church. In 1872 Mary was hired to organize a woman's missionary society. She gathered existing societies into the woman's auxiliary and developed a model for its operation. When she left in 1876 to marry the domestic missionary secretary, the Rev. A. T. Twing, Julia replaced her as national secretary. Twing led the campaign to create an order of deaconesses within the Episcopal Church, officially approved by the 1889 General Convention, and then taught missionary classes at the newly organized New York Training School for Deaconesses. In 1876 Margaret joined Julia in the national office as editor of the *Young Christian Soldier* (a missionary magazine for children) and organizer of the "box work" (local parishes provisioning foreign and domestic missionaries). Julia remained on the national staff until 1916, Margaret until 1919. Under their leadership, auxiliary chapters were organized in all local and missionary dioceses of the Episcopal Church. A triennial meeting of churchwomen was established to meet in conjunction with the General Convention. The United Thank Offering was created to raise funds for salaries and retirement benefits for women mission workers and to build schools and hospitals in missionary districts. Julia promoted the work at home and visited missionaries abroad, while Margaret oversaw the national office. Helen remained in Massachusetts to care for their disabled sister and widowed mother; when they died, she moved to New York to keep house for her sisters.

ANB (Julia Emery); Mary S. Donovan, *A Different Call* (1986); Julia Chester Emery, *A Century of Endeavor* (1921); Mary Abbot Emery, *Twice around the World* (1898).

MARY SUDMAN DONOVAN

Ettenberg, Sylvia Cutler (1917–). Jewish educator. Born and raised in Brooklyn, New York, Sylvia Cutler Ettenberg received degrees from the Teachers Institute (TI) of the Jewish Theological Seminary and Brooklyn College. During the 1930s and 1940s she was a key member of the Hebrew Youth Movement in New York and the Hebrew Arts Committee; she was a founder of Massad, an important Hebrew immersion summer camp. In 1947 she helped establish Camp Ramah, the first in the Conservative movement's nationwide network of summer camps. At the Jewish Theological Seminary, Ettenberg served as registrar of the TI, associate dean of the undergraduate college, and dean of educational development. She has been recognized throughout her career for her contributions to Jewish education.

JWA; Sylvia C. Ettenberg and Geraldine Rosenfeld, ed., *The Ramah Experience* (1989); Oral History Interview, Ratner Center, Jewish Theological Seminary.

EMILY ALICE KATZ

Evald, Emmy Carlsson (1857–1946). Lutheran churchwoman. After Emmy Carlsson graduated from college she organized the young people in her father's congregation in Andover, Illinois. In the late 1870s she organized young people's societies in the Lutheran Church. She married Carl Evald in 1883. At the 1892 annual synod meeting held in Lindsborg, Kansas, Evald, *Alma Swensson, and other women received permission to convene the Augustana Synod's Woman's Foreign and Home Missionary Society (WMS), and Evald became its first president, a post she held until 1942. The society raised money for 79 hospitals and schools located in India, China, Palestine, America, and Africa. The society's financial clout gave Evald leverage within the synod, but no formal authority. Evald used her support among Swedish American immigrant women to promote women's rights and women's suffrage. While tensions existed in Swedish congregations between male leadership and female determination, Evald channeled these tensions into creative endeavors.

Jane Telleen, "'Yours in the Master's Service': Emmy Evald and the Woman's

Missionary Society of the Augustana Lutheran Church, 1892–1942," *Swedish Pioneer Historical Quarterly* 30 (July 1979); WMS, *What God Hath Wrought* (1942); Angela Howard Zophy with Frances M. Kavenik, eds., *Handbook of American Women's History* (1990); Archives of the Evangelical Lutheran Church in America.

MARIA ERLING

Evangelical and Ecumenical Women's Caucus (1973–). Christian feminist organization. A group of socially concerned evangelicals, later known as Evangelicals for Social Action (ESA), met in 1973 and drafted the Chicago Declaration. At a second consultation six task forces were formed. Among these was the Evangelical Women's Caucus (EWC). The EWC fought for various causes including inclusive language in biblical translations, support of the Equal Rights Amendment, and the ordination of women. With the 1978 publication of *Virginia Mollenkott's and Letha Scanzoni's book, *Is the Homosexual My Neighbor?* a fissure between conservative and liberal elements in the organization became apparent. At a 1986 meeting, a resolution to support civil rights protection for homosexuals was hotly debated but ultimately passed. Conservative participants in the organization feared that identification with homosexual rights would call into question their credibility within the wider evangelical community and were compelled to leave. In order to reflect the increasing inclusiveness of the organization, its name was changed in 1990 to the Evangelical and Ecumenical Women's Caucus (EEWC). The EEWC publishes a quarterly newsletter, *Christian Feminism Today* (formerly called the *EEWC Update*), which includes articles that support its witness of Christian feminism, gender equality, and social justice; Letha Dawson Scanzoni has been its editor since 1994.

EE; S. Sue Horner, "Trying to Be God in the World: The Story of the Evangelical Women's Caucus and the Crisis over Homosexuality," in *Gender, Ethnicity, and Religion*, ed. Rosemary Radford Ruether (2002).

JUDITH L. GIBBARD

Evans, Jane (1907–2004). Jewish leader and peace activist. Raised in a Reform Jewish home in New York City, Jane Evans was lecturing on art at the Young Men's/Young Women's Hebrew Association (YM/YWHA) in St. Louis in 1928 when one of her students, impressed by her Jewish education and speaking ability, invited her to become the first executive director of the National Federation of Temple Sisterhoods (NFTS), of which the student happened to be the president. During Evans's 48-year tenure NFTS went beyond its focus on Reform religious life, becoming involved in issues of world peace and international relations, feminism, civil rights, and more. She expanded the presence of NFTS to Reform congregations outside North America and led NFTS to be among the founders of the Jewish Braille Institute, of which she became president in 1979. A lifelong religious pacifist, Evans was a founder and leader of the Jewish Peace Fellowship and president of the National Peace Conference. After World War II she chaired the Commission on Displaced Persons of the American Jewish Conference and was a consultant to the American delegation to the United Nations.

Kerry Olitzky et al., eds., *Reform Judaism in America: A Biographical Dictionary and Sourcebook* (1993).

JOAN S. FRIEDMAN

Eynon, Elizabeth Dart (1792–1857). Bible Christian preacher. Born in Marhamchurch, England, Elizabeth Dart was one of a small company of women and men who met with William O'Bryan in 1815 to form what came to be called the Bible Christian Church. The following year she became the group's first itinerant. In 1833 she married John Hicks Eynon, one of her converts, and two months later they set out for Upper Canada (now Ontario) as missionaries. Eynon preached her first Canadian sermon in Cobourg in July 1833. She and her husband served a 200-mile circuit; when John was ill, Elizabeth took on his ministry in addition to maintaining her own. In 1848 they went to England but returned a year later to Cobourg, where Eynon, despite ill health, remained active in the church until her death.

DCB; Elizabeth Gillan Muir, *Petticoats in the Pulpit* (1991).

MARILYN FÄRDIG WHITELEY

Fahrni, Mildred Osterhout (1900–1992). Socialist and peace activist. A child of the Methodist manse and rooted in the social gospel movement of Western Canada, Mildred Osterhout Fahrni forged her own path of passionate crusading for peace and social justice. Living in the company of Mahatma Gandhi in 1931 inspired her to absolute pacifism and defending the rights of the disenfranchised. In 1933 Fahrni helped found the Co-operative Commonwealth Federation. During World War II she taught Japanese students at an internment camp, and in the 1950s she joined the American civil rights movement. In the 1960s Fahrni resisted the Vietnam War, and from the 1970s she fostered Quaker projects in Mexico. She was a leader in the antinuclear movement, and worked for many organizations including the Fellowship of Reconciliation and the Women's International League for Peace and Freedom. Fahrni's home was an informal international hostel to refugees and strangers, to whom she provided hospitality.

Nancy Knickerbocker, *No Plaster Saint* (2001); Special Collections, University of British Columbia.

JANET SILMAN

Fahs, Sophia Lyon (1876–1978). Religious educator and Unitarian minister. Sophia Lyon was born in Hangchow, China, to Presbyterian missionaries. She graduated from the College of Wooster in 1897. In 1902 she married Harvey Fahs and they had five children. She received a master's degree from Columbia University Teachers College (1904) and a divinity degree from Union Theological Seminary (UTS) (1926). She taught religious education at UTS from 1927 to 1944 and directed the church school of Riverside Church from 1933 to 1942. As curriculum editor for the American Unitarian Association (1937–51), Fahs launched the New Beacon Series in Religious Education and revolutionized liberal religious education. Fahs believed children should discover their own religious truths through story, biography, and nature before learning Bible stories. She was, in 1958, one of the first Unitarian women ordained to ministry.

ANB; DARB; UU; Barbara Anna Keely, ed., *Faith of Our Foremothers* (1997); Stephen Kendrick, *A Faith People Make* (1988); Papers, Andover-Harvard Theological Library, Harvard Divinity School.

BARBARA COEYMAN

Fargo, Mary Ann Drake (ca. 1818–92). Episcopal Church clubwoman. Married to Mortimer Fargo, cofounder of Wells Fargo, Mary Ann Fargo led other women of the Church of the Holy Communion in New York City to found the Church Periodical Club in 1888. The club distributed books, magazines, and newspapers to domestic and foreign church missions and engaged women around the country in its work. Fargo ran the club from an office in her home (with the help of staff), and she shipped materials free through her husband's firm. After her death, Fargo's husband provided the club with a small endowment for operations. Fargo also founded and served as trustee on the endowment fund for a parish-sponsored orphanage known as the Babies' Shelter.

Barbara Braun, "Mary Ann Fargo: Woman of Vision," *Timelines: The Newsletter of the Episcopal Women's History Project* 21 (2001); *New York Times*, 12 January 1909, 13 January 1893, 14 February 1882.

JOAN R. GUNDERSEN

Farmer, Sarah Jane (1844–1916). Transcendentalist and Bahá'í. Raised by Transcendentalist parents active in the Underground Railroad, Jane Farmer and four partners opened a hotel in Eliot, Maine, in 1890. The poet John Greenleaf Whittier named it Green Acre. Following an 1892 vision, Farmer initiated the progressive Green Acre Conferences, drawing renowned speakers from around the world. A year after the 1893 World Parliament of Religions in Chicago, she dedicated the site to world peace and religious unity, raising the world's first known peace flag. In 1900, while undergoing a personal crisis, Farmer traveled to Palestine and met Abdu'l-Bahá, the son of Bahá'u'lláh, the founder of the Bahá'í Faith. She became a devotee, integrating Bahá'í teachings into the conferences. Green Acre became a gathering site and school for the Bahá'í community. Abdu'l-Bahá visited it in 1912. Farmer was posthumously named a Disciple of Bahá'u'lláh in 1926.

EAWR; Portsmouth Peace Treaty, portsmouthpeacetreaty.org/BahaCenter treaty.cfm.

AMY BLACK VOORHEES

Farrar, Cynthia (1795–1862). First American single woman missionary sent overseas. Cynthia Farrar was born and raised in New Hampshire and was a teacher there and in Boston. In 1815 she underwent a religious conversion and joined the Congregational Church in Marlborough, Massachusetts. Because of prevailing concepts of female delicacy and dependence, American mission boards were slow to send unmarried women to foreign fields. However, American churchwomen began to pressure these boards to appoint single women as missionaries to work with women and children. Eventually the Congregational Church, through its American Board of Commissioners for Foreign Missions, selected Farrar to organize and direct schools for girls in Bombay, India. She broke through initial resistance from Indian parents and succeeded in enrolling over 400 girls by 1928. Farrar served in India for 34 years and established a large network of primary and secondary schools.

NoAW; R. Pierce Beaver, *American Protestant Women in World Mission*, rev. ed. (1980) [1968].

BETH SPAULDING

Fearing, Maria (1838–1937). Teacher and Presbyterian missionary to the Congo (Zaire). Born to slave parents on a plantation near Gainesville, Alabama, Maria gained her surname only after emancipation. At age 33 she learned to read, then trained and worked as a teacher. In 1894 she applied to go to Africa with the Presbyterian Congo Mission. Turned down due to her age (56), Fearing sold her home, received a small financial pledge from the local Congregationalists, and paid her own expenses for the journey. Based at the Luebo mission station, she created the Pantops Home for Girls to provide academic, domestic, and Christian spiritual training for up to 100 girls, mostly orphans. The home's success prompted the Presbyterians to grant it funding. Fearing ran Pantops until 1915, when she reluctantly retired to Alabama.

BWA; BWARC; Sylvia M. Jacobs, ed., *Black Americans and the Missionary Movement in Africa* (1982).

SANDRA L. BEARDSALL

Fedde, Elizabeth Tonette (1850–1921). Deaconess. Following early domestic employment and influenced by Haugean pietism, Elizabeth Fedde joined the Deaconess Institute in Christiania (Oslo), Norway, where she received religious and nursing education. She served as a nurse in Tromso and other Norwegian cities prior to responding to the plight of her country folk in the U.S. in 1883. Within days of her arrival in Brooklyn Fedde organized a voluntary relief society to minister to sick and poor Norwegians. In the next years she cooperated with the Norwegian Seaman's Mission and various congregations in a Sunday school. She also organized direct aid through a hospital and an ambulance service for all residents, not only Norwegians. The hospital grew from nine to 30 beds and was reincorporated as Norwegian Lutheran Deaconess Home and Hospital, later the Lutheran Medical Center. In the late 1880s she helped establish similar institutions among Norwegian Americans in Minneapolis. She returned to Norway in 1896, married, and settled on a farm.

EAWR; NoAW; RLA; Frederick S. Weiser, comp., *Pioneers of God's Future* (1991); "Elizabeth Fedde's Diary, 1883–88," *Norwegian American Studies and Record* 20 (1959); L. DeAne Lagerquist, *The Lutherans* (1999); Erling Nicolai Rolfsrud, *The Borrowed Sister* (1953).

L. DEANE LAGERQUIST

Feld Carr, Judy (Leve) (1938–). Humanitarian and musicologist. Judy Feld Carr was born in Montreal. She studied at the University of Toronto and received a bachelor's degree in music (1957) and master's degree in music (1968). She became a music specialist with the Toronto Secondary School Board. In 1973 Feld Carr and her husband learned of the difficulties Jews were experiencing in Syria and established contact with them. After her husband's death, Feld Carr continued to raise funds and to develop networks across the Middle East that allowed Jewish families to leave Syria. This was dangerous for both the families and for her. Twenty-eight years of clandestine efforts enabled 3,228 Syrian Jews to reestablish themselves in Israel and in other parts of the world. Feld Carr has been the recipient of many awards. She was appointed, for example, to the Order of Canada in 2000. She continues to volunteer within her community and to advocate for human rights. She is often known simply as "Mrs. Judy." She was an advisor for the 1991 documentary film *In The Shadows: The Tragedy of Syrian Jews* (produced and directed by Cayle Chernin). Her unswerving determination and passion demonstrate the power of one individual to make a difference.

Andrew Chung, *The Toronto Star* (6 June 2002); Perlitta Ettedgui, *Macleans* (18 June 2001); Edmond Lipsitz, *Canadian Jewry at Year 2000 and Beyond* (2000); *Who's Who of Canadian Women*, 7th ed. (1997).

TRUDY FLYNN

Feller, Henriette Odin (1800–1868). French Canadian Protestant evangelist and educator. Henriette Feller arrived in Lower Canada (Quebec) in 1835 under the sponsorship of the Evangelical Mission Society of Lausanne. Born into a privileged family in Switzerland, Feller's spirituality was shaped by the Swiss Genevan Revival, which upheld individual righteousness over doctrinal conformity. Feller was determined to spread Protestantism within Roman Catholic Quebec, and, to this end, she distributed Bibles, conducted Bible studies, founded churches, and opened schools. She was instrumental in the 1840 organization of the French Canadian Missionary Society. A strong and charismatic woman, she often faced hostility because of her Protestantism and her gender. Theologically opposed to denominational alliances, she nevertheless associated with the small Baptist community in Quebec.

DCB; EE; Randall Balmer and Catharine Randall, "'Her Duty to Canada': Henriette Feller and French Protestantism in Quebec," *Church History: Studies in Christianity and Culture* 70, no. 1 (March 2001).

ELEANOR J. STEBNER

Female Hebrew Benevolent Society (FHBS) (1819–1990). First nonsynagogal Jewish charity in the U.S. Founded by *Rebecca Gratz and women of her Philadelphia synagogue to assist Jewish women, the FHBS was a model for similar organizations formed elsewhere, but its fiscal solvency and reliability made it exceptional. The FHBS strove to keep families together but also helped women become financially independent. In 1838 it became the parent organization to the Hebrew Sunday School, the first Jewish Sunday school and the first Jewish religious educational organization run by women. Choosing to remain independent of Philadelphia's United Hebrew Charities when that was formed in 1869 the FHBS received funds in the 20th century from Philadelphia's Federation of Jewish Charities but still continued to operate on its own until it disbanded.

DARB; EAWR; JWA; Dianne Ashton, *Rebecca Gratz: Women and Judaism in Antebellum America* (1997); *When Philadelphia Was the Capital of Jewish America* (1993); Murray Friedman, ed., *Jewish Life in Philadelphia, 1830–1940* (1983).

DIANNE ASHTON

Ferguson, Abbie Park (1837–1919). Educator and missionary. Born into a Congregationalist family, Abbie Ferguson graduated from Mount Holyoke Seminary in 1856. She taught school before she responded to an appeal to help establish a work-study school for girls in Cape Colony, South Africa. She and *Anna Elvira Bliss founded the Huguenot Girls High School in 1874; it expanded to include branch campuses and a college. As president of the college, Ferguson raised funds and lobbied for a governmental charter. Ferguson also helped organize the Vrouwen Zending Bond in 1889.

NoAW; Papers, Mount Holyoke College Archives and Special Collections.

SCOTT D. SEAY

Ferguson, Catherine ("Katy") (ca. 1779–1854). Educator and reformer. Born into slavery, little else is known about the early life of Catherine Ferguson. She joined the Murray Street Church (Presbyterian) in New York City by the age of 16. She purchased her freedom (ca. 1792), married, and had two children, but her children and husband soon died. By 1797 she became a client of a new almshouse under the leadership of Isabella Graham and soon was a leader in Graham's diversified social reform movement. By 1803 she was teaching in a popular Sunday school and advocating for orphaned children. The Murray Street School, the first of its kind in New York City, continued under her leadership for almost 50 years. The Katy Ferguson Home for unwed mothers and their children continues her pioneering work.

BWA; NBAW; Allen Hartvik, "Catherine Ferguson: Black Founder of a Sunday School," *Negro History Bulletin* (January–September 1996).

SCOTT D. SEAY

Fillmore, Mary ("Myrtle") Page (1845–1931). Cofounder of the Unity School of Christianity. In 1886, as a young mother suffering from tuberculosis, Myrtle Fillmore attended lectures in Kansas City, Missouri, by a student of *Emma Curtis Hopkins; she hoped for healing. Her health improved, and she soon brought healing to others. At first skeptical, her husband Charles Fillmore later joined her in Chicago to study under Hopkins, who ordained her in 1891. Over the next decade, the couple founded the Unity School of Christianity, which became the largest of the New Thought groups. Fillmore's voluminous letters and writings emphasize thought-based approaches to overcoming illness and poverty. Based at Unity Farm near Kansas City, Unity flourishes as a Christian presence in the New Age movement.

ANB; DARB; EAWR; NoAW; RLA; Thomas E. Witherspoon, *Myrtle Fillmore,* 3rd ed. (2000) [1977]; Myrtle Page Fillmore, *How I Used Truth* (1916).

GRAEME SHARROCK

Finley, Martha (1828–1909). Author. Born in Chillicothe, Ohio, to James Brown Finley and Maria Theresa Brown Finley, Martha Finley was educated privately and spent her youth in Ohio and Indiana. She taught school in New York and Philadelphia before moving in 1876 to Elkton, Maryland, where she made her home for the remainder of her life. In 1867 Finley published the first of 28 books about the life and kin of the fictional Elsie Dinsmore, a wealthy southerner with a sensitive conscience and pious inclinations, much given to tears and Bible quotations. Finley's public manifested an insatiable appetite for stories that romanticized the South and promoted Sabbath observance, temperance, traditional gender roles, and obedience to parents. Finley produced a related seven-volume series about a heroine named Mildred Keith, a more realistic figure than her distant relative, the sentimental Elsie. The Presbyterian Board of Publications printed more than 50 of Finley's shorter works, and her total output exceeded 100 works. The Elsie Dinsmore series sold tens of millions of copies in North America and Britain, and sales of up-to-date editions remain brisk in the Christian market.

ANB; NoAW: Candy Gunther Brown, *Word in the World: Evangelical Writing, Publishing, and Reading in America* (2004); Taryn Benbow-Pfalzgraf, ed., *American Women Writers,* vol. 2 (2000); David Reynolds, *Faith in Fiction* (1981); Janet Elder Brown, *The Saga of Elsie Dinsmore: A Study in Nineteenth-Century Sensibility* (1945).

EDITH BLUMHOFER

Finson, Shelley Davis (1936–2008). Feminist theologian and educator. Born in England, Shelley Finson's childhood was disrupted by World War II. In 1956 Finson moved to Canada, where the bowling alley in Toronto's Queen Street United Church lured her into church involvement and her eventual call to ministry. She began working with troubled youth and later pursued a master's degree in social work. The feminist movement led Finson to a "seeing with new eyes" form of spiritual awakening. She became the coordinator of the Movement for Christian Feminism. Finson's career concluded as an educator at the Centre for Christian Studies (Toronto) and the Atlantic School of Theology (Halifax). She completed a DMin at Boston University in 1985. At a time when many feminists left the church, Finson recognized its transformative potential and worked for change from within.

Shelley Davis Finson, "Seeing with New Eyes: Moment of Spiritual Awakening," *Consciousness Rising* (1999), "Travelling to a Distant Shore," *No Name Newsletter* (April 1993).

SARAH BRUER

Fisher, Mary (ca. 1623–1698). Quaker preacher and missionary. Mary Fisher was repeatedly imprisoned and flogged in England for her activities as a Quaker between 1652 and 1655. She then traveled as a missionary to Barbados, New England, the Mediterranean, and the Near East. She and *Ann Austin were the first Quakers to arrive in—and be deported from—Boston in 1656. She returned to England in 1662, married, and raised three children. After her husband's death she married again and moved in 1682 to Charleston, South Carolina, where she died.

ANB; NoAW; Phyllis Mack, *Visionary Women* (1992).

SCOTT D. SEAY

Fisher, Welthy Honsinger (1879–1980). Educator, missionary, and author. Welthy Fisher was born in Rome, New York, to a family of blacksmiths. She graduated from Syracuse University and later worked as an educator in various New York schools, including Rosebud College and Englewood High School. While living in New York City she attended a religious meeting led by missionary Robert Speers. During the meeting Fisher was convinced that she should spend her life in service as a Christian missionary. In 1906 Fisher traveled to China to teach at a mission school in Nanchang, and worked diligently to learn the Mandarin language so that she could better influence her pupils. She later worked in India and spent time with Mohandas Gandhi. Fisher sought to eradicate global poverty and to empower women through literacy. During her lifetime she received honorary doctorates from Syracuse University and Delhi University. She died in Southbury, Connecticut.

Sally Swenson, *Welthy Honsinger Fisher* (1988); Nolan B. Harmon, ed., *The Encyclopedia of World Methodism* (1974); Welthy Honsinger Fisher, *To Light a Candle* (1963).

CHRISTOPHER J. ANDERSON

Fiske, Fidelia (1816–64). Missionary. Fidelia Fiske was the first of many graduates of Mount Holyoke Female Seminary to leave the school for a missionary career. In 1843 Fiske traveled to Orumiyeh, Persia, where she began a boarding school for girls modeled on her alma mater. Fiske emphasized self-sufficiency and self-sacrifice in her students, and was also instrumental in the conversion of many of the girls (as well as their parents). After 15 years in Persia, and with failing health, Fiske returned to the U.S. She spent the last six years of her life teaching at Mount Holyoke and writing a book about the teaching and influence of *Mary Lyon, the beloved founder of the school.

NoAW; Daniel Taggart Fiske, *Faith Working by Love: As Exemplified in the Life of Fidelia Fiske*, digitized (2006) [1868]; Dana Lee Robert, *American Women in Mission: A Social History of Their Thought and Practice* (1997).

LYDIA HUFFMAN HOYLE

Fitkin, Susan Norris (1870–1951). Evangelist and advocate of world missions. Susan Norris was born to Quaker parents in Quebec. Influenced by the evangelical wing of the Society of Friends, she became an evangelist and pastor while still in her early 20s. She married Abram Fitkin in 1896, and they founded a congregation that they affiliated with the Association of Pentecostal Churches in America. She later became an ordained elder in the Pentecostal Church of the Nazarene. Fitkin helped organize the Nazarene World Mission Society, became in 1915 its first president, and continued to serve in that capacity for more than 30 years. She was an important leader in the early Nazarene tradition.

Phyllis H. Perkins, *Women in Nazarene Missions* (1994); Rebecca Laird, *Ordained Women in the Church of the Nazarene* (1993).

ELEANOR J. STEBNER

Fleming, Louise ("Lulu") Cecilia (1862–99). Missionary. Born into slavery in Florida, Louise Fleming graduated valedictorian of her class from Shaw University in 1885. The first African American woman commissioned by the Woman's Baptist Foreign Missionary

Society of the West (1886), she taught at Palabala, Congo, from 1887 to 1891, when ill health forced her to accept a furlough. Determined to return to Africa, she studied at the Leonard Medical School of Shaw University and graduated from the Woman's Medical College of Philadelphia in 1895. The Woman's Baptist Foreign Missionary Society (East) appointed her as a medical missionary to Irebu, Upper Congo, in 1895. Infected with African sleeping sickness, she returned to the U.S., where she died.

BWA; BWARC; Courtenay Bachan Cannady, "Send Forth the Trumpet! God's Truth Is Marching On," *American Baptist Quarterly* 12 (1993); L. C. Fleming, "A Day at Palabala," *Baptist Missionary Magazine* 68 (1888).

KENDAL P. MOBLEY

Flower(s), Amanda Cameron (1863–1940). Medium, Spiritualist pastor, founder of the Independent Spiritualist Association. Canadian by birth and attracted to Spiritualism from a young age, Amanda Flower settled in Michigan as a young adult. She bought a church building in Grand Rapids and opened the First Church of Truth, where she served as pastor from 1904 to 1939. She opened Spiritualist churches in the Midwest affiliated with the National Spiritualist Association of Churches, but in the 1920s she began to chafe against their regulations regarding ministers and teachings. In 1924 Flower founded the Independent Spiritualist Association, established their newsletter, and edited it until 1935. In 1931 she was elected president of the association for life. (Editor's note: Flower's name is sometimes spelled "Flowers" and appears in both forms in materials of the Independent Spiritualist Association.)

EAWR; RLA; J. Stillson Judah, *The History and Philosophy of the Metaphysical Movements in America* (1967).

MARY FARRELL BEDNAROWSKI

Fontbonne, Delphine (Marie-Antoinette) (1813–56). First superior and founder of the Congregation of the Sisters of St. Joseph of Toronto. Marie-Antoinette Fontbonne was born in Bas-en-Basset, France, and entered the *Sisters of St. Joseph in Lyons in 1832, taking the name Sister Delphine. In 1836 her aunt, Mother St. John, sent Sister Delphine, her sister Antoinette, and four other members of the community to the U.S., accompanied by Sister Delphine's brother, Father Jacques Fontbonne. After studying English for a short time, Sister Delphine became superior of a log cabin convent in Carondelet (St. Louis). In 1851, at the request of Bishop Charbonnel of Toronto, she and two other sisters opened an orphanage there. By the time Sister Delphine died of typhus while nursing the sick in 1856 she had established a novitiate, an orphanage, and the House of Providence for the elderly.

DCB; M. B. Young, *The Dawn of a New Day* (1983).

ELAINE GUILLEMIN

Foote, Julia A. J. (1823–1900). Ordained elder and evangelist in the African Methodist Episcopal Zion (AMEZ) Church. Born in Schenectady, New York, to former slaves, Julia was converted at 15 years of age. Several years later, she married George Foote, moved to Boston, and joined an AMEZ church, where she began to testify about her experiences of conversion and sanctification. Her husband and pastor disapproved of her teaching on sanctification, but she persisted. She received a call from God to preach, which she answered affirmatively, despite opposition. For over 50 years she traveled as an evangelist, preaching in cities and towns in the northern U.S. and as far west as Ohio. She was the first woman to be ordained a deacon (1894) and the second to be ordained an elder (1900) in the AMEZ church.

BWA; EAWR; EE; NBAW; NoAW; William L. Andrews, ed., *Sisters of the Spirit* (1986); Julia Foote, *A Brand Plucked from the Fire* (1879).

PRISCILLA POPE-LEVISON

Forbes, Lilian Stevenson (1869–1945). Southern Baptist pioneer in elementary Sunday school work. Lillian Forbes worked several years as a pastor's assistant and as a church secretary in Mississippi, Kentucky, and Alabama, before serving five years as the state elementary Sunday school secretary in Alabama. The Southern Baptist Convention hired her to serve as the secretary of the elementary department of the Sunday school board, a position she held for 17 years. She started the *Elementary Messenger* for children's workers. A popular teacher, Forbes traveled often to speak at Sunday school training sessions. She authored two books, *The Home Department of the Sunday School* (1916) and *Program Material for Beginner and Primary Workers* (1922), three church manuals, and numerous magazine articles.

EAWR; Norman W. Cox, ed., *Encyclopedia of Southern Baptists*, 4 vols. (1958–1982); Allene Bryan, "Lilian Stevenson Forbes," in *Baptist Leaders in Religious Education*, ed. J.M. Price (1943).

KEITH DURSO

Ford, Ita (1940–80). Catholic religious and missionary. A *Maryknoll sister, Ita Ford served the poor in areas torn by violence and corruption, first in Chile and then in El Salvador. Ford continued her work in El Salvador despite escalating violence and the military's open hostility toward church workers. On 2 December 1980 Ford was traveling in the company of *Dorothy Kazel, *Maura Clarke, and *Jean Donovan when all four were arrested, assaulted, and assassinated by El Salvadoran national guardsmen at the command of officials in the El Salvadoran army.

Ita Ford and Jeanne Evans, *Here I Am, Lord* (2005); Judith Noone, *The Same Fate as the Poor* (1995).

MARY J. HENOLD

Foster, Abigail ("Abby") Kelley (ca. 1810–87). Abolitionist and activist. A Massachusetts Quaker, Abby Kelley attended and taught at Friends schools. Inspired by William Lloyd Garrison, she served as secretary of the Lynn Female Antislavery Society and helped found the New England Non-Resistant Society. She spoke on the abolitionist circuit and stood up to threatening crowds and misogynous clerics. She played a part in the 1840 American Anti-Slavery Society schism over several issues, including the role of women. She left the Quakers for equivocating on slavery and became interested in spiritualism. Married to fellow abolitionist Stephen Foster in 1848, she continued to agitate for abolitionism and women's rights after the birth of her only daughter. A tireless crusader, she remained active in reform politics until her death.

ANB; NoAW; Dorothy Sterling, *Ahead of Her Time: Abby Kelley and the Politics of Antislavery* (1991); Elizabeth Cady Stanton et al., *History of Woman Suffrage* (1881).

JANET MOORE LINDMAN

Foster, Mary Elizabeth Mikahala Robinson (1844–1930). Founder of Hawaiian Theosophical society and patron of Buddhism. Mary Foster's mother was Maui royalty and her father was James Robinson, an influential English shipbuilder. After a Christian missionary upbringing, Foster began to resist Christian dominance in Hawaii. She was a member of the underground organization, Ho'Inaba Ba'ayao, a group that sought to combine Hawaiian and Christian spiritual teachings. Foster founded the Aloha Branch of the Theosophical Society with Auguste Marques in 1894. She became a supporter of Anagarika Dharmapala; he called her the "Queen of the Empire of Righteousness" for her support of Buddhist teachings. She supported Buddhist projects in Sri Lanka, India, and Hawaii, and donated land for the first Jodo Shinshu temple (1899), Hongwanji High School (1907), and Honpa Hongwanji Betsuin (1918).

Patricia Lee Masters and Karma Lekshe Tsomo, "Mary Foster: The First Hawaiian Buddhist," in *Innovative Buddhist Women*, ed. Karma Tsomo (2000).

BARBARA E. REED

Fox, Selena (1949–). Wiccan high priestess and founder of the Church of Circle Wicca. As a child Selena Fox had out-of-body experiences and psychic visions, and as a teenager she became interested in parapsychology. She holds a BS in psychology and an MS in counseling. She founded the Church of Circle Wicca (now known as Circle Sanctuary or just Circle) in 1974 near Madison, Wisconsin. Her church was one of the first Wiccan churches to receive official recognition by the federal and state governments. Fox founded the Circle Network (1978) to serve practitioners of nature religions. In the 1980s at Mount Horeb, Wisconsin, she established the School for Priestesses to educate adherents of goddess worship. Fox has been active in religious liberty issues and in protecting Native American sacred burial grounds.

EAWR; RLA; Rosemary Ellen Guiley, *The Encyclopedia of Witches and Witchcraft* (1989).

KEITH DURSO

Fox Sisters, Anne Leah (ca. 1814–90), **Margaret** (ca. 1835–93), **Catherine ("Kate")** (ca. 1836–92). Spiritualist mediums. In the spring of 1848 Kate and Margaret Fox, daughters of nominal Methodist parents living in an old haunted house in Hydesville, New York, reported strange rappings in their bedroom, and locals tried to extricate messages from spirits of the departed through the girls. In 1849 the sisters began public, paid demonstrations that eventually took them to England and Europe. Although the girls vacillated in their belief in spirits, others welcomed such belief. Some supporters of women's rights and other reforms were Spiritualists, and the Civil War, with its thousands of young dead, was a boon to the movement. Kate was courted by the rich and famous to conduct séances, but was unable to control her drinking; in 1888 she lost care of her children. Leah was an adept medium, but accepted no money. Margaret gave up spiritualist practices after converting to Roman Catholicism in 1858 and explained in 1888 that the rappings were the product of toe cracking; her recantation seemed as fragile as the claims it annulled. Margaret's remaining years were shrouded in controversy, poverty, and alcoholism.

ANB; EAWR; NoAW; RLA; Barbara Weisberg, *Talking to the Dead* (2004); Ann Braude, *Radical Spirits*, 2nd ed. (2001) [1989].

GRAEME SHARROCK

Frame, Alice Seymour Browne (1879–1941). Missionary educator and evangelist. Born in Turkey to Congregational missionaries, Alice Seymour Browne received her BA from Mount Holyoke College and bachelor of divinity degree from Hartford Theological Seminary (1903). She was secretary of the American Board of Commissioners for Foreign Missions (ABCFM) women's board before arriving in China in 1905, where she initially taught at the Tong Xian Girls' School and North China Union College and served as a village evangelist. In 1913 she married Murray Frame and relocated to Peking, where she taught at North China Union

Women's College (NCUWC) and continued village evangelism. Despite sudden widowhood and single motherhood, Frame was dean of NCUWC from 1918 to 1931, during and after the challenging affiliation with Yenching University. Frame was a rural evangelist for the last decade of her life, focusing on religious education, and also served on national missionary committees and boards.

NoAW; Dwight Edwards, *Yenching University* (1959); Harold S. Matthews, *Seventy-Five Years of the North China Mission* (1942); Papers, Archives and Special Collections, Mount Holyoke College; Papers, Special Collections and University Archives, University of Oregon.

JANE HARRIS

Franciscan Sisters (13th century). Congregations of Roman Catholic religious. Italian Francis of Assisi (1181–1226) founded several religious orders of women and men. Most Franciscan sisters in North America follow the Third Order Regular Rule of St. Francis; they comprise the largest group of religious women under one rule. Members profess simple vows of poverty, chastity, and obedience. Franciscan sisters began to immigrate to the U.S. in the mid-19th century to serve Roman Catholic immigrant populations, settling in places like Wisconsin, Indiana, Pennsylvania, New York, Illinois, Minnesota, and Iowa. New groups continued to be formed, either from Europe or indigenously, well into the 20th century. Each congregation is governed by constitutions designed according to its specialized mission and particular ministries. The Sisters of St. Francis of Philadelphia, for example, exemplify service to the poor in a variety of ministries, as do the Franciscan Missionaries of Mary in the U.S. and across the globe. Many other Franciscan congregations have focused on education and health care; in the early days, many cared for orphans. The Franciscan Federation represents many of these congregations. Founded in the 1960s the federation promotes communication, collaboration, and education among its members. As of 1994 there were 77 official communities of these sisters in the U.S.

EACH; NCE; ROWUS; Raffaele Pazzelli, *The Franciscan Sisters* (1996); Elise Saggau, *The Franciscan Federation* (1995); G. C. Stewart Jr., *Marvels of Charity: History of American Sisters and Nuns* (1994); Pierre Peano, *Bearing Christ to the People, the Franciscan Sisters* (1989).

ELLEN WHELAN, OSF

Frank Litman, Rachel ("Ray") (1861–1948). Jewish religious leader. In 1890, when Ray Frank preached on the Jewish New Year, she launched her remarkable career as the "Girl Rabbi of the Golden West." Frank, a teacher, religious school principal, and journalist, spent the next decade preaching to America's Jews in diverse settings. Her prayer opened the Jewish Woman's Congress of the 1893 Columbian World's Exposition. Even as she claimed she had no intention of becoming a rabbi, the popular attention she received in the press, which erroneously called her the first woman rabbi, raised debate about Jewish women's ordination. Frank's marriage to Professor Simon Litman in 1901 ended her public career, but she remained active in Jewish life as a faculty wife.

ANB; JWA; Pamela S. Nadell, *Women Who Would Be Rabbis* (1998); Simon Litman, *Ray Frank Litman* (1957); *Papers of the Jewish Women's Congress* (1894); Jewish Women's Archive.

PAMELA S. NADELL

Franklin, Ursula Martius (1921–). Feminist, educator, Quaker, and physicist. Ursula Franklin is University Professor Emerita at the University of Toronto, the recipient of the 2001 Pearson Medal of Peace for her work in human rights, and a companion of the Order of Canada. She is one of Canada's foremost advocates and practitioners of pacifism. She is the author of *Real World Technology* (1990) and *The Ursula Franklin Reader: Pacifism as a Map* (2006). Born Ursula Martius in Germany to a Jewish mother, Martius was imprisoned in a Nazi work camp during World War II. In 1948 she received her PhD in experimental physics from the Technical University of Berlin. She moved to Canada in 1949 and worked for 15 years for the Ontario Research Foundation. Her work on strontium 90, a radioactive isotope fallout from nuclear weapons testing, was instrumental in the cessation of atmospheric weapons testing.

Canadian Women in Science, www.collectionscanada.ca/women/002026-404-e.html.

LOUISE GRAVES

Freehof, Lillian Simon (1906–98). Author. Lillian Simon, secretary of the K. A. M. Temple in Chicago, married Rabbi Solomon B. Freehof in 1934. Freehof's husband was the rabbi of Rodef Shalom (Pittsburgh) from 1934 to 1966. Lillian Freehof wrote children's books, drawing upon the *aggadah* (homiletical biblical interpretation), but she also wrote *The Right Way* (1957), a religious school ethics textbook. A skilled crocheter, she also wrote books on crafts for adults. She led the Rodef Shalom sisterhood in creating programs for the blind in the 1930s, including services with Braille prayer books, and wrote short plays about Jewish holidays for performance by synagogue members. Her other books include *The Bible Legend Book* (1948), *Candle Light Stories* (1951), *Stories of King David* (1952), *Second Bible Legend Book* (1952), *The Captive Rabbi: The Story of R. Meir of Rothenburg* (1965), and *Embroideries and Fabrics for Synagogue and Home* (1966).

Jo Marks Rifkin, "Lillian Freehof, Author and Rebbetzin, Dies," *Pittsburgh Jewish Chronicle*, 1 December 2004; Solomon B. Freehof Papers, American Jewish Archives, Hebrew Union College.

JOAN S. FRIEDMAN

Freiberg, Stella Heinsheimer (1862–1962). Patron of the arts and Reform Judaism. Daughter of a prosperous Cincinnati German Jewish family with established ties to Reform Judaism, Stella Heinsheimer received a music teacher's education. She married J. Walter Freiberg, a Cincinnati businessman and president of the Union of American Hebrew Congregations (UAHC). Freiberg established the National Federation of Temple Sisterhoods (NFTS) and served as its national vice president (1913–23) and president (1923–29). She secured funds for a dormitory and donated a gymnasium (1923) for Hebrew Union College and sat on the board of directors of the *National Council of Jewish Women and Jewish Social Agencies in Cincinnati. She was one of ten women to found the Cincinnati Symphony Orchestra in 1894, and also directed the Cincinnati Art Museum in the 1930s. An independent businesswoman into her 80s, Freiberg proved that Jewish women could achieve civic and religious excellence in the U.S.

JWA; Karla Goldman, "Reform Judaism," in *Encyclopedia of Women and Religion in North America*, ed. Rosemary Skinner Keller et al. (2006).

MICHAEL A. SINGER

Freiman, Lillian Bilsky (1885–1940). Community leader. Born in Mattawa, Ontario, Lillian Freiman was active in a wide variety of Jewish and nonsectarian organizations. As president of the Canadian *Hadassah, she helped to organize chapters in all Canadian provinces. An active Zionist, her fund-raising campaign to alleviate poverty in Palestine established a new hallmark for fund-raising within the

Canadian Jewish community. She was active in promoting the education and well-being of young women and worked for a variety of charitable organizations. In 1920 she helped organize the Jewish War Veterans Committee and then lobbied to bring Jewish war orphans to Canada. She traveled to Europe and helped to send more than 150 orphans to Canada. Numerous honors were bestowed upon her, including a lifetime membership in the Canadian Legion for her work on behalf of war veterans. In 1934 she was made a member of the Order of the British Empire, in recognition of her leadership in Jewish charitable organizations.

Gerald Tulchinsky, *Taking Root: Origins of the Canadian Jewish Community* (1992); Simon Belkin, *Through Narrow Gates* (1966).

TRUDY FLYNN

Frost, Yvonne Wilson (1931–). Wiccan, teacher, and author. Born in Los Angeles to a conservative Baptist family originally from Kentucky, Yvonne Wilson rejected her religious upbringing early and explored alternative spiritual paths. After divorce ended a 10-year marriage in 1960, she earned an AA degree from Fullerton Junior College and in 1970 married Gavin Frost, a British aerospace scientist interested in the occult. With the goal of reconstructing the practice of witchcraft, they cofounded the Church and School of Wicca. The church was recognized legally as a religious association in 1972, and the school has offered correspondence courses to thousands of students. Frost has coauthored multiple books with her husband, such as *The Witch's Bible* (1972), controversial because of references to the sexual initiation of children, and reissued with changes as *The Good Witch's Bible* (1976). Unlike most practitioners of Wicca, Frost considers herself a monotheist, not a pagan. She works with her husband to counter negative popular images of witchcraft and on behalf of civil rights for witches.

EAWR; RLA; Margot Adler, *Drawing Down the Moon* (2006).

MARY FARRELL BEDNAROWSKI

Fujinkai of Buddhist Churches of America (BCA) (1914–). Women's organization of Japanese American Buddhist temples. Fujinkai is the women's organization of the BCA, and has often been the backbone of Japanese Buddhist communities in the U.S. It serves religious and social purposes for the Japanese American community. The fujinkai are often responsible for the primary fund raising of Japanese American temples or Buddhist churches. The largest Japanese American Buddhist organization, the BCA, continues to rely on fujinkai, which increasingly consists of older women.

Richard Hughes Seager, *Buddhism in America* (1999).

BARBARA E. REED

Fuller Ossoli, Margaret (1810–50). Intellectual, journalist, and Transcendentalist. Raised by a Unitarian mother, Margaret Fuller became a charter member of the Transcendentalist Club in 1837. In 1839 she published translations of Goethe and became editor of the Transcendentalist publication, the *Dial*. She hosted popular conversations (discussion groups) in the 1840s, ending them in a trancelike state inveighing social injustices and articulating a loosely formed mystical utopianism. In 1844 Horace Greeley invited her to become a literary critic at his *New York Daily Tribune*. In 1845 she wrote her best-known work, *Woman in the Nineteenth Century*. In 1846 she left for Europe to work as a foreign correspondent. She wrote a manuscript in Rome during its revolution and French occupation, volunteered as a hospital director, had a son Angelo, and probably married Marchese Giovanni Angelo d'Ossoli. In 1850 the Ossolis sailed for New York, but drowned in a storm near Fire Island. Scholarship on Fuller has become increasingly interdisciplinary, reflecting her intense depth of intellect and broad-ranging abilities.

ANB; DARB; DUUB; EAWR; NoAW; UU; *The Letters of Margaret Fuller*, ed. Robert Hudspeth, 6 vols. (1983–94); Joan von Mehren, *Minerva and the Muse* (1994); Charles Capper, *Margaret Fuller*, 2 vols. (1992, 2007).

AMY BLACK VOORHEES

Fulton, Mary Hannah (1854–1927). Medical missionary. Mary Fulton was born in Ohio into a prominent Presbyterian family. She received a BS (1874) and an MS (1877) from Hillsdale College (Michigan) and an MD (1884) from the Woman's Medical College of Pennsylvania. The Presbyterian Board of Foreign Missions commissioned her to join her brother and sister-in-law, Albert and Florence (Wishard) Fulton, as a medical missionary in southern China. Based in Guangzhou for over 30 years, Fulton provided direct care, taught pediatrics at the missionary hospital, and served as its director from 1899 to 1915. In 1902 she organized the David Gregg Hospital for Women and Children and Hackett Medical College to train Cantonese-speaking women in medical science. Failing health forced her to relocate to Shanghai in 1915, where she translated medical texts and helped establish two churches devoted to ecumenical mission work. She retired to Pasadena, California, in 1918.

NoAW; Mary Hannah Fulton, *Inasmuch: Extracts from Letters, Journals, Papers, Etc.* (1915).

SCOTT D. SEAY

Gable, Mariella (1898–1985). Professor, poet, and literary critic. Originally from Wisconsin, Mary Margaret Gable received the name Mariella at Saint Benedict's Convent (St. Joseph, Minnesota) in 1916. After earning a PhD from Cornell University (1934), she chaired the English Department of the College of St. Benedict (1934–58). Gable was a pioneer in shaping mid-20th-century standards of Catholic fiction in the U.S., Great Britain, and Ireland through her edited anthologies of short stories, *Great Modern Catholic Short Stories* (1942), *Our Father's House* (1945), *Many-Colored Fleece* (1950), and her many essays. Gable insisted that literature about moral and religious values must be good art and not sentimental propaganda. She was among the first to recognize the greatness of J. F. Powers and *Flannery O'Connor.

EACH; *The Literature of Spiritual Values*, intro. Nancy J. Hynes (1996); Mariella Gable, *This Is Catholic Fiction* (1948), *Blind Man's Stick* (1938).

NANCY J. HYNES, OSB

Gage, Matilda Joslyn (1826–98). Women's rights advocate. Matilda Joslyn's family home in Cicero, New York, was a gathering place for reformers and intellectuals. In 1845 she married Henry Gage and settled in Fayetteville, New York. Family burdens and a heart condition did not prevent Gage from entering the public sphere of women's rights. An original member and officer of the National Woman Suffrage Association (NWSA) and the New York association, Gage was among the most radical leaders of the movement. She was concerned with the broad oppression of women by religious and civil institutions. She claimed that a matriarchate once existed but was overthrown by men who used Christianity to maintain their power, a position articulated in her 1893 book, *Woman, Church and State.* Frustrated by the merger of the NWSA with the more conservative American Woman Suffrage Association (AWSA), Gage founded the Woman's National

Liberal Union (WNLU) in 1890. Gage documented the unacknowledged achievements of women in *Woman as Inventor* (1870) and collaborated on *History of Woman Suffrage* (1881). She was a member of the Fayetteville Baptist Church but developed an interest in theosophy and spiritualism later in life.

ANB; EAWR; NoAW; Leila R. Brammer, *Excluded from Suffrage History* (2000); Sally Roesch Wagner, *Matilda Joslyn Gage* (1998).

BARBARA J. MACHAFFIE

Gallagher, Carol (1955–). Episcopal church bishop. Carol Gallagher was consecrated in 2002 in the Diocese of Southern Virginia, becoming the first Native American woman bishop in the Episcopal Church in the U.S.A. (ECUSA) and in the worldwide Anglican Communion. She has devoted much of her life and ministry to women and Native Americans through writing, preaching, and retreat leadership. She resigned her diocesan position in 2005, citing personal and professional concerns. In that same year Gallagher received a PhD in urban affairs from the University of Delaware. Her dissertation addressed leadership issues in the Episcopal Church relative to Native Americans. In September 2005 she became an assistant bishop in the Diocese of Newark.

Carol J. Gallagher, "Relating Circles: The Future of Native Leadership in the Episcopal Church" (PhD diss., University of Delaware, 2005); Gallagher, "A Native American Response," in *Ethics and World Religions*, ed. Regina Wentzel Wolfe and Christine E. Gudorf (1999).

ANNIE RUSSELL

Gambold, Anna Rosina Kliest (1762–1821). Missionary, educator, and scientist. Anna Rosina Kliest was born in the Moravian village of Bethlehem, Pennsylvania, in 1762 and was educated in the single sisters choir (see *Moravian Women Choirs). From 1788 to 1805 she served as the head teacher of the Seminary for Young Ladies in Bethlehem. She taught natural science (among other subjects) and later made the first botanical survey of northern Georgia. In 1805 she married John Gambold so that she could become a missionary to the Cherokee. They did evangelical work at Springplace, Georgia, where they also established a school. Hampered by the difficulties of the Cherokee language, the mission still progressed primarily because of Anna Rosina, who kept a detailed diary of the mission. The U.S. government closed the mission as part of the removal of the Cherokee.

Rowena McClinton, *The Moravian Spring Mission to the Cherokees*, 2 vols. (2007); Rose Simon, "Saved: The Gambold Collection of Moravian Devotional Books," *North Carolina Libraries* (1998); Edmund Schwarze, *History of the Moravian Mission among the Southern Indian Tribes* (1923).

CRAIG D. ATWOOD

Ganley, Rosemary Anne (1937–). Educator, journalist, and cofounder of Jamaican Self-Help. A pioneering Canadian feminist ever alert to the signs of the times, Rosemary Ganley is assistant editor of *Catholic New Times*, an independent faith and justice national newspaper. She is noted for her insightful social commentaries, activism for social and gender justice, and theological reflections on feminist concerns. In the late 1970s Ganley and her husband, John, founded the Peterborough (Ontario)-based Jamaican Self-Help (JSH) organization to work in partnership with Jamaican communities. Ganley represented Canadian women at the Fourth United Nations Conference on Women (Beijing, 1995) and the Beijing Plus Five Review. She leads workshops across Canada and Jamaica on journalism, global women's issues, and justice in cross-cultural contexts. She has received numerous awards, among them the Government of Canada 150th Anniversary Medal in 1992.

JSH, www.jshcanada.org.
VERONICA M. DUNNE, RNDM

Gardener, Helen Hamilton (1853–1925). Author, lecturer, and public official. Born Alice Chenoweth to a Calvinist mother and an Episcopal father (who became a Methodist circuit rider), Helen Gardner studied biology at Columbia University in the 1880s, wrote for newspapers under male pseudonyms, and published a popular novel, *Is This Your Son, My Lord?* in 1890. She gave freethinking lectures published as *Men, Women and Gods, and Other Lectures* (1885) and became well known for her study, "Sex in Brain" (1888), that refuted the theory that women's smaller brain weight indicated less intelligence. She participated in the *Woman's Bible* project (1895). Her friendships with Woodrow Wilson and members of Congress furthered her work with the National American Woman Suffrage Association. In 1920 Wilson appointed her the first woman on the U.S. Civil Service Commission.

EAWR; NoAW; RLA; Elizabeth C. Stanton et al., *History of Woman Suffrage*, vols. 4 and 5 (1902, 1922); Papers, Schlesinger Library, Radcliffe Institute, Harvard University.
MARY FARRELL BEDNAROWSKI

Garvey, Amy Ashwood (1897–1969). Pan-Africanist, feminist, and political activist. Born in Jamaica, Amy Ashwood helped found the Universal Negro Improvement Association (UNIA), the ladies' auxiliary of the UNIA, and the weekly *Negro World*. She was married briefly to Marcus Garvey, founder of the UNIA, after serving as his chief aide and secretary of the UNIA New York branch. She challenged his 1922 divorce action, considering herself rather than his second wife, *Amy Jacques Garvey, the true heir to his legacy. Her later career included world travel, residencies in Liberia and London, pan-African advocacy for women, cabaret ownership, and theater work. In the 1940s she was involved in politics in Jamaica and New York, and worked for equality for women in U.S. seasonal immigration policies related to Jamaica and the West Indies, an activity that brought her under the scrutiny of the FBI.

BWA; Tony Martin, *Amy Ashwood Garvey* (2006).
MARY FARRELL BEDNAROWSKI

Garvey, Amy Jacques (1885–1973). Pan-African activist, intellectual, and author. Born in Jamaica to an affluent, mixed-race family and educated at an Anglican-sponsored deaconess school, Amy Jacques moved to the U.S. in 1917. In 1919 she served as secretary of the Universal Negro Improvement Association (UNIA), and in 1922 she became the second wife of its founder, Marcus Garvey. She was well known as a major publicist of Garvey's anticolonialist, pan-African nationalist thought and edited volume 1 (1923) and volume 2 (1925) of *The Philosophy and Opinions of Marcus Garvey*. In 1963 she wrote *Garvey and Garveyism*. Amy Jacques Garvey was highly regarded for her own women- and worker-oriented efforts in the U.S. and Africa, serving as editor of the weekly *Negro World* women's page column, "Our Women and What They Think." She supported workers' movements in Africa and the black liberation movement in the U.S., was involved in organizing the fifth Pan-African Congress (1945), and helped sponsor the sixth congress (1974).

BWA; Ula Yvette Taylor, *The Veiled Garvey* (2002).
MARY FARRELL BEDNAROWSKI

Gates, Susan Young (1856–1933). Mormon writer and women's leader.

Susan Young was the 41st child of Mormon leader Brigham Young. One of the founders of the Mormon's genealogical work, Gates was the first person baptized for the dead in the Mormon temple at St. George, Utah, in 1877. Under the pseudonym Homespun, she wrote many articles for church publications during the 1880s. She and her second husband spent four years, beginning in 1885, as missionaries in Hawaii. Gates founded the *Young Woman's Journal* and founded and edited the *Relief Society Magazine*. The only woman to have an office in the Mormon Church's office building, her influence and power earned her the nickname the "13th apostle." She authored several books, including *Surname Book and Racial History*, *History of the Young Ladies' Mutual Improvement Association*, and (with her daughter) *The Life Story of Brigham Young*.

EAWR; RLA; Daniel H. Ludlow, ed., *Encyclopedia of Mormonism* (1992).

KEITH DURSO

Gérin-Lajoie, Marie (1890–1971). Social work pioneer, founder and superior of the Institut Notre-Dame du Bon-Conseil. Daughter of suffragist activist Marie Lacoste-Gérin Lajoie, the young Gérin-Lajoie found in her mother a powerful role model. In contrast to her mother, however, she chose the routes of higher education and religious life to impact a highly clericalized Quebec society. After a period of extensive travel, education, and activism, she earned a degree in social work at Columbia University. She returned to Quebec, where she created and taught a course in social work; it was developed widely by the province. In 1923 the socially avant-garde religious order she created received papal approval. Throughout the remainder of her life she pushed her church's boundaries toward gender equality and social justice and against ecclesiastical patriarchal structures.

Alison Prentice and Susan Mann Trofimenkoff, eds., *The Neglected Majority* (1987); Hélène Pelletier-Baillargeon, *Marie Gérin-Lajoie* (1985).

OSCAR COLE-ARNAL

Gezari, Temima (Fruma) Nimtzowitz (1905–). Artist, educator, and humanist. Temima Nimtzowitz was raised in New York City after immigrating to the U.S. with her family as an infant. She received degrees from the Teachers Institute of the Jewish Theological Seminary and the Master Institute of United Arts (New York City). As director of the art department in the Board of Jewish Education of New York, Gezari advocated for the arts in the Jewish school curriculum and introduced such practices as an annual public exhibition of Jewish children's art. In addition to working as an artist and teacher, Gezari published articles and books on art education, and illustrated many Jewish children's books.

JWA; Temima Gezari, *Mama, Papa and Me* (2002), *Footprints and New Worlds* (1964); Daniel Gezari, ed., *The Art of Temima Gezari* (1985); Oral History Collection, Dorot Jewish Division, New York Public Library.

EMILY ALICE KATZ

Gillespie, Angela ("Elizabeth") (1824–87). Catholic religious leader, teacher, writer. American-born and educated at Visitation Academy, Georgetown (Washington, DC), Elizabeth Gillespie joined the French immigrant congregation of Marianites of the Holy Cross (MSC) in 1853. She returned from novitiate training in France to direct St. Mary's Academy in Indiana (predecessor to St. Mary's College). After supervising the work of 80 sister-nurses at Union Military Hospital during the Civil War, she resumed her teaching career. She served as de facto editor of the Catholic weekly *Ave Maria*, and edited

Metropolitan Readers, a popular series of graded literature textbooks. As superior of her congregation (1867–82), she expanded its work in education and drew on her Civil War experience to introduce work in health care.

EACH; NoAWMP; M. Georgia Costin, *Priceless Spirit* (1994); Anna Shannon McAllister, *Flame in the Wilderness* (1944).
KAREN M. KENNELLY, CSJ

Gilman, Charlotte Anna Perkins Stetson (1860–1935). Author, speaker, and women's rights activist. Charlotte Perkins studied at the Rhode Island School of Design. She married Charles Walter Stetson in 1884, and their daughter Katherine was born in 1885, after which she experienced postpartum depression. She divorced Stetson and moved to California, but she allowed Stetson to keep their daughter and was criticized for being a bad mother. She published a short story, "The Yellow Wall-paper" (1892), about a woman who was treated for neurasthenia (depression) following childbirth. In 1898 she published *Women and Economics*. She married George Gilman in 1900. Charlotte Gilman wrote and spoke about women, children, and suffrage for the remainder of her life. She advocated for communal kitchens, cleaning services, laundries, and child care as a way to free women from the burdens of household work and permit them to work outside the home. She edited and published the *Forerunner*, a monthly magazine. With *Jane Addams she founded the Woman's Peace Party in 1915. Gilman committed suicide after being diagnosed with inoperable breast cancer.

ANB; NoAW; Charlotte Gilman, *His Religion and Hers* (2003) [1923], *The Living of Charlotte Perkins Gilman* (1935), *Women and Economics* (1898); Gary Scharnhorst, *Charlotte Perkins Gilman* (1985); Mary Hill, *Charlotte Perkins Gilman* (1980).
LYNN JAPINGA

Ginzberg, Adele Katzenstein (1886–1980). Leader in Conservative Judaism. In 1909 Adele Katzenstein married Louis Ginzberg, a professor of Talmud at the Jewish Theological Seminary (JTS). She was a longtime monthly columnist for the National Women's League *Outlook* magazine and initiated work on what eventually became the Menorah Award merit badge for Girl Scouts. She was an early and strong supporter of equal participation by women in synagogue ritual. She and her husband played the unofficial role of "Mr. and Mrs. Seminary" (previously filled by Solomon and *Mathilde Schechter) at JTS, holding open houses on Shabbat and holidays and thereby contributing greatly to the institution's sense of community. Ginzberg was honored as New York State Mother of the Year in 1966, was named a member of the seminary's Honorary Society of Fellows in 1976, and received the Mathilde Schechter Award posthumously in 1980.

JWA; Oral History Collection, Dorot Jewish Division, New York Public Library.
JOAN S. FRIEDMAN

Goldstein, Rebecca Fischel (1891–1961). Activist, community builder, and educator. One of four sisters, Rebecca Fischel received a thorough Jewish education in an Orthodox home, earned a BA at Barnard College, and continued her Jewish studies at the Teachers Institute of the Jewish Theological Seminary. To demonstrate their shared commitment to learning and teaching Torah, she and her soon-to-be-husband, Rabbi Herbert Goldstein, translated and published an 18th-century Hebrew ethical treatise. Goldstein was an equal partner with her husband in founding the Institutional Synagogue of Harlem. She led in promoting educational efforts in the community and founded the Daughters of the Institutional Synagogue, through which she became a mother figure and role model to numerous young women.

Goldstein was the first president of the *Union of Orthodox Jewish Congregations of America and a vice chair of the women's committee of the Rabbi Isaac Elchanan Theological Seminary.

JWA.

JOAN S. FRIEDMAN

Gooding, Margaret (Peg) King (1922–2003). Unitarian Universalist educator. Born a fifth-generation Universalist in Claremont, New Hampshire, Margaret King received a BS from Wheelock College (Boston). She was a director of religious education at the Unitarian Church in Phoenix, Arizona, and then at Ottawa, Ontario. She was ordained a minister of religious education in 1981. She retired as minister emerita in 1992. Gooding conducted educational workshops around North America. She wrote *The Canadians . . . Adventures of Our People*, *Growing Up Times*, and *Exploring Our Roots*. Her "Shake Hands with the Dragon" New Year's worship service advised facing fears. She was awarded honorary doctorates by Starr King School for Ministry and Meadville Lombard Theological School (where she taught from 1989 to 1992). She questioned neglecting the Universalist tradition.

Irene Baros-Johnson and Mary Lu MacDonald, *Concise Portraits of Canadian Unitarian and Universalist Women* (2006); Papers, Meadville Lombard Theological School.

IRENE BAROS-JOHNSON

Goodwin, Marsha Baset (d. 1885). Editor and publisher. Marsha Baset Goodwin was probably the first woman editor and publisher in the Stone-Campbell movement. Two of her publications are noteworthy. The longest-running and most important of her religious periodicals was the *Christian Companion* (1863–88), devoted to women's mission work, while the *Christian Monitor* (1866–85) was widely regarded as the principal venue for reports on the work of Stone-Campbell women. Goodwin was also an important leader of the Christian Women's Board of Mission and served on the committee that drafted the organization's constitution.

ES-CM.

SCOTT D. SEAY

Gordon, Anna Adams (1853–1931). Temperance leader, author, and hymn writer. Anna Gordon became the personal secretary of *Frances Willard, leader of the National *Woman's Christian Temperance Union (NWCTU), in 1877. She held this post for 21 years, during which time she also built the Loyal Temperance Legion (LTL), the children's wing of the NWCTU. At Willard's death in 1898 Gordon became vice president of the NWCTU, and in 1914 she became the fourth president of the organization. Through the World War I era, she led the NWCTU to patriotically support America's war effort and toward the passage of the 18th (Prohibition) Amendment in 1919. She was elected president of the World's WCTU in 1922. She published books on the life and sayings of Willard, as well as a few collections of songs.

ANB; NoAW; WBC; Randall Jimerson et al., eds., *Temperance and Prohibition Papers* (1977, microfilm); *Union Signal* (27 June 1931).

CAROLYN DESWARTE GIFFORD

Gordon, Eleanor Elizabeth (1852–1942). Minister and women's rights advocate. Born in Hamilton, Illinois, Eleanor Gordon attended the University of Iowa from 1873 to 1874. Minister *Mary Safford invited her to assist with the Humboldt and Sioux City Unitarian churches. Gordon studied at Cornell University for one semester and was ordained in 1889. She encouraged and financially supported college for women, and served four other congregations. She and Safford published the magazine *Old and New* from 1891 to 1908. Gordon was field secretary of the Unitarian Conference of Iowa (1907–10) and facilitated its communication for 10 years. She lived at the Roadside Settlement House in Des Moines from 1906 to 1910. In 1912 she organized a Unitarian church in Orlando, Florida. She retired from ministry in 1918. In 1937 she wrote that women seemed unwelcome in denominational positions of authority.

UUWM; Dorothy May Emerson, *Standing Before Us* (2000); Cynthia Grant Tucker, *Prophetic Sisterhood* (1990).

IRENE BAROS-JOHNSON

Gordon, Nora Antonia (1866–1901). Missionary. Born in Georgia, Nora Gordon embraced Christianity at Spelman Seminary (now Spelman College), where she became an effective evangelist and an intrepid Christian worker. After her graduation in 1888 the Woman's Baptist Foreign Missionary Society of the West appointed her to the Congo. Stationed at Palabala she worked briefly with *Lulu Fleming. In 1891 she was transferred to Lukunga. When ill health forced her to return to the U.S. in 1893 she brought two young African women to be educated at Spelman. She returned to the Congo in 1895 as the wife of Rev. S. C. Gordon, a Jamaican who served as an English Baptist missionary, but political difficulties and her fragile health inhibited their work at Stanley Pool. After her second child perished the couple returned to the U.S. in 1900. She died at Spelman College.

BWA; BWARC; NBAW; Benjamin Brawley, *Women of Achievement* (1919).

KENDAL P. MOBLEY

Gorham, Sarah E. (1832–94). Missionary, church leader, and social worker. Sarah Gorham was born at Fredericksburg, Maryland. Little is known of her life until 1880, when she visited family members in Liberia and became interested in the peoples of Africa and the work of Christian missionaries. Gorham returned to the U.S. and became active in Boston's Charles Street African Methodist Episcopal (AME) Church. In 1888 she became the first woman missionary to serve overseas for the AME Church. Gorham was sponsored by the Woman's Parent Mite Missionary Society and worked at the Magbelle mission in Sierra Leone. She later established the Sarah Gorham Mission School. Gorham is buried at the Kissy Road Cemetery in Freetown.

BWARC; Octavia Dandridge, *A History of the Women's Missionary Society of the African Methodist Episcopal Church* (1987); *Women in New Worlds*, vol. 2, ed. Rosemary S. Keller, Louise L. Queen, and Hilah F. Thomas (1982).

CHRISTOPHER J. ANDERSON

Grant, Amy (1960–). Singer. Born in Augusta, Georgia, Amy Grant is one of the most popular and controversial Contemporary Christian Music (CCM) artists. Her 20 albums to date have been among the bestsellers in CCM. She crossed over successfully to the secular market in the 1980s. In 1982 she released her breakout album, *Age to Age*. As Grant's popularity grew she sought to reach a wider audience by transforming her overtly Christian songs into songs that presented a Christian perspective, and used images that appealed to both CCM and secular audiences. Grant has won 22 Dove and 5 Grammy awards in her 25 years in the recording business. Her success as a crossover artist challenged how Christian music is defined.

EE; RLA; Amy Grant, *Mosaic: Pieces of My Life So Far* (2007); William D. Romanowski, "Where's the Gospel?" *Christianity Today* 41, no. 14 (8 December 1997); Bob Millard, *Amy Grant* (1996).

SUSAN B. RIDGELY

Grant, Jacquelyn (1948–). Womanist theologian and minister. Jacquelyn Grant completed her PhD at Union Theological Seminary in New York City. In the 1970s she helped create the women's studies in religion program at Harvard Divinity School. A decade later she founded the Center for Black Women in Church and Society at the Interdenominational Theological Seminary. Grant's theological approach focuses on the experiences of black women. Criticizing white feminist theologians for overlooking their own racial privilege, Grant reclaims and articulates the theological contributions of black women. Her work also challenges black theology and the black church to recognize that unless black women are made visible and their needs addressed, both entities will fail to attain their goal of liberation.

Jacquelyn Grant, *White Women's Christ and Black Women's Jesus* (1989); Grant, "Black Theology and the Black Woman," in *Black Theology*, vol. 1, ed. James H. Cone and Gayraud S. Wilmore (1979).

LYNN S. NEAL

Grant Banister, Zilpah Polly (1794–1874). Educator. Born in Norfolk, Connecticut, and raised by her mother, Zilpah Grant attended district school and began teaching at the age of 15. Her health was precarious, but her faith held strong and was lived out in her Congregational church membership. As a student at the Byfield Seminary in Massachusetts, Grant became interested in women's education. In 1823 she was called to organize and take charge of the Adams Female Academy in Londonderry, New Hampshire. The academy flourished under her direction, and she was later asked to establish a similar seminary in Ipswich, Massachusetts. *Mary Lyon, the well-known founder of Mount Holyoke Seminary, was one of Grant's teachers at the Ipswich school. Grant left Ipswich and teaching in 1839 for health reasons. In 1841 she married William Banister and continued recruiting teachers and advocating for women's formal education.

NoAW; Linday Thayer Guilford, *The Use of a Life: Memorials of Mrs. Zilpah Polly Grant Banister* (1885); Papers, Archives and Special Collections, Mount Holyoke College.

BETH SPAULDING

Gratz, Rebecca (1781–1869). Philanthropist and founder of the Jewish Sunday school movement. Born in Philadelphia, Rebecca Gratz helped to found the Female Association (1801), the Philadelphia Orphan Asylum (1815), the *Female Hebrew Benevolent Society (1819), the Hebrew Sunday School (1838), and the Jewish Foster Home (1855). Her love of literature, exceptional education, and talent for writing led her to assume the responsibilities of secretary rather than president in these organizations. As secretary she shaped organizational decisions, publicity, and memories. She assisted similar Jewish institutions in Savannah (Georgia), New York City, Richmond (Virginia), and Charleston (South Carolina), as well as an orphan asylum in Lexington (Kentucky). Gratz attended synagogue regularly, encouraged her rabbi to deliver sermons at a time when these were unusual in synagogues, recruited educated women to teach Hebrew Sunday school, and promoted works by Jewish British theologian Grace Aguilar. Gratz hoped her charities and schools would strengthen belief among Jewish women and children.

ANB; DARB; EAWR; JWA; NoAW; Dianne Ashton, *Rebecca Gratz* (1997); David Philipson, ed., *Letters of Rebecca Gratz* (1929).

DIANNE ASHTON

Greenberg, Blu (1936–). Jewish feminist. Blu Greenberg was born to

Orthodox parents in Seattle, Washington, but her family relocated to New York City so that she and her sister could continue their Jewish education. She earned master's degrees in clinical psychology and Jewish history. For most of her early life Greenberg accepted that women had fewer public obligations and less access to Jewish learning than men. When she read Betty Friedan's *The Feminist Mystique* (1963) she began questioning gender divisions in Judaism. Ten years later she gave the opening address at the First National Jewish Women's Conference in New York. Her groundbreaking book is *On Women and Judaism* (1981). In 1997 she helped found the *Jewish Orthodox Feminist Alliance. Her work has inspired countless Jews to champion greater women's participation in Jewish ritual, prayer, education, and synagogue life.

JWA; Blu Greenburg, in *Transforming the Faiths of Our Fathers*, ed. Ann Braude (2004); Papers, Schlesinger Library, Radcliffe Institute, Harvard University.

LILA CORWIN BERMAN

Grimké, Sarah Moore (1792–1873), and **Grimké Weld, Angelina Emily** (1805–79). Abolitionists and women's rights pioneers. Born into the upper class of Charleston, South Carolina, both Grimké sisters were educated for motherhood and domestic management. They moved to Philadelphia and, attracted by their piety and simplicity, first Sarah and then Angelina joined the Quakers. Early in their lives both women had become sensitive to the brutality and injustice of slavery. Angelina became convinced that her vocation lay with the antislavery movement. Sarah's conversion to the cause was slower, but eventually she followed Angelina to New York to pursue antislavery activities. In 1836 Angelina's *Appeal to the Christian Women of the South*, which argued for black equality and the slave's right to freedom, was published, and was followed by Sarah's *Epistle to the Clergy of the Southern States*. The latter pamphlet claimed that Christianity and slavery were contradictory; as with all the writings of the sisters, it used the biblical text as a basis for argument. The Grimké sisters also became the first female agents of the American Anti-Slavery Society and lectured widely, first to small groups of women and then to large crowds that included men. Since they came from a leading southern family, their lectures and their writing aroused intense public interest. They were denounced because they stepped beyond the appropriate private sphere for women. In response to this criticism Sarah wrote her *Letters on the Equality of the Sexes*, where she claimed that the cause of abolition could not move forward until women were liberated. Angelina's marriage to non-Quaker Theodore Weld resulted in the dismissal of both sisters from the Quakers. They retired from public life, and Sarah went to live with the Welds to help with childcare and domestic duties. They both aided Theodore Weld in writing his *American Slavery As It Is* (1839). The sisters became increasingly distanced from Protestant orthodoxy and established religious communities.

ANB; DARB; EAWR; EE; NoAW; Katharine Du Pre Lumpkin, *The Emancipation of Angelina Grimké* (1974); Gerda Lerner, *The Grimké Sisters from South Carolina* (1967); Gilbert Barnes and Dwight Dumond, eds., *Letters of Theodore Dwight Weld, Angelina Grimké Weld, and Sarah Grimké*, 2 vols. (1934); Catherine Hoffman Birney, *The Grimké Sisters* (1885).

BARBARA J. MACHAFFIE

Gruchy, Lydia Emelie (1894–1992). First woman ordained by the United Church of Canada. Lydia Gruchy was born in Asnière, France. She moved in her teens with her family to Saskatchewan, where she taught school and obtained her bachelor's degree. At the encouragement of its principal, Edmund Oliver, Gruchy entered Saskatoon's Presbyterian Theological College (later St. Andrew's College), graduating with high honors in 1923. The Presbyterian Church declined to ordain her, in view of the impending 1925 union with Methodists and Congregationalists that would form the United Church of Canada. While the new United Church debated women's ordination, Gruchy served Saskatchewan congregations as a "home missionary." In 1934 the national United Church sent a remit to all its presbyteries to test approval for the ordination of women. It passed decisively (79 to 26), and the 1936 General Council accepted the results. Gruchy was ordained in Moose Jaw, Saskatchewan, on 4 November 1936. Gruchy worked for the national church in Toronto and in congregational ministry in Saskatchewan until retiring in 1962. In 1953 she became the first woman to receive the St. Andrew's College honorary doctor of divinity degree.

Mary Hallett, "Ladies—We Give You the Pulpit" and "Lydia Gruchy: First Woman Ordained in the United Church of Canada," *Touchstone: Heritage and Theology in a New Age* 4, no. 1 (January 1986).

SANDRA L. BEARDSALL

Grumm, Christine Helen (1950–). Lay leader and fund-raiser. Christine Grumm was born into a Lutheran Church Missouri Synod missionary family. She has been a lay leader in the Association of Evangelical Lutheran Congregations and the first vice president of the Evangelical Lutheran Church in America (1987–1991). Grumm served as deputy general secretary of the Lutheran World Federation, based in Geneva. After returning to the U.S., she was executive director of the Chicago Foundation for Women and then of the Women's Funding Network.

Caroline Bennett, "Seven Who Create New Pathways for Success," *Women's Enews* (23 December 2003), www.womensenews.org/article-cfm/dry/aid/1639; "Christine Grumm," *Mother Jones Radio* (24 December 2006), www.motherjones.com/radio/2006/12/grumm.bio.html.

L. DEANE LAGERQUIST

Guerin, Anne-Therese (Mother Theodore) (1798–1856). Roman Catholic saint and founder of a women's college. Born in a fishing village in France, Guerin entered religious life in 1823 and quickly rose to leadership within her congregation. Chosen to lead a missionary trip to the new world in 1840 she traveled to what is now central Indiana with five other *Sisters of Providence. There she established an academy for girls and, in 1846, St. Mary-of-the-Woods College for women. Over the next decade, Guerin established schools throughout the region, founded an orphanage for girls and another for boys, and established pharmacies that dispensed free medications to the poor. She was canonized as St. Mother Theodore Guerin in 2006.

EACH; ROWUS ("Sisters of Providence"); Katherine Burton and Mary K. Doyle, *The Eighth American Saint* (2006); Penny Mitchell, *Mother Theodore Guerin: A Woman for Our Time* (1998).

COLLEEN CARPENTER CULLINAN

Gulick, Alice Winfield Gordon (1847–1903). Congregational missionary and educator. Born in Boston of Scottish and English ancestry, Alice Gordon was given an understanding of the missionary life through her father, who served as treasurer of the American Board of Commissioners for Foreign Missions (ABCFM). Upon completing her education in public schools and at Mount Holyoke Seminary, she became a teacher. In 1871 she married the Reverend William Gulick and the two sailed for Spain, the first missionaries sent to that country by the ABCFM. Gulick opened a boarding school for girls that grew rapidly; encouraged by this, she decided to open a nondenominational institution for the higher education of girls modeled on Mount Holyoke and Wellesley. The International Institute for Girls continues to prepare Spanish women for professional training, either in Spain or abroad.

NoAW; Elizabeth Putnam Gordon, *Alice Gordon Gulick* (1917); Papers, Archives and Special Collections, Mount Holyoke College.

BETH SPAULDING

Gurney, Eliza P. (1801–81). Quaker minister and pacifist. Born in Philadelphia, Eliza Paul Kirkbride married Joseph J. Gurney, a prominent English evangelical Quaker in 1836. She was known in her own right as a minister and preacher in the U.S. and Europe. In 1862 she convened a prayer meeting with three Friends and President Abraham Lincoln in the White House in order to provide him with comfort during the Civil War. After their meeting, Gurney's inner conflict between her antiwar and antislavery views prompted her to write to Lincoln. Their subsequent correspondence lasted for several years. Her letters are frequently cited as important keys to understanding Lincoln's own inner conflicts during the war, as well as his religious beliefs.

ANB; NoAW; Ronald C. White Jr., *Lincoln's Greatest Speech* (2002); Eliza Gurney, *Memoirs and Correspondence of Eliza P. Gurney* (1884).

ANNIE RUSSELL

Guyart Martin, Marie ("Marie de l'Incarnation") (1599–1672). Founder of the *Ursulines in Quebec. Marie Guyart was born in Tours, France. Although she felt called to religious life, she married Claude Martin at the age of 17 but was soon widowed. In 1631 Martin entrusted her son to her sister and entered the Ursuline convent; she became Marie de l'Incarnation. At the urging of Madame de la Peltrie, Marie and her companions left in 1639 for Quebec to begin educating French and native children in the new colony. Marie was a mystic imbued with a sense of action, and she was responsible for her religious foundation for the next 32 years. Supported by Jesuit spiritual advisors, she exerted enormous influence on the leaders and people of New France. She was beatified in 1980.

DCB; Elizabeth C. Goldsmith, *Publishing Women's Life Stories in France* (2001); Joyce Marshall, ed., *Word from New France* (1967).

ELAINE GUILLEMIN

Hadassah (1912–). Zionist organization. Founded under *Henrietta Szold's leadership in New York as a women's study group, Hadassah was reshaped to provide medical care in Palestine, promote Jewish ideals, and educate Jewish women. Its motto, "the Healing of the Daughter of my people," referred to benefits to be reaped by American women, for whom Hadassah offered Jewish education and a sense of purpose, and by the women and children of Palestine—Arabs and Jews—who were cared for by the visiting nurses and free milk stations Hadassah provided. Local Hadassah chapters often initiated additional activities like sewing circles and English and Yiddish language groups. During the late 1930s Hadassah helped fund Youth Aliyah, which rescued children and teens from Nazi Europe and resettled them on kibbutzim in Jewish territories in Palestine. Although Hadassah began as an arm of the Zionist Organization of America, in 1933 it became independent. Hadassah founded many small health centers and in 1952 began building Hadassah Hospital in Jerusalem, today the leading medical and research facility in the Middle East. By 1991 Hadassah counted 385,000 members, the largest Zionist organization in the world.

DARB; EAWR; JWA; Miriam Freund-Rosenthal, *A Tapestry of Hadassah Memories* (1994); Marlin Levin, *Balm in Gilead* (1973).

DIANNE ASHTON

Hall, Rosetta Sherwood (1865–1951). Medical missionary and educator. Rosetta Sherwood taught school until she heard an appeal for medical missionaries. She attended the Woman's Medical College in Philadelphia, graduating in 1889. She became engaged to William James Hall, who also planned to become a Methodist medical missionary. She was sent to Seoul, Korea, in 1890. He obtained an appointment there also, and the two were married in 1892. Hall founded a dispensary in Seoul before she and her husband moved to Pyongyang in 1894. Following her husband's death later that year, Hall took her son to New York, and gave birth to a daughter soon after her arrival. In 1897 Hall returned to Korea, where she established a women's hospital in Pyong Yang and a medical training institute for women in Seoul. In 1933 she returned to the U.S.

NoAWMP; Sherwood Hall, *With Stethescope in Asia: Korea* (1978).

MARILYN FÄRDIG WHITELEY

Hamer, Fannie Lou Townsend (1917–77). Civil rights leader. Fannie Lou Townsend was born into a sharecropping family in Montgomery County, Mississippi. After receiving a rudimentary education, she began working in the cotton fields with her parents and 19 siblings. Her plantation owner learned in 1944 that she was literate, and he appointed her to be his record keeper, a position that she held for the next 18 years. In 1945 she married Perry "Pap" Hamer. In 1962 Hamer was inspired by Student Non-violent Coordinating Committee (SNCC) volunteers and, along with 17 others, went to the county seat to register to vote. The group was jailed briefly; as a result, Hamer was forced off the plantation where she worked. Hamer volunteered with the SNCC and was appointed to be a field secretary. In 1964 she helped found the Mississippi Freedom Democratic Party (MFDP) and unsuccessfully ran for Congress. Hamer founded the Freedom Farms Corporation in 1969, a nonprofit organization aimed at providing economic assistance, social services, and scholarships for needy black families. Hamer's determination, courage, and frank openness about the civil rights struggle won her numerous recognitions, awards, and honorary degrees.

ANB; BWA; NBAW; NoAWC; Chana Kai Lee, *For Freedom's Sake* (1999); Kay Mills, *This Little Light of Mine* (1993).

SCOTT D. SEAY

Hammond, Lily Hardy (1859–1925). Author, church leader, and civil rights activist. Lily Hardy Hammond was the daughter of slave owners and an active leader, speaker, and writer for the Woman's Missionary Council of the Methodist Episcopal Church, South. She was active in the Commission on Interracial Cooperation and called upon white women to seek out personal friendships with black women. Hammond authored 10 books, including an important social commentary entitled *In Black and White* (1914), where she openly criticized the racial attitudes of white women in the U.S. She was concerned about issues of social justice, such as lynching and the sharecropper system. Hammond believed that inequality and racial injustice would always permeate American society until whites viewed African Americans as equally created in the image of God.

DARB; Alice G. Knotts, *Fellowship of Love: Methodist Women Changing American Racial Attitudes* (1996).

CHRISTOPHER J. ANDERSON

Han, Jung Mi (1943–). First Korean woman to be ordained by the Presbyterian Church (U.S.A.) (PCUSA). Born in Korea, Jung Mi Han came to the U.S. as a foreign exchange student in 1965. She studied at Nyack Missionary College and earned her BA in psychology from the Lehmann College of the City University of New York in 1975. During her studies at Columbia Theological Seminary in Decatur, Georgia, Jung Mi Han was the director of Christian education at the Korean Community Presbyterian Church in Atlanta. Following her graduation from Columbia, she was ordained as the first Korean woman in the PCUSA by the Presbytery of Greater Atlanta in 1986. Among other positions, she served as the organizing pastor of the Han Mi Presbyterian Church of Atlanta, a new church development, from 1990 to 1995. During those years the church increased its size to 200 members. She also was the founder and director of the Immanuel Spiritual Center in Atlanta from 1996 to 2006, and she has served as the chair of the ecumenical Korean clergywomen's group in Atlanta since 1998.

Alice Brasfield and Elisabeth Lunz, eds., *Voices of Experience: Life Stories of Clergywomen in the Presbyterian Church (USA)* (1991).

LINDA B. BREBNER

Hanaford, Phoebe Ann Coffin (1829–1921). Universalist minister, activist, and writer. Phoebe Coffin was born on Nantucket, where her parents' Quaker faith shaped her religious authority and intellectual development. In 1848 she married Joseph Hanaford. She wrote prolifically and edited the *Ladies' Repository* from 1866 to 1868. After converting to Universalism, Hanaford became a licensed preacher and was ordained in Hingham, Massachusetts, in 1868, becoming the first ordained woman in New England. She was called by the Universalist church in New Haven (1870 and 1884) and Jersey City (1874). Her most famous book was *Women of the Century* (1876). She helped edit *The Woman's Bible* in the 1890s. Hanaford worked for *Julia Ward Howe's Women's Peace Conference (1870), and for temperance, abolition, and women's suffrage. She preached funeral orations for *Elizabeth Cady Stanton and *Susan B. Anthony.

EAWR; NoAW; RLA; UU; UUWM; Dorothy Emerson, ed., *Standing Before Us*, (2000); E. R. Hanson, *Our Woman Workers* (1884).

BARBARA COEYMAN

Hardey, Mary ("Aloysia") (1809–86). Mother superior of the Society of the Sacred Heart. In 1825 Mary Hardey entered the novitiate at the convent of the Sacred Heart in Grand Coteau, Louisiana, and took the name Aloysia. In 1833 she took her vows and cofounded the convent at St. Michael's, Louisiana, of which she became the superior in 1836. Hardey founded her society's first house in New York City in 1841 and three years later became the superior of all the society's convents on the East Coast and in Canada. In 1872 she moved to Paris, France, where, as assistant general, she represented the society's houses in the British Empire and North America. During her ministry Hardey helped found 30 convents in the U.S. and Canada.

ANB; NCE; NoAW; ROWUS; *New Advent Catholic Encyclopedia* [online]; Margaret A. Williams, *Second Sowing* (1942).

KEITH DURSO

Harkness, Georgia Elma (1891–1974). Theologian and religious educator. Georgia Harkness entered the field of religious education after receiving both the MRE and PhD degrees from Boston University. An active Methodist since childhood, she was ordained as a local deacon in 1926 and as a local elder in 1938, but was denied membership in the Methodist Annual Conference until 1956. Her early career was marked by striving toward an ideal of philosophical objectivity that would enable people to live religiously. Her two years of study (1936–37) at Union Theological Seminary (New York City) changed her, however, and she began to describe herself as an evangelical liberal. Her position as the only female member of the Younger Theologian's Group, which included Reinhold Niebuhr and Paul Tillich among its members, also played a significant part in shaping her theological thinking. She became the first female professor of theology at a Protestant seminary in the U.S. when she accepted a position at Garrett Biblical Institute in Evanston, Illinois, in 1939. She subsequently held a similar position at the Pacific School of Religion in Berkeley, California, from 1950 until her retirement in 1961. Harkness was a prolific author, an active pacifist, and a participant in the international ecumenical movement. She was part of the founding convention of the World Council of Churches in 1948, where she argued against Karl Barth for women's equality in the church. She was the most visible female theologian in mid-20th century America. Harkness's teaching and public commitment to social justice made her a role model for a generation of women in the church and academia alike.

ANBO; DARB; EAWR; NoAWMP; RLA; Gary Dorrien, *The Making of American Liberal Theology* (2003); Rosemary Skinner Keller, *Georgia Harkness* (1993); Georgia Harkness, *Grace Abounding* (1963).

ANNIE RUSSELL

Harper, Frances Ellen Watkins (1825–1911). Author and social reformer. Internationally known as an extraordinarily gifted and prolific African American literary figure, Frances Harper was also involved in social reform. She was an abolitionist lecturer, an activist in the Underground Railroad, friend to William Still and supporter of John Brown, a founder of the American Woman Suffrage Association and the *National Association of Colored Women, member of the *Woman's Christian Temperance Union national board, developer of Sunday schools in the black community, and supporter of the African Methodist Episcopal Church (although she belonged to the First Unitarian Church in Philadelphia). Harper was born to free parents in Baltimore, orphaned at age three, and educated at her uncle's prestigious William Watkins Academy for Negro Youth. Biblical themes and Gospel mandates appear regularly in her novels, poetry, speeches, and letters, testimony to the religious foundation of her life.

BWA; DUUB; NoAW; Frances Smith Foster, *A Brighter Coming Day: A Frances Ellen Watkins Harper Reader* (1990).

MARGARET MCMANUS

Harris, Barbara Clementine (1930–). Episcopal bishop. Barbara Harris was the first woman bishop in the Episcopal Church in the U.S.A. (ECUSA) and the first black woman bishop in the worldwide Anglican communion. A baptized and confirmed Episcopalian, Barbara Harris was born in Philadelphia and became a public relations professional. Active in the civil rights movement, in 1968 she joined the Church of the Advocate (North Philadelphia) and was instrumental in founding the Union of Black Episcopalians. After women were admitted to the Episcopal priesthood in the U.S. in 1976, Harris began to study toward ordination. She was ordained deacon in 1979 and priest in 1980. She became executive director of the Episcopal Church Publishing Company in 1984. Harris was interim rector of the Church of the Advocate when she was elected suffragan bishop of the Diocese of Massachusetts in 1989. She retired in 2002 and became assisting bishop in the Diocese of Washington, DC.

BWA; BWARC; EAWR; NBAW; Mark Francisco Bozzuti-Jones, *The Mitre Fits Just Fine* (2003).

SHERYL A. KUJAWA-HOLBROOK

Harris, Elizabeth Bache (ca. 1630–89). Quaker missionary. Elizabeth Bache married William Harris in 1649, and they became converts to Quakerism. She conducted a missionary trip to the Chesapeake in 1655 or 1656. She returned to England in 1657, where she was eventually arrested, imprisoned, and banished to Jamaica. Historians differ as to where and when she died, but she may have returned to the Chesapeake and continued her Quaker efforts in New Jersey between 1677 and 1689.

Jay Worrall Jr., "A Response to 'America's First Quakers—Where, When and by Whom?' by Kenneth L. Carroll," *Quaker History* 86 (Spring 1997); Kenneth L. Carroll, "Elizabeth Harris, The Founder of American Quakerism," *Quaker History* 57 (Autumn 1968).

JOAN R. GUNDERSEN

Hauptman, Judith (1943–). Scholar and Jewish feminist. After graduating with a BA in economics from Barnard College, Judith Hauptman received her MA and PhD in Talmud at the Jewish Theological Seminary of America. Specializing in issues of women's roles in Jewish thought and the exploration of Talmudic texts to illuminate historical realities, she became the first woman appointed to teach Talmud at her alma mater, which stands as the primary institution of Judaism's Conservative movement. In addition to her academic achievements, she promoted gender equality within the Conservative movement and in the larger Jewish community. She became one of the early activists in Ezrat Nashim, a 1970s group composed of educated young women from the Conservative movement. They supported ordaining women as rabbis and cantors, allowing women to count as members of the minyan (quorum) needed for prayer services, and granting them equal status under Jewish law in divorce proceedings. She holds the E. Billi Ivry Professor of Talmud and Rabbinic Culture at the Jewish Theological Seminary of America. She was ordained a rabbi by the Academy for Jewish Religion in 2003.

Jewish Theological Seminary, www.jtsa.edu; Judith Hauptman, "The Challenge Facing Conservative Judaism," *The Jewish Week* (8 July 2005).

SHIRA M. KOHN

Haviland, Laura Smith (1808–98). Abolitionist, educator. Born a Quaker but influenced by the evangelical revivalism of western New York, Laura Smith moved to Michigan and helped found the first antislavery society in that state. She eventually withdrew from the Society of Friends and became a Methodist minister. In 1844 she and her husband opened a trade school for boys and girls of all races. An operative for the Underground Railroad, she traveled south to rescue slaves. She taught in black schools, lectured on abolitionism, and supported temperance and women's rights. During the Civil War she worked as a nurse and a paid agent for the Michigan Freedmen's Aid Commission. In 1879 she moved to Kansas to help black migrants settle in the West.

ANB; NoAW; Mildred E. Danforth, *A Quaker Pioneer* (1961); Laura Sarah Haviland, *A Woman's Life Work* (1881).

JANET MOORE LINDMAN

Hayden, Margaret ("Mother Bridget") (1814–90). Catholic religious sister, educator. Margaret Hayden emigrated with her parents from Ireland to Missouri when she was six years old.

In 1841 she joined the *Sisters of Loretto at the Foot of the Cross and was given the name Sister Bridget. In 1847 she volunteered to help create a Native American girls school among the Osage in Kansas. She became mother superior in 1859. Although she eventually left Kansas she continued to advocate fiercely for the education of Osage girls throughout her career, ensuring they were taught academic subjects as well as the domestic arts.

ANB; NoAW; Barbara Misner, *"Highly Respectable and Accomplished Ladies": Catholic Women Religious in America* (1988); William W. Graves, *Life and Times of Mother Bridget Hayden* (1938).

SUSAN B. RIDGELY

Haygood, Laura Askew (1845–1900). Teacher, administrator, and missionary. Laura Haygood was born in Georgia to a family of educators and Methodist ministers. She attended Wesleyan Female College in Macon and in 1865 began her teaching career in Oxford. In 1877 she became principal of the Atlanta Girls' High School, where she also taught Latin, English, moral science, philosophy, and teacher training courses. Despite poor health she resigned in 1884 to become a missionary to China, where she established and oversaw several schools, led Bible studies for expatriates, and evangelized. Upon returning to the U.S., she became the head of the Woman's Board of Foreign Missions of the Methodist Episcopal Church, South. Her work earned her the reputation of the quintessential foreign missionary, and a school in China was named in her honor.

ANBO; NoAW; Oswald E. and Anna M. Brown, *Life and Letters of Laura Askew Haygood* (1987 [1904]).

ANDREW H. STERN

Haynes, Elizabeth Ross (1883–1953). Reformer, writer, and community leader. The daughter of former slaves, Elizabeth Ross was born in Lowndes County, Alabama. She earned a BA from Fisk University and an MA in sociology from Columbia. Ross began working for the national board of the *YWCA (Young Women's Christian Association) in 1908, resigning in 1910 to marry George Edmund Haynes. In addition to helping her husband in his work, she dedicated her life to temperance, racial uplift, women's rights, and other social causes. She was the first African American on the YWCA national board and the only woman appointed to the New York State Temporary Commission on the Condition of the Urban Colored Population.

ANB; NoAWMP; Elizabeth Ross Haynes, *Unsung Heroes* (2007) [1921]; Iris Carlton-LaNey, "Elizabeth Ross Haynes: An African American Reformer of Womanist Consciousness," *Social Work* 42, no. 6 (1997).

MANDY E. MCMICHAEL

Healy, Mary Elisa (1813–50). Wife and mother. Born a mulatto slave near Macon, Georgia, Mary Elisa became in 1829 the common-law wife of Michael Morris Healy, an Irish immigrant and plantation owner. Although Michael Healy loved Mary Elisa devotedly, it was illegal for him to marry or free her. The couple had 10 children who, while legally slaves, were not raised as slaves. All were sent north for education. Both Michael and Mary Elisa Healy died in 1850, but, through their estate, all the children achieved their freedom. Three of the older sons were ordained priests in the Roman Catholic Church: James became the bishop of Portland, Maine; Alexander Sherwood became a theologian and administrator; and Patrick became president of Georgetown College. Two daughters, Josephine and Eliza, became religious sisters in Canada.

Cyprian Davis, *The History of Black Catholics in the United States* (1995); Albert S. Foley, SJ, *God's Men of Color* (1955).

JUDITH METZ, SC

Heck, Barbara Ruckle (1734–1804). Traditional founder of Methodism in North America. Born into a family that fled from Ireland to Germany, Barbara Ruckle became one of the Methodist converts among the Palatines. In 1760 she and her husband Paul Heck joined others from the community to immigrate to New York City. There were no Methodist services in New York at the time. According to tradition, in 1766 Barbara Heck became enraged upon seeing some of her neighbors playing cards. She threw the cards into the fire and encouraged her cousin, Philip Embury, to preach to the small group she drew together. A Methodist congregation was formed, and two years later they built John Street Church. In 1770 some of the immigrants moved to Camden Valley, New York, where again they held Methodist services. As revolution loomed, they remained loyal to Britain, so the Hecks and others in the group fled to Canada, settling first in Montreal, then near present-day Prescott, Ontario. Once again Barbara Heck, her husband, and some neighbors formed a Methodist group. In 1790, when the first Methodist preacher arrived, he held his initial service in the Heck home.

ANB; DARB; DCB; EAWR; EE; NoAW; Eula C. Lapp, *To Their Heirs Forever* (1977).

MARILYN FÄRDIG WHITELEY

Heinemann Landmann, Barbara (1795–1883). Cofounder of the Amana communities. During her adolescence in Alsace, France, Barbara Heinemann's (or Heynemann's) quest for the "true presence of God" led her to the Community of True Inspiration, a pietistic group led by Christian Metz. At age 23 she received the gift of oral inspiration (or prophecy), but after her marriage it was lost and not recovered until 1849. In the meanwhile, to escape religious oppression, Metz led his group in the mid-1840s to upstate New York, then in 1854 to Iowa, where he and Heinemann established seven collectivist Amana colonies. After Metz's death in 1867, Heinemann, as religious leader and prophet, maintained tight control over the membership until her death. In 1932 the Amana Society was liberalized and reconstituted on free-enterprise principles.

ANB; NoAW; Peter Hoehnle, *Amana People* (2003); Bertha H. M. Shambaugh, *Amana* (1988).

GRAEME SHARROCK

Hellwig, Monika Konrad Hildegard (1929–2005). Catholic theologian. Born in Germany to a Roman Catholic father and a Jewish mother, Monika Hellwig left Germany in 1935. Raised primarily in Britain, Hellwig joined the Medical Mission Sisters in 1951 and was sent to the U.S. to study theology. She was in Rome during the Second Vatican Council. After being released from her vows, she completed her doctorate in 1968 at the Catholic University of America. A professor at Georgetown University for 28 years, Hellwig published two dozen books (including *Understanding Catholicism*, 2nd ed. (2002) [1981]), edited major theological journals, and served on international academic boards. She also raised three adopted children as a single mother. After leaving Georgetown she served as president of the Association of Catholic Colleges and Universities (ACCU) for nine years.

Joe Feuerherd, "Monika Hellwig, Noted Theologian, Dies," *National Catholic Reporter* (14 October 2005); Patricia Sullivan, "Monika Hellwig; Theologian Challenged Vatican," *Washington Post* (7 October 2005).

COLLEEN CARPENTER CULLINAN

Hemenway, Abby Maria (1828–90). Writer, editor, and historian. Abby Hemenway's life work was the compilation and editing of the five-volume, multiauthor *Vermont Historical Gazetteer*, a history of nearly every community in Vermont, which she began in 1859. Born in Vermont of Yankee ancestry to a Methodist father and Baptist mother, Hemenway converted to Roman Catholicism in 1863. She participated in the company of American Catholic intellectuals and the arena of Catholic letters, publishing such works as *The Mystical Rose* (1865). For decades Hemenway was judged condescendingly as an undiscriminating gatherer of antiquarian facts. More recently she has been recognized for the immense scope of her undertaking, her inclusive perspective on what people and events count as significant in the history of a town, and her foreshadowing of the discipline now known as social history.

NoAW; Deborah Pickman Clifford, *The Passion of Abby Hemenway* (2001); Abby Maria Hemenway, ed., *Vermont Historical Gazetteer* (1867–91).

MARY FARRELL BEDNAROWSKI

Henderlite, Rachel (1905–91). Christian educator and clergywoman of the Presbyterian Church in the U.S. (PCUS). The daughter of a Presbyterian minister, Rachel Henderlite taught Christian education at the training school of the PCUS in Richmond, Virginia, following her own theological education. She wrote several books on Christian education and the Christian life, as well as church school curriculum. She had a lifelong interest in the global church, civil rights, and ecumenism, and served as a member of the World Alliance of Reformed Churches and as a delegate to, and later president of, the Consultation on Church Union. She was ordained as the first clergywoman of the PCUS in May 1965 by Hanover Presbytery (Virginia). From 1965 until her retirement in 1972, she was professor of Christian education at Austin Theological Seminary, the first woman to serve as a full professor in a seminary of the PCUS.

EAWR; Presbyterian Historical Society Staff, "Rachel Henderlite and Myra Scovel: Lives of Dedication," *Presbyterian Heritage* (Winter 2005); Estelle Rountree McCarthy, "Rachel Henderlite," Christian Educators of the 20th Century, www.talbot.edu/ce20.

BEVERLY ZINK-SAWYER

Henrichsen, Margaret Kimball (1900–1976). American Methodism's first woman district superintendent. Born in Plainfield, New Jersey, Margaret Henrichsen earned her teacher's certificate in 1921, but after her husband's death in 1943 she moved to Maine to become a minister. She worked tirelessly to serve her seven congregations and complete her theological course of study. Her book, *Seven Steeples*, chronicles her time in Sullivan and reflects upon the challenges she faced as a clergywoman. Henrichsen was ordained a deacon in 1947 and an elder in 1949. In 1956 she was among the first women to be granted trial membership in the Annual Conferences of the Methodist Church, receiving full connection in 1958. In 1967 Henrichsen became district superintendent of Maine's Bangor District.

Nolan B. Harmon, ed., *Encyclopedia of World Methodism* (1974); Margaret Henrichsen, *Seven Steeples* (1953); Papers, New England Conference, Commission on Archives and History, United Methodist Church.

MANDY E. MCMICHAEL

Heron, Claire Elizabeth (1940–). Catholic educator and ecumenist. A compassionate bridge builder, Claire Heron's work in education, ecumenism, equity, and advocacy has been guided by her vision of a time when all people will be acknowledged for their innate giftedness and everyone will have a place at the table. The vocations of women in the churches and the visions ignited by the Second Vatican Council have been pivotal dynamics to Heron's life. Through the *Catholic Women's League (CWL) of Canada, she involved herself in the struggles and commitments of women of faith. Heron served as national CWL president, delegate to the Non-Governmental Organization (NGO) Women's Conference in Beijing, and elected member to the World Union of Catholic Women's Organizations (WUCWO). She was the Roman Catholic appointee to the ecumenical Women's Inter-Church Council of Canada (WICC) and past president.

VERONICA M. DUNNE, RNDM

Herron, Carrie Rand (1867–1914). Teacher and philanthropist. Carrie Rand was raised in Burlington, Iowa. In 1891 a new pastor, George Herron, and his wife came to the congregational church in her town. After two controversial years (because of Herron's socialism) Rand's mother, *Caroline Rand, gave $35,000 to Iowa College (now Grinnell) to endow a chair in Applied Christianity for George Herron. The Herrons and the Rands moved to Grinnell, where Rand served as instructor in physical education and principal for women. Herron's socialism was also controversial at the college, and he resigned in 1899. Mrs. Herron filed for divorce from him in 1900, and Herron and Rand married in 1901. They received so much negative publicity for the divorce and his remarriage that they moved to Italy in 1904, where they continued to work for social change. The Herrons had two sons.

ANB; NoAW; George D. Herron papers, Grinnell College Archives.

LYNN JAPINGA

Hiatt, Suzanne Radley (1936–2001). Episcopal priest and pastoral theology professor. Suzanne Hiatt was one of the first women ordained to the priesthood in the Episcopal Church in the U.S.A. (ECUSA). Born in Minneapolis, Suzanne ("Sue") Hiatt graduated from Radcliffe College (1958), the Episcopal Theological School (1964) and Boston University (1965). She was ordained deacon in 1971. A trained community organizer, Hiatt organized the first "irregular" ordinations of women to the Episcopal priesthood in Philadelphia on 29 July 1974. (Refer to the *Philadelphia 11.) In 1975 she joined the faculty of the Episcopal Divinity School (EDS), where she taught until her retirement in 1998. Hiatt was referred to as "the bishop of women" and traveled throughout the worldwide Anglican Communion in support of women's ordination.

Carter Heyward, *A Priest Forever* (1999) [1976]; Pamela Darling, *New Wine* (1994); Emily C. Hewitt and Suzanne R. Hiatt, *Women Priests Yes or No?* (1973); Papers, Archives of Women in Theological Scholarship, Burke Library, Union Theological Seminary.

SHERYL A. KUJAWA-HOLBROOK

Hill, Frances Maria Mulligan (1799–1884). Episcopal missionary and educator. Born in New York City, Frances Hill and her husband, the Reverend Henry Hill, volunteered as missionaries to Greece in the first foreign mission of the Episcopal Church. Hill ran all the schools at the mission for girls and women, including a boarding school, an elementary school, and an industrial school, while managing a household of 80. Her schools flourished throughout the 1830s, eventually serving over 5,000 students, and her teacher-training course was commended by educator Emma Willard. The girls' elementary school became one of the best in the country, with a curriculum that included ancient Greek, geography, and arithmetic. During her husband's furlough in the U.S. in 1841 Hill oversaw the entire mission.

NoAW; Sheryl A. Kujawa-Holbrook, *Freedom Is a Dream* (2002); Charles T. Bridgeman, "Mediterranean Missions," *Historical*

Magazine of the Episcopal Church (June 1962); Sarah Josepha Hale, ed., *Woman's Record* (1853).

SHERYL A. KUJAWA-HOLBROOK

Hill, Grace Livingston (1865–1947). Author. Grace Livingston was born to Charles M. and Marcia Macdonald Livingston in Wellsville, New York. She married Thomas Franklin Hill in 1892, and they had two daughters. Hill followed in the footsteps of her maternal aunt, *Isabella Macdonald Alden, and her mother, both of whom supplemented their husband's ministerial incomes through writing. Grace Hill's earliest work promoted the programs at Chautauqua as well as the young Christian Endeavor movement. After the death of her first husband in 1899 she pursued a writing career in earnest. She published several historical novels but found her niche in contemporary religious fiction. Hill was a prolific and financially successful author, producing two to three novels per year for her publisher, J. B. Lippincott Co. She built a large home in Swarthmore, Pennsylvania, where she resided until her death. Hill was a lifelong Presbyterian and became an active proponent of dispensational theology. She was a popular speaker at youth meetings and on the Bible conference circuit. She married Flavius Josephus Lutz in 1904, but they later separated. Hill's most popular novels include *The Witness, The Enchanted Barn,* and *Matched Pearls.*

Robert Munce, *Grace Livingston Hill* (1986); Jean Karr, *Grace Livingston Hill: Her Story and Her Writings* (1948).

VALERIE REMPEL

Hill, Mary Theresa Mehegan (1846–1921). Philanthropist. Mary Mehegan was born in New York City of Irish immigrant parents; the family moved to St. Paul, Minnesota, in 1850. Mehegan graduated from St. Joseph Academy and then worked as a waitress at the Merchant Hotel, where she met a young entrepreneur, James J. Hill. They married in 1867. Wife, mother of 10, and family administrator, she was also a gracious hostess who welcomed to their mansion millionaires of the Gilded Age, churchly dignitaries, and a U.S. president. She was involved in Catholic educational and charitable causes. Her Methodist millionaire husband built the Saint Paul Seminary and dedicated it to her, and she made substantial donations to the College (now University) of St. Thomas and the Saint Paul Seminary.

Mary Christine Athans, *To Work for the Whole People* (2002); Clara Hill Lindley, *James J. Hill and Mary T. Hill* (1948); James Jerome Hill and Family Papers, Minnesota Historical Society.

MARY CHRISTINE ATHANS

Hills, Marilla Turner Marks Hutchins (1807–1901). Educator and missionary. Marilla Turner was born in Arlington, Vermont. In 1829 she converted and married her first husband, Freewill Baptist leader and itinerant preacher David Marks. She attended Oberlin College from 1842 to 1845, but her studies were cut short by the death of her husband. She then married another Freewill Baptist leader, Elias Hutchins. She was active in support of the Underground Railway. For over 20 years, she was treasurer and then secretary of the Freewill Baptist Female Mission Society. In 1870 she married Orsemus Hills. In 1885, under the auspices of the Women's Missionary Society, she published her memoirs and correspondence with missionaries working in India.

EE; G. A. Burgess and J. T. Ward, *Free Baptist Cyclopedia* (1889); Marilla Turner Hills, *Missionary Reminiscences* (1885).

JUDITH L. GIBBARD

Hitschmanova, Lotta (1909–90). Humanitarian. Born in Prague, where she earned a PhD, Lotta Hitschmanova studied journalism in Paris and worked in Czechoslovakia as a freelance writer. She went into exile to escape the Nazis, and in 1944 she immigrated to Canada. (Her parents had died in the Holocaust.) She secured the help of the Ottawa Unitarian Congregation in forming a branch of the U.S. Unitarian Service Committee (USC) to collect clothes for European refugees. In 1948 the independent Unitarian Service Committee of Canada (USC) was chartered, thereby expanding a denominational project into a nondenominational international aid agency. Under her direction the USC went to Asia and Africa and innovatively advertised on television. Honored by the governments of France, Greece, South Korea, India, and Lesotho she received her country's highest award as Companion of the Order of Canada in 1979.

DUUB; Phillip Hewett, *Unitarians in Canada* (1995); Clyde Sanger, *Lotta and the Unitarian Service Committee Story* (1986).

IRENE BAROS-JOHNSON

Hockin, Katharine Boehner (1910–93). Missionary and educator. The daughter of Methodist missionaries, Katharine Hockin was born and raised in China. Hockin traveled to Canada at age 16 to complete high school, undergraduate studies, and diplomas in social work and education. She was among Emmanuel College's (Toronto) first female students, completed the first Woman's Missionary Society–sponsored doctorate and study in India. Hockin taught at the Ahousat (Vancouver Island) residential school and at the United Church Training School (Toronto). She worked with the Student Christian Movement as a missionary in China, and held administrative responsibilities at the Canadian School of Mission and Ecumenical Institute. She did volunteer work within the United Church of Canada and ecumenically. Hockin was instrumental in the evolution of missiology within the church.

M. Lucille Marr, "Naming Valiant Women," CSCH Historical Papers (1994); Mary Rose Donnelly and Heather Dau, *Katharine* (1992); Katharine Hockin, "My Pilgrimage in Mission," *International Bulletin of Missionary Research* 12, no. 1 (1988).

SARAH BRUER

Hoffer, Clara Schwartz (1887–1975). Author and pioneer. Clara Schwartz was born in Austria and immigrated to Canada in 1903, where she married another young Jewish immigrant, Israel Hoffer. She chronicled the stories of the Schwartz and Hoffer families in southeastern Saskatchewan in the books *Township Twenty-five* and *Land of Hope*. Originally written in Yiddish and then translated into English, these memoirs describe the determination and initiative that were necessary to maintain traditional Jewish life and to endure the harshness of the prairies.

Gerald Tulchinsky, *Taking Root: Origins of the Canadian Jewish Community* (1992); Clara Hoffer and F. H. Katan, *Township Twenty-five* [online] (1975), *Land of Hope* (1960); Simon Belkin, *Through Narrow Gates* (1966); Jewish Women's Archive, www.jwa.org; Personal papers, National Archives of Canada (Ottawa, Ontario).

TRUDY FLYNN

Hoffman, Fanny Binswanger (1862–1948). Jewish educator and lay leader. Fanny Binswanger was a well-traveled and highly educated daughter of a rabbi. Her father led Philadelphia's Maimonides School, the first Jewish American institution of higher learning, and she became the first principal of Mikveh Israel's Sunday school. Binswanger married a rabbi, Charles Hoffman. Hoffman's passion for children's religious education united her myriad commitments. She founded and led Philadelphia's *National Council of Jewish Women and the city's Young Women's Union. Hoffman also helped to found the *Women's League for Conservative Judaism (WLCJ) and served as its second president from 1919 to 1928. (The league's pioneering first president, *Mathilde Schechter, personally selected Hoffman as her successor.) Hoffman focused on the league's childhood education program. In 1940 the WLCJ crowned Hoffman's career, honoring her as Mother in Israel.

JWA; National Women's League, *They Dared to Dream* (1967); Obituary, *New York Times* (16 August 1948).

DEBORAH SKOLNICK EINHORN

Hoge, Jane Currie Blaikie ("Mrs. A. H. Hoge") (1811–90). Relief and welfare worker, churchwoman. *Dorothea Dix appointed Jane Blaikie Hoge and Mary Livermore to serve as general army nurses and recruiters for army hospitals during the Civil War. In March 1862 Hoge toured hospitals in Illinois, Kentucky, Missouri, and elsewhere. Recognizing the unsanitary conditions for patient care she became a leader in sanitary reform. Hoge and Livermore were appointed directors of the Chicago branch of the U.S. Sanitary Commission at the general conference in Washington, DC, in December 1862. They instigated a campaign that motivated aid societies in the Northwest to gather clothing, medical supplies, food, and other necessities for hospitals. Hoge's experiences are recorded in *The Boys in Blue* (1867). Hoge also served as general secretary of the Pittsburgh Orphan Asylum, helped to create the Home for the Friendless in Chicago, and headed the Woman's Presbyterian Board of Foreign Missions in the Northwest.

NoAW; WBC.

ELIZABETH HINSON-HASTY

Hooten, Elizabeth (ca. 1600–1672). Quaker missionary. Elizabeth Hooten, wife of Oliver Hooten, a prosperous farmer in Nottinghamshire, became George Fox's first convert and the first woman Quaker preacher. Her final 20 years were spent in and out of prison as she preached, traveled, and published. During her three trips to New England in the 1660s, officials repeatedly imprisoned, whipped, and banished her. She died in Jamaica while traveling with George Fox.

EE; Phyllis Mack, "Gender and Spirituality in Early England Quakerism, 1650–1665," in *Witness for Change: Quaker Women over Three Centuries*, ed. Elizabeth Potts Brown and Susan Mosher Stuard (1989); Emily Manners, *Elizabeth Hooten* (1914); James Bowden, *The History of the Society of Friends in America*, vol. 1 (1850).

JOAN R. GUNDERSEN

Hope, Lugenia Burns (1871–1947). Community leader and social reformer. In 1897 Lugenia Burns married John Hope, future president of Atlanta Baptist College (Morehouse College). The following year she collaborated with W. E. B. DuBois and Gertrude Ware in a project that launched her 25 years of visionary leadership in Atlanta's Neighborhood Union. An internationally renowned organization that modeled community development and justice advocacy, the Neighborhood Union's core leaders were educated, middle-class African American women. Establishing and funding a wide range of services in the black community (e.g., public health, sanitation, education, playgrounds), the union also exerted political pressure against government neglect of the city's black neighborhoods and against the blatant discrimination of separate-but-equal education. Adept at alliance building and uncompromisingly committed to justice, Hope led the African American *YWCA in demanding autonomous status and created cross-race alliances in the antilynching movement. As Atlanta NAACP officer in 1932, she developed citizenship schools, a strategy replicated in the later civil rights movement.

BWA; BWARC; NBAW; Jacqueline A. Rouse, *Lugenia Burns Hope* (1989); Papers, Robert W. Woodruff Library, Atlanta University Center.

MARGARET MCMANUS

Hopkins, Emma Curtis (1849–1925). New Thought thinker and teacher. Raised in New England, Emma Hopkins heard a talk in 1883 by *Mary Baker Eddy and enrolled in Eddy's courses. Eddy appointed her editor of the *Journal of Christian Science* in 1884, but expelled her from Christian Science a year later. She moved to Chicago without her husband and cofounded the Emma Curtis Hopkins College of Christian Science and *Truth: A Magazine of Christian Science*, but split with her female colleague. When the first college class graduated in 1889 Hopkins ordained them without regard to gender, the first woman in American history to ordain other women. She realized that this was both a feminist and a religious act; she believed God's feminine side was revealing itself on earth through women's leadership. In 1894 she closed the college and moved to New York, where she saw private students and patients. Hopkins divorced in 1901 and lived celibately thereafter, writing and publishing her studies in *High Mysticism*. She was arguably the most important thinker in the New Thought movement. Her students included the founders of the Unity School of Christianity, Religious Science, Homes of Truth, and Divine Science.

ANB; DARB; EAWR; NoAW; RLA; WBC; Gail M. Harley, *Emma Curtis Hopkins* (2002).

GRAEME SHARROCK

Hopkins, Mattie (1917–88). Episcopal educator and social activist. Mattie Hopkins received degrees from the Tuskegee Institute and the University of Chicago. She taught in the South, and for the Chicago school system from 1951 to 1983. Hopkins was active in many Chicago civic, educational, and church organizations. In the 1960s she was the president of the Chicago chapter of the Episcopal Society for Cultural and Racial Unity (ESCRU) and sought employment for African Americans in the construction of the Diocese of Chicago headquarters. She was instrumental in the founding of the Union of Black Episcopalians and was also a board member of the Episcopal Urban Caucus. In 1988 Hopkins received the prestigious Vida Scudder Award for outstanding contributions to the social mission of the church, presented by the Episcopal Publishing Company.

"Hopkins: Taught by Being, Doing," *The Witness* 71 (September 1988).

SHERYL A. KUJAWA-HOLBROOK

Hopkins, Sarah Winnemucca (ca. 1844–91). Intercultural mediator. As a young woman, Sarah Winnemucca (Paiute) worked as an interpreter for the U.S. Army at Fort McDermitt (Nevada) and Camp Harney (Oregon). After a brief marriage to a lieutenant, she moved to the Malheur Reservation (Oregon) and worked as a teacher and interpreter. She translated for the military during the Bannock War of 1878 and then moved to the Yakima Reservation (Washington), where she witnessed the ill treatment of Paiute prisoners. Angered by the government's refusal to restore the Malheur lands to the Paiute people, Winnemucca gave lectures to publicize their plight, traveling to Washington, DC, in 1880. Rebuffed, she continued to lecture and published her *Life among the Piutes* (1883). She returned to Nevada to establish a school for Paiute children. Discouraged and ending her second marriage to former soldier Lewis H. Hopkins, she moved to

Idaho to be with her sister and died soon thereafter.

NaAW; Gae W. Canfield, *Sarah Winnemucca of the Northern Paiutes* (1983).

LISA J. POIRIER

Horton, Isabelle (1852–1933). Methodist deaconess, editor, and writer. Isabelle Horton grew up in Michigan, where she taught in public schools for 14 years. She graduated from the Chicago [Deaconess] Training School (CTS) in 1893. After a year in Milwaukee she returned to Chicago to become editor of the *Messenger* (later *Deaconess Advocate*) for eight years and an instructor at CTS. During the 1900s and 1910s she served as superintendent of deaconess homes in Chicago, St. Louis, and New York City, and spent seven years developing a vigorous program of friendly visiting and organized activities for the neighborhood at the Halsted Street Institutional Church on Chicago's West Side. Through her writing, teaching, and active service, Horton helped to define the nature and scope of deaconess work at the turn of the 19th century.

Carolyn DeSwarte Gifford, *The American Deaconess Movement in the Early 20th Century* (1987); Isabelle Horton, *The Builders* (1910), *High Adventure* (1928).

CAROLYN DESWARTE GIFFORD

Hosmer, Elizabeth ("Sister Rachel") (1908–88). Episcopal religious, priest, and founding member of the Order of Saint Helena. Born in Massachusetts, Elizabeth Hosmer was exposed to Christianity through friends and was confirmed in the Episcopal Church at age 16. Academically and artistically gifted she studied painting and had contact with various religious communities. Hosmer made her life profession in the Order of Saint Anne in 1935. She served several years as a school principal and then felt called to a more monastic form of the religious life. In 1945 she helped found the Order of Saint Helena. Sister Rachel was a popular retreat leader, teacher, spiritual director, and writer, and was active in civil disobedience and the peace movement. She worked for three years in West Africa, and later she worked in New York City, where she was ordained to the diaconate (1975) and the priesthood (1977).

Sheryl A. Kujawa-Holbrook, *Freedom Is a Dream* (2002); Rachel Hosmer, *My Life Remembered* (1991).

SHERYL A. KUJAWA-HOLBROOK

Howard, Clara (d. 1935). Baptist missionary and educator. Clara Howard entered Spelman Seminary in 1881, graduated as valedictorian of the first high school class in 1887, and taught in schools throughout rural Georgia. Under the auspices of the Woman's American Baptist Foreign Mission Society, she served as a missionary in the Congo from 1890 to 1895, where she administered Lukungu Seminary, a primary school. She then worked in Panama until frail health forced her to return to the U.S. in 1897. She was the matron of the boarding department at Spelman and taught in the school of missions until her retirement in 1928. She helped to organize the Spelman alumnae association, and served as its president from 1892 to 1923. Her adopted daughter, Congolese orphan Flora Zeto, graduated from Spelman in 1915 and settled in Nyasaland (Malawi) as a Baptist missionary.

BWARC; Beverly Guy-Sheftall and Jo Moore Stewart, *Spelman: A Centennial Celebration* (1981); Florence Matilda Read, *The Story of Spelman College* (1961).

SCOTT D. SEAY

Howe, Julia Ward (1819–1910). Abolitionist, poet, preacher, and social activist. Julia Ward received little formal education but learned music, several languages, and read widely on her own. She married Dr. Samuel Howe in 1843. Her husband was 18 years older than she, and although they had six children, their marriage was not a particularly happy one. Howe wrote "The Battle Hymn of the Republic" in 1861, but she also published poetry, plays, articles, a biography of *Margaret Fuller Ossoli, and a memoir. During the last four decades of her life she traveled, organized, administered, and lectured for women's suffrage, the peace movement, and women's clubs. She was president of the New England Woman Suffrage Association (1868–77, 1893–1910) and worked with the American Woman Suffrage Association. She wanted to help free women from restrictive marriages, gender roles, and the ideology of separate spheres. She called for a Mother's Peace Day, which developed into the May Mother's Day observance. She was the first woman named to the American Academy of Arts and Letters, and received honorary degrees from Tufts, Brown, and Smith College.

ANB; DUUB; EAWR; EE; NoAW; Valarie Ziegler, *Diva Julia* (2003); Mary Grant, *Private Woman, Public Person* (1994); Julia Ward Howe, *Reminiscences* (1899).

LYNN JAPINGA

Huber, Jane Parker (1926–). Presbyterian laywoman, elder, and hymn text writer. Jane Parker was born in Jinan, China, to Presbyterian missionaries, but grew up on the campus of Hanover College in Indiana, where her father served as president. She graduated from Wellesley College and in 1947 married William Huber, a future Presbyterian pastor. In 1976, after raising six children and carrying out the many responsibilities of a pastor's wife, Huber began a new venture of writing hymn texts that were inclusive and contemporary. She is the author of *A Singing Faith* (1987) and *Singing in Celebration* (1996), and served on the Presbyterian Hymnal Committee chaired by Melva W. Costen. Huber served the church on all levels, including on the national executive committee of United Presbyterian Women (1973–76) and on the council on Women and the Church (1979–87). She is a strong advocate for social justice issues throughout the church and society. Huber was honored as a Valiant Woman by *Church Women United (1991) and was given a Presbyterian Women Honorary Life Membership (1992).

Patricia Lloyd-Sidle, ed., *Celebrating Our Call* (2006); Howard Rice and Lamar Williamson, eds., *A Book of Reformed Prayers* (1998); Elizabeth Howell Verdesi and Sylvia Thorson-Smith, *A Sampler of Saints* (1988).

LINDA B. BREBNER

Huerta, Dolores (1930–). Labor organizer, activist, and cofounder of the United Farm Workers of America (UFW). Raised in the Central San Joaquin Valley, Dolores Huerta developed her concern for migrant families when she was a teacher to the farm workers' children and saw firsthand the privations and indignities they suffered daily. Prompted by the legendary labor organizer Fred Ross, Huerta began what would be her life's work. She was a community activist in Stockton, California, and then cofounded with César Chávez and others the UFA in 1962. Huerta became the first vice president of the UFA. A highly skilled strategist and negotiator, Huerta helped create a powerful leverage for migrants, surely among the most exploited laborers in the country.

NoHAW; Alicia Chávez, "Dolores Huerta and the United Farm Workers," in *Latina Legacies*, ed. Vicki L. Ruiz and Virginia Sánchez Korrol (2005); UFW Collection, Walter P. Reuther Library Archives, Wayne State University.

MARY JANE O'DONNELL

Hull, Hannah Hallowell Clothier (1872–1958). Peace activist and suffragist. From a wealthy Philadelphia family, Hannah Clothier graduated from Swarthmore College in 1891 and married William Hull in 1898. Hull was active in settlement house work and women's suffrage, and served as vice president of the Pennsylvania Woman Suffrage Association (1913–14). Pacifism drew her into the Woman's Peace Party, and she headed the Pennsylvania chapter. A founding member of the Women's International League for Peace and Freedom (WILPF), she held many leadership positions, advocating total disarmament through petition drives, lobbying, and international agitation. Active in the American Friends Service Committee, the American Association of University Women, and the Association for Social and Educational Work with Negroes, she remained honorary president of the WILPF until her death.

ANB; NoAWMP; Harriet Hyman Alonso, *Peace as a Woman's Issue* (1993); Gertrude Bussey and Margaret Tims, *Pioneers for Peace* (1965); Papers, Swarthmore College Peace Collection.

JANET MOORE LINDMAN

Hultin, Ida C. (1858–1938). Unitarian minister and suffragist. Raised a Congregationalist, Ida Hultin took teacher training at the University of Michigan. She taught at liberal churches in Battle Creek, Sherwood, and Athens, Michigan, sometimes traveling 40 miles a day on her horse. She replaced *Mary Safford in Algona, Iowa. Hultin was ordained in 1886. She served in Des Moines (1886–91) and in Moline, Illinois (1891–98). She was an Illinois delegate to the National Suffrage Convention held in Washington, DC, in 1887. Throughout the 1890s she campaigned for suffrage in Michigan, Illinois, Nebraska, and Minnesota. She was settled in Allston, Massachusetts, in 1900, and represented that state at the suffrage convention, preaching to a great crowd at the Unitarian Church in Washington, DC. She ministered in Sudbury, Massachusetts (1903–16).

UUWM; ; Cynthia Grant Tucker, *Prophetic Sisterhood* (1990); Susan B. Anthony and Ida Husted Harper, *History of Woman Suffrage*, vol. 4 (1902).

IRENE BAROS-JOHNSON

Hume, Sophia Wigington (ca. 1702–74). Quaker preacher. Born into a prosperous Charleston, South Carolina, family, Sophia Wigington was reared as an Anglican, the tradition of her father. Her mother was a Quaker, as was her maternal grandmother, *Mary Fisher. In 1721 she married Robert Hume, a lawyer and wealthy landowner. Hume became accustomed to a life of luxury. By 1740, however, two serious illnesses and the death of her husband convinced her to move to London, join the Society of Friends, and dedicate herself to a life of simplicity. In 1747 she returned to Charleston to call the self-indulgent to repentance. After a year she returned to London, where she preached a similar message and published numerous tracts. The city's meeting recognized her as a minister in 1763. She made one final journey to Charleston in 1767 to revive the dying Quaker community. Unable to win enough support to construct a new meetinghouse she returned to London, where she died.

ANB; NoAW.

SCOTT D. SEAY

Hunton, Addie D. Waites (1875–1943). Advocate and suffragist. An Episcopalian, Addie Hunton was a lifelong advocate for African Americans. She married a YMCA official, William Hurton, and she traveled extensively to encourage African Americans to become involved in the organization. She worked for the YMCA after her husband's death in 1916, and organized religious and educational programs for over 1,000 African American troops in northern France. In the three years before her return to the U.S., Hunton observed many injustices faced by African American soldiers. Once home, she focused on causes associated with African American women. Hunton held leadership positions with the Women's International League for Peace and Freedom, the *YWCA, and the suffrage department of the NAACP. She was also instrumental in challenging the National Woman's Party to support black women voters in the South.

BWARC; NBAW; NoAW; Paula Giddings, *When and Where I Enter* (1984); Sylvia Dannett, *Profiles of Negro Womanhood* (1966); Elizabeth Lindsay Davis, *Lifting As They Climb* (1933).

SHERYL A. KUJAWA-HOLBROOK

Hutchinson, Anne Marbury (1591–1643). Religious dissenter. The daughter of an Anglican clergyman who encouraged her study of Scripture and doctrine, Anne Marbury was born in Alford, England. She married businessman William Hutchinson and gave birth to 12 children. Hutchinson was a skilled midwife and herbalist, and a supporter of Puritan vicar John Cotton. In 1634 the family followed Cotton to the Massachusetts Bay Colony. Hutchinson started a weekly meeting in her home for women to discuss Cotton's sermons and exchange household advice. Soon she added a second meeting, and men began to attend her gatherings; Hutchinson was then accused of spreading antinomianism. Instead of looking to laws of church and state to regulate behavior, antinomians relied on the inner guidance of Christ. Hutchinson was brought to civil trial in November 1637. Puritans believed that women were adept at spreading false doctrine; also, Hutchinson seemed to exemplify antinomian chaos by leading gender-mixed meetings. To violate divine law was to court divine wrath in a colony already threatened by Native Americans and new immigrants. Hutchinson refuted the charges against her, revealing her knowledge of the Bible and church history. Just as the case against her seemed to be collapsing, however, she claimed that God spoke directly to her. Since Puritans condemned direct revelation, she was banished from the colony. The family moved to Rhode Island and then to the shores of Long Island Sound, where they were later killed by Native Americans.

ANB; DARB; EAWR; NoAW; David Hall, *The Antinomian Controversy* (1990).

BARBARA J. MACHAFFIE

Immaculate Heart Community (1969–). Ecumenical Christian community. The community resulted from a dispute between the California Institute of the Sisters of the Most Holy and *Immaculate Heart of Mary (IHM) Sisters and Los Angeles Cardinal James F. McIntyre. Independent of their Spanish origins since 1924, the California IHMs ministered in education, health care, and retreat work. In the 1960s tensions developed over reforms the community's governing chapters had approved. When the dispute with the cardinal could not be resolved, some 400 sisters reluctantly requested dispensations from their vows. Led by *Anita Caspary, about 300 sisters established the Immaculate Heart Community, and about 50 sisters remained in the canonical congregation. In 2000 the canonical group had about 20 sisters, while the new community had about 175 women and men, single and married, from different Christian denominations, who engaged in various ministries.

NCE; Anita M. Caspary, *Witness to Integrity* (2003).

ANNE E. PATRICK, SNJM

Immaculate Heart of Mary (IHM) Sisters (1845–). Roman Catholic congregations of women religious. Founded as *Sisters of Providence at Monroe, Michigan, by Rev. Louis Gillet and *Oblate Sister of Providence *Theresa Maxis Duchemin, the community changed its name in 1847 to Sisters, Servants of the Immaculate Heart of Mary. In 1857 Detroit Bishop Peter Paul Lefevere installed Rev. Edward Joos as superior over Duchemin, who in 1858 sent sisters to teach in Pennsylvania. After a conflict with Lefevere, the congregation divided in 1859; 12 sisters remained in Michigan and 12 sisters remained in Pennsylvania with Duchemin. The latter group became two foundations in 1871, one in Scranton and the other near Philadelphia. Each congregation staffed schools and founded a college: Marygrove (Detroit), Marywood (Scranton), and Immaculata (Philadelphia). For decades the groups had little contact, but in the 1960s Tri-IHM collaboration began with educational conferences, blossoming in the 1990s with celebrations that inspired IHMs to reconnect also with the Oblates, the first congregation for women religious of African American descent. A historic Oblate/Tri-IHM gathering took place at Immaculata in 2005, attended by some 950 sisters from the four congregations. The combined IHM membership was then about 2,100, with sisters engaged in educational, pastoral, and other ministries in the U.S. and abroad.

EACH; NCE; ROWUS; Michel Keenan, *The Sisters, Servants of the Immaculate Heart of Mary—Scranton, Pennsylvania* (2005); IHM Sisters, *Building Sisterhood* (1997); Margaret Gannon, *Paths of Daring, Deeds of Hope* (1992); Rosalita Kelly, *No Greater Service* (1948).

ANNE E. PATRICK, SNJM

International Association of Women Ministers (IAWM) (1919–). Interdenominational professional association. Begun in St. Louis by Methodist preacher M. Madeline Southard (1877–1967), the IAWM offered resources and social support for female clergy long before denominations developed their own ministerial groups for women. Its periodical, the *Woman's Pulpit*, has reported on the status of gender equality in denominations, nationally and internationally, since 1922. Although initially a largely Methodist and midwestern undertaking, its social base has become increasingly diverse and international. After more than 75 years of work, this small group of mostly mainline Protestants continues to strive for women's access to religious leadership.

Kendra Weddle Irons, *Preaching on the Plains* (2007); Margaret Bendroth, *Women and Twentieth-Century Protestantism* (2002); Records, Archives of Women in Theological Scholarship, Burke Library, Union Theological Seminary (New York City).

CATHERINE BOWLER

Ireland, Ellen ("Mother Seraphine") (1842–1930). Catholic religious leader. Born in Ireland, Ellen Ireland immigrated with her family at age eight to Vermont. They settled in Minnesota, where she met women in the *Sisters of St. Joseph of Carondelet. She joined the congregation in 1858 and quickly demonstrated a genius for leadership. She assumed directorship of St. Joseph Academy, St. Paul, at age 19. She went on to open several parochial schools and to direct an orphanage before being named superior of the St. Paul Province in 1882. She traveled extensively in the U.S., Canada, and Europe and guided the establishment of 48 institutions, including the College of St. Catherine for women, St. Agatha's Conservatory of Music and Art, several academies, over 30 parochial schools, and five hospitals. The St. Paul province membership grew from 160 at the time she assumed its leadership in 1882 to 913 in the year of her death.

Ann Thomasine Sampson, *Seeds on Good Ground: Biographies of 16 Pioneer Sisters of St. Joseph of Carondelet* (2000); Judy Barrett Litoff and Judith McDonnell, eds., *European Immigrant Women in the United States* (1994); Patricia Johnston, "Reflected Glory: The Story of Ellen Ireland," *Minnesota History* 48, no. 1 (Spring 1982); Helen Angela Hurley, *On Good Ground* (1951).

KAREN M. KENNELLY, CSJ

Isasi-Diaz, Ada-Maria (1943–). Latina activist and theologian. Born in Havana, Ada-Maria Isasi-Diaz left Cuba as a political refugee in 1960. She attended college in the U.S. and then traveled to Lima, Peru, in 1967 as a missionary sister with the Order of St. Ursula. In Peru she became committed to social justice and solidarity with the poor. Back in the U.S. in 1975, she attended the first *Women's Ordination Conference and realized that oppression is linked to poverty and gender. She received a PhD from Union Theological Seminary (New York City) in 1990. Her writing and research focus on theology from the perspective of Latina women in the U.S. She has been professor of ethics and theology at Drew University in New Jersey since 1991.

Ann Braude, ed., *Transforming the Faiths of Our Fathers* (2004); Ada-Maria Isasi-Diaz, *En La Lucha/In the Struggle*, 2nd ed. (2003) [1994].

COLLEEN CARPENTER CULLINAN

Jackson, Mahalia (1911–72). Gospel singer. Mahalia Jackson was born into poverty in New Orleans, Louisiana, but moved to Chicago at the age of 15. She blended the sacred music of her strict Baptist roots with the energetic worship of the Holiness tradition and the sounds of jazz and blues, an eclectic mélange that shaped the emergence of African American gospel music. Despite her limited formal education, Jackson was a shrewd entrepreneur. She refused to perform jazz or blues because of her religious convictions, but she helped make gospel music commercially successful. Her breakthrough 1946 recording, "Move On Up a Little Higher," sold over 8 million copies and made her an international star. She was active in the civil rights movement of the 1950s and 1960s. She was twice married and divorced.

ANB; BWA; EAWR; NBAW; NoAWMP; RLA; WBC; Laurraine Goreau, *Just Mahalia, Baby* (1975); Mahalia Jackson, *Movin' On Up* (1966).

KENDAL P. MOBLEY

Jackson, Rebecca Cox (1795–1871). Founder of a Shaker community for blacks. Born black and free, Rebecca Cox grew up close to the Bethel African Methodist Episcopal Church in Philadelphia, where her older brother Joseph was an elder and the famed Richard Allen was pastor. She married Samuel S. Jackson in 1830, but that same year she was spiritually awakened and began to preach in favor of holiness and against sexual union. Shunned by local churches, she was increasingly attracted to the feminine aspect of deity offered in Shaker theology, to the practice of celibacy, and to spiritualism. She lived in the predominantly white Shaker community at Watervliet, New York, until 1851, when she left with Rebecca Perot to start a community in Philadelphia for blacks that lasted until about 1900. Her extraordinary diary, *Gifts of Power*, shows how visions and dreams empowered her radical actions.

ANB; BWA; NBAW; Jean McMahon Humez, ed., *Gifts of Power* (1981).

GRAEME SHARROCK

Jacobs, Ruth Krehbiel (1897–1960). Music educator and founder of the Chorister's Guild. Born to Henry J. and Lydia D. Ruth Krehbiel, Ruth Krehbiel was educated at Bluffton College (Ohio), a Mennonite school, and the Hochschule für Musik at the University of Berlin. In 1929 she married Arthur Leslie Jacobs. Ruth Jacobs began her teaching career at the high school and college levels before accepting a job as a church musician. Her work with children brought her national recognition, and she became a frequent lecturer at music festivals and seminars as well as a staff member at Marlborough School in Los Angeles. In 1949 she founded the Choristers Guild, serving as its first president. The guild was founded to nurture the spiritual life of children through children's choirs. She also founded the Brotherhood of Song in 1958 to work internationally.

Art Clemens, "Recollections and Remembrances of Ruth and Leslie Jacobs," *The Chorister* (September 1999); Ruth Unrau, "Letting the Children Sing," in *Encircled: Stories of Mennonite Women* (1986).

VALERIE REMPEL

Jameelah, Maryam (1934–). Muslim convert and author. Maryam Jameelah was born Margaret Marcus in New Rochelle, New York, of nonobservant Jewish parents. In 1960 she began corresponding with Mawlana Abdul Ala Mawdudi of the Islamic Society of Pakistan, and then formally converted in 1961. At Mawdudi's invitation and with the support of Muslim leaders in the U.S. and abroad she moved to Pakistan in 1962. She became the second wife of Mohammad Yusuf Khan. Her many writings in English (translated into many other languages) defend orthodox Islam from secularist and modernist critics. She views Westernization and modernization as threats to the universal truth of Islam, and defends the superiority of Islamic teachings of polygamy and purdah.

John L. Esposito and John O. Voll, *Makers of Contemporary Islam* (2001); Papers, Manuscripts, and Archives Division, Humanities and Social Science Library, New York Public Library.

BARBARA E. REED

Jetsunma Ahkon Lhamo (Catharine Burroughs) (1949–). First Western woman recognized as a reincarnated Tibetan lama. Born Alyce Zeoli in Brooklyn, New York, and raised as a Roman Catholic, Zeoli married Michael Burroughs and changed her name to Catharine Burroughs. Burroughs met H. H. Penor Rinpoche, a high-ranking Tibetan lama, in 1985. She had not been a practicing Buddhist prior to Penor Rinpoche's recognition of her as a bodhisattva, but had been leading a New Age spiritual group in her basement. In 1988 she was enthroned as the reincarnation of a 16th-century Tibetan saint, one of the founders of the Nyingma sect's Palyul tradition, becoming the first U.S. woman *tulku* or reincarnated lama. Jetsunma established a thriving temple in rural Maryland, the Kunzang Palyul Chöling (KPC), which is one of the largest ordained communities in North America.

Martha Sherrill, *The Buddha from Brooklyn* (2000).

BARBARA E. REED

Jeunesse Ouvrière Chrétienne Féminine (JOCF) (1931–). Youth movement for female Catholic workers. Originating in Belgium, the JOCF and its male counterpart, the Jeunesse Ouvrière Catholique (JOC), received official papal approval in 1925. Under the influence of the Oblate priest, Henri Roy, the movement came to Canada where a local JOCF unit emerged in Montreal. The movement recruited blue-collar Catholic youth who entered the workforce in their early teen years. Even though the church's leadership used the JOCF as a base to train adolescent women to be dutiful wives and mothers, the presence of these women on the assembly lines drove them to more independent thinking and action. Soon they engaged in social analysis, public speaking, journalistic endeavors, union organizing, and strike actions that led them outside the boundaries advocated by their church. By the 1960s JOCF members gradually abandoned their more traditional views and challenged their male comrades through feminist analysis in order to buttress gender egalitarianism.

Susan B. Whitney, "Gender, Class, and Generation in Interwar French Catholicism," *Journal of Family History* 26, no. 4 (Oct. 2001); ; Jean Hamelin, *Histoire du catholicisme québécois*, vol. 2 (1984); Gabriel Clément, *Histoire de l'action catholique au Canada français* (1972).

OSCAR COLE-ARNAL

Jewish Orthodox Feminist Alliance (JOFA) (1997–). Feminist organization. Founded in the wake of a successful conference on feminism and Orthodoxy, JOFA is committed to expanding the role of women within the framework of Orthodox Judaism. *Blu Greenberg helped lead the organization from a small group to an internationally known presence in the Jewish world. JOFA organizes biannual conferences that bring together Jewish scholars, religious leaders, and laypeople to discuss ways to increase women's participation in Judaism. It also publishes a quarterly newsletter. It has demanded greater attention from the Orthodox community to women's issues, including infertility, women's education, and meaningful leadership roles for women, as well as advocating for the status of women whose husbands do not grant them religiously valid divorces. By arguing that these matters are concerns of the entire Jewish community, JOFA has worked to bring them from the periphery to the center of Orthodox life. Some Orthodox leaders believe that the activism of JOFA places it on the fringes—or even outside of—Orthodoxy, while others see it as leading the way toward a more vibrant Orthodox Judaism.

Debra Nussbaum Cohen, "Successful Conference Spawns New Orthodox Feminist Alliance," *Jewish Telegraphic Agency* (July 4, 1997).

LILA CORWIN BERMAN

Johnson, Sonia Harris (1936–). Educator and activist for the Equal Rights Amendment (ERA). Sonia Harris was raised in a devout Latter-day Saints Church (LDS) or Mormon family. She graduated from Utah State University and later earned an MA and an EdD. She married Richard Johnson, and they had four children. She began to work for the ERA in 1977 and was a cofounder of Mormons for the ERA. She testified at a U.S. Senate Constitutional Rights Subcommittee in 1978 to ask for more time to ratify the ERA. In September 1979 she gave a speech entitled "Patriarchal Panic: Sexual Politics in the Mormon Church" at the American Psychological Association in New York City. She protested in favor of the ERA and opposed the LDS's efforts to defeat it. Excommunicated by the LDS in December 1979 she wrote about her experiences in *From Housewife to Heretic* (1981).

EAWR; Collection, J. Willard Marriot Library, University of Utah.

LYNN JAPINGA

Johnson, Susan Christine (1958–). First woman national bishop, Evangelical Lutheran Church in Canada (ELCIC). Born in Saskatchewan, Susan Johnson grew up in London, Ontario, and Vancouver, British Columbia. Johnson began her career as a parish pastor in London, Ontario (1992–94). She has served as an advisor to the Lutheran World Federation Council (LWF) since 1998 and as a member of the North American regional committee for LWF since 2005. She sits on numerous national and synodical-level boards, committees, and task forces. From 2001 to 2005 she served as vice president of the ELCIC. In 2003 she was appointed an Ecumenical Canon in the Anglican Diocese of Niagara. From 1994 to her 2007 election as national bishop, Johnson was assistant to the bishop of the Eastern Synod of the ELCIC. Johnson is a visionary, a strong leader, and committed to helping the church to be in mission for others.

News Release, ELCIC (22 June 2007), www.elcic.ca.

ALAN KA LUN LAI

Jones, Martha Garner (1866–1959). Unitarian Universalist minister and equal rights advocate. Martha Garner was ordained by the Unitarian Universalist Church in New Salem, Illinois, in 1894. Shortly thereafter she married circuit rider minister Leon Jones, and together they formed one of the first husband-and-wife coministry teams. They shared ministrial responsibilities, such as preaching, education, and pastoral care, and served parishes in southern Ontario and the U.S. Midwest. While serving at Olinda, Ontario, they spearheaded the successful fight to win an amendment to the Ontario marriage law that recognized the right of women clergy to solemnize marriages. Canadian Unitarian Universalists recognize her birthday, August 24, in their liturgical almanac and calendar.

UUWM; Unitarian Fellowship: Historical Overview, cuuf.net/uusi/uusi.html.

LOUISE GRAVES

Jones, Rebecca (1739–1818). Quaker preacher. Born in Philadelphia to Anglican parents, Rebecca Jones was educated in the school that her mother conducted in their home. She attended Quaker meetings with some of her friends, and their faith made a deep impression upon her. By 1758 she had become a Quaker. Upon her mother's death in 1761 Jones took over her school and administered it for the next 20 years. She also became a powerful preacher among the Philadelphia Quakers. Beginning in 1784 she undertook four years of missionary work in England, Wales, and Scotland. Upon her return to Philadelphia in 1788 she opened a small fabric store to earn a living. She continued preaching, especially in New Jersey and New England, and was instrumental in founding the Westtown (Pennsylvania) Boarding School, which began operation in 1799.

ANB; NoAW.

SCOTT D. SEAY

Jones, Sybil (1808–73). Quaker minister and educator. Born in Brunswick, Maine, Sybil Jones attended the Friends School in Providence, Rhode Island; became a Quaker minister; and taught public school. In 1833 she married fellow schoolteacher Eli Jones; the couple had five children. The Joneses were Gurneyite Quakers, those influenced by evangelicals, and served as ministers in Canada and in the U.S. Despite fragile health Jones felt called in 1851 to preach in Liberia. After two months in Africa, the couple traveled throughout Western Europe. During the American Civil War they ministered to wounded soldiers. After the assassination of President Lincoln, Sybil Jones consoled his widow and counseled his successor. In 1867 the Joneses journeyed to Palestine and Syria and established a girls' school in Ramallah.

ANB; NoAW; Rufus Jones, *Eli and Sybil Jones* (1889); Ellen Clare Miller, *Eastern Sketches* (1871); Jones Family Papers, Special Collections, Haverford College.

JANET MOORE LINDMAN

Joseph Gaudet, Frances (1861–1934). Prison reformer and educator. Frances Joseph was born in Mississippi of African American and Native American descent. Widowed young, she dedicated her life to prison reform. Beginning in 1894 she held prayer meetings, wrote letters, delivered messages, and secured clothing for black prisoners, and later, for white prisoners. She won the respect of prison officials, city authorities, the governor, and the Prison Reform Association. A delegate to the *Woman's Christian Temperance Union international convention in 1900, she advocated for black youth arrested for misdemeanors. Joseph Gaudet was the first woman to support homeless juvenile offenders in Louisiana and helped found the juvenile court. In 1902 she purchased a farm and founded the Gaudet Normal and Industrial School. Joseph Gaudet served as principal until 1921, when it was donated to the Episcopal Diocese of Louisiana. Closed in 1950, the Gaudet Episcopal Home opened in the same location four years later to serve African American children. The Frances Joseph Gaudet endowment fund supports African American children through Episcopal Community Services in the Diocese of Louisiana.

NBAW; "Frances Joseph Gaudet," *Louisiana Leaders: Notable Women in History* (LSU Libraries, 1995–98); Girault M. Jones, *Some Personal Recollections of the Episcopal Church in Louisana* (1980); Carter Hodding and Betty Werlein Carter, *So Great a Good* (1955); Frances Joseph-Gaudet, *He Leadeth Me* (1913).

SHERYL A. KUJAWA-HOLBROOK

Judson, Ann Hasseltine (1789–1826). Baptist missionary. Born in Bradford, Massachusetts, Ann Hasseltine married Adoniram Judson two weeks before they sailed for India as Congregational missionaries in 1812. During the long voyage, Judson's husband began to question the validity of infant baptism on New Testament grounds, but she resisted it. Both finally adopted Baptist sentiments in India and were baptized. Appealing to Baptists in the U.S. for support, they sailed to Burma in 1813 to escape deportation by the British. Judson returned only once to the U.S., for the sake of her health, during 1822 and 1823. In Burma, Judson evangelized women, educated girls, translated biblical texts and religious literature, and maintained an invaluable correspondence. Her husband probably would not have survived 11 months in a Burmese prison without her heroic intervention. Her first child was stillborn; her second, a son, died at seven months; her third, a daughter, died when she was just over two years old—six months after Judson's death.

ANB; EAWR; EE; HDB; NoAW; James D. Knowles, comp., *Memoir of Mrs. Ann H. Judson* (1831); Ann Hasseltine Judson, *A Particular Relation of the American Baptist Mission to the Burman Empire* (1823).

KENDAL P. MOBLEY

Judson, Emily Chubbock (1817–54). Writer and Baptist missionary. Emily Chubbock emerged from childhood poverty to become a successful writer, often writing as "Fanny Forester," and was a teacher at the Utica Female Seminary from 1841 to 1846. Adoniram Judson recruited her to write *Sarah Hall Boardman Judson's memoir. After a whirlwind romance, they were married and left for Burma in 1846. Despite frail health and illness, she published the memoir in 1848 and cared for her husband and stepsons. She bore a daughter in 1847 and, 10 days after her husband's death in 1850, a son, who died within hours. She returned to the U.S. the next year, resumed her literary work, and assisted Francis Wayland with his biography of Adoniram Judson.

ANB; EAWR; EE; HDB; NoAW; Arabella Stuart, *The Lives of the Three Mrs. Judsons* (1999); Asahel Clark Kendrick, *The Life and Letters of Mrs. Emily C. Judson* (1860).

KENDAL P. MOBLEY

Judson, Sarah Hall Boardman (1803–45). Baptist missionary. Born in Alstead, New Hampshire, Sarah Hall married George Dana Boardman in 1825, and they sailed to Burma to become pioneer missionaries among the Karens. Despite frequent illness and many hardships, Judson established schools, translated biblical texts and religious literature, and wrote hymns. She bore three children, one of whom died in infancy and another in early childhood. After her husband's death in 1831 Judson remained in Burma with her surviving son and continued her missionary work. She married Adoniram Judson in 1834 and bore eight children, one of whom was stillborn and two who died in infancy. After an extended illness, she died in the port of St. Helena en route to the U.S.

ANB; EAWR; EE; HDB; NoAW; Arabella Stuart, *The Lives of the Three Mrs. Judsons* (1999); Emily C. Judson, *Memoir of Sarah B. Judson* (1848).

KENDAL P. MOBLEY

Jung, Irma Rothschild (1897–1993). Philanthropist, communal leader, activist, and *rebbetzin* (rabbi's wife). Raised with a deep commitment to Judaism and to the physical welfare of Jews, the German-born Irma Jung worked tirelessly, for over seven decades, to assist needy Jews in Europe, America, and Israel. As director of several Jewish agencies after World War I she organized free camps in Switzerland for refugee children. After immigrating to the U.S. in 1922 with her husband, influential Orthodox rabbi Leo Jung, she collected and distributed funds to impoverished Yeshiva University students during the Great Depression and to Holocaust victims after World War II. Jung was vice president of the Yeshiva College Women's Organization (1934–35) and founded the women's league of the *Union of Orthodox Jewish Congregations of America (UOJCA). Extraordinarily generous with her resources, Jung left a lasting imprint upon 20th-century Jewry.

JWA; *Who's Who in American Jewry* (1938).

MICHAEL A. SINGER

Jungreis, Esther Jungreisz (1936–). Jewish religious leader. Born in Hungary, Esther Jungreisz survived the Bergen-Belson concentration camp during World War II and immigrated to the U.S. in 1947. After completing her education, Jungreisz, a committed Orthodox Jew, married Meshulem Halevi Jungreis, a fifth cousin. They established a synagogue in suburban New York, and Jungreis immediately took over the institution's educational endeavors. While raising the couple's four children and serving her community as *rebbetzin*, or rabbi's wife, Jungreis called for the return of Jews to Jewish traditions and practices. Her most notable achievement was the creation of Hineni (in Hebrew, "I am here") in the early 1970s, a movement that inspired college-aged Jews to participate in a spiritual revival. Hineni appeared at the height of Jewish communal concerns about the influence of New Age religions and cults over Jewish youths, and Jungreis was committed to combating the conversion efforts of such groups. Her charismatic speaking and national campaigns paralleled those of Billy Graham, a Christian evangelist whose style she admired. Jungreis filled a niche in American Jewish life by offering young adults a venue for attaining Jewish knowledge and spirituality.

JWA; Shuly Rubin Schwartz, *The Rabbi's Wife* (2006): "Reb. Esther Jungreis," the Harry Walker Agency Inc., www.harry-walker.com.

SHIRA M. KOHN

Ka'ahumanu (ca. 1768–1832). Ruler and intercultural mediator. Born on Maui of noble lineage, Ka'ahumanu became the favorite wife of Kamehameha the Great. After his 1819 death Ka'ahumanu assumed rule with the new king, Kamehameha II (Liholiho), the first implemented role of *kuhina nui* (coruler). When the *kapu* (taboo) system was suspended in mourning for Kamehameha, Ka'ahumanu prevented the restoration of *kapu*. Soon, in a revolutionary rejection of traditional religion, she and Liholiho ordered the destruction of the *heiaus* (temples). When Protestant missionaries (notably, Hiram Bingham) arrived in 1820, Ka'ahumanu resisted, but eventually embraced many Christian teachings. She saw in Christianity a means to power and a way to reunify Hawaii. In 1827 Ka'ahumanu established laws based on Christian teachings. She was loyal to Bingham, expelled Catholic missionaries, but never compromised her dedication to Hawaiian sovereignty.

NoAW; Lilikala Kameeleihiwa, *Na Wahine Kapu* (1999); Samuel Manaiakalani Kamakau, *Ruling Chiefs of Hawaii*, rev. ed. (1992); Jane L. Silverman, *Ka'ahumanu* (1987).

LISA J. POIRIER

Kander, Lizzie Black (1858–1940). Cookbook author and philanthropist. Born and educated in Milwaukee, Lizzie Black married businessman and later Wisconsin state legislator Simon Kander in 1881. Chief among her philanthropic pursuits was the Milwaukee Jewish Mission (called the Settlement), incorporated to "provide free instructions in industrial pursuits" to poor (mostly Jewish) immigrants, which she served as president for many years. At the settlement Kander began teaching the popular cooking classes that became the basis for *The Settlement Cook Book* (1901). The cookbook has since appeared in roughly 40 editions and has sold over a million and a half copies. It included recipes for fashionable nonkosher dishes, such as fried oysters, and Jewish specialties like matzah balls and gefilte fish; it also offered household tips.

ANB; JWA; NoAW; Barbara Kirshenblatt-Gimblett, "Kitchen Judaism," in *Getting Comfortable in New York* (1990); Papers ("Mrs. Simon Kander"), Milwaukee Manuscript Collection DN, State Historical Society of Wisconsin, University of Wisconsin–Milwaukee.

EMILY ALICE KATZ

Kapiolani (1834–99). Monarch and philanthropist. Granddaughter of Kaumualii (the last king of Kauai prior to the unification of the Hawaiian Islands by Kamehameha the Great), Kapiolani was raised in the court of Kamehameha III. In 1852 Kapiolani was married briefly to Chief Bennet Namakeha, but was soon widowed. Her second marriage was to the king's brother, David Laamea Kalakaua, within weeks of the death of Kamehameha IV in 1863. Some regarded their marriage as violating proper mourning practices. Kalakaua became king in 1874, and the royal couple traveled to the U.S. and England. Kapiolani's reign as queen was characterized by works of charity. She established the Kapiolani Home for Girls and the Kapiolani Maternity Home. After the death of her husband in 1891, Kapiolani retired to Waikiki. The Kapiolani Medical Center for Women and Children remains her lasting legacy.

NoAW; Maili Yardley and Miriam Rogers, *Queen Kapiolani* (1985); Emily V. Warinner, *A Royal Journey to London* (1975).

LISA J. POIRIER

Karma Lekshe Tsomo (Patricia Jean Zenn) (1944–). Ordained Buddhist nun, scholar, and activist. Karma Lekshe Tsomo was first ordained as a novice in 1977 by the 16th Gyalwa Karmapa, head of the Karma Kagyu tradition of Tibetan Buddhism. Because the Tibetan tradition lacked full ordination for women, she went through full ordination as a *bhikkhuni* in Taiwan. Her scholarship and activism have focused on interfaith dialogue and the status of women in Buddhism throughout the world. She has served as president of Sakyadhita: International Association of Buddhist Women and director of Jamyang Foundation, an initiative to provide educational opportunities for women in India.

Karma Lekshe Tsomo, ed., *Buddhism and Social Justice* (2004), *Buddhism through American Women's Eyes* (1995); Richard Hughes Seager, *Buddhism in America* (1999).

BARBARA E. REED

Kazel, Dorothy (1939–80). Catholic woman religious and mission worker. Dorothy Kazel dedicated her life to serving the poor and living her commitment as an *Ursuline sister in El Salvador. Kazel worked in El Salvador despite escalating violence and the military's open hostility toward church workers. On 2 December 1980 Kazel was traveling in the company of *Ita Ford, *Maura Clarke, and *Jean Donovan when all four were arrested, assaulted, and assassinated by El Salvadoran national guardsmen at the command of officials in the El Salvadoran army.

Cynthia Glavac, *In the Fullness of Life* (1996).

MARY J. HENOLD

Kelly, Leontine Turpeau Current (1920–). First African American United Methodist woman bishop. Leontine Turpeau was steeped in Methodism from childhood. She married her second husband, James David Kelly, in 1958. She served as a schoolteacher, pastor, and staff member of the Virginia Annual Conference Council on Ministries. She earned a BA from Virginia Union University (Richmond) and an MDiv from Union Theological Seminary (Richmond). Ordained a deacon in 1972 and an elder in 1977 Kelly was elected a bishop by the western jurisdiction and consecrated in 1984. Kelly believes that the church and politics can join together to effect change. She retired in 1988, but remains active in community service work. The recipient of several honorary doctorates, Kelly was elected in 2000 to the National Women's Hall of Fame in Seneca Falls, New York.

BWARC; EAWR; RLA; Nathan Aaseng, *African-American Religious Leaders* (2003); *African-American Almanac*, 6th ed. (1994).

ANGELA D. SIMS

Kennedy, Ethne (1921–2005). Founding president of the *National Assembly of Religious Women (NARW). (NARW was originally known as the National Assembly of Women Religious.) Sister Ethne Kennedy was a member of the Society of Helpers. She worked for the full participation of women in the Catholic Church after the Second Vatican Council and was the editor of *Probe*, the newsletter of the organization of U.S. sisters' councils. At the NARW, an independent organization for Catholic sisters, she facilitated means by which sisters could cooperate with and participate in decision making and the implementation of processes at national, regional, and local levels of the church and in society. Under her leadership the NAWR promoted a new sense of identity for Catholic sisters as religious women. In the last years of her life Kennedy worked with AIDS patients in New York, and participated in antiwar demonstrations at the United Nations.

Ethne Kennedy, *Women in Ministry: A Sister's View* (1972); NARW Records, University of Notre Dame Archives.

SUSAN MARIE MALONEY, SNJM

Kent, Mary Corita ("Sister Corita") (1918–86). Artist. Mary Corita Kent became a sister of the *Immaculate Heart of Mary in 1936. She joined the faculty of Immaculate Heart College in 1950 as an art instructor. In the 1960s she began to utilize her art as a means of protest, and several antiwar exhibits brought her national recognition. Among Kent's friends were people such as Buckminster Fuller and the Berrigan brothers. She left her religious order in 1968 and relocated to Boston, where she produced numerous serigraphs with spiritual themes. Her 1971 rainbow mural on a Boston Gas Company storage tank and her 1985 "Love" postage stamp are considered her most enduring works.

ANB; EACH; NoAWC; Julie Ault, *Come Alive* (2007); Corita Kent, "The Artist as Social Activist," in *Sacred Dimensions of Women's Experience*, ed. Elizabeth Dodson Gray (1988); Harvey Cox and Samuel Eisenstein, *Sister Corita* (1968).

ANNIE RUSSELL

Keyser, Harriette Amelia (1841–1936). Labor reformer, author, and suffragist. An Episcopal laywoman, Harriette Keyser was the driving force behind the Church Association for the Interests of Labor (CAIL), serving as its executive secretary and chief publicist from 1896 to 1926. Her investigations of labor conditions in New England fisheries and the New York garment industry appeared in the CAIL periodical *Hammer and Pen* and in *Survey Magazine*. Active in the Working Woman's Society and the Consumer League, Keyser championed the cause of working women in the suffrage movement. Her study, "The Economic Value of Women to the State," used statistics to justify women's inclusion in the body politic. She was an active member of the *Society of the Companions of the Holy Cross. She wrote the biography of Bishop Henry C. Potter (1910) and two social-issue novels, *On the Borderland* (1882) and *Thorns in Your Side* (1884).

Harriette A. Keyser, "A Woman to the Rescue," *The Spirit of Missions* (1914).

MARY SUDMAN DONOVAN

Khandro (1967–). Tibetan lama and teacher. Venerable Khandro Rinpoche is one of the most renowned Tibetan lamas currently teaching in the West. She is the eldest daughter of Mindrolling Trichen Rinpoche. She was recognized at the age of two by His Holiness the 16th Karmapa as the reincarnation of Khandro Ugyen Tsomo, one of the most renowned female masters of her time. She holds lineages in both the Nyingma and Kagyu schools and has been teaching internationally for 12 years. She teaches extensively in Europe and North America. She is the author of *This Precious Life: Tibetan Buddhist Teachings on the Path to Enlightenment* (2003). Khandro established and heads the Samten Tse Retreat Center in Mussoori, India, and is also resident teacher at the Lotus Garden Retreat Center in rural Virginia, in the U.S. Khandro is also involved with the Mindrolling Monastery in Dehra Dun, India.

Venerable Khando Rinpoche, www.vkr.org.

LOUISE GRAVES

Kikuchi, Shigeo (d. 1985). Japanese teacher and leader of Shin Buddhism in Hawaii. Shigeo Kikuchi was one of the many pioneering *bomori* (minister's wives) who brought Buddhism to Japanese immigrants in the plantation villages of Hawaii. She and her husband were missionaries of the Shin sect of Japanese Buddhism, which teaches devotion to Amida Buddha. Born in Japan (date unknown), she arrived in Hawaii in 1914 and spent over 40 years teaching Japanese classes and serving the Japanese American community in the remote village of Naalehu. While her husband traveled by horseback to serve the Japanese working in the sugarcane fields and sugar plantation mill, Kikuchi taught Japanese to the youth, wrote letters and legal documents for the illiterate, managed the dharma hall, acted as a matchmaker, and hosted visitors. She was active in *Fujinkai, the Young Buddhist Association, Sunday school, and Japanese school. During World War II Kikuchi continued to serve the immigrant community after her husband was interred in Hawaii and later on the mainland. She learned English so that she could write to the interred Japanese who were not allowed any Japanese language letters.

Shigeo Kikuchi, *Memoirs of a Buddhist Woman Missionary in Hawaii* (1991).

BARBARA E. REED

King, Coretta Scott (1927–2006). Civil rights leader. Coretta Scott began her civil rights career while attending Antioch College (Yellow Springs, Ohio), where she studied music and elementary education. After graduation, she furthered her education in Boston at the New England Conservatory of Music. She married Martin Luther King Jr. in June 1953. The couple moved to Montgomery, Alabama, in 1954, where her husband had accepted a pastorate and where she participated in the civil rights movement. The couple had four children, Yolanda Denise (1955–2007), Martin Luther III (b. 1957), Dexter Scott (b. 1961), and Bernice Albertine (b. 1963). After her husband's assassination in 1968 Coretta Scott King continued promoting nonviolence and civil rights. She was the keynote speaker at the Poor People's Campaign held at Washington, DC (June 1969), the first woman to preach during a worship service at St. Paul's Cathedral (London), and the first woman to deliver a Class Day address at Harvard University. King founded the Martin Luther King Jr. Center for Nonviolent Change in Atlanta (1968).

BWA; EAWR; NBAW; RLA; Cynthia Fitterer Klingel, *Coretta Scott King* (1999); Sondra Henry and Emily Taitz, *Coretta Scott King* (1992); Coretta Scott King, *My Life with Martin Luther King, Jr.* (1969).

KEITH DURSO

Kingston, Maxine Hong (1940–). Author and Buddhist leader. Maxine Hong was born in Stockton, California, and graduated from the University of California at Berkeley. She is best known as a writer who introduced Chinese traditions and themes to the English-reading world in her mixed writing of memoir and fiction—*The Woman Warrior: Memoirs of a Childhood among Ghosts* (1976), *China Men* (1980), *Tripmaster Monkey: His Fake Book* (1989), *The Fifth Book of Peace* (2003). Kingston is a leader among American Buddhists. She came to Buddhism gradually, partly through reading the Buddhist-influenced Beat poets. Under the influence of the Vietnamese Buddhist monk and peace activist Thich Nhat Hanh, Kingston began leading writing retreats for Vietnam veterans. Her contributions to understanding Buddhism also include her essay in Thich Nhat Hanh's *For a Future to Be Possible* (1993).

Mary Zeiss Stange, "Treading the Narrative Way between Myth and Madness," *Journal of Feminist Studies in Religion* 3, no. 1 (1987).

BARBARA E. REED

Kitomaquund, Mary (ca. 1633–54?). Intercultural mediator. Mary Kitomaquund, daughter of the Piscataway *tayac* (chief), was brought by him in 1640 to Jesuit Father Andrew White as a means toward alliance with the English. She was educated at St. Mary's, capital of the colony of Maryland. Her legal guardians were Margaret Brent, the most powerful woman in colonial Maryland, and Leonard Calvert, the governor of Maryland and the brother of Lord Baltimore. She was baptized in 1642. Brent appears in legal documents as Kitomaquund's guardian, and Kitomaquund likely lived in her household. In 1644 Kitomaquund was married to Giles Brent (the brother of Margaret Brent), likely as a strategy for the Brents to gain title to more Piscataway land, circumventing the need for a proprietary grant, and thereby gaining more power in the colony. Their marriage seems to have led to a land dispute between Lord Baltimore and Giles Brent. The Brents soon left Maryland and established a plantation near Aquia Creek (Stafford County, Virginia). There are no records of Kitomaquund's death. Local lore is divided as to whether she died in 1654 or, having separated from Giles Brent, lived to 1670.

Lois Green Carr, *Maryland . . . at the Beginning* (1978).

LISA J. POIRIER

Klirs, Tracy Guren (1955–). First female rabbi to head a congregation in Canada. Tracy Guren was born in Vancouver, British Columbia, and raised in San Mateo, California, and Seattle, Washington. She completed an undergraduate degree in Yiddish literature at the University of Chicago and married Elisha Klirs in 1977. She studied for the rabbinate at Hebrew Union College–Jewish Institute of Religion. She was ordained in Cincinnati in 1984, and was the rabbi of Temple Shalom in Winnipeg, Manitoba, from 1984 to 1986. She returned to the U.S. to work as a congregational rabbi in Texas and as a leader in several Jewish educational organizations across the U.S. Klirs is the principal author of *The Merit of Our Mothers* (1992) and has also published a number of articles. She is featured in *Godtalk: Women of God (series b)*, an interfaith television show.

The Jewish Post, 17 May and 13 September 1984.

TRUDY FLYNN

Knapp, Susan Trevor (1862–1941). Episcopal deaconess and dean of the New York Training School for Deaconesses. Susan Knapp was set apart (i.e., recognized as a deaconess through a religious service) in 1899 and was appointed dean of the New York Training School for Deaconesses in 1903. She considered her vocation to be a lifetime commitment requiring a celibate lifestyle. Having studied the organization of English deaconesses, Knapp made the curriculum academically rigorous, expanded practical training, diversified placements, and recruited top students. She revitalized the worship life of the school, encouraged students in their prayer lives, and cultivated communal spirituality. Knapp traveled, wrote, and lectured extensively on the deaconess movement throughout the U.S. and abroad. She resigned the deanship when threatened with the reorganization of the board. She retired to Japan to teach English and the Bible for 25 years.

Sheryl A. Kujawa-Holbrook, *Freedom Is a Dream* (2002); Mary Sudman Donovan, "Paving the Way: Deaconess Susan Trevor Knapp," *Anglican and Episcopal History* 63 (1994).

SHERYL A. KUJAWA-HOLBROOK

Kohler, Rose (1873–1947). Jewish artist, sculptor, and reformer. A member of Reform Judaism, Rose Kohler worked for the equality of Jewish women. She advocated women being counted in determining a quorum in synagogues and worked for their formal membership in their congregations. She also worked for women's suffrage. Kohler was active in the *National Council of Jewish Women (NCJW) and at one time was its chairperson. She openly questioned the Jewish practice of treating boys and girls equally as children but unequally as teenagers and adults. Kohler wrote numerous articles on the origin and development of Jewish art, and on how art has been used to persecute Jews.

EAWR; JWA; Ann Braude, "The Jewish Woman's Encounter with American

Culture," in *Women and Religion in America*, vol. 1, ed. Rosemary Radford Ruether and Rosemary Skinner Keller (1981); Kaufmann Kohler Papers, Jacob Rader Marcus Center, American Jewish Archives.

KEITH DURSO

Kohut, Rebekah Bettelheim (1864–1951). Jewish activist. Born to Hungarian Jewish parents who immigrated to the U.S. when she was three, Rebekah Bettelheim grew up in Jewish communal life. After attending two years of classes at the University of California, she met and married Alexander Kohut, who served as a rabbi in New York. She assisted him with his work, raised his young children from a previous marriage, and also organized a sisterhood at her husband's synagogue. After her husband's death in 1894, Kohut became active in the *National Council of Jewish Women (NCJW) and instituted a program to assist the war-ravaged Jewish communities of Europe after World War I. Kohut supported women's suffrage and created employment opportunities in Jewish and non-Jewish communities.

ANBO; EAWR; JWA; NoAW; Linda Gordon Kuzmack, *Woman's Cause* (1990); Rebekah Bettelheim Kohut, *More Yesterdays* (1950), *My Portion* (1925).

SHIRA M. KOHN

Koulomzin, Sophie Shidlovsky (1903–2000). Orthodox Christian educator. Born in St. Petersburg, Sophie Shidlovsky in 1927 became the first Orthodox woman to receive a master's degree in religious education from Columbia University. Founder of the Orthodox Christian Education Commission (1957) in North America, she was the director of the Russian Student Christian Movement in France. A major force in youth education in both North America and Europe, Koulomzin wrote a dozen books about church school education, founded *Young Life Magazine* (1948), and was its editor for the next two decades. In 1948 Koulomzin, her husband (whom she married in 1932), and their children immigrated to the U.S. She spent the rest of her life working in youth education. In 1999 she was awarded the Order of St. Olga by Patriarch Aleksy of Moscow.

Sophie Koulimzin, *Many Worlds: A Russian Life* (1980); Helen Creticos Theodoropoulos "Sophie Shidlovsky Koulomzin: An Extraordinary Life," *St. Nina Quarterly* 2, no. 4 (Fall 1998); "Sophie Koulimzin: Renowned Orthodox Christian Religious Educator," St. Vladimir's Orthodox Theological Seminary [online].

REBEKAH GOODYEAR

Kugler, Anna Sarah (1856–1930). Lutheran medical missionary. Anna Sarah Kugler graduated from the Woman's Medical College in Philadelphia in 1879. The Reverend A. D. Row asked her to take up medical work alongside the missionary station in Guntur, southern India. The Lutheran General Synod, however, was not ready to send a woman into this field and sent her instead as a general missionary. She worked initially among secluded Hindu and Muslim women, but her medical knowledge was a great asset to her general work. Kugler was finally appointed a medical missionary in 1883. She opened a women's hospital, the American Evangelical Lutheran Mission Hospital, in Guntur in 1897. Kugler (and other Christian women doctors, like *Clara Swain) endured many trying situations, especially regarding the strict caste rules that governed social interaction. Kugler maintained that her role was not only that of head physician and administrator, but also that of evangelical teacher. She spent 47 years in India.

Maina Chawla Singh, "Women, Mission, and Medicine: Clara Swain, Anna Kugler, and Early Medical Endeavors in Colonial

India" in *International Bulletin of Missionary Research* (2005); Margaret R. Seebach, *Indian Goddess: The Story of Anna Kugler* (1942); Anna Kugler, *Guntur Mission Hospital* (1928).

MARIA ERLING

Kuhlman, Kathryn (1907–76). Evangelist and healer. In her teen years, Kathryn Kuhlman experienced a spiritual awakening and left school to join her brother-in-law as a tent revival preacher. She was ordained by the Evangelical Church Alliance and in 1934 opened the Kuhlman Revival Tabernacle in Denver. After a scandalous affair with a visiting preacher, whom she married, Kuhlman moved to Los Angeles. Seven years later Kuhlman left her husband and moved to Franklin, Pennsylvania, to set up the Gospel Revival Tabernacle. Her ministry encouraged a special relationship to the Holy Spirit, and soon reports of healing began to emerge. In 1947 she began weekly radio broadcasts, in addition to serving congregations in three states. By 1962, when she published *I Believe in Miracles*, she was a national figure and leader in the emerging charismatic movement. In the decade before her death she produced the top-rated religious television program in the U.S.

DARB; EAWR; EE; RLA; Jamie Buckingham, *Daughter of Destiny* (1999).

GRAEME SHARROCK

Kussy, Sarah (1869–1956). Jewish leader. Born into a Jewish family in Newark, New Jersey, Sarah Kussy became involved in Jewish communal activities at an early age. She was a member of the first graduating class of the Jewish Theological Seminary's Teachers Institute and taught in several of New Jersey's religious and Hebrew schools. While a teacher, she combated Christian missionary activities among Jewish children. She was active in her synagogue, Ohev Shalom (which her parents helped to found), served as secretary of the Ladies' Patriotic Relief Society, and raised funds for Miriam's Auxiliary, one of her congregation's philanthropic projects. She also assisted *Henrietta Szold in creating *Hadassah and helped found the National Women's League of the United Synagogue of America. Her commitment to Zionism led to her participation as a delegate to five World Zionist congresses.

JWA; Obituary, *New York Times* (3 October 1956); Papers, American Jewish Historical Society Archives.

SHIRA M. KOHN

Kwon, Elizabeth (1922–97). First Presbyterian Korean woman minister ordained. In 1944 Elizabeth (Young Hee) Kwon was ordained by the United Church of Christ in Japan (Kyodan); her ordination was recognized by the Presbytery of the Pacific of the United Presbyterian Church in the U.S.A. (UPCUSA) in 1974. Born in Korea, Kwon grew up in China with her missionary parents and received her initial college and seminary education in Japan. Kwon served in pastoral and teaching positions in Korea and Japan. She later studied at Barrington University (Providence, Rhode Island), Hartford Seminary (Connecticut), and the University of Southern California (Los Angeles). In 1952 she married Peter Kwon, a Presbyterian pastor, and they became the first Asian clergy couple in the UPCUSA, serving churches mostly in California. In addition to her work within the church, she was a junior high school teacher for 24 years.

Shin-Hwa Park, "The Pioneering Life of the Rev. Elizabeth Kwon, the First Korean Clergywoman," (unpublished), based on *The Life Journey of Elizabeth and Peter Kwon*, ed. Jung Nam Lee (1999).

LINDA B. BREBNER

LaHaye, Beverly Ratcliffe (1929–). Author and founder of *Concerned

Women for America (CWA). Beverly Ratcliffe met her husband Tim LaHaye at Bob Jones University, but she left school to raise four children and travel with her husband to various church assignments. Beverly LaHaye teamed with her husband to coauthor several books, produce television programs, and conduct Family Life Seminars. She also authored books on being a Christian wife and mother. By the end of the 1970s the LaHayes began to crusade against secular humanism, which led Beverly LaHaye into national politics. In 1979 she founded CWA, a public policy organization lobbying for traditional family values and supporting the election of conservative candidates. Her organizational and communication skills mobilize thousands of fundamentalist women to pray and to be politically active.

EAWR; EE; David Garrison, "Tim and Beverly LaHaye," in *Twentieth-Century Shapers of American Popular Religion*, ed. Charles H. Lippy (1989); Kim A. Lawton, "Powerhouse of the Religious Right?" *Christianity Today* (6 November 1987).

BARBARA J. MACHAFFIE

Lampkin, Daisy Elizabeth Adams (ca. 1883–1965). Civil and women's rights activist. Daisy Adams was born in Washington, DC. In 1909 she moved to Pittsburgh, and in 1912 she married William Lampkin. Best known for her work as the national field secretary for the National Association for the Advancement of Colored People (NAACP), Lampkin traveled tirelessly to raise funds, recruit new members, and establish NAACP chapters. She was involved with the *National Association of Colored Women (NACW) and the *National Council of Negro Women (NCNW), and received the first Eleanor Roosevelt–Mary McLeod Bethune World Citizenship Award given by the NCNW in 1964. Lampkin served as vice president of the *Pittsburgh Courier* for three decades and was active in Grace Memorial Presbyterian Church, serving as one of its first woman elders. She spent her life battling discrimination and creating space for women and African Americans in the public sphere.

ANB; BWA; NoAWMP.

MANDY E. MCMICHAEL

Laney, Lucy Craft (1854–1933). Presbyterian educator. Born of free parents in Macon, Georgia, Lucy Laney graduated as a teacher with the first class of Atlanta University in 1873. Frustrated by the lack of school facilities for African American children, Laney made an unsuccessful financial appeal at the 1883 General Assembly of the Presbyterian Church, U.S.A. The church's women's department, however, under Francine E. H. Haines, took up the cause, and Augusta's Haines Normal and Industrial School was chartered in 1886; the school became a cultural center for the African American community. Laney founded other centers for African American education, including a kindergarten and the Lamar School of Nursing. Laney consistently promoted dignity and self-worth. Her portrait hangs in the Georgia state Capitol.

ANB; BWA; NBAW; NoAW; Frank T. Wilson, ed., "Lucy Craft Laney—Educator," *Journal of Presbyterian History* 51 (1973); Georgia Women of Achievement, www.gawomen.org.

SANDRA L. BEARDSALL

Lange, Elizabeth Clovis (Mother Mary Elizabeth) (1784–1882). Educator and founder of the *Oblate Sisters of Providence, the first black Catholic order in the U.S. Born in a French colony in Haiti, Elizabeth Lange came to the U.S. in 1817 because of the Haitian revolution. Highly educated and wealthy, she settled in Baltimore, Maryland, in 1827. Lange used her inheritance to open the first school for black French-speaking immigrants. As a black woman in a slaveholding state and as a single woman in a male-dominated society, she met strong opposition. Lange persisted nevertheless. She established schools for blacks in Maryland, Philadelphia, New York, and St. Louis. At her death the influence of the Oblate order extended to the Caribbean and Central America. Efforts have been made to make her the first African American female canonized by the Roman Catholic Church.

ANB; BWA; EACH; EAWR; NBAW; ROWUS.

SUSAN MARIE MALONEY, SNJM

Larcom, Lucy (1824–93). Author, seminary teacher, and magazine editor. Descended from the Huguenots, Lucy Larcom was raised in Lowell, Massachusetts, the ninth of 10 children. She worked for a decade at various mill jobs. She began writing at a young age and made the acquaintance of the poet John Whittier; he and his sister became lifelong friends of Larcom. In 1846 Larcom moved to Illinois, where she taught school and received college training at the Monticello Seminary in Godfrey. She returned to Massachusetts and taught English literature and rhetoric at Wheaton Seminary. She pioneered a system of lecturing and conducting discussions, a departure from the usual textbook-centered recitation method. Larcom contributed frequently to magazines and edited a children's periodical. The binding force of her life was her Christian faith, mostly nonsectarian in nature, although she did find a home in the Episcopal Church.

NoAW; Daniel Dulany Addison, *Lucy Larcom* (1894).

BETH SPAULDING

Larson, April C. Ulring (1950–). First woman bishop of the Evangelical Lutheran Church in America (ELCA). April Larson and her husband, Judd Larson, were the first married couple to attend Wartburg Seminary. At her ordination in 1978 she joined the fewer than 10 female clergy in the American Lutheran Church (ALC). In 1992 she was elected bishop of the LaCrosse Area Synod of the ELCA.

Who's Who of American Women (1993); ELCA, *Biographical Directory of Clergy* (1988).

L. DEANE LAGERQUIST

Las Hermanas (1971–). Chicana/Latina organization. Formed in Houston and later moved to offices on the campus of Our Lady of the Lake University in San Antonio, Texas, Las Hermanas originally united Hispanic members of women's religious congregations in the U.S. for the purpose of maintaining solidarity in the struggle for justice motivated by faith. Founded by a group of 50 Mexican American women religious from eight states and 20 congregations under the leadership of Chicana activists Gloria Gallardo and Gloria Ortega, membership has expanded to include all Hispanic Catholic women supportive of the cause of gender equity in church and society. A principal collaborator in the founding of the Mexican American Cultural Council in San Antonio, Las Hermanas serves as a clearinghouse to raise awareness of Hispanic community need. It has organized projects to meet specific social needs, to educate women domestic workers for occupations that pay higher wages and afford them broader opportunities for ministry, and to train women in leadership skills. Overall, it promotes Hispanic women as change agents with a uniquely Latina faith perspective.

Lara Medina, *Las Hermanas* (2005); Sarah Slavin, ed., *U.S. Women's Interest Groups* (1995).

KAREN M. KENNELLY, CSJ

Lathrop, Julia Clifford (1858–1932). Social reformer. Born in Rockford, Illinois,

Julia Lathrop graduated from Vassar College in 1880. After serving as a secretary in her father's law firm, she joined *Jane Addams at Hull House in 1890. Lathrop was appointed to the Illinois Board of Charities in 1893 and made regular visits to the state's poorhouses. Her growing concern for competent staffing for these charities led her to establish a training institute that would later become the University of Chicago's School of Social Service Administration. In 1912 Lathrop moved to Washington, DC, to become director of the newly created U.S. Children's Bureau. She lobbied regularly before Congress concerning juvenile delinquency, parental education, child labor, and treatment of the mentally ill. She retired to Rockford in 1922 and continued in various causes.

ANB; NoAW; WBC; Eleanor J. Stebner, *The Women of Hull House* (1997); Jane Addams, *My Friend: Julia Lathrop* (1935).

SCOTT D. SEAY

Lathrop, Rose Hawthorne (Mother Mary Alphonsa) (1851–1926). Author and founder of a Catholic religious community. Rose Hawthorne was the youngest daughter of Nathaniel and Sophia Hawthorne. She married George Parsons Lathrop in 1871, and their only child died at age four. She published *Along the Shore* (1888) and, with her husband, *A Story of Courage* (1894) and *Memories of Hawthorne* (1897). The couple converted to Roman Catholicism in 1891. Lathrop left her alcoholic husband in 1893, prior to his 1898 death. She founded the third order *Dominican congregation of St. Rose of Lima, Servants of Relief for Incurable Cancer in 1900. With Sister Mary Rose (born Alice Huber), she established St. Rose's Home and Rosary Hill; both sites became havens for destitute cancer victims.

ANB; DARB; EACH; EAWR; NoAW; RLA; Patricia Valenti, *To Myself a Stranger* (1991); Katherine Burton, *Sorrow Built a Bridge* (1937); Hawthorne Family Papers, Special Collections, Green Library, Stanford University.

SANDRA YOCUM MIZE

Laveau, Marie (ca. 1801–81). Roman Catholic and voodoo queen. Marie Laveau was a controversial free woman of color living in New Orleans in the 19th century. She dedicated great portions of her life to working as a prison chaplain and helping the sick, the poor, and the dying. She was a symbol of resistance, functioned as an assertion of female power in a patriarchal society, and embodied outrage over the unjust distribution of power, wealth, and privilege in a profoundly class-stratified environment. By preserving and practicing African traditions, Laveau gave people of African descent a meaningful sense of identity. She is one of the most popular figures in the history of New Orleans.

ANB; BWA; NBAW; Carolyn Morrow Long, *A New Orleans Voudou Priestess* (2006); Ina Johanna Fandrich, *The Mysterious Voodoo Queen, Marie Laveaux* (2005); Martha Ward, *Voodoo Queen* (2004).

ANGELA D. SIMS

Lazarus, Emma (1849–87). Poet, author, and social reformer. Emma Lazarus was born in New York City to a family of upper-class Sephardic Jews who had been in the U.S. for several generations. She became interested in the lives of recent Jewish immigrants and in the persecution of Jews in Russia and Eastern Europe when the Russian pogroms intensified in the 1880s. She advocated a homeland for Jews in Palestine, and spent two years in Europe working to resettle persecuted Jews. She also opposed the growing exclusion of Jews from hotels, universities, and social organizations in the U.S., and helped found the Hebrew Technical Institute for Vocational Training in New York City. She wrote poems, plays, and essays, and many of them explored what it meant to be Jewish. Her most well-known poem was "The New Colossus," which she wrote in 1883. An excerpt—"Give me your tired, your poor / Your huddled masses yearning to breathe free"—was inscribed on the pedestal of the Statue of Liberty.

ANB; EAWR; NoAW; Emma Klein, ed., *Emma Lazarus* (1997); Daniel Vogel, *Emma Lazarus* (1980); Heinrich E. Jacob, *The World of Emma Lazarus* (1949); Jewish Women's Archives, www.jwa.org.

LYNN JAPINGA

Lazarus, Josephine (1846–1910). Essayist and critic. Born in New York City to a wealthy Jewish family, Josephine Lazarus began publishing her writing after the death of her famous sister, the poet *Emma Lazarus. She began to explore the subject of Judaism as a speaker at the Congress of Religions at the World Columbian Exposition in Chicago (1893), collecting and publishing her essays on the subject as *The Spirit of Judaism* (1895). Lazarus was critical of both traditional Judaism and the radical revisions of the Reform movement. She advocated a universalist religion that would combine the best of Judaism and Christianity. In her last published essays, Lazarus explored a new appreciation for political Zionism. Her writings reflect the waning milieu of Sephardic Jewry in America, who were assimilated into Gentile high society but proud of their privileged Jewish pedigree.

JWA; Joe Rooks Rapport, "The Lazarus Sisters: A Family Portrait" (PhD diss., Washington University in St. Louis, 1988).

EMILY ALICE KATZ

Leadership Conference of Women Religious (LCWR) (1956–). Organization for Catholic women religious in elected leadership. The LCWR began as the Conference of Major Superiors of Women (CMSW), the first national organization to represent the interests of women religious in the U.S. By 1971 the conference adopted its current name, hoping to deemphasize the hierarchical connotations associated with the term "major superiors." The LCWR aimed to train and provide a support network for women religious in leadership, promote the spiritual welfare of nuns and sisters, and foster cooperation with the church hierarchy. Over time, the LCWR expanded its mission by engaging in struggles for human rights and social justice in the U.S. and throughout the world. The LCWR became outspoken on issues of women's rights, espousing a feminist agenda in the early 1970s. It continues to pursue justice for women in and outside the Roman Catholic Church.

EACH; Records, University of Notre Dame Archives.

MARY J. HENOLD

Leddy, Mary Jo (1946–). Author, scholar, and social activist. Inspired by the Second Vatican Council, Mary Jo Leddy entered the Sisters of Our Lady of Sion, a religious order known for its work in Jewish-Christian dialogue. Her PhD is from the University of Toronto. She was the founding editor of the progressive *Catholic New Times*. In 1992 she set up Romero House, an organization that works in the resettlement of refugees. She left the Sisters of Sion in 1994. A tireless activist, she also teaches at the Jesuit Regis College as an adjunct professor. Her reputation has grown out of a combination of activism, public speaking, and numerous books. Her 2002 book, *Radical Gratitude*, underscores a profound spirituality of gratitude that she calls the "most radical attitude to life." She received the Order of Canada in 1996.

Mary Jo Leddy, *Memories of War, Promises of Peace* (1989).

OSCAR COLE-ARNAL

Lee, Ann ("Mother Ann") (1736–84). Visionary and founder of the Shakers (United Society of Believers in Christ's Second Coming). Ann Lee grew up in the textile manufacturing culture of Manchester, England. Impressed by the expressive Christian worship of the "Shaking Quakers," she joined a group expecting the imminent return of Christ as a woman. After an arranged marriage, Lee gave birth to four children, all of whom died in infancy, convincing her that sexual union was the source of pain and evil. In 1770 she had a vision that confirmed her belief that sexual intercourse was Adam and Eve's original sin and where Christ appointed her "Mother of the New Creation." After several arrests and confinement in an asylum, she had a second vision in which Christ revealed that Lee was his successor. Another vision in 1774 convinced her to escape religious persecution by moving with a handful of followers to New York City. The group later founded a settlement near Albany. They initially proved as controversial in America as they had been in England, given their British origin, pacifism, and their unusual religious ideas. By Mother Ann's death in 1783, however, 11 celibate communities were established and growing. Lee's legacy includes a theology in which God is both feminine and masculine, and community ideals of sharing and equality for both sexes. Today several Shaker communities offer historical tours, but only a handful of believers remain.

ANB; DARB; EAWR; NoAW; Richard Francis, *Ann the Word* (2002); Ken Burns, dir., *The Shakers* [DVD] (2004).

GRAEME SHARROCK

Lee, Jarena (ca. 1783–?). African Methodist Episcopal (AME) evangelist. Born in Cape May, New Jersey, Jarena Lee spent her early years working as a domestic servant. In her 20s, she was converted, sanctified, and received a call to preach. The AME Church rebuffed her request for approval to preach, so she married a minister; he subsequently died. As a widow with two young children, Lee repeated her request to Richard Allen, who granted her official church approval to preach. Her evangelistic meetings ranged from her home base of Philadelphia throughout New England, as well as north into Canada and west into Ohio. She recounted her meetings in her 1836 autobiography (the first to be published in the U.S. by an African American woman), and mentions frequently the denominational and racial composition of her audience, which, in both cases, was quite inclusive. There is no recorded history about her between 1849 and 1857. The last known event in her life was a visit she made to the home of *Rebecca Cox Jackson, a Shaker leader, on New Year's Day in 1857.

ANB; BWA; EAWR; EE; NBAW; Jarena Lee, *Religious Experience and Journal of Mrs. Jarena Lee* (1849).

PRISCILLA POPE-LEVISON

Lee, Mabel (1893–1966). Leader of Chinese American Baptists. Mabel Lee was the daughter of the Reverend Lee To, the pastor of the Chinese Baptist Mission in New York City. She received a PhD in economics in 1922 from Columbia University and then succeeded her father as the leader of the mission. Lee was a liberal Christian and a Chinese nationalist acquainted with Hu Shih. She sought to emphasize a Christianity of social service. She believed that Christianity would be the salvation of the Chinese people, but that it must be Chinese Christianity and not white European American Protestantism.

Timothy Tseng, "Chinese Protestant Nationalism in the United States, 1880–1927," in *New Spiritual Homes: Religion and Asian Americans*, ed. David K. Yoo

(1999); Tseng, "The Interstitial Career of a Protestant Chinese American Woman, 1924–1950" (paper presented at OAH annual meeting, 1996).

BARBARA E. REED

Lee, Sara (1933–). Educator and interfaith activist. Sara Lee was not raised as an observant Jew, but she grew up in a neighborhood that nurtured her Jewish identity. While a student at Radcliffe College, she spent a semester in Israel, where her interest in her Jewish education formed. After her husband died unexpectedly in 1974, Lee pursued the study of education. In 1980 she was appointed director of the Rhea Hirsch School of Education at Hebrew Union College in Los Angeles, a position she continues to hold. In 2005 she was awarded the president's award for Distinguished Leadership of Jewish Education in the Diaspora by the president of Israel. She is active in the Jewish-Christian interfaith movement and is committed to building deeper understanding between the two communities.

Jean Bloch Rosensaft, "From Girls Latin School to Beit Ha-Nasi: Sara Lee on 25 Years at HUC-JIR," *Hebrew Union College Chronicle* 65 (2005).

LILA CORWIN BERMAN

Lehmann, Katherine (1876–1960). Lutheran leader. Born into a leading family of moderate Lutheranism, Katherine Lehmann made a career of leadership in women's auxiliaries, first in the Ohio Synod and then in the American Lutheran Church (ALC). Although her father was president of Capital University and she was later one of the first women on its board of regents, Lehmann attended Lima College. For two decades she was congregational organist and music director in Bellevue, Ohio. Lehmann's primary work within women's organizations began with her election as recording secretary. Soon thereafter she began editing the women's department in the *Lutheran Standard*. In 1921 she was elected president of the Women's Missionary Federation. Unlike many of her peers, Lehmann was paid for this work, which she continued until her retirement in 1950. The federation expanded its activities under her leadership. Shortly after the formation of the ALC she traveled to India to visit work supported by the women's federation. Lehmann was also a director of Milwaukee Hospital and advised the ALC's foreign mission board.

L. DeAne Lagerquist, *The Lutherans* (1999); L. DeAne Lagerquist, "Katherine Lehmann and Church Work in India," *Concordia Historical Missionary Quarterly* (Winter 1988).

L. DEANE LAGERQUIST

Leonard, Ellen Margaret (1933–). Theologian, educator, and Catholic religious. Ellen Leonard joined the *Sisters of St. Joseph of Toronto in 1951. Born into a family of women educators, she too embraced teaching as a primary school teacher, principal, and religious education consultant. After the Second Vatican Council, Leonard pursued postgraduate theological education. During her years as professor at the University of St. Michael's College (Toronto School of Theology), Leonard taught, served on church committees at many levels, and wrote about Christology, ecclesiology, ecumenism, feminist theology, religious life, and Roman Catholic modernism. Known as a mentor to her many students, Leonard retired in 1999 but continues to serve the university as professor emeritus.

Sheila M. Dabu, "A Woman of Distinction: St. Ellen Leonard," *Catholic New Times* (10 April 2005); Ellen M. Leonard, *Creative Tension* (1997); "Meet Sister Ellen," Sisters of St. Joseph, www.csj-to.ca.

TRACY J. TROTHEN

Li, Tim Oi ("Florence") (1907–92). First Anglican woman priest. Born into a Christian family in rural Hong Kong, Tim Oi Li went at the age of 21 for secondary education in Hong Kong. She adopted the name Florence and became a teacher. In 1937 she gained family permission to attend Union Theological College in Canton. Ordained deacon in 1941 she had charge of a large parish and refugee service in Macao. With no priests available she was authorized to administer communion and in 1944 was ordained priest. In 1946 she reluctantly surrendered her license to ease criticism of her bishop. From 1951 to 1979 China suppressed all religion. Allowed to join family in Canada in 1983 and reinstated priest in 1984, she is commemorated in the Episcopal Book of Lesser Feasts and Fasts.

Florence Tim-Oi Li, *Raindrops of My Life* (1996); Robert Browne, *Return to Hepu* [VHS] (1987).

JOAN R. GUNDERSEN

Lichtenstein, Tehilla Hirschenson (1893–1973). Cofounder and leader of the Society of Jewish Science. Daughter of an Orthodox rabbi, Tehilla Hirschenson received a BA from Hunter College and an MA from Columbia University. She and her husband, Reform rabbi Morris Lichtenstein, founded the Society of Jewish Science in New York City in 1922. At a time when the warmth and spirituality of Christian Science attracted a number of Reform Jews who were unsatisfied by the cool rationalism of the classical Reform synagogue, the Lichtensteins offered an alternative rooted within Judaism, but drawing on insights and techniques from Christian Science and New Thought. Lichtenstein directed the society's religious school and edited its monthly journal. After her husband's death in 1938 she became its spiritual leader and preached at its weekly Sunday service until 1972.

ANBO; JWA; Ellen Umansky, *From Christian Science to Jewish Science* (2005); Doris Friedman, *Applied Judaism* (1989); Papers, Jacob Rader Marcus Center, American Jewish Archives.

JOAN S. FRIEDMAN

Lieberman, Judith Berlin (1903–78). Principal of Shulamith, one of the first yeshivahs for young women. Judith Berlin came from an established rabbinic family. Her paternal grandfather, Rabbi Naftali-Zvi, headed the Volozhin Yeshivah, and her father, Rabbi Meyer Berlin, directed the world Mizrachi Organization. While trapped in Belorussia and Lithuania with her grandmother during World War I Berlin found solace in a private library, where she absorbed the works of Lord Byron and Leo Tolstoy, among others. In 1918 Berlin was reunited with other family members in the U.S., where she completed a BA at Hunter College. She later completed her PhD at the University of Zurich. She married rabbinic academic Saul Lieberman and lived in Jerusalem from 1932 to 1940, where she taught at the Mizrachi Teachers Training School for Girls. The couple returned to U.S. in 1940 and Lieberman became principal of Shulamith in Brooklyn.

JWA.

KAREN-MARIE WOODS

Liliuokalani, Queen Lydia (1838–1917). Last Hawaiian monarch. Lydia Liliuokalani was born in Honolulu to high chief Kapaakea and the chiefess Keohokalole, and then was adopted by Abner Paki and his wife, Konia. As a child she attended the Royal School, where she became fluent in English and acquainted with Congregational missionaries. Liliuokalani ascended to the throne of Hawaii in January 1891 after the death of her brother, King Kalakauam, who had given away much of the power of the monarchy. In 1893 Queen Liliuokalani sought to empower herself and preserve Hawaiian traditions through a new constitution that she herself had drawn up. In 1894 the queen was deposed by Americans of European descent with help from American military forces. In 1898 the U.S. annexed Hawaii, but she continued to live in Honolulu.

NoAW; Helena G. Allen, *The Betrayal of Liliuokalani* (1982); Collections, Archives of Hawaii and Bishop Museum (Honolulu).

BARBARA E. REED

Lincoln Mowry, Salome (1807–41). Reformed Methodist and Free Will Baptist preacher. Salome Lincoln was the eldest of six children born to Ambrose and Susanna Weston Lincoln. She was born in Raynham, Massachusetts; grew up in a Christian home; and experienced a religious conversion at age 15. While Lincoln preached her first sermon in 1827 she financially supported herself by working in factories. In 1829 she led the weavers at Taunton in a walkout when the owners reduced their wages. Shortly after, Lincoln became a full-time itinerant minister, preaching 12 revival meetings in Boston and on many occasions at Martha's Vineyard. She married a clergyman in 1835 and continued to preach occasionally, delivering her last sermon in 1840.

EAWR; Catherine A. Brekus, *Strangers and Pilgrims* (1998); Gerda Lerner, *The Female Experience* (1977); Almond H. Davis, *The Female Preacher, or Memoir of Salome Lincoln* (1972) [1843].

MANDY E. MCMICHAEL

Lindheim, Irma Levy (1886–1978). Zionist leader. Born into a wealthy, assimilated Jewish family, Irma Levy Lindheim's epiphany—her discovery of Zionism when she was 21—changed the course of her life. In less than a decade, she had founded a Zionist cultural center in New York City, studied for the rabbinate, journeyed to Palestine, become national president of *Hadassah (the women's Zionist organization of America), and published the first of her two books, *The Immortal Adventure* (1928), an account of her Palestine trip. In 1933, after her husband's death, she abandoned organizational work to settle on a kibbutz in Palestine. Lindheim lived there for the remainder of her life, returning periodically to the U.S. for extended stays to promote the Zionist dream.

JWA; Shulamit Reinharz, "Irma 'Rama' Lindheim: An Independent Zionist Woman," *Nashim* 1 (1988); Irma Levy Lindheim, *Parallel Quest* (1962).

PAMELA S. NADELL

Lindley, Grace (1875–1955). Mission work administrator. From 1919 until 1940 Lindley was the executive secretary of the Woman's Auxiliary to the Board of Missions for the Episcopal Church. Under her leadership, the auxiliary recruited, trained, and supported women for mission work in Asia and Latin America, and within the United States. She was instrumental in the founding of two church training schools for women in the 1920s: the Bishop Tuttle Memorial School in North Carolina trained black women, and Windham House in New York City was strongly supported by General Seminary. Both schools provided theological education for women in an era when seminaries were closed to them.

Patricia N. Page, "Looking Backward—To Look Forward: Grace Lindley, Margaret Sherman, and Frances Young," in *Deeper Joy: Lay Women and Vocation in the 20th-Century Episcopal Church*, ed. Fredrica Harris Thompsett and Sheryl Kujawa-Holbrook (2005).

ANNIE RUSSELL

Little Sisters of the Poor (LSP) (1839–). Congregation of Roman Catholic women. The LSP was founded in France when Jeanne Jugan opened her home to an elderly blind and paralyzed woman. Other young laywomen joined her to serve increasing numbers of elderly poor. They moved to larger accommodations and began the practice of begging daily for the needs of those under their care. Within a short time, they formally became a religious congregation, with Jeanne Jugan as the superior. In 1868 the sisters opened their first American home in Brooklyn, New York. The congregation currently has more than 30 homes in North America. Three thousand Little Sisters of the Poor serve in 31 countries worldwide. The sisters take vows of poverty, chastity, and obedience, and add a fourth vow: hospitality to the aged poor. Totally dependent on charity, they have no fixed income or endowments; most of their income is procured through begging.

NCE; ROWUS; George C. Stewart, *Marvels of Charity* (1994); Gabriel-Marie Garrone, *Poor in Spirit* (1975); *New Advent Catholic Encyclopedia* [online].

ELLEN WHELAN, OSF

Livermore, Harriet (1788–1868). Itinerant preacher and author. Born into an elite New England family, Harriet Livermore spent several years in the social limelight of Washington, DC, while her father was in Congress. At the age of 23, she resolved to put away frivolities and pursue religion seriously. She became a well-known preacher. On January 8, 1827, with President John Quincy Adams in attendance, she preached to members of Congress, the first of four times. Her beliefs became increasingly apocalyptic, and she developed an interest in Native Americans, who she believed were descendants of the lost tribes of Israel. Between 1836 and 1858 she traveled four times to Jerusalem, believing it to be the epicenter of Jesus' return. She lived her last years in poverty and died alone in a Philadelphia almshouse.

ANB; NoAW; Catherine A. Brekus, "Harriet Livermore, the Pilgrim Stranger," *Church History* 65, no. 3 (September 1996); Samuel Livermore, *Harriet Livermore* (1884).

PRISCILLA POPE-LEVISON

Lomax, Judith (1774–1828). Writer and poet. A member of a prominent family, Judith Lomax was the first Virginia woman to publish a volume of poetry entirely of her own writing. Family financial reverses in 1815, which partially estranged her from her family, forced Lomax to spend the last 14 years of her life supporting herself while living in Port Royal, Virginia. In poor health she moved to Fredricksburg in 1827 to live with a sister. From 1819 until her death she kept a notebook of religious writings that demonstrate both women's participation in the rebuilding efforts of Episcopalians in Virginia. Her notebook illustrates the piety and beliefs of an evangelical Episcopalian.

Joan R. Gundersen and Madeleine F. Marshall, eds., *Poetry, Piety, and Politics: The World and Writings of Judith Lomax* (unpublished); Laura Hobgood-Ostler, ed., *The Sabbath Journal of Judith Lomax* (1999); Judith Lomax, *Notes of an American Lyre* (1813).

JOAN R. GUNDERSEN

Longacre, Doris Janzen (1940–79). Author and lecturer on world hunger. Doris Janzen was born to John P. and Helene Claassen Janzen. She received a BA from Goshen College (Indiana) and pursued graduate studies at Kansas State University and Goshen Biblical Seminary. She married Paul M. Longacre, and they had two daughters. They worked for Mennonite Central Committee (MCC) in Vietnam (1964–67) and

Indonesia (1971–72). While working for MCC she compiled a collection of recipes from Mennonites around the world that became *The More-With-Less Cookbook* (1976). Her emphasis on healthy foods and suggestions on ways to reduce consumption of the world's resources propelled the book far beyond Mennonite circles. A second book, *Living More with Less* (1980), was published shortly after her death.

The Mennonite Encyclopedia, vol. 5, ed. Cornelius J. Dyck and Dennis D. Marten (1990); "Author Modeled More-With-Less," *Mennonite Weekly Review* (29 November 1979); *Gospel Herald* 72, no. 49 (4 December 1979).

VALERIE REMPEL

Louis, Minnie Dessau (1841–1922). Educator and writer. Born in Philadelphia, raised in Georgia, and educated in New York, Minnie Dessau married businessman Adolph H. Louis in 1866. She centered her philanthropic work on poor, uneducated Jewish children. In 1880 she opened the Louis Downtown Sabbath School for Jewish immigrant families. Louis became a leader in vocational education when her school refocused as the Hebrew Technical School for Girls. Louis was one of the founders of the *National Council of Jewish Women and its New York section, a leader of the Mount Sinai Training School for Nurses, and field secretary for the Jewish Chautauqua Society. Besides publishing her poems and essays Louis was also editor of the personal service department of the *American Hebrew.*

JWA; Melissa Klapper, "Jewish Women and Vocational Education in New York City, 1885–1925," *American Jewish Archives Journal* 53, nos. 1 and 2 (2001).

JUDITH METZ, SC

Lowry, Edith Elizabeth (1897–1970). Ecumenical home missions leader. A 1920 Wellesley College graduate, Lowry began work for the board of missions of the Presbyterian Church in the U.S.A. in 1922, although she was a Baptist. Starting at the ecumenical council of women for home missions in 1926, she rose through the ranks to become director of migrant ministries (1929) and executive secretary (1936). In 1939 she was the first woman invited to speak on the National Radio Pulpit. Through a process of mergers she became the first secretary of the board of home missions of the National Council of Churches in 1950. She retired in 1962.

ANB; EAWR; NoAWMP; RLA; Edith E. Lowry, Velma Shotwell, and Helen White, *Tales of Americans on Trek* (1940); Edith E. Lowry, *Migrants of the Crops* (1938).

KENDAL P. MOBLEY

Lucas, Helen Geatros (1931–). Artist. Born to an immigrant Greek family on the Canadian prairies, Helen Lucas processed her life story, including her relationships with family, church, and God, through her artwork. Lucas worked through misogynist Christian theology and patriarchal Greek cultural norms in her earlier charcoal drawings. Her art, two daughters, and women friends helped Lucas through a bad marriage and divorce. She subsequently reclaimed her sexuality and faith through her art. Her paintings include *Angelica*, a liberating nude angel, and a crucifix sprouting flowers. The colors bursting forth in her acrylic paintings of flowers reflect Lucas's vibrant life.

Sylvia Fraser, "Helen Lucas Inside Out," *Homemaker's* (September 1998); Margaret Laurence, *The Christmas Birthday Story*, Helen Lucas, illus. (1980); Helen Lucas, *This Is My Beloved—Sometimes* (1981), *Angelica* (1973); Donna Davey, prod., *Helen Lucas . . . Her Journey—Our Journey* [VHS] (1996); Fonds, York University Archives and Special Collections.

TRACY J. TROTHEN

Lund, Henriette (1887–1984). Social worker and welfare consultant. The child of Danish immigrants, Henriette Lund spent her adult life providing social services to a variety of persons. Her interest in social issues was cultivated at Macalester College. Beginning in Minneapolis she worked for several religious and secular agencies, such as the Red Cross and the North Dakota State Children's Bureau. In addition she conducted a study of the Blackfoot people for the Bureau of Indian Affairs. During the Depression years of the 1930s, Lund headed Staten Island (New York) Social Services. Her involvement with religious agencies included participation in the resettlement of refugees by the National Lutheran Council (1943–55) and the World Council of Churches, and a study of Lutheran work among Alaskan natives. In retirement Lund was a nongovernment observer at the United Nations. She was awarded the UN peace medallion in 1975. In 1981 the University of North Dakota established a student scholarship in the field of social work in her honor.

L. DeAne Lagerquist, *The Lutherans* (1999); Willmar Thorkelson, "The 'Grande' Dame of Lutheranism," *The Lutheran Bond* 57 (1980); Henriette Lund, *Of Eskimos and Missionaries* (1974).

L. DEANE LAGERQUIST

Luu, Dam (1932–99). Vietnamese American nun who founded the first Vietnamese convent in the U.S. Venerable Dam Luu was born in Han Dong province and lived from the age of two in Cu Da Temple under the care of Abbess Dam Soan. She was ordained as a Bhiksuni in Hanoi (1951) and graduated from Duoc Su Seminary (1960). She was the director of the Lam Ty Ni Orphanage until the collapse of the South Vietnamese government. She escaped South Vietnam (after four unsuccessful tries) and came to the U.S. in 1980, where she founded Duc Vien Temple in San Jose along with a Buddhist convent. She was an international leader for Buddhist women within the Sakyadhita organization and made Buddhist teachings more accessible in vernacular Vietnamese. According to her followers, after she died and was cremated, her body left behind colorful relics distinctive of Buddhists of high realization.

Thich Minh Duc, "Dam Luu: An Eminent Vietnamese Buddhist Nun," in *Innovative Buddhist Women*, ed. Karma Lekshe Tsomo (2000).

BARBARA E. REED

Lyman, Mary Ely (1887–1975). Congregationalist minister and biblical scholar. After graduating from Mount Holyoke College (Massachusetts) in 1911 Lyman taught high school for two years and then served as general secretary of the *YWCA (Young Women's Christian Association) at Mount Holyoke. She entered Union Theological Seminary (New York City) in 1916 and was the only woman in her 1919 graduating class, where she was prohibited from participating in her graduation ceremony because of her gender. Lyman published *Paul the Conqueror* in 1919, the first of several books. She earned a PhD from the University of Chicago in 1924 and was ordained as a Congregationalist minister in 1949. She became the first woman professor at Union Theological Seminary in 1950, the first woman to hold a full professorship at a U.S. seminary. Lyman was a member of the World Council of Churches Commission on Life and Work in the Churches.

ANB; DARB; EAWR; NoAWMP; RLA; Papers, Union Theological Seminary Archives.

KEITH DURSO

Lynch, Mary B. (1924–79). Catholic feminist and cofounder of the *Women's Ordination Conference (WOC). Mary

Lynch discerned a call to ordination at a young age, but since she was denied that option she embarked on a wide-ranging and distinguished career in education and social service. At the age of 47 Lynch became one of the first women to study theology at a Roman Catholic seminary. In 1970 she assumed leadership of the Deaconess Movement, an early Catholic feminist organization, devoting seemingly limitless energy to supporting the struggle for women's ordination. Lynch was known for her dedication, prayerfulness, generosity, and gentle spirit. Her work for women's ordination culminated in the 1975 Women's Ordination Conference, the first major gathering of Catholic feminists in the U.S.

Anne Marie Gardiner, ed., *Women and Catholic Priesthood* (1975); Papers, University of Notre Dame Archives.

MARY J. HENOLD

Lyon, Mary (1797–1849). Educator. Born on a farm in Buckland, Massachusetts, Mary Lyon attended school until age 13, when she was forced to quit to help run the family farm. Thereafter she gained her education by attending lectures at male academies and colleges. She got her first teaching job at age 17 and developed an interest in women's education. After teaching at Adams Female Academy and Ipswich Female Seminary, she left Ipswich to organize her own institution of higher education for women. She spent three years planning curriculum, raising support, and hiring teachers before Mount Holyoke Female Seminary, the first college for women in the U.S., opened in 1837 in South Hadley, Massachusetts. It reflected Lyon's innovative philosophy of equal education for women with a curriculum comparable to that offered at men's colleges, including an emphasis on science. Mount Holyoke also reflected Lyon's devout Christian convictions; it required religious observances on the part of students and staff, and emphasized training women for mission and benevolent work. The school became one of the most consistent producers of women missionaries for several decades. Viewing female education as both mission and ministry, Mount Holyoke graduates carried Lyon's educational ideas and methods to schools they served and founded across the U.S. and around the globe; they made Lyon's school a model for women's education.

ANB; EAWR; EE; NoAW; Amanda Porterfield, *Mary Lyon and the Mount Holyoke Missionaries* (1997); Elizabeth Alden Green, *Mary Lyon and Mount Holyoke* (1979); Mount Holyoke College Archives and Special Collections.

BEVERLY ZINK-SAWYER

Macdonald, Katherine ("Sister Kay") (1931–). Interreligious dialogue advocate and former superior of Sisters of Our Lady of Sion, Canada. Katherine Macdonald began her links with her congregation as a high school student in Saskatoon, Saskatchewan, and became a leader in the international Roman Catholic Church. She has advocated passionately for healthy and progressive relations with Jews, the raison d'être of her sisterhood since its French inception in 1842. With the Second Vatican Council, the Catholic effort to convert Jews was abandoned in favor of mutual respect and understanding. Sister Kay embodied the new spirit of openness, so much so that she found herself in conflict with the Vatican for pushing the new policy further than the papacy wished. She extended her outreach to other major world religions.

Kate Daffern, "Sister Kay," *Catholic Insight* (September 2002); National Film Board of Canada, *Sister Kay* [VHS] (2002).

OSCAR COLE-ARNAL

Machar, Agnes Maule (1837–1927). Writer, feminist, and social reformer. Born in Kingston, Ontario, to a Presbyterian minister who became the principal of Queen's University, Agnes Machar advocated for the higher education of women, temperance, and improved workplace conditions. She wrote children's books, fiction, history, poetry, and biography. While some scholars call her conservative, others see her as moderate with radical moments. For example, she agitated for women's access to higher education but did not challenge gender stereotypes. Although she did not seek substantive change in the social order, she sought a vision of a better world informed by, but not limited to, the Presbyterian Christianity of her time.

DCB; Dianne Hallman, "Rights, Justice, Power: Gendered Perspectives on Prohibition in Late Nineteenth-Century Canada," *History of Intellectual Culture* 2, no. 1 (2002) [online]; Dianne M. Hallman, *Religion and Gender in the Writing and Work of Agnes Maule Machar* (PhD diss., University of Toronto, 1994); Ruth Compton Brouwer, "Moral Nationalism in Victorian Canada: The Case of Agnes Machar," *Journal of Canadian Studies* 20 (Spring 1985).

TRACY J. TROTHEN

MacInnes, Elaine (1924–) Catholic religious, Zen master, and author. Sister Elaine MacInnes is a member of Our Lady's Missionaries, a Canadian Catholic foreign mission community. She studied with Rinzai Buddhist nuns in Kyoto and became a Zen master after koan studies at the Soto Zen Sanbo Kyodan at Kamakura, Japan. For over 30 years she encouraged prisoners to meditate and do yoga. She was director of the Prison Phoenix Trust in Oxford, England, and established a program in meditation and yoga for inmates of Canadian correctional institutions. She became an officer of the Order of Canada in 2001, and in 2002 she was awarded the Queen's Golden Jubilee Medal. MacInnes has authored three books on Zen and Christianity.

John Kasimow et al., eds., *Beside Still Waters* (2003); Elaine MacInnes, *Light Sitting in Light* (1997); Hilary Pryor, dir., *The Fires That Burn* [DVD] (2005).

ELAINE GUILLEMIN

MacKay, Amanda Norris (1858–1942). Presbyterian churchwoman. Amanda MacKay taught school in her native Nova Scotia before moving to Manitoba with her husband in 1879. In 1886 she helped organize a local Indian Missionary Society to assist Sioux families living near Portage la Prairie. After moving to Winnipeg in 1893 MacKay held various local, regional, and national offices in the Presbyterian Women's Foreign Missionary Society. She also helped to found and oversee mission shelters, free kindergartens, and other programs to serve the large European immigrant population of north Winnipeg.

Margaret E. McPherson, "Head, Heart, and Purse: The Presbyterian Women's Missionary Society in Canada, 1876–1925," in Dennis L. Butcher et al., *Prairie Spirit* (1985).

SANDRA L. BEARDSALL

Mackenzie, Jean Kenyon (1874–1936). Missionary and author. The Women's Foreign Missionary Society of the Presbyterian Church sent Jean Kenyon Mackenzie to Cameroon in 1904. She lived among tribal peoples and served as a missionary in Africa until 1913. While on the mission field she developed a sense of special mission to women. She held a genuine appreciation for non-Western culture, but also became concerned about women's cultural oppression as evidenced by practices such as polygamy. Mackenzie advocated for modernization and thought that Christianity offered African men and women greater freedom. She also showed some awareness of the impact that modernization had on tribal peoples. Her experiences were recorded in textbooks published by the United Study of Foreign Missions, including *Black Sheep* (1916), *An African Trail* (1917), and *African Clearings* (1924). *An African Trail* sold more than 130,000 copies to missionary auxiliaries.

NoAW; Patricia R. Hill, *The World Their Household* (1985).

ELIZABETH HINSON-HASTY

MacLeish, Martha Hillard (1856–1947). Educator and Baptist leader. A graduate of Vassar College, Martha Hillard was the principal of Rockford (Illinois) Seminary from 1884 to 1888, during which time she doubled the enrollment and prepared it for collegiate status. She resigned to marry Chicago merchant Andrew MacLeish. They had five children, including poet Archibald MacLeish and artist Norman H. MacLeish. Martha MacLeish published papers on child development, based on observations of her own children. As president of the Woman's Baptist Foreign Missionary Society of the West (1910–14) she was instrumental in merging the society with its eastern counterpart. She organized two Baptist mission education groups, the World Wide Guild in 1915 and the Children's World Crusade in 1917. She was a lifelong supporter of progressive education and social and municipal reform.

ANB; NoAW; Louise A. Cattan, *Lamps Are for Lighting* (1972); Martha Hillard MacLeish, *Martha Hillard MacLeish* (1949).

KENDAL P. MOBLEY

MacNamara, Geraldine (1938–84). Roman Catholic youth and community advocate. A convert to Roman Catholicism, Geraldine MacNamara entered the *Sisters of the Holy Names of Jesus and Mary (SNJM) in 1962, took her first vows in 1964, and taught in numerous Catholic schools in northern Manitoba and Winnipeg. Influenced by the directives of Vatican II, she decided to focus on teaching and mentoring poor children. She also studied law so she could better help at-risk young people. After she and several other sisters moved into an inner-city Winnipeg neighborhood, she founded Rossbrook House. Rossbrook became a place for young people to socialize (especially aboriginal and Métis youth), the location of alternative schooling, and the hub of political neighborhood organizing. Sister Mac, as she was affectionately called, became a well-known local and national leader. She was awarded the Order of Canada in 1983.

Eleanor J. Stebner, *Gem: The Life of Sister Mac* (2001).

ELEANOR J. STEBNER

MacPhail, Agnes (1890–1954). Canadian politician and social reformer. Agnes MacPhail was the first woman member of Canada's federal Parliament, elected on the Progressive Party's ticket in 1921. Serving continually until her defeat in 1940 MacPhail associated herself with the parliamentary left, first with the Progressives; then with the "Ginger Group" of social gospelers under the leadership of J. S. Woodsworth; and finally as a founding and continuing member of Canada's socialist party, the Cooperative Commonwealth Federation (CCF). MacPhail entered politics through the Ontario farm movement and championed labor rights, social welfare systems, international peace, prison reform, and rights for women. As an adolescent she joined the socially conscious Reorganized Church of Jesus Christ of Latter-day Saints and ended her career in the United Church of Canada. Her faith reflected the broad liberalism of the Protestant social gospel.

Terry Crowley, *Agnes MacPhail* (1990); Doris Pennington, *A Brave and Glorious Adventure* (1989).

OSCAR COLE-ARNAL

Macy, Joanna Rogers (1929–). Buddhist activist and author. Joanna Rogers received her bachelor's degree from Wellesley College (1950) and her doctorate from the State University of New York (1978). She married Francis Macy in 1953. Joanna Macy has been in the forefront of contemporary Buddhist movements, such as engaged Buddhism, deep ecology, and peace activism. In addition to academic positions, she has led workshops dealing with the psychology of personal and social change with the goal of turning despair into collaborative action. Her books include *Despair and Personal Power in the Nuclear Age* (1983), *Dharma and Development* (1985), *Mutual Causality in Buddhism and General Systems Theory* (1991), *World as Lover, World as Self* (1991), and *Widening Circles* (2000).

RLA; Sandy Boucher, *Turning the Wheel* (1993); Joanna Macy, *World as Lover, World as Self* (1991).

BARBARA E. REED

Mallory, Arenia (1904–77). Educator and Pentecostal lay leader. As a young woman, a curious Arenia Mallory attended a Pentecostal tent meeting and left with a deep religious awakening. Trained as a musician by her entertainer parents, she completed a bachelor's degree at Simmons College (1927) and a master's degree at the University of Illinois (1950). In 1926 Mallory began teaching piano at the Saints Academy (later the Saints Academy and Junior College) in Lexington, Mississippi. She served as school president for over 50 years. Under her direction the school modernized, expanded, and came to include an elementary and a high school (the first for black students in the county). Mallory was elected as the only female delegate from the Church of God in Christ (COGIC) to the World Pentecostal Convention in 1952.

NBAW; Dovie Marie Simmons and Olivia Martin, *Down behind the Sun* (1983).

LORETTA LONG HUNNICUTT

Mallory, Kathleen Moore (1879–1954). Southern Baptist Convention churchwoman. Kathleen Mallory—the daughter of the mayor of Selma, Alabama, and a 1902 graduate of the Woman's College of Baltimore (later Goucher College)—turned a privileged southern heritage into a legacy of service. After her fiancé's death in 1907 she immersed herself in church work. Her election as secretary of the Alabama Woman's Missionary Union (WMU) in 1909 brought her to the attention of the national WMU leadership. She was the executive secretary of the WMU from 1912 to 1948. Mallory led through simplicity, frugality, systematic efficiency, and single-hearted devotion to the missionary cause. Her prayerful and disciplined leadership raised WMU's contributions by 2,817 percent and helped keep the Southern Baptist Convention afloat.

EAWR; RLA; Catherine Allen, *Laborers Together with God* (1987); Anne Wright Ussery, *The Story of Kathleen Mallory* (1956); Kathleen Mallory, *Manual of WMU Methods*, rev. ed. (1949) [1917].

KENDAL P. MOBLEY

Malone, Mary Teresa (1938–). Educator. A feminist educator, Mary Malone was among the first Canadians to challenge the Roman Catholic Church in advocating for women's ordination to the priesthood. She taught principally at the Toronto School of Theology and at St. Jerome's University (Waterloo), and was active in providing popular theological education to thousands of persons through lectures, workshops, and retreats. Her major writing has retrieved the stories of women of the Christian tradition, whose silenced voices can now illuminate dark corners of women's Christian history. She opens the lives of these women as an alternative version of Christianity rooted in the experience of women, thereby helping women alter their effective historical consciousness and begin to establish an alternative psychic history.

"A Chat with Mary Malone," *Catholic New Times* (20 October 2002); Mary T. Malone, *Women and Christianity*, 3 vols. (2001–03); Gerry McCarthy, "*The Social Edge* Interview: Author, Historian, and Theologian Mary Malone," *The Social Edge.com* (June 2002) [online].

VERONICA M. DUNNE, RNDM

Manning, Joanna (1943–). Roman Catholic author and activist. A voice of conscience in the Catholic Church, Joanna Manning is a dedicated and prophetic educator engaged in works of justice. Prompted by the 1987 Canadian clergy sexual abuse scandals, she founded the Coalition of Concerned Canadian Catholics (CCCC). Consequently, Toronto's archbishop pressured the Catholic school board to remove her from teaching religion. Manning and the teachers' union mounted a legal challenge, with the landmark decision going in her favor. She opened the Anne Frank House (Toronto), a nonprofit housing cooperative for refugees, in 1993. In 1995 she received the Marion Tyrell Award for distinguished contributions to Catholic education. Manning's publications have amplified her voice and enabled her to lead diverse national and international workshops. She is a frequent commentator in Canadian media on church affairs.

Joanna Manning, *Take Back the Truth* (2003), *Is the Pope Catholic?* (1999).

VERONICA M. DUNNE, RNDM

Markley, Mary Elizabeth (1881–1954). First woman on the national staff of a Lutheran denomination. Mary Markley, daughter of the Reverend A. B. Markley, was born in Hillerdale, Pennsylvania. She graduated from Ursinus College (1902) and received a master's degree in English from Columbia University (1907). She taught at Elizabethtown College and Agnes Scott College in Decatur, Georgia, before becoming supervisor of the Service House for the National Commission for Soldiers' and Sailors' Welfare (1918–19). Markley became secretary for the Board of Education of the United Lutheran Church in 1919 and served until 1946. Her responsibilities included visitation to colleges and seminaries and recruiting missionaries for overseas work. She was a board member of the Lutheran Nurses Guild, the Women's Missionary Society, the Lutheran Student Association, and the National Christian Council. Her efforts opened doors for other women to enter professional church work.

Archives of the Evangelical Lutheran Church in America.

MARIA ERLING

Marshall, Martha Stearns (18th century). Baptist preacher. Little is known about Martha Marshall, except the facts that can be established by her relationships with her brother, Shubal Stearns (1706–71), and her husband, Daniel Marshall (1706–84), whom she married in 1747. Both of these men were key leaders of the Separate Baptists as they migrated out of New England and settled in the southern colonies in the 1750s and 1760s. Marshall was among those Baptists jailed several times in New England for advocating adult baptism and women's preaching. She apparently was an important leader in her own right, being remembered by Baptist historians as an eloquent revivalist preacher. The Baptist Women in Ministry have established the first Sunday of

February as the annual Martha Stearns Marshall Day of Preaching.

Dictionary of Baptists in America (1994).

SCOTT D. SEAY

Marshall LeSourd, Sarah Catherine Wood (1914–83). Author and publisher. Catherine Wood, the daughter of a Presbyterian minister was born in Johnson City, Tennessee. She graduated from Agnes Scott College in 1936 and married Presbyterian minister Peter Marshall. After his death in 1949 she compiled a volume of his sermons. Her second book, a biography of his life entitled *A Man Called Peter* (1951), was on *The New York Times* bestseller list for over 50 consecutive weeks. In 1959 Marshall married Leonard LeSourd. They founded a religious publishing house, Chosen Books, with another couple. Marshall authored more than 20 books that together sold over 18 million copies. Her books resonated with people so deeply that one was made into a movie (*A Man Called Peter*) and another into a television series (*Christy*).

EAWR; NoAWC; Special Collections, McCain Library, Agnes Scott College.

MANDY E. MCMICHAEL

Maryknoll Sisters (1912–). U.S.-based Catholic congregation serving foreign missions and minority groups in the U.S. Founded by *Mary Josephine ("Mollie") Rogers ("Mother Mary Joseph"), the Maryknoll Sisters were the first U.S. congregation dedicated to foreign missions. Mollie Rogers graduated from Smith College and credited her education and the example of Protestant women missionaries for influencing her life and missionary call. In 1912 she and six other laywomen went to Hawthorne, New York, to assist the Maryknoll Fathers with missionary publications; the small community later moved to nearby Ossining, New York. The group grew steadily and in 1920 formally became a religious congregation. The next year, six sisters went to Hong Kong and China. The congregation expanded missions in Asia until World War II interrupted their work. After the war, Maryknoll sisters founded new missions in Latin America, Africa, and several islands in the South Pacific; they also increased their missions to minority groups in the U.S. The ministry of Maryknoll sisters is service to the poor and oppressed. To that end, sisters earn degrees in nursing, medicine, education, and community development. Working with local groups, the sisters adapt their services to the needs of specific cultures. The congregation presently has over 700 members from 22 nations, and they serve in 31 countries worldwide.

EACH; NCE; Cindy Yik-Yi Chu, ed., *Diaries of the Maryknoll Sisters in Hong Kong* (2007), *The Maryknoll Sisters in Hong Kong* (2004); Jean-Paul Wiest, *Maryknoll in China* (1997); Penny Lernoux, *Hearts on Fire* (1993).

ELLEN WHELAN, OSF

Mason, Lucy Randolph (1882–1959). Labor activist and reformer. Born of the first families of Virginia, the daughter and granddaughter of Episcopal priests, Lucy Mason was raised with a strong sense of Christian service and social responsibility. Throughout the 1930s she advocated for better working conditions for women and children, minimum wage laws, and social security legislation. In 1937 the Congress of Industrial Organizations (CIO) invited Mason to join the Textile Workers organizing committee to promote the need for unions in the South. In this capacity she traveled extensively and worked with religious and community leaders and the media in supporting the interests of labor. At a time when southern community leaders easily associated labor unions with communism, "Miss Lucy" was successful in advocating for the needs of workers.

ANB; NoAWMP; Sheryl A. Kujawa-Holbrook, *Freedom Is a Dream* (2002); Lucy Randolph Mason, *To Win These Rights* (1952).

SHERYL A. KUJAWA-HOLBROOK

Mathews, Ann Teresa (Mother Bernardina) (1732–1800). Founder of first U.S. Roman Catholic monastic community. Ann Mathews was born in Charles County, Maryland, in the English Catholic colonial community. Her deeply religious upbringing fostered her desire to enter a religious community. Restrictions enforced against Catholics under British colonial rule forced Mathews to seek entrance in an English Discalced *Carmelite community in Hoogstraeten, Belgium. In 1754 she became Sister Bernardina and professed final vows in 1755. Mathews became the community's prioress in 1774. In 1790 she returned to Maryland with four other women to found a Carmelite monastery, the first in the newly established U.S. The community increased to 14 in the first decade and continues to thrive. She is buried in the Bonnie Brae cemetery in Baltimore, Maryland.

ANB; EACH; EAWR; NoAW; Charles Warren Currier, *Carmel in America* (1989).

SANDRA YOCUM MIZE

Matthews, Marjorie Swank (1916–86). Methodist pastor and bishop. An active laywoman in the United Methodist Church, Matthews became a part-time pastor at the age of 46, even though she lacked any formal education. While pastoring churches in New York, Michigan, and Florida, she graduated (with highest honors) from Central Michigan University (BA 1968), Colgate Rochester Divinity School (BA 1972), and Florida State University (MA 1974; PhD 1976). Matthews was appointed as a district superintendent in western Michigan and then elected delegate to the church's General Conference. In 1980 Methodists elected Matthews a bishop, then age 64 and battling breast cancer, making her the first woman to hold such a position in a mainline denomination practicing episcopal polity. As bishop she supervised 522 churches, 399 ministers, and 135,000 congregants.

EAWR; RLA; Jean Caffey Lyles, "An Improbable Episcopal Choice," *Christian Century* 97, no. 31 (13–20 August 1980).

KEITH DURSO

Matthews, Victoria Earle (1861–1907). Author and reformer. Born into slavery in Georgia, Victoria Matthews turned to writing soon after her marriage and the birth of a son. Her work as an author and lecturer led to leadership positions in clubs for African American women in New York and Brooklyn. In 1892 she organized the antilynching crusade for *Ida B. Wells in New York. In 1895 she founded the National Federation of Afro-American Women in Boston with *Josephine St. Pierre Ruffin and others. The death of her 16-year-old son ignited her interest in social, political, and educational improvement for African Americans. In 1897 she founded the White Rose Mission in New York City, a shelter and community center for African American women and girls. She was a member of St. Philips Episcopal Church in Brooklyn.

NBAW; NoAW; Hallie Q. Brown, *Homespun Heroine and Other Women of Distinction* (1988) [1926]; Gilbert Osofsky, *Harlem* (1971); Elizabeth Lindsay Davis, *Lifting As They Climb* (1933).

SHERYL A. KUJAWA-HOLBROOK

Mattson, Ingrid (1963–). Muslim leader. Ingrid Mattson was born into a Canadian Roman Catholic household and converted to Islam when she was 23 years old. She is the first Muslim convert and first woman to be elected as president of the Islamic Society of North America. Mattson holds a BA from the University of Waterloo (1987) and a PhD from the University of Chicago (1999), and teaches Islamic studies at Hartford Seminary. She and her husband, Amer Aatek, have two children.

Sarah Childress, "Ingrid Mattson; Islam: Raised Catholic, This Muslim Professor Is Bringing the Moderate Viewpoint to the World," *Newsweek* (25 December 2006); Jane Lampman, "Muslim Convert Takes On Leadership Role," *Christian Science Monitor* (13 December 2001).

ELEANOR J. STEBNER

Matz, Mary Jane Dill (1931–). Moravian pastor and educator. Mary Matz was the first ordained woman in the Moravian Church in America, Northern Province. The 1957 Unity Synod of the worldwide Moravian Church affirmed the ordination of women and the autonomy of each province to proceed toward it. The Moravian Church in America endorsed the ordination of women in 1970, and Matz was ordained in 1975. Mary Dill, raised Lutheran, was a 1953 graduate of Grove City College and a director of Christian education in the First Presbyterian Church (Athens, Ohio) before her marriage to William Matz in 1955. Mary Matz graduated with a master's degree from Moravian Theological Seminary in 1975. After her ordination, she served as a pastor at the Central Moravian Church (Bethlehem, PA) and in educational ministry with the Eastern District of the church.

Mark Liebenow, comp., *Women of the Moravian Church* (1987).

ELEANOR J. STEBNER

Mayes, Martha Jane ("Mattie") Warner (1859–1953). Baptist leader. Born a slave in Georgia, Mattie Warner moved with her family to Tennessee after the Civil War. There she met and married Joseph Mayes, a Baptist minister, and they moved to Oklahoma in search of land to farm. Life in Oklahoma was difficult because of floods and the escalation of Jim Crow laws in the early 1900s. They decided to move to Canada after hearing about the availability of free homesteads. Along with 10 other families associated with their Baptist church, the Mayeses and their 13 children arrived in Saskatchewan in 1910. They farmed near Maidstone and built the Shiloh Baptist Church. Grannie Mayes, as she was called, became the spiritual leader and matriarch of the black community on the Canadian prairies.

Mona Holmlund and Gail Youngberg, eds., *Inspiring Women: A Celebration of Herstory* (2003); North of the Gully History Book Committee, *North of the Gully* (1981).

ELEANOR J. STEBNER

McBeth, Susan ("Sue") Law (1830–93), and **Kate Christine McBeth** (1833–1915?). Presbyterian missionary educators. Born near Stirling, Scotland, Sue McBeth was brought as an infant by her parents to Ohio, where Kate was born. In 1873 Sue was appointed by the Presbyterian Board of Foreign Missions to the reservation school at Lapwai, Idaho Territory. She moved 60 miles east to Kamiah, where Kate joined her in 1879. Kate taught the women of the community, while Sue taught theology to the men. Sue prepared several Nez Perce men for Presbyterian ordination, as did Kate after her sister's death. The McBeth sisters were fiercely devoted to the Nez Perce people, but, in their European American ethnocentricity, they suppressed the indigenous culture and reconfigured the community's power structures. As a result of ongoing conflict with the reservation agent, the McBeths left Kamiah in 1885 and spent the rest of their lives in nearby Mount Idaho, just outside the reservation boundaries.

ANB; EAWR; NoAW; Allen Conrad Morrill and Eleanor Dunlap Morrill, *Out of the Blanket* (1978); Michael C. Coleman, "Christianizing and Americanizing the Nez Perce: Sue L. McBeth and Her Attitudes to the Indians," *Journal of Presbyterian History* 53 (1975); "Kate and Sue McBeth," University of Idaho Library, www.lib.uidaho.edu/mcbeth/index.htm.

SANDRA L. BEARDSALL

McClung, Nellie Letitia Mooney (1873–1951). Author, social activist, and politician. When Nellie Mooney was seven years old, her family moved from Ontario to homestead in Manitoba. She began teaching at age 16, and at age 23 she married Robert Wesley McClung. She became active in the *Woman's Christian Temperance Union (WCTU) and also began writing, with a first novel published in 1908. While living in Winnipeg she became an effective speaker on behalf of women's rights and Prohibition, and she also developed her concern for urban laborers, farmers, and immigrants. The family moved to Alberta, where from 1921 until 1926 she served as a member of the provincial legislature. An active Methodist, she addressed the ecumenical council of the Methodist Church in London in 1921 as one of Canada's delegates. She spoke extensively in Canada and the U.S. in support of women religious leadership and even ordination. McClung was one of five women who brought forward the Person's Case that eventually resulted in the verdict that women were legally "persons." She was an effective reformer and proponent of social gospel ideals.

DCB; Mary Hallett and Marilyn Davis, *Firing the Heather* (1993); Randi R. Warne, *Literature as Pulpit* (1993); Nellie McClung, *Clearing in the West* (1976) [1935], *The Stream Runs Fast* (1965) [1945].

MARILYN FÄRDIG WHITELEY

McDade, Carolyn Annette McGehee (1935–). Songwriter and activist. Carolyn McGehee grew up in a Southern Baptist Louisiana family. The post–World War II context shaped her antiwar, antiracist, and feminist consciousness. She trained as a teacher, married, had three daughters, and later divorced. In 1970 she composed the music for the first women's service at her Unitarian Universalist (UU) congregation in Boston. In 1983 she founded with Sister Chris Loughlin the Womancenter (Plainville, Massachusetts). McDade was active in numerous social justice causes in the 1980s, including the sanctuary movement. Earth-centered spirituality and the preservation of species has been her passion from the 1990s. McDade empowers and transforms the lives of women through song. She has nurtured a "sacred web" of activist women's singing circles across Canada and the U.S. Several of her songs are published in Christian and UU hymnals.

Kimberly French, "Carolyn McDade's Spirit of Life," *UU World Magazine* (18 August 2007); Carolyn McDade, www.carolynmcdademusic.com.

JANET SILMAN

McDowell, Mary Eliza (1854–1936). Settlement house leader and social reformer. Mary McDowell was educated in the public schools of Chicago and became active in Methodist social service work in the 1870s and 1880s. After four years with Hull House, she was appointed director of the University of Chicago Settlement, a position that she held from 1894 to 1929. The house grew into a place that provided child care, education, economic assistance, and other social services. She was a founder of the Women's Trade Union League. McDowell worked to improve race relations in Chicago and joined both the National Association for the Advancement of Colored People (NAACP) and the Chicago Urban League. She was convinced that democracy, informed by Christian virtues, was the most effective means to bring about social reform.

ANB; NoAW; WBC; Caroline Hill, ed., *Mary McDowell and Municipal Housekeeping* (1938); Howard Wilson, *Mary McDowell, Neighbor* (1928).

SCOTT D. SEAY

McGroarty, Susan ("Sister Julia") (1827–1901). Catholic educator. Born in Ireland, Susan McGroarty immigrated to Cincinnati in 1831. Joining the *Sisters of Notre Dame de Namur in 1846 she received the name "Sister Julia" and began a career as an educator in academies and free schools for poor children in Cincinnati, Philadelphia, and Roxbury (Massachusetts). In 1887 she became superior of the U.S. houses of her congregation and was responsible for the education of her sisters as teaching professionals. In this capacity she wrote a standardized course of instruction and established common general examinations for the schools. In 1897 McGroarty established Trinity College, a national Catholic college for women in Washington, DC. Modeled after the Seven Sisters colleges, Trinity developed a reputation for high academic standards.

ANBO; EACH; NoAW; ROWUS; Mary Hayes, "The Founding Years of Trinity College: A Case Study in Christian Feminism," *U.S. Catholic Historian* 10, nos. 1 and 2 (Winter/Spring 1992).

JUDITH METZ, SC

McIntosh Bell, Martha E. (1848–1922). Southern Baptist Convention churchwoman. The daughter of a wealthy planter and slave owner in South Carolina, Martha McIntosh entered organized missionary work as the first secretary and treasurer for the South Carolina Central Women's Committee (1875–1894). She became the founding president of Woman's Missionary Union (WMU), and led the organization to sponsor an annual Christmas offering for foreign missions. After four years as president (1888–92), McIntosh declined reelection, serving instead as vice president from South Carolina (1892–95). After she married T. P. Bell in 1895 she declined all WMU leadership positions beyond her local church. Her husband died in 1916, and in 1918 she went to live with her stepdaughter, a missionary in Tengchow, North China. Three years later they returned to the Ridgecrest Baptist Assembly in North Carolina, where she died.

EAWR; RLA; Catherine Allen, *Laborers Together with God* (1987).

KENDAL P. MOBLEY

McKim, LindaJo Horton (1946–). Hymnal editor. LindaJo McKim was the editor of *The Presbyterian Hymnal: Hymns, Psalms, and Spiritual Songs* (1990), a hymnal of the Presbyterian Church (U.S.A.). She was chosen as editor from over 200 applicants and is the first woman editor of a Presbyterian hymnal. An ordained Presbyterian minister, she has served as a pastor of several congregations and an adjunct theological professor, and has also worked as a professional opera singer and music engraver. She is the author of *The Presbyterian Hymnal Companion* (1993). She married Donald K. McKim in 1976, and they have two sons.

ELEANOR J. STEBNER

McMain, Eleanor Laura (1866–1934). Settlement house worker. Eleanor McMain attended the Episcopal church and schools, and worked as a teacher and governess in her early years. She began her 30-year settlement house career around 1900 by taking courses at the University of Chicago and studying the settlement house movement. In 1902 she reorganized Kingsley House in New Orleans and established a vacation school, free clinic, playgrounds, and an antituberculosis league. Within seven years, a day nursery association, summer retreat, program for blind children, and school for public service were opened. A new Kinsley House was built in 1925, and it included a residence, library, gymnasium, and trade school rooms. McMain also worked for child welfare throughout the state of Louisiana, and in national and international settlement movements.

NoAW; Isabelle Dubroca, *Good Neighbor Eleanor McMain of Kingsley House* (1955).

SHERYL A. KUJAWA-HOLBROOK

McPherson, Aimee Elizabeth Kennedy Semple ("Sister Aimee") (1890–1944). Faith healing Pentecostal evangelist and denominational founder. Born on a farm in rural Ontario, Aimee Kennedy was converted as a teenager and called to evangelistic work at a Pentecostal revival led by Robert Semple, whom she married. Their mission to China was brief due to Robert's death from malaria. She returned to the U.S. with their daughter and married Harold Stewart McPherson, with whom she had a son. Discontented with her domestic life she vowed, against her husband's wishes, to follow the call to evangelism. She held evangelistic meetings up and down the East Coast in a portable tent for several years. In 1918 she settled in Los Angeles with her two children and her mother. Within several years she built a monumental church building, Angelus Temple, the epicenter of her evangelistic enterprise and headquarters for her denomination, the International Church of the Foursquare Gospel. In addition to nine worship services a week, Angelus Temple hosted a commissary, prayer tower, radio station, and Bible college. Her disappearance for six weeks in May 1926 remains a mystery; she maintained that she was kidnapped, and she was acquitted in court of the charge of obstructing justice. For nearly two more decades Sister Aimee held expansive evangelistic meetings in many cities and solidified her denomination. Her health began to deteriorate; she had another brief marriage and divorce, and irreparable quarrels with her mother and daughter. Her death in a hotel room from an overdose of sleeping pills was deemed accidental by the autopsy report.

ANB; EAWR; EE; NoAW; Matthew A. Sutton, *Aimee Semple McPherson and the Resurrection of Christian America* (2007); Edith Blumhofer, *Aimee Semple McPherson* (1993); Daniel Mark Epstein, *Sister Aimee* (1993); Linda Garmon, dir., *American Experience: Sister Aimee* [DVD] (2007); Richard Rossi, dir., *Aimee Semple McPherson* [DVD] (2006); Ephemera, Billy Graham Center Archives, Wheaton, Illinois.

PRISCILLA POPE-LEVISON

Mears, Henrietta Cornelia (1890–1963). Christian educator. Henrietta Mears was raised in Minnesota, attended a Baptist church, and graduated from the University of Minnesota. She taught high school chemistry and a popular Sunday school class for young women. In 1928 she hosted the pastor of the First Presbyterian Church of Hollywood, California, for a Sunday dinner; he was so impressed with her that he invited her to become the director of Christian education at his church. She served there until her death. The Sunday school grew from 450 to 4,000 in three years. She taught the college class and developed an extensive training program for all the teachers. She wrote curriculum for all grade levels, founded Gospel Light Publications, and developed the Forest Home Christian Conference Center. She was a mentor to Bill Bright (Campus Crusade), Billy Graham, Richard Halverson (chaplain of the Senate), and many others. A number of Presbyterian ministers were "Miss Mears's boys" and valued deeply her role in their formation. She was known for her wisdom, excellent teaching, enthusiasm, energy, and brightly colored hats.

EAWR; RLA; Earl O. Roe, ed., *Dream Big* (1990); Barbara Powers, *The Henrietta*

Mears Story (1957); Richard J. Leyda, "Henrietta Cornelia Mears," Christian Educators of the 20th Century, www.talbot.edu/ce20.

LYNN JAPINGA

Melton, Florence Spurgeon Zacks (1911–2007). Jewish philanthropist and educator. Born into a Jewish family in Philadelphia, Florence Spurgeon's grandmother inspired her to live a life committed to Jewish values. She and her first husband, Aaron Zacks, married in 1930 and had two children. They founded jointly R. G. Barry Corporation, the largest manufacturer of soled slippers. Zacks used that success to help children in need, by creating a foundation that provided prostheses to those unable to afford them. After Aaron Zacks's death in 1965, Florence Zacks met and married Samuel Mendel Melton (an engineer and philanthropist), who was also dedicated to the Jewish community. Frances Melton then created the Florence Melton Adult Mini School to educate adults about Jewish traditions and values. The community-based curriculum utilized a two-year program. The program gained momentum quickly and now operates in over 25 communities across North America and Australia. Melton also cofounded the Center for the Advancement of Jewish Education, the largest organization of Jewish educators in the Americas.

JWA; Jewish Women's Archive, "JWA—In Memoriam—Florence Melton" (26 July 2007), www.jwa.org/discover/inmemoriam/melton; "About Us: Florence Melton," Florence Melton Adult Mini School, www.fmams.org.il.

SHIRA M. KOHN

Meyer, Annie Nathan (1867–1951). Founder of Barnard College and writer. Annie Nathan was born into a prominent New York Jewish family. She enrolled in Columbia University's collegiate course for women, but wanted women educated at the same level as their male peers and argued for the creation of a women's college annexed to Columbia. She put forth a petition that listed names of several prominent New York clergy and citizens. With the help of her physician husband, Meyer leased the building that became the first home to Barnard College in 1889. While supporting educational and professional opportunities for women, she disliked suffragists, whom she felt were extreme. Meyer's commitment to enhancing women's lives was a prominent theme in several of her published plays, stories, and articles.

ANB; JWA; Judith Solar, "Annie Nathan Meyer," *Barnard Alumnae* (Summer 1978); Annie Nathan Meyer, *It's Been Fun* (1951); Papers, Jacob Rader Marcus Center, American Jewish Archives, Hebrew Union College.

SHIRA M. KOHN

Meyer, Lucy Jane Rider (1849–1922). Educator and deaconess organizer. Born in Vermont and converted in her teens, Lucy Rider studied and taught in Vermont and at a Quaker school in Greensboro, North Carolina, before attending Oberlin College (BA 1872). After further study and teaching, she became a field secretary in 1880 for the Illinois State Sunday School Association. Rider married Josiah Shelly Meyer in 1885, and they soon opened the Chicago Training School (CTS) for City, Home, and Foreign Missions. The Meyers had one son, born in 1887, the same year Meyer received an MD from Woman's Medical College of Chicago. A prolific writer in numerous fields including Christian education, hymnology, and science, Meyer taught in the training school on subjects that ranged from biblical studies to medical training and visitation among the urban poor. The Meyers also established a deaconess home, Wesley Memorial Hospital, Chicago Old People's Home, and Lake

Bluff Orphanage. Meyer was an advocate for deaconess work in the Methodist Episcopal (ME) Church. In 1888, with the endorsement of the Rock River Annual Conference and Bishop James Thoburn, the General Conference of the ME Church (although reluctant to support other ecclesiastical rights for women) recognized the role of deaconess as a church office. Meyer trained deaconesses at CTS and edited the *Deaconess Advocate* (earlier known as the *Message*) from 1886 to 1914. Deaconesses at CTS chose from two concentrations: evangelistic visitation or nursing. Although they took no vows, deaconesses remained unmarried, wore a simple uniform, and received no salary (only room and board). A debate developed, persisting until Meyer's death, between her vision for the office of deaconess alongside elders and deacons, and *Jane Bancroft Robinson's vision for their inclusion within the Woman's Home Missionary Society.

ANB; EAWR; EE; NoAW; WBC; Isabelle Horton, *High Adventure: Life of Lucy Rider Meyer* (1928).

LACEYE C. WARNER

Michael, Olga ("Matushka Olga," "Olinka") (1916–79). Orthodox Christian midwife and spiritual leader among the Yup'ik people of Alaska. Until her death in 1979 Olga Michael lived a life of bare subsistence in Kwethluk, Alaska. She married the village postmaster, who later became Archpriest Nicolai Michael. Well known as a skilled midwife in her region, Michael was also highly regarded by the Yup'ik people as a spiritual mother. Her influence exemplifies the enculturation of the Orthodox faith, from its roots in the 18th-century Russian mission to Alaska, within the indigenous communities of the region. Matushka Olga transmitted many of the hymns of the Orthodox Church to her own community in the Yup'ik language. Although not formally canonized, Orthodox believers, not only in Alaska but also increasingly throughout North America, revere her as a saint. Icons of Michael often depict her against a backdrop featuring the Northern Lights.

Kevin Wigglesworth, "Matushka Olga Michael of Alaska," *The Canadian Journal of Orthodox Christianity* 3, no. 1 (2008); Michael Oleksa, *Orthodox Alaska: A Theology of Mission* (1998).

MATTHEW FRANCIS

Militz, Annie Rix (1855–1924). New Thought leader. In 1887 Annie Rix attended a class offered in San Francisco by *Emma Curtis Hopkins and found healing and a career. In 1890 she studied with Hopkins in Chicago. She married and returned to California, where she founded Homes of Truth all along the West Coast. She wrote New Thought texts, founded the University of Christ (Los Angeles), and traveled internationally as a lecturer. After she failed to rise from the dead in three days (as she had promised), the network of homes dwindled to the current one in Alameda.

EAWR; RLA.

GRAEME SHARROCK

Miller, Emily Clark Huntington (1833–1913). Author and educator. Emily Huntington graduated from Oberlin College in 1857 and taught there briefly. In 1860 she married John Edwin Miller, and they moved several times before settling in Evanston, Illinois. Miller, already a published writer, became editor of the *Little Corporal*, a children's magazine, of which her husband was the publisher. Miller was active in the Methodist Woman's Foreign Missionary Society and contributed to the establishment of Evanston College for Ladies (which later merged with Northwestern University). She was an active participant in the *Woman's Christian Temperance Union. In 1891, some years after the death of her husband, Miller became dean of women and assistant professor of English literature at Northwestern; she retired as dean in 1898 and as professor in 1900. Miller continued to write for periodicals and published poetry, novels, and children's stories until her death.

NoAW.

MARILYN FÄRDIG WHITELEY

Mills, Susan Lincoln Tolman (1825–1912). Educator. A graduate of Mount Holyoke Female Seminary (now Mount Holyoke College), Susan Tolman taught on the faculty there until she married Cyrus Mills in 1848. The couple then served as Presbyterian missionaries to Sri Lanka, where they both worked at Batticota College. They resigned as missionaries shortly after they returned to the U.S. in 1854. From 1860 to 1864 Mills's husband served as president of Oahu College in Hawaii while she was a member of the faculty. They returned to the U.S. and established a Young Ladies Seminary in Benecia, California. The seminary was later moved to Oakland and renamed Mills Seminary; in 1885 the school became known as Mills College. It was the only Protestant college for women in California at the time, and Mills was its president from 1890 to 1909.

NoAW; Frederik Ohles et al., *Biographical Dictionary of Modern American Educators* (1997).

ELIZABETH HINSON-HASTY

Miner, Sarah Luella (1861–1936). Missionary educator. Inspired by the Student Volunteer Movement (SVM) and her Oberlin College education, Sarah Miner arrived in China in 1888. She was an American Board of Commissioners for Foreign Missions (ABCFM) missionary teacher, and she worked at Luhe Boys' Academy and North China Union College. After surviving and writing about the Boxer Uprising, Miner established the North China Union (later Yenching) Women's College, China's first women's college, in 1904, where she taught science and served as dean. In 1911, as revolution started, Chinese leaders elected her president of Peking's Society for the Protection of Women and Children. She was the only woman on the advisory council of China's Christian Educational Association, one of 50 members of the interdenominational China Continuation Committee/National Christian Council, and one of six Chinese missionary representatives to the 1936 International Missionary Council in Jerusalem. Her career ended at Shandong Christian University.

NoAW; Luella Miner, *China's Book of Martyrs* (1903); *Two Heroes of Cathay* (1903).

JANE HARRIS

Minor, Clorinda S. (ca. 1809–55). Millennialist. As a Philadelphia millennialist in the 1840s, Clorinda Minor edited (with Emily C. Clemons) a periodical for women entitled *Advent Message to the Daughters of Zion*. She resolved her disappointment with the failure of William Miller's prophecies by advocating that Christ could not return until the Jews were returned to their ancestral homeland. She migrated in 1852 to Palestine, cofounded an interfaith settlement at Artas, became a key figure in the agricultural development of Palestine, and helped introduce U.S. diplomacy to the region.

Barbara Krieger with Shalom Goldman, *Divine Expectations* (1999).

GRAEME SHARROCK

Modesto, Ruby Eleanor (1913–80). Medicine woman and anthropologist. Ruby Modesto was a Cahuilla Indian born on the Martinez Reservation of Southern California. Descended from a family of ceremonial leaders and medicine men, she grew up attending a Moravian church but left it when she discovered her own shamanistic powers. She served the Cahuilla as a *pul* (medicine woman) and worked to preserve their culture. She taught Cahuilla language classes, lectured at local colleges, and collaborated with anthropologists studying the indigenous peoples of Southern California. In 1976 she coauthored *Not for Innocent Ears*, a collection of autobiographical information and Cahuilla folktales. She intended the work, published shortly after her death, to preserve information about the Cahuilla and their beliefs.

NaAW; Ruby Modesto and Guy Mount, *Not for Innocent Ears* (1980); Richard Lando and Ruby Modesto, "Temal Wakish: A Desert Cahilla Village," *Journal of California Anthropology* 4 (1977).

ANDREW H. STERN

Moes, Mother Alfred (Marie Catherine) (1828–99). Catholic religious founder. Born in Luxembourg, Mother Alfred immigrated as a laywoman to the U.S. in 1851 and founded two Franciscan congregations, one in Joliet, Illinois (1865), and one in Rochester, Minnesota (1877). Following Rochester's devastating tornado of 1883, Mother Alfred convinced a respected country doctor, Dr. W. W. Mayo, that Rochester needed a hospital. She promised him that the sisters would build the hospital if Dr. Mayo and his sons would staff it. Her vision and resolve persuaded the doctor to agree, and Saint Marys Hospital opened in 1889. The Mayo Clinic, which has its roots in this frontier hospital, became world renowned, as did Dr. W. W. Mayo's surgeon sons, the Mayo Brothers. The *Franciscan Sisters of Rochester continue to sponsor Saint Marys Hospital.

Ellen Whelan, *The Sisters' Story*, 2 vols. (2002, 2007); Carlan Kraman, *Odyssey in Faith* (1990); Ursula Stepsis and Dolores Liptak, *Pioneer Healers* (1989).

ELLEN WHELAN, OSF

Moise, Penina (1797–1880). Jewish poet. Called the poet laureate of Charleston, South Carolina, Penina Moise's work appeared in many magazines. In 1833 she published her collection, *Fancy's Sketch Book*, the first by a Jewish woman in the U.S. In 1824 she helped organize the first Reform Jewish society in the U.S. Later they rejoined and then reshaped Charleston's Beth Elohim congregation. Moise composed most of the hymns for its hymnal, the first Jewish hymnal in America, and ultimately wrote 190 hymns. Thirteen of these were included in the Reform movement's 1932 *Union Hymnal*. In 1845 Moise became superintendent of her congregation's Sunday school. She lost her vision late in life and was assisted by her niece, with whom she ran a small school in her home.

ANB; JWA; NoAW; Gary Phillip Zola, *Isaac Harby of Charleston* (1994); Elzas Barnett, *The Jews of South Carolina* (1905).

DIANNE ASHTON

Mollenkott, Virginia Ramey (1932–). Evangelical feminist and author. Virginia Ramey was raised as an evangelical fundamentalist in the Plymouth Brethren Assemblies. She earned a BA from Bob Jones University, an MA from Temple University, and a PhD from New York University. She taught at Carl McIntire's Shelton College, Nyack Missionary College, and William Paterson College. In 1978, as both a founding member of the Evangelical Women's Caucus (EWC) and a then-closeted lesbian, she published a book with Letha Scanzoni entitled *Is the Homosexual My Neighbor?* The book defended gay rights and precipitated a division within the EWC. Mollenkott is a founder of the *Evangelical and Ecumenical Women's Caucus and continues to publish and articulate her vision of Christian biblical feminism.

EE; Virginia Mollenkott, in *Transforming the Faiths of Our Fathers*, ed. Ann Brande

(2004); Virginia Ramey Mollenkott and Letha Sconzoni, *Is the Homosexual My Neighbor?* rev. ed. (1994) [1978].

JUDITH L. GIBBARD

Montgomery, Carrie Judd (1858–1946). Author, editor, and pastor. Born in Buffalo, New York, as the fourth of eight children, Carrie Judd was confirmed in an Episcopal church. In 1877 a fall left her an invalid. Healed in 1879 in response to the prayers of the African American evangelist Sarah Mix, Judd published her testimony as *The Prayer of Faith* (1880). She identified with an emerging evangelical interest in divine healing, spoke and wrote on the subject, and prayed for the sick. In 1890 she moved to Oakland, California, where she married businessman George Montgomery. They opened the House of Peace, a home for missionaries on furlough (1893), an orphanage (1895), and a missionary training school, and sponsored an annual camp meeting. They also began publishing *Triumphs of Faith* (edited by Carrie Montgomery), a monthly digest of testimonies, exhortations to holiness, sermons, missionary reports, and announcements. From 1908 onward Montgomery identified with Pentecostalism. Her publication is a rich source for the study of the emergence of global interest in the new movement.

EAWR; EE; RLA; Edith Blumhofer, *Restoring the Faith* (1993); Daniel Albrecht, "The Life and Teachings of Carrie Judd Montgomery" (MA thesis, Western Evangelical Seminary, 1984); Carrie Judd Montgomery, *Under His Wings* (1936); Papers, Flower Pentecostal Heritage Center.

EDITH BLUMHOFER

Montgomery, Helen Barrett (1861–1934). Social reformer, Baptist, and ecumenical churchwoman. An 1884 Wellesley College graduate, Helen Montgomery was the first president (1893–1911) of the Women's Educational and Industrial Union of Rochester, New York, and the first woman on the Rochester school board (1900–1910). For a decade she worked with *Susan B. Anthony on women's issues. Social reform was crucial to her missiology. In *Western Women in Eastern Lands* (1910), Montgomery made women's emancipation a rationale for global mission. She wrote six textbooks and numerous study guides for the central committee for the United Study of Foreign Missions and was a driving force behind women's ecumenical cooperation in mission. Montgomery served from 1914 to 1924 as the first president of the Woman's American Baptist Foreign Mission Society and in 1921 as the first woman president of the Northern Baptist Convention. She was one of two women to address the 1923 congress of the Baptist World Alliance in Stockholm, Sweden. The American Baptist Publication Society published her English translation of the Greek New Testament to celebrate its centenary in 1924.

ANB; EAWR; HDB; NoAW; Conda D. H. Abbott, *Envoy of Grace* (1997); Louise A. Cattan, *Lamps Are for Lighting* (1972); Helen Barrett Montgomery, *Helen Barrett Montgomery* (1940).

KENDAL P. MOBLEY

Moody, Deborah Dunch ("Lady Moody") (ca. 1586–1659). Colony founder and religious leader. Member of a prominent Wiltshire County, England, family, Deborah Dunch married Henry Moody in 1605 or 1606 and took the title Lady after her husband was knighted. Widowed in 1629 she moved to London and then to Massachusetts in 1639, after her Nonconformist views put her at odds in England. She had Anabaptist leanings and led a group of friends and followers to New Netherland in 1643, where the Dutch allowed her to found the first English settlement in what is now Brooklyn, New York. Moody's settlement at Gravesend received a charter from the Dutch in 1645, granting it freedom of worship and self-government. In 1657 Moody welcomed Quaker missionaries to her home, and the community became a center for their activity.

ANB; NoAW; Victor H. Cooper, *A Dangerous Woman* (1995).

JOAN R. GUNDERSEN

Moon, Charlotte ("Lottie") Digges (1840–1912). Southern Baptist missionary icon. Born in Virginia, Lottie Moon earned a master's degree from the Albermarle Female Institute in 1861. She returned home during the Civil War and became a teacher. One of the first single women appointed by Southern Baptists, Moon sailed for China's Shantung Province in 1873. For 39 years she was an itinerant evangelist and educator. She also studied the Bible in Greek and Hebrew, cultivated a deep spirituality, shaped missionary policy, trained new missionaries, and endured controversies among her colleagues. Moon encouraged respect for Chinese culture, but she opposed foot binding and fought for the education of girls and women. When she could no longer itinerate, she opened her home to poor women and supported them at her own expense. In 1887 Moon encouraged Southern Baptist women to collect a Christmas offering to fund women missionaries for China. *Annie Armstrong and *Martha McIntosh organized the Woman's Missionary Union (WMU) in 1888 and collected about $3,000 in the first offering. The WMU named the offering for Moon in 1918; its cumulative gifts total more than $2.4 billion.

ANB; DARB; EAWR; HDB; NoAW; Keith Harper, ed., *Send the Light* (2002); Catherine B. Allen, *The New Lottie Moon Story* (1980).

KENDAL P. MOBLEY

Moore, Joanna P. (1832–1916). Missionary. In 1863 Joanna P. Moore was the first white woman missionary appointed by the American Baptist Home Missionary Society. She was sent to Island Number Ten in the Mississippi River near Memphis to work with more than 1,000 black women and children who had gone to the island for protection by the Union Army. From that time until her death, Moore dedicated her life to work in black communities in the American South. She established a series of mothers' training schools, which provided literacy instruction and the development of practical domestic skills for women. She also assisted in organizing women's societies as a means of developing black Baptist women's leadership. In 1885 Moore founded a monthly nondenominational magazine, *Hope*. This magazine contained Sunday school lessons and guides for Bible Bands, thereby promoting biblical literacy. *Hope* also published letters from black women and ministers and served as an important source of communication and information among black women's organizations within black Baptist churches.

EAWR; HDB; NBAW; RLA; Evelyn Brooks Higginbotham, *Righteous Discontent: The Women's Movement in the Black Baptist Church* (1993); Joanna P. Moore, *"In Christ's Stead": Autobiographical Sketches* (1902) [online, Documenting the American South, University of North Carolina at Chapel Hill, http://docsouth.unc.edu.].

ANNIE RUSSELL

Moravian Women Choirs (18th–19th centuries). Collective living groups. The most distinctive aspect of the Moravian Church in the 18th and early 19th centuries was the choir system. The choirs were not singing groups, but bands—or groups of people intentionally sharing their social and religious lives—based on age, gender, and marital status. In Herrnhut, Germany, the first choir was formed by the single men in 1728. In 1730 Anna Nitschmann gathered a group of single women in a similar covenant. By the mid-1740s the entire population had been divided into choirs, and the system was the basis of all Moravian societies in America. At the onset of puberty, Moravian children typically moved into the single sisters or single brothers house, where they lived until they married. The choirs provided specialized care for the emotional, intellectual, physical, and spiritual needs of women in childhood, puberty, marriage, pregnancy, motherhood, and widowhood. It also provided support for women who chose to remain single. Except for the community-wide sermon, almost all of the pastoral care of women was carried out by ordained women. Women had a surprisingly good education in the Moravian choirs, and the system meant that there was a remarkable symmetry in masculine and feminine roles in Moravian communities.

Craig D. Atwood, *Community of the Cross* (2005); Beverly Prior Smaby, *The Transformation of Moravian Bethlehem from Communal Mission to Family Economy* (1988).

CRAIG D. ATWOOD

Morgan, Emily Malbone (1872–1937). Founder of the *Society of the Companions of the Holy Cross (SCHC). Born to a wealthy Episcopal family, Emily Morgan founded the SCHC with friends in response to a request for prayers from Adelyn Howard, a girl who struggled with an incurable bone disease. The society's activities centered on intercessory prayer, communal spirituality, and social reform, and had a flexible structure to accommodate professional women. Chapters extended nationwide soon after the organization's founding in 1884. Beginning in 1889 Morgan financed summer hospitality for women mill workers and their children. Gifted with a keen business mind, she earned funds for her philanthropy by giving lectures on the arts and publishing travel stories in a Sunday school paper.

EAWR; Sheryl A. Kujawa-Holbrook, *Freedom Is a Dream* (2002); Mary Sudman Donovan, *A Different Call: Women's Ministries in the Episcopal Church* (1986); Emily Malbone Morgan, *Letters to Her Companions* (1944).

SHERYL A. KUJAWA-HOLBROOK

Morgan, Mary Kimball (1861–1948). Christian Science practitioner and educator. Mary Kimball was born in Wisconsin to native New England parents. She was educated in public schools in St. Louis, where she engaged in youth work in a Methodist congregation. She sought Christian Science healing as a young married woman, and she and her husband joined a small group that became the first Christian Science church in St. Louis. The philosophy of education, including character development, by which she homeschooled her sons and other Christian Science children formed the foundation of what became the Principia in Elsah, Illinois. The Principia is a Christian Science multileveled (the first college class graduated in 1934) educational institution independent of the Church of Christ, Scientist, but staffed by committed Christian Scientists.

ANB; NoAW; Mary Kimball Morgan, *Education at the Principia* (1965); Edwin S. Leonard Jr., *At the Sowing* (1948).

MARY FARRELL BEDNAROWSKI

Morton, Nelle (1905–87). Scholar, church leader, and social activist. Nelle Morton was educated at Flora MacDonald College (now St. Andrews Presbyterian College) and the General Assembly Training School (now Union-PSCE). Before joining the faculty of the Theological School of Drew University in 1956, she served as a director of religious education and as assistant director of youth work for the board of education of the Presbyterian Church in the U.S. In 1969 she taught what is thought to be the first course in theological education on the topic of women in church and society. As she became more involved in the women's movement, her writing focused almost exclusively on feminist theology. She emphasized the education and empowerment of those who are marginalized and wholeness in theological education. Morton's most significant published contribution to the field of religious education is her collection of essays entitled *The Journey Is Home* (1985).

NoAWC; *The Journey Is Home* [video] (1989); Elizabeth F. Caldwell, "Nelle Katherine Morton," Christian Educators of the 20th Century, www.talbot.edu.

ELIZABETH HINSON-HASTY

Mosteller, Sue (1933–). L'Arche leader. Sue Mosteller went as an Episcopal girl from Ohio to Toronto, Ontario, for schooling with the *Sisters of St. Joseph (CSJ), the congregation she later joined. After teaching in various provinces in Canada, Sister Sue was introduced to Jean Vanier and his work with people with disabilities at L'Arche. Mosteller was eventually won over by Vanier's dedication to living in community with handicapped people. In 1972 she requested and was granted permission to live and work at L'Arche, an unusual privilege at the time. She has served as a director of Daybreak, the Toronto house of L'Arche, and also as the international coordinator of L'Arche. She worked with writer-priest Henri Nouwen for the 10 years he was at Daybreak and was Nouwen's literary executrix when he died.

Sue Mosteller, *A Place to Hold My Shaky Heart* (1998), *My Brother, My Sister* (1974).

ELAINE GUILLEMIN

Mott, Lucretia Coffin (1793–1880). Social reformer, abolitionist, and Quaker minister. Lucretia Coffin spent her childhood in Nantucket, Massachusetts, and then attended and later taught at Nine Partners School near Poughkeepsie, New York. She was angry when she found that female teachers were paid half the salary of male teachers. Coffin met James Mott there and married him in 1811; they had six children, and five lived to adulthood. Mott was recognized as a minister in the Society of Friends (Quakers) in 1821. She was active in the antislavery movement and helped organize the Philadelphia Female Anti-Slavery Society in 1833 because women were not accepted as full members in other societies. She and her husband went to London in 1840 as delegates to the World's Anti-Slavery Convention only to find, when they arrived, that women were not permitted to be official delegates. Mott met *Elizabeth Cady Stanton in London, and they pledged to do something about women's rights. In 1848 she and Stanton organized the Seneca Falls Woman's Rights Convention. Mott, Stanton, and *Susan B. Anthony organized the National Woman Suffrage Association in 1869. Mott traveled extensively throughout her life giving speeches and sermons in favor of abolition, women's rights, and pacifism.

ANB; DARB; EAWR; NoAW; Beverly Wilson Palmer, ed., *Selected Letters of Lucretia Coffin Mott* (2001); Margaret Hope Bacon, *Valiant Friend* (1980); Dana D. Green, ed., *Lucretia Mott: Her Complete Speeches and Sermons* (1980); Otelia Cromwell, *Lucretia Mott* (1971); the Lucretia Coffin Mott Papers Project, Pomona College.

LYNN JAPINGA

Mountain Wolf Woman (Kéhachiwinga) (1884–1960). Winnebago autobiographer and medicine woman. Mountain Wolf Woman served as a medicine woman of the Winnebago tribe in Wisconsin. Because of an early childhood illness, she was named Kéhachiwinga (or Xehaciwinga)—meaning to live on a bluff like a wolf—as a way to make her healthy. She received some formal education in white schools, and she encouraged tribal children to receive non-Indian education. She also welcomed the end of arranged marriages. She joined the Native American Church, which blends Indian and Christian rituals and centers around the sacrament of using the fruit of the peyote cactus to cause a psychedelic experience. In her willingness to share her story, Mountain Wolf Woman has inspired many Native American women to share their stories.

EAWR; NaAW; RLA; Nancy Oestreich Lurie, ed., *Mountain Wolf Woman, Sister of Crashing Thunder* (1961); Jocelyn Riley, prod., *Mountain Wolf Woman* [DVD] (2004).

KEITH DURSO

Muhammad, Clara Evans ("Sister Clara") (1898–1972). First Lady of the Nation of Islam (NOI). As the wife of Elijah Muhammad, the leader who led the NOI to its greatest prominence in the 1950s and 1960s, Sister Clara played a central, if often unheralded, role in the growth and leadership of the NOI. She assumed many of her husband's duties when he was in hiding or imprisoned (often for years), and became the first teacher at the University of Islam. The school, which began around Sister Clara's dining room table, later became a nationwide network of elementary and secondary schools designed to instill in students the key tenets of the NOI: self-improvement, racial pride, and self-discipline.

Debra Mubashir Majeed, "Clara Evans Muhammad," in *Encyclopedia of Women and Religion in North America*, vol. 2, ed. Rosemary Skinner Keller et al. (2006); Claude Andrew Clegg III, *An Original Man* (1997).

MARY JANE O'DONNELL

Murray, Anna Pauline ("Pauli") (1911–85). Episcopal priest, writer, and civil rights activist. The first African American woman ordained to the Episcopal Church in the U.S.A. priesthood, Pauli Murray was proud of her African, American Indian, and European ancestry. She believed that racial and cultural differences were potential sources of enrichment, rather than obstacles to relationship and community, despite her own encounters with both racism and sexism. Murray held many prominent positions in law and education. She was a civil rights activist and a founder of the National Organization for Women (NOW) before her ordination to the priesthood in 1977. Thereafter Murray served at the Church of the Atonement in Washington, DC. A popular speaker and preacher, she assisted at her home church, Holy Nativity in Baltimore, after her retirement in 1982.

ANB; BWA; BWARC; NBAW; Sheryl A. Kujawa-Holbrook, *Freedom Is a Dream* (2002); Pauli Murray, *Song in a Weary Throat* (1987), *Proud Shoes* (1956).

SHERYL A. KUJAWA-HOLBROOK

Murray, Judith Sargeant Stevens (1751–1820). Writer and women's advocate. Born in Gloucester, Massachusetts, Judith Sargeant was a ship owner's daughter. She married Captain John Stevens in 1769, and they converted to Universalism. The first Universalist church in the U.S. was built for their friend, the Reverend John Murray, on land her father donated. Her first published essay in 1784 was anonymously signed "Constantia," and her catechism of 1782 seems the earliest writing by a Universalist woman. Widowed in 1786 she married the Reverend Murray in 1788 and accompanied him on preaching tours; they attended the first Universalist convention in Philadelphia in 1790, and ministered in Boston from 1793. Hers was the first American play at Federal Street Theater in 1795. Her pseudonymous essays and poems in *Massachusetts Magazine* from 1789 to 1794 included the essay "On the Equality of the Sexes."

Murray valued the inspiration of the classics and American literature, as well as women's self-reverence and the education of women for paid employment. In 1803 she cofounded a female academy in Dorchester, Massachusetts. After her husband's 1809 stroke, she edited his letters and sermons, and issued his autobiography after his 1815 death.

DUUB; Bonnie Hurd Smith, ed., *The Letters I Left Behind, Judith Sargent Murray Papers* (2005), *From Gloucester to Philadelphia in 1790* (1998); Sheila L. Skemp, *Judith Sargeant Murray* (1998); Marianne Dunlop, ed., *Judith Sargeant Murray* (1995); Sharon M. Harris, ed., *Selected Writings of Judith Sargeant Murray* (1995); Nina Baym, "Introduction" to Judith Sargeant Murray's *The Gleaner* (1992); Vena Bernadette Field, *Constantia* (1931).

IRENE BAROS-JOHNSON

Musgrove Matthews Bosomworth, Mary (Coosaponakeesa) (ca. 1700–1766). Interpreter, Creek leader, and intercultural mediator. The daughter of an English trader and Creek woman, Coosaponakeesa received a European education and religious training. About 1715 she married John Musgrove, and they operated a trading post on the Savannah River. Twice widowed, Musgrove married John Matthews in 1737 and the Reverend Thomas Bosomworth in 1744. As a trader and translator Musgrove wielded great influence in the early years of Georgia and helped secure the colony's safety. She asserted her claims against Georgia for compensation in 1749, and in 1754 she and Bosomworth traveled to England to plead their cause. After a compromise settlement was reached in 1759 she continued acting as cultural go-between until her death.

ANBO; NaAW; NoAW; Michele Gillespie, "The Sexual Politics of Race and Gender: Mary Musgrove and the Georgia Trustees," in *The Devil's Lane*, ed. Catherine Clinton and Michele Gillespie (1997).

JOAN R. GUNDERSEN

Muslim Women's League (MWL) (1992–). Muslim nonprofit organization. The MWL was established to "implement the values of Islam and thereby reclaim the status of women as free, equal and vital contributors to society." It seeks the end of oppression of women based on the understanding of the Qur'an. It sponsors forums, publications, and educational events to inform the broader public about issues related to Muslim women. The MWL has organized camps and athletic events for Muslim women and girls.

Muslim Women's League, www.mwlusa.org.

BARBARA E. REED

Nathan, Maud (1862–1946). Jewish activist. Maud Nathan taught English to Jewish immigrants in New York City and served as a director of the Mount Sinai Training School for Nurses. She was one of the first members of the Consumers' League of New York City, an organization dedicated to promoting better working conditions, especially in factories and shops. In 1897 Nathan became president of the Consumers' League of New York, a position she held for 21 years. She became an executive board member of the National Consumers' League in 1898. A gifted speaker, Nathan presented in 1897 a paper (not a sermon) called "The Heart of Judaism" during the worship service at Temple Beth-El in New York City. An active participant in the suffrage movement, she gave 24 speeches in one day from the backseat of a car. She was a delegate to the 1913 convention of the International Women's Suffrage Alliance in Budapest. Nathan authored three books: *Justice and the Expediency of Woman Suffrage* (1917), *The Story of an Epoch-making Movement* (1926), and *Once upon a Time and Today* (1933), her autobiography.

ANB; EAWR; JWA; NoAW; Linda Gordon Kuzmack, *Woman's Cause* (1990);

Jacob R. Marcus, *The American Jewish Woman* (1981).

KEITH DURSO

Nation, Carry (or Carrie) Amelia Moore Gloyd (1846–1911). Temperance activist. Carry Moore had a difficult childhood with minimal formal education. She married Charles Gloyd in 1867, and he died of complications from alcoholism in 1869, leaving her with a daughter and no money. She married David Nation in 1874, and they divorced in 1901. She was shaped by several different religious traditions, including the Disciples of Christ, slave religion, and faith healing. During her life she worked as a hotel operator, cotton farmer, osteopathic medicine practitioner, lecturer, and social reformer. She was convinced that saloons and alcohol endangered not only those who drank, but also their family members and society. Because women lacked the vote, she argued that their only recourse against saloons was "smashing" them, which she did in several highly publicized efforts. She believed that this was her calling from God.

ANB; NoAW; Fran Grace, *Carry A. Nation* (2001).

LYNN JAPINGA

National Assembly of Religious Women (NARW) (1970–95). Catholic social justice organization. Founded by Roman Catholic sisters as the National Assembly of Women Religious (NAWR), the NAWR became the NARW in 1982 to signify the full inclusion of laywomen. Founding president *Ethne Kennedy helped build an organization that by 1975 had 103 diocesan council members with direct ties to tens of thousands of sisters, along with some 3,500 sisters as grassroots members, and some clergy and lay associates. NAWR published the newsletter *Probe*, books about post–Second Vatican Council developments among sisters, and justice education materials. The themes of ministry and social justice marked the meetings and activities of NAWR/NARW, with *Marjorie Tuite and Judy Vaughn providing significant leadership. Although NARW disbanded for financial reasons, its influence has continued through other organizations that its members helped to establish, especially the Catholic social justice lobby *NETWORK and the *Women's Ordination Conference.

Anne E. Patrick, "A Ministry of Justice," in *What's Left: Liberal American Catholics*, ed. Mary Jo Weaver (1999); Judy Vaughn, "National Assembly of Religious Women (NARW)," in *U.S. Women's Interest Groups*, ed. Sarah Slavin (1995); Ethne Kennedy, ed., *Gospel Dimensions of Ministry* (1973), *Women in Ministry* (1972).

ANNE E. PATRICK, SNJM

National Association of Colored Women (NACW) (1896–). Reform society. Denied entrance into white women's associations, African American women forged their own organizations for social change. In 1896 the National League of Colored Women and the National Federation of Afro-American Women merged to form the NACW. Selecting "lifting as we climb" as their motto, this group of elite women promoted self-help, moral purity, and temperance. It combatted negative stereotypes of black women and equipped them with the skills to be better wives and mothers. The NACW established mother's clubs, sponsored homemaking demonstrations, and built educational centers. Its 50,000 members supported women's suffrage and lobbied against lynching. The NACW purchased the Frederick Douglass House in 1916, established the National Scholarship Loan Fund in the 1920s, and founded the National Association of Colored Girls' Clubs in the 1930s. While not as powerful as it once was, the NACW, now known as the National

Association of Colored Women's Clubs (NACWC), is the oldest existing African American secular organization, one that throughout its history has been an advocate for social change and racial justice.

BWA; BWARC; DARB; NBAW; Marcia Y. Riggs, "'Lifting As We Climb': NACW/NCNW," in *Encyclopedia of Women and Religion in North America*, ed. Rosemary Skinner Keller et al. (2006); Beverly Jones, "Mary Church Terrell and the National Association of Colored Women," in *Church and Community among Black Southerners*, ed. Donald G. Nieman (1994); Charles Harris Wesley, *The History of the National Association of Women's Clubs* (1984); Elizabeth Lindsay Davis, *Lifting As They Climb* (1933).

LYNN S. NEAL

National Black Sisters' Conference (NBSC) (1968–). Catholic religious organization. Instrumental in the resurgent black Catholic activism stirred by the U.S. civil rights movement and the Second Vatican Council, the NBSC began under the leadership of Sister Mary Martin de Porres Grey (now Dr. Patricia Grey Tyree). Initially composed of black Roman Catholic nuns, it now includes associate members (other black Catholics) and auxiliary members (persons supportive of the NBSC vision). At the 2004 NBSC national gathering for black Catholic women, attendance numbered over 500. Throughout its history the conference national office, now in Washington, DC, has coordinated pathbreaking initiatives to forward NBSC's vision: regular conferences and workshops to develop individual sisters' resources; encouragement of black laywomen's leadership and of the gifts within black Catholic communities; trainings to assist white religious in addressing racism; advocacy for Catholic schools in black communities; a 1970s collaborative tutorial and recreational program for Louisiana sugarcane workers' children; formal participation in the National Black Political Assembly; and development and maintenance of Project DESIGN, a five-year effort directed at the educational crisis in black communities.

BWA; BWARC; M. Shawn Copeland, "A Cadre of Women Religious Committed to Black Liberation: The National Black Sisters' Conference," *U.S. Catholic Historian* 14 (1996); Special Collections, Raynor Memorial Libraries, Marquette University.

MARGARET MCMANUS

National Coalition of American Nuns (NCAN) (1969–). Feminist Catholic women religious organization. NCAN drew together liberal and radical women religious dedicated to working for social justice in and outside the Roman Catholic Church. Under the leadership of *Margaret Ellen Traxler in the early 1970s, NCAN spoke out strongly on a range of justice issues. Traxler described the women of NCAN as "icebreakers which prepare the way for frailer crafts," a phrase illuminating both their sense of mission and their dispositions. Feminist in its orientation, NCAN agitated for women's rights in the church, particularly sisters' rights to govern their own communities, and women's ordination. Often controversial, NCAN affirmed abortion rights in the mid-1980s and same-sex marriage in the early 2000s. It continues to support issues of social justice and human rights.

Frances Kissling, "Women's Freedom and Reproductive Rights," in *Encyclopedia of Women and Religion in North America*, ed. Rosemary Skinner Keller et al. (2006); NCAN, *If Anyone Can NCAN: Twenty Years of Speaking Out* (1989).

MARY J. HENOLD

National Council of Catholic Women (NCCW) (1920–). Catholic organization. The NCCW was founded under the direction of U.S. Catholic bishops to promote traditional female and family values. It is composed of affiliated parish, diocesan, and national organizations, and individual members. It holds observer status at the U.S. Conference of Catholic Bishops. The NCCW acts through its affiliates to support, educate, and empower Roman Catholic women in spirituality, leadership, and service. Although NCCW has held conservative perspectives in regard to family and women's roles, it has taken progressive stances in areas of social welfare and some international issues. For example, in 1981 it passed a resolution in support of disarmament and the abolition of nuclear weapons, and in 2005 it called, in unison with the United Nations, for the recognition of water as a basic human right. In addition to existing as a federation of organizations, NCCW is a service agency. Its services are implemented through six commissions: church, family concerns, community concerns, international concerns, legislation, and organization. NCCW represents U.S. Catholic women at national and international meetings of government and nongovernmental agencies concerned with the welfare of women and the moral and religious welfare of humanity.

EACH; EAWR; NCE; RLA.

SUSAN MARIE MALONEY, SNJM

National Council of Jewish Women (NCJW) (1893–). First national Jewish women's organization in the U.S. Founded by *Hannah Greenebaum Solomon and Sadie American, the NCJW was formed on the heels of the Jewish Women's Congress at the Chicago World Columbian Exhibition, a meeting Solomon used to spark interest among Jewish women around the country. The council provided informal education to its members, who in turn provided assistance to needy Jewish women. Over its lifetime, council women assisted immigrant women traveling alone and refugees abroad. Various committees were developed to serve American synagogues and religious schools and to enhance Jewish domestic life. The organization has supported expanded legal rights for women, including abortion rights, and strives to assist Jewish women at home and abroad. The National Council of Jewish Women of Canada (NCJWC) was formed in 1897, the first such organization in Canada.

EAWR; JWA; Faith Rogow, *Gone to Another Meeting* (1993); Jewish Publication Society, *Papers of the Jewish Women's Congress, 1893* (1894); Papers, Manuscript Division, Library of Congress.

DIANNE ASHTON

National Council of Negro Women (NCNW) (1935–). Association of clubs and professional societies. The NCNW was organized by *Mary McLeod Bethune in 1935. Shaped by her experiences with the Franklin Roosevelt administration and with the *National Association of Colored Women (NACW), Bethune envisioned a comprehensive organization to pursue the political, spiritual, social, and economic interests of black women. Her efforts, however, eventually split the black women's club movement. Bethune criticized the much older NACW for neglecting feminist issues and the concerns of poor and working-class black women. Under the leadership of Bethune and successive presidents, the NCNW championed many causes to improve the lives of black women, including programs to improve housing conditions, reduce malnutrition, promote civil rights, address delinquency among black youth, and attend to women's health issues. Since 1939 the NCNW has sponsored the National Archives of Black Women's History, which has played a major role in preserving materials of interest in black women's studies. The NCNW struggled initially with a lack of resources. A key turning point occurred in 1966 when, under the leadership of Dorothy Height (the fifth president), they obtained tax-exempt status. Afterward, the NCNW attracted more large grants from nonprofit foundations, catapulting the organization into the national leadership role it enjoys today.

BWARC; NBAW; Marcia Y. Riggs, "'Lifting As We Climb': NACW/NCNW," in *Encyclopedia of Women and Religion in North America*, ed. Rosemary Skinner Keller et al. (2006); NCNW, *Voice of Vision: African American Women on the Issues* (1996); Bettye Collier-Thomas, *N.C.N.W.* (1981).

LORETTA LONG HUNNICUTT

NETWORK (1971–). Catholic social justice lobby. Founded by 47 Catholic sisters, it was the first woman-led registered Catholic social justice lobby in the U.S. Staffed predominantly by Catholic sisters and laypersons, NETWORK's identity is distinct from that of the official church hierarchy. Informed by the Catholic social justice tradition in general and the prophetic charism characteristic of congregations of women religious in particular, its mission is to influence the formation of U.S. federal legislation to promote economic and social justice on behalf of the poor, especially women and children. Comprising over 12,000 individual and institutional memberships, its collaborative organizational structure promotes a participatory consultation-affirmation process to ensure that it represents the concerns of its members. NETWORK evaluates pending legislation for its adherence to Catholic social principles and the gospel, the life experiences of people who are poor, and a feminist/womanist/*mujerista* perspective that values women as contributing members of society. NETWORK works in collaboration with other faith-based and secular organizations that share its goals.

Kristin E. Heyer, *Prophetic and Public* (2006); Stephanie Niedringhaus, "Celebrating 30 Years Action on Behalf of Justice: The Evolution of Network," *Network Connection* 30, no. 3 (May/June 2002).

SUSAN MARIE MALONEY, SNJM

Neumark Montor, Martha (1904–81). Jewish activist. In 1921, when 17-year old Martha Neumark petitioned Reform Judaism's Hebrew Union College for a High Holiday pulpit, she launched a two-year debate among America's Jews over women's ordination. Her challenge prodded Reform rabbis to declare that women could not justly be denied ordination. Yet the college's board of governors, refusing to cross this threshold, certified Neumark as a Sunday school superintendent and not as a rabbi. Even as Jewish interests, especially Zionism, remained a thread coursing through her life, other talents shaped her subsequent careers, notably teaching, composing music, and counseling for New York City's Department of Corrections.

JWA ("Rabbis"); Pamela S. Nadell, *Women Who Would Be Rabbis* (1998); Papers (correspondence), Jacob Rader Marcus Center, American Jewish Archives, Hebrew Union College.

PAMELA S. NADELL

Newell, Harriet Atwood (1793–1812). Missionary. Harriet Atwood was born in Haverhill, Massachusetts, to Moses Atwood (a successful merchant) and Mary Tenny Atwood. She attended Bradford Academy, where she experienced a religious conversion. In 1810 she met Samuel Newell, who was preparing for the mission field. They married in 1812 and almost immediately sailed for Calcutta. They arrived in India, but were not allowed to stay. While on their way to the Isle of France, Harriet Newell contracted consumption, dying shortly after they came ashore. Her husband published her memoirs, and Newell subsequently became a model of self-sacrifice for Christian women, who celebrated her faithfulness and remembered her as the first U.S. missionary martyr.

NoAW; Dana Robert, *American Women in Mission* (1997); Harriet Newell, *Memoirs of Mrs. Harriet Newell* (1814).

MANDY E. MCMICHAEL

Newman, Angelia Louise French Thurston Kilmore (1837–1910). Reformer and Methodist churchwoman. Angelia Thurston was born in Connecticut but moved with her family to Wisconsin. When she was 18 years old, she married Frank Kilmore. Widowed within a year, she married David Newman in 1859. For some years her health was poor, but following a move to Nebraska in 1871, it improved. She was active in the Woman's Foreign Missionary Society of the Methodist Episcopal Church. In 1876 she visited Salt Lake City and developed a concern for Mormon women in polygamous marriages. She worked through the Methodist Woman's Home Missionary Society and the *Woman's Christian Temperance Union, and was instrumental in the founding of a home for plural wives in Salt Lake City. She was one of five Methodist women elected to the General Conference of the Methodist Church in 1888, but the conference refused to break precedent and seat any female delegates.

NoAW.

MARILYN FÄRDIG WHITELEY

Newman, Emma E. (1838–1921). Congregational licensed minister, women's suffrage and temperance organizer, and homeopathic healer. Emma Newman's father was from a prominent family related to Andover Theological Seminary and Phillips Academy, and her mother was from Maine; both were staunch orthodox Congregationalists. Newman was the first woman to receive a license to preach from a Congregational association, the Northwest Association of Congregational Churches in Kansas in 1883. At least two women had been ordained before her by congregations acting on their own. Lacking support from the powerful Home Missionary Society, she was never ordained. In addition to serving small Congregational churches in the Midwest and California, Newman organized temperance and women's suffrage efforts and participated in meetings of the Women Ministers' Association. She studied homeopathic medicine and mental healing and practiced these in addition to preaching and serving as pastor.

Randi Jones Walker, *Emma Newman* (2000).

RANDI JONES WALKER

Nurse, Rebecca Towne (1621–92). Victim of Salem witchcraft hysteria. Rebecca Towne married around 1645, raised eight children, and was a churchgoer renowned for her piety. She was deaf and blind when charged with witchcraft and hanged. By 1712 her conviction had been nullified and restitution paid to her heirs, her accusers had published a statement of remorse, and the Salem congregation had reinstated her membership.

ANB; NoAW; Paul Boyer and Stephen Nissenbaum, eds., *The Salem Witchcraft Papers* (1977); Charles Tapley, *Rebecca Nurse* (1930).

SCOTT D. SEAY

Oblate Sisters of Providence (OSP) (1829–). Roman Catholic congregation. The world's first congregation of women of African descent, the OSP was founded in Baltimore by Haitian immigrant *Elizabeth Clovis ("Mother Mary") Lange and Father James Hector Joubert. The sisters took in orphaned children and also established St. Frances Academy, the oldest continuously operating black Catholic school in the U.S. Their early years were marked by Baltimore's nativist suspicion of Catholics and the fact that slave owning was still legal; indeed, in the 1840s slave-owning bishop Samuel Eccleston saw no purpose to the continued existence of the sisters and ordered them to accept no new members. The Redemptorist Fathers, in the person of Thaddeus Anwander, came to the aid of the sisters and facilitated their continued existence, growth, and financial stability. In 1900 the sisters opened their first foreign mission in Havana, Cuba. They have missions today not only in Cuba and in 25 U.S. cities, but also in Costa Rica, the Dominican Republic, and Africa. In 2005 the Mother Mary Lange Catholic School opened in Baltimore, extending the educational work and mission of the Oblate sisters. Their other ministries include early education, child care, a reading tutorial center, parish-based religious education, Hispanic ministry, and a home for teenage girls in need of shelter.

BWARC; EAWR; NBAW; NCE; ROWUS; Diane Batts Morrow, *Persons of Color and Religious at the Same Time* (2002); Maria M. Lannon, *Response to Love* (1992); Grace H. Sherwood, *The Oblates' Hundred and One Years* (1931).

COLLEEN CARPENTER CULLINAN

O'Connell, Mary ("Sister Anthony") (1814–97). Catholic religious sister. Born in Limerick, Ireland, Mary O'Connell immigrated to Maine in the late 1820s. In June 1835 she joined the *Sisters of Charity. Sister Anthony helped to form an independent foundation, the Sisters of Charity of Cincinnati, in 1853. In that same year she opened St. John's Hotel for Invalids, later renamed the Good Samaritan. In 1873, after serving as a nurse during the Civil War, she opened St. Joseph's Maternity Hospital to care for unwed mothers and their children. Seven years later she retired as superior of both St. Joseph's and the Good Samaritan.

ANBO; NCE; NoAW; ROWUS; Barbara Misner, *Highly Respectable and Accomplished Ladies: Catholic Women Religious in America* (1988).

SUSAN B. RIDGELY

O'Connor, (Mary) Flannery (1925–64). Writer. Writing and religion were early interests that became lifelong passions for Flannery O'Connor. She began college as a sociology major, but her work on the college literary magazine brought her to the University of Iowa Writers' Workshop where, in her first year, she won a prize for a short story that later became her first novel, *Wise Blood*. In 1950, as she was beginning her literary career, she was diagnosed with lupus, a degenerative disease. She returned to Georgia, where she lived on a farm with her mother and maintained a relationship with a nearby community of nuns. O'Connor's Roman Catholic faith and her upbringing as a Catholic in a primarily Protestant area informed her writings. Her two novels, *Wise Blood* (1952) and *The Violent Bear It Away* (1960), feature characters that wrestle with their relationship to Jesus Christ, portrayed in graphic and occasionally disturbing fashion.

ANBO; EAWR; NoAWMP; Ralph C. Wood, *Flannery O'Connor and the Christ-Haunted South* (2004); Paul Elie, *The Life You Save May Be Your Own* (2003); Flannery O'Connor, *The Habit of Being*, ed. Sally Fitzgerald (1979); Special Collections, Ina Dillard Russell Library, Georgia College and State University.

ANNIE RUSSELL

O'Hair, Madalyn Mays Murray (1919–95). Atheist activist. In 1968 Madalyn O'Hair started the *American Atheist Magazine* and in 1969 published *What on Earth Is an Atheist?* In 1970 she founded the Society of Separationists (now American Atheists) and opened the Charles E. Stevens American Atheist Library and Archives. She publicly debated the existence of God and instigated numerous lawsuits (some of which were heard by the Supreme Court) to prevent the public expression of religion. When her autocratic leadership style angered many members of American Atheists, she left to form the Freedom from Religion Foundation. In August 1995 O'Hair and two family members were reported missing from their home in Austin, Texas. Victims of a brutal murder, authorities found their remains on a Texas ranch in January 2001.

EAWR; NoAWC; RLA; Gordon Stein, ed., *Encyclopedia of Unbelief* (1985); William J. Murray, *My Life without God* (1982).

KEITH DURSO

O'Reilly, Leonora (1870–1927). Labor organizer and socialist. Leonora O'Reilly attended labor meetings as a young child with her mother, an Irish immigrant garment worker on New York's East Side. In 1886 she joined the Knights of Labor, thereby establishing her lifelong commitment to Irish working-class traditions of social radicalism. Although Roman Catholic by birth, the labor movement, rather than the church, received O'Reilly's passionate devotion, yet she still valued connections with religious reformers such as James O. S. Huntington. From 1881 until 1897 O'Reilly labored as a garment worker and also engaged in trade union organizing. Such experiences equipped her for influential leadership in the National Women's Trade Union League, the Socialist Party, the 1910–11 New York garment workers' strike, and investigation of the 1912 Triangle Shirtwaist Factory fire. In over 30 years of speaking, writing, and organizing, O'Reilly consistently urged working women to gain equality—in politics and in pay.

NoAW; Mary J. Bularzik, "The Bonds of Belonging: Leonora O'Reilly and Social Reform," *Labor History* 24 (1983); Papers of the Women's Trade Union League and Its Principal Leaders: A Guide to the Microfilm Edition, ed. Edward T. James (1981).

MARGARET MCMANUS

Ortega, Ofelia Miriam (1936–). Minister, scholar, and ecumenist. Ofelia Miriam Ortega was the first Hispanic woman ordained as a minister of the Word and Sacrament (1967) in the Presbyterian Reformed Church of Cuba/Iglesia Presbiteriana Reformada en Cuba (IPRC) and the first woman rector of the Evangelical Theological Seminary (ETS) in Cuba. Born in Cuba into a Roman Catholic family, Ortega's mother valued education and sent her to the best school in her area, which was sponsored by the Presbyterian Church. She studied Christian education at the ETS in Matanzas, Cuba, and became a professor upon her 1959 graduation. (Professors were needed because many foreign professors had left Cuba following the revolution.) She later earned her bachelor of divinity degree, the first woman to do so in the seminary's history, and was ordained by the IPRC. Ortega married Daniel Montoya in 1970; Montoya was a Baptist minister who became a Presbyterian because his Baptist Convention would not validate Ortega's pastoral credentials. Ortega and Montoya have one daughter, Greta, who is a nurse and is at the time of publication studying theology. Ortega served a number of parishes and continued teaching, and in 1985 she became a professor at the Ecumenical Institute in Bossey, Switzerland. Three years later she began to direct a program focusing on theological education for future women leaders in Latin America for the World Council of Churches (WCC). In 1997 Ortega returned to the ETS to become its rector, a position she held until 2004. In 2006 she was elected one of the WCC's eight presidents representing the Latin American and Caribbean regions. She currently directs the Christian Institute of Gender Studies, related to the seminary, where she continues to teach.

Ofelia Miriam Ortega, "Encounters and Visions," in *Celebrating Our Call: Ordination Stories of Presbyterian Women*, ed. Patricia Lloyd-Sidle (2006).

LINDA B. BREBNER

Osborn, Sarah Haggar Wheaten (1714–96). Evangelical leader. With her mother, Sarah Haggar emigrated from England to Boston in 1722. Her first husband died, and she was left with an infant son. She later married Henry Osborn of Newport, Rhode Island. Sarah Osborn became a teacher, and in the 1740s she became leader of an evangelical prayer meeting for women. Beginning in the 1760s her home served as a meeting place every night of the week for over 10 years. Osborn believed that the prerogative of congregational leadership belonged to men, but that women could, through the Holy Spirit, be revival leaders and educators.

ANB; EAWR; Catherine A. Brekus, *Sarah Osborn's World* (forthcoming); Marilyn Westerkamp, *Women and Religion in Early America* (1999); Charles E. Hambrick-Stowe, "The Spiritual Pilgrimage of Sara Osborn," *Church History* 61, no. 4 (1992); Samuel Hopkins, ed., *Memoirs of the Life of Mrs. Sarah Osborn* (1796).

SCOTT D. SEAY

O'Sullivan, Mary Kenney (1864–1943). Labor leader and social reformer. Born to immigrant Irish Catholic parents, Mary Kenney inherited their commitment to Catholicism and to the working class. She joined the workforce at age 14 and learned early and firsthand about the injustices of economic life in the U.S. While working at a Chicago bookbindery in 1892, she became the first salaried woman organizer for the American Federation of Labor, despite her consistent demand that unskilled workers, along with tradespeople, be included in organizing efforts. Kenney was married to John O'Sullivan, labor editor for the *Boston Globe*, until his death in 1902. The couple was closely associated with Boston's Denison House Settlement and its commitment to the labor movement. Kenney O'Sullivan was a founding member in 1903 of the National Women's Trade Union League and a significant figure in the 1912 Lawrence textile workers' strike. She served for 20 years as a Massachusetts factory inspector.

NoAW; Kathleen Banks Nutter, *"The Necessity of Organization": Mary Kenney O'Sullivan and Trade Unionism for Women* (2000); Mary Kenney O'Sullivan, "The Labor War at Lawrence," *The Survey* 28 (1912); Papers, Schlesinger Library, Radcliffe Institute, Harvard University.

MARGARET MCMANUS

Ozman LaBerge, Agnes N. (1870–1937). Pentecostal leader. Agnes Ozman grew up in a Methodist Episcopal family in Nebraska. On January 1, 1901, while attending Charles Fox Parham's Bethel Bible College (Kansas), Parham laid hands on Ozman and asked God that she be baptized in the Holy Spirit. She began to "speak in tongues." Parham viewed this as evidence of his teachings on spiritual baptism. Many others agreed with him, and Ozman's experience became emblematic of the rise in Pentecostalism; Ozman herself identified with the movement. In 1911 she married a Pentecostal preacher, Philemon LaBerge, and they held meetings throughout the U.S. In 1917 she joined the Assemblies of God and was given the title of evangelist.

EE; Edith L. Blumhofer, *Restoring the Faith* (1993), *Assemblies of God* (1989); Agnes N. Ozman LaBerge, *What God Hath Wrought* (1921).

JUDITH L. GIBBARD

Packard, Sophia B. (1824–91). Baptist educator. Sophia Packard began her long teaching career at the age of 14. She was pastoral assistant to George C. Lorimer (Boston) from 1870 to 1879. A principal organizer of the Woman's American Baptist Home Mission Society in 1877 she toured the South on the society's behalf in 1880 to survey the postwar conditions and needs among African Americans, especially women and girls. With the society's reluctant sponsorship and the assistance of Frank Quarles, Packard and Harriet E. Giles opened the Atlanta Baptist Female Seminary in the basement of the Friendship Baptist Church in 1881. The school expanded and was financially supported by John D. Rockefeller. It was renamed Spelman Seminary in 1884 and Spelman College in 1924, in honor of Mrs. Laura Rockefeller and her parents, Harvey Buel and Lucy Henry Spelman, who had been abolitionists.

ANB; EAWR; NoAW; RLA; Florence M. Read, *The Story of Spelman College* (1961).

KENDAL P. MOBLEY

Padgham, Estella Elizabeth (1874–1952). Unitarian minister. Born in Syracuse, New York, Elizabeth Padgham went to Smith College and graduated from Meadville Theological School in 1901. She was ordained at her home church in Syracuse, with participation of her high school friend, the Reverend Marie Jenney Howe, who had inspired her ministerial aspirations. She always used her title and left her first church of Perry, Iowa, debtless, serving it from 1901 to 1904. She then settled in Rutherford, New Jersey, for 22 years. She was the first woman chaplain of the New Jersey House and president of the state ministers' association in 1924. Padgham was a longtime member of the executive board of the Middle States and Canada, was on the national board of religious education, and chaired the metropolitan religious education association in 1926. She retired early for health reasons and returned to Syracuse, where the church celebrated the 50th anniversary of her ordination.

UUWM; Cynthia Grant Tucker, *Prophetic Sisterhood* (1990).

IRENE BAROS-JOHNSON

Palmer, Phoebe Worrall (1807–74). Holiness evangelist. Born in New York and raised in a Methodist family—her father had heard John Wesley preach—at age 19 Phoebe Worrall married physician Walter Palmer. The tragic loss of their first two sons in infancy led the Palmers to focus more fervently upon their Christian faith. In 1835 Palmer joined her sister, Sarah Lankford, in leading the Tuesday Meetings for the Promotion of Holiness. These meetings consisted of Bible study, prayer, and testimonies; they persisted for 37 years and helped to form many influential leaders, such as Nathan Bangs, Catherine Booth, *Amanda Berry Smith, and *Frances Willard. A prolific writer and international preacher, Palmer emerged as a leader of the holiness movement with her sometimes controversial "altar theology." She and her husband led revivals in North America for as much as six months of the year and spent 1859 to 1863 in Great Britain, where they promoted the holiness movement. Expanding upon Wesley's doctrine of entire sanctification, Palmer emphasized the immediate accessibility of perfection. In 1859 one of Palmer's many publications appeared, *Promise of the Father*, a defense of women's preaching. Although a proponent of women's preaching, Palmer did not advocate for women's rights generally or for abolition. She worked among the urban poor, including prisons and orphanages, and contributed to the establishment in 1850 of the Five Points Mission in New York City.

ANB; DARB; EAWR; EE; NoAW; Nancy A. Hardesty, "Holiness Movements," in *Encyclopedia of Women and Religion in North America*, ed. Rosemary Skinner Keller et al. (2006); Susan Lindley, *"You Have Stept Out of Your Place": A History of Women and Religion in America* (1996); Charles Wallace, *The Beauty of Holiness: Phoebe Palmer as Theologian, Revivalist, Feminist, and Humanitarian* (1986).

LACEYE C. WARNER

Pardy, Marion (1942–). United Church of Canada minister. Having explored her call to ministry at the Atlantic Christian Training Centre (Nova Scotia), Marion Pardy left her Newfoundland home in 1961. She worked at Albert College in Belleville, Ontario, while completing prerequisites for her deaconess training at Covenant College in Toronto. Pardy then ministered with United Church congregations and conferences in Saskatchewan, Manitoba, Ontario, and Newfoundland. She has four academic degrees, including a DMin from Boston University. Pardy has made a significant contribution in the field of children's ministry through faith formation work at the church's national office in the 1980s and her DMin thesis on teaching the Bible to children. In 2000 Pardy became the first woman with diaconal training to be elected moderator for the United Church of Canada.

United Church of Canada, "Moderator: Profile of the Very Rev. Dr. Marion Pardy," www.united-church.ca/organization/moderator/pardy/profile; Assorted papers, United Church/Victoria University Archives, University of Toronto.

SARAH BRUER

Parker, Ethel Dodds (1890–1977). Pioneer in social work and settlement houses. Ethel Dodds graduated from the University of Toronto in 1915, a member of the first graduating class from the faculty of social work. While studying in Toronto, Dodds worked at St. Christopher's Settlement House. She became the head worker of the Toronto University Settlement in 1916. The city of Toronto created a welfare division under public health in 1921 and named Dodds as staff supervisor and then director in 1927. Forced to resign her position when she married in 1931 Parker went on to serve in community organizations in Toronto and Hamilton. Parker considered her childhood with her father, an ordained lay clergyman working in Presbyterian missions on Indian reserves in Manitoba, as the source of her passion for community service. Her father's example of developing relationships with the people he served was the model for her career.

Cathy James, "Practical Visionary: Tracing the Life of Ethel Dodds Parker," *Touchstone: Heritage and Theology in a New Age* 25, no. 1 (January 2007); Ethel (Dodds) Parker, "The Origins and Early History of the Presbyterian Settlement Houses," in *The Social Gospel in Canada*, ed. Richard Allen (1975).

BARBARA ADLE

Parks, Rosa Louise McCauley (1913–2005). Civil rights activist. Rosa Parks was a major catalyst in the 1960s U.S. civil rights movement and is often called its "mother." Parks served as a local National Association for the Advancement of Colored People (NAACP) secretary in the 1950s. On 1 December 1955 she defied custom and law in refusing to surrender her bus seat to a white passenger. Her act of dignity inspired African Americans in Montgomery, Alabama, to fight for their rights by staging one of the longest boycotts in history. Because of the harassment that she and her family received during and after the boycott, Parks relocated to Detroit, Michigan. A member of Congressman John Conyers's staff from 1965 to 1988, Parks continued to be involved in the civil rights struggle. She was awarded the Martin Luther King Jr. Nonviolent Peace Prize in 1980 and the Congressional Gold Medal in 1999. Ten years after her husband's 1977 death, Parks founded the Rosa and Raymond Parks Institute for Self-Development to offer youth programs in communication, health, economics, and political skills.

ANBO; BWA; NBAW; Henry Louis Gates Jr. and Cornel West, *The African-American Century* (2000); *African-American Almanac*, 6th ed. (1994); Robert Houston, dir., *Mighty Times: The Legacy of Rosa Parks* [VHS] (2002).

ANGELA D. SIMS

Patrick, Mary Mills (1850–1940). Missionary, author, and educator. Born in Canterbury, New Hampshire, Mary Patrick graduated from the Lyons Collegiate Institute in 1869. The American Board of Commissioners for Foreign Missions (ABCFM) appointed her to a mission school in eastern Turkey in 1871, where she pioneered education for women in the Middle East. After four years she was reassigned to the American High School for Girls (later Constantinople Woman's College), and became the principal in 1889. She served as the college president from its inception in 1890 until 1924. Patrick studied during summer breaks and earned a PhD from the University of Bern (Switzerland) in 1897. She learned Turkish and Greek, and wrote several books on Greek philosophy, an autobiography, and a history of Constantinople Woman's College.

Mary Mills Patrick, *A Bosporus Adventure* (1934), *The Greek Sceptics* (1929), *Under Five Sultans* (1929).

MANDY E. MCMICHAEL

Paulssen, Bertha (1891–1973). First female professor at a U.S. Lutheran seminary. Bertha Paulssen received her schooling through graduate training in Leipzig and received her doctorate in 1917. At the age of 32 she moved to Hamburg and led a staff of 800 social workers. When Hitler assumed power in 1933 Paulssen lost her position and later became a wartime refugee. At the Henry Street Settlement House (New York City) she met Mildred Winston, the Lutheran Student Association organizer working with the United Lutheran Church. Winston enabled Paulssen to network with Lutheran churchwomen. These connections helped her get a teaching position at Wagner College (Staten Island, New York). She became a professor at Gettysburg Seminary in 1945. Paulssen's tenure at Gettysburg (until 1963) influenced many graduates to enter social service and public ministries. Lutheran urban and social ministries during the second half of the 20th century were deeply influenced by her.

Carl T. Uehling, "Bertha Paulssen: Seeing Ministry Interface with Society," in *Witness at the Crossroads*, ed. Frederick K. Wentz (2001); Richard Luecke, "Themes of Lutheran Urban Ministry," *Churches, Cities, and Human Community*, ed. Clifford Green (1996).

MARIA ERLING

Peabody, Elizabeth Palmer (1804–94). Transcendentalist, educator, and reformer. Influenced by her mother and mentored by Unitarian William Ellery Channing, Elizabeth Peabody's concept of education merged moral, spiritual, physical, and intellectual development. She collaborated with Bronson Alcott at Temple School in the 1830s. She was an 1837 charter member of the Transcendentalist Club, and from 1840 to 1850 she was a transcendentalist bookseller, librarian, and publisher. In 1860, influenced by German educator Friedrich Froebel, Peabody opened in Boston the first kindergarten in the U.S. She established the kindergarten system by training teachers, lecturing, writing articles, and editing the influential *Kindergarten Messenger* (1873–77). In the 1880s she lectured at Alcott's Concord School of Philosophy. She and her sister Mary advocated for Paiute rights and education with Sarah Winnemucca.

ANB; DUUB; NoAW; UU; Bruce A. Ronda, *Elizabeth Palmer Peabody* (1999); *The Letters of Elizabeth Palmer Peabody*, ed. Bruce A. Ronda (1984); Ruth M. Baylor, *Elizabeth Palmer Peabody* (1965).

AMY BLACK VOORHEES

Peabody, Lucy Whitehead McGill Waterbury (1861–1949). Baptist missionary and ecumenical leader. After five years in India, Lucy Waterbury's missionary career ended when her husband died in 1886. She became corresponding secretary of the Woman's American Baptist Foreign Missionary Society (1890–1906) and later its vice president (1914–21). Her second husband, Henry Peabody, died in 1908 and left an estate with which she funded her subsequent endeavors. Peabody published and edited *Everyland,* a mission magazine for children (1906–18). She chaired the central committee for the United Study of Foreign Missions (1902–29) and produced ecumenical mission study texts; she was the chief organizer of the 1910 Golden Jubilee. She led a campaign to raise $3 million for women's education in Asia for the joint committee on Women's Union Christian Colleges. Disagreement with Northern Baptist missionary policy led her to establish the Association of Baptists for World Evangelism in the Orient and serve as its first president (1927–35). She chaired the Woman's National Committee for Law Enforcement (1922–34) and wrote *Kidnaping* [sic] *the Constitution* (1934) to protest the repeal of the 18th Amendment.

ANB; EAWR; HDB; NoAW; Louise A. Cattan, *Lamps Are for Lighting* (1972).

KENDAL P. MOBLEY

Pearre, Caroline ("Carrie") Neville (1831–1910). Educator and missionary. Born near Clarksville, Tennessee, Carrie Neville affiliated early in her life with the emerging Stone-Campbell movement. She trained as a teacher and taught at a number of educational institutions for women in the Midwest and Upper South. In 1869 she married Sterling Pearre, an influential Stone-Campbell preacher, and settled in Iowa City. Along with several other prominent women in the movement, she helped found the Christian Women's Board of Missions (CWBM) in 1874. The CWBM consolidated many local mission organizations into a cooperative effort. She was primarily responsible for writing its constitution, served as its first corresponding secretary, and spoke nationally on behalf of the board and its work. When she died in Danville, Kentucky, she left an envelope on her dressing table containing an offering to the CWBM.

ES-CM; Lester McAllister and William Tucker, *Journey in Faith* (1975).

SCOTT D. SEAY

Pennington, Edith Mae Patterson (1902–74). Pentecostal evangelist. Born in Pine Bluff, Arkansas, Edith Pennington won the title "The Most Beautiful Girl in the United States" in 1921, the year before the first Miss America competition. Using her celebrity status, she crossed the country en route to an acting career in Hollywood by speaking in civic clubs and modeling fashions. By 1924 she abandoned Hollywood and was converted in a Pentecostal Holiness Church in Oklahoma City. She became an ordained Assemblies of God minister in 1929 and itinerated as a tent revivalist before founding her own church, the Gospel Temple, in Shreveport, Louisiana, where she was pastor until her death. Her legacy continues today in the ministries of the Plant of Renown, an interdenominational organization that blends Pentecostalism and Jewish culture.

William Lindsey, *Religion and Public Life in the Southern Crossroads: Showdown States* (2005); "Beauty Pageant Winner-Turned-Evangelist Edith Mae Pennington," *Assemblies of God Heritage Magazine* 25, nos. 2 and 3 (Summer–Fall 2005); Grant Wacker, *Heaven Below* (2001).

JANE HARRIS

Penrose, Romania Pratt (1839–1932). Mormon physician and women's suffrage advocate. Acting on Brigham Young's admonition that women should study medicine, Romania Penrose left her five children in her mother's care in Utah and traveled to New York City to study medicine at the Woman's Medical

College; she then studied obstetrics and pediatrics at the Woman's Medical College in Philadelphia. After graduation in 1877 Penrose studied the treatment of eye and ear diseases. Upon returning to Salt Lake City she opened her own medical practice, taught medical courses, and wrote articles on hygiene for women's magazines. Penrose also participated in the women's suffrage movement. She attended the 1882 Woman's Suffrage Convention and spoke at the 1908 Woman's International Suffrage Alliance in Amsterdam. In 1911 she became a counselor to the president of the Mormon Church.

EAWR; RLA; Daniel H. Ludlow, ed., *Encyclopedia of Mormonism* (1992).

KEITH DURSO

Perkins, Frances Coralie (1880–1965). Labor reformer. Although Frances Perkins is best known for her role as secretary of labor (1933–45), her longtime work as a reformer was informed by her religious commitments. She was born in Boston and graduated from Mount Holyoke College. She joined the Episcopal Church while living at Hull House in Chicago. After she moved to New York City, she earned an MA from Columbia University and lived at Greenwich House. The 1911 Triangle Shirtwaist fire impelled her to campaign for factory regulations. Perkins was appointed to the New York Industrial Commission in 1919 and became the state industrial commissioner in 1929. She became an associate of All Saints' Sisters of the Poor after her move to Washington, DC, and made monthly retreats at their convent throughout her years as secretary of labor.

ANB; DARB; NoAWMP; Sheryl Kujawa-Holbrook and Fredrica Harris Thompsett, eds., *Deeper Joy* (2005); George W. Martin, *Madam Secretary* (1976); Oral History Collection, Columbia University.

MARY SUDMAN DONOVAN

Peter, Sarah Worthington King (1800–1877). Social activist and philanthropist. Born near Chillicothe, Ohio, into a prominent family, Sarah Worthington married Edward King in 1816. When she and her family moved to Cincinnati in 1831 she became one of the founders of the Cincinnati Protestant Orphan Asylum (1833). After her husband's death she lived in Philadelphia, where she married William Peter in 1844. She was active in organizations that protected and supported women in their need to earn a livelihood. Out of these efforts she began the Philadelphia School of Design (1848). After the death of her second husband Peter returned to Cincinnati and converted to Roman Catholicism. She expended substantial energy and resources furthering the work of her new church and was instrumental in bringing four women's religious congregations to the city. She left her substantial fortune to several charitable organizations.

ANBO; NoAW; John Lamott, *History of the Archdiocese of Cincinnati* (1921).

JUDITH METZ, SC

Peterson (Pjetursson), Jennie E. McCain (1838–1918). Unitarian missionary and minister. Born into an active Unitarian family in New Hampshire, Jennie McCain moved with her family to Minnesota. She became general secretary of the Post Office mission of the Minnesota Unitarian Conference; her work consisted of placing advertisements in liberal papers and responding to queries with information about Unitarianism. Through this work she met and converted Bjorn Pjetursson, a well-educated Icelandic immigrant from North Dakota, whom she married in early 1890. She then persuaded the American Unitarian Association to sponsor him as a missionary to the Icelandic community in and near Winnipeg, Manitoba, where the couple founded the First Icelandic Unitarian

Church in 1891. When her husband died in 1893 Peterson remained in Winnipeg and succeeded him as minister.

Dorothy Boroush, *Notable Universalist and Unitarian Women* (2000); Heather Watts, "The Canadian Unitarian-Universalist Record Survey," *Archivaria* 30 (1991); Church records, Provincial Archives of Manitoba.

ROBYNNE ROGERS HEALEY

Phelps, Elizabeth Wooster Stuart (1815–52). Author. Born and raised in Andover, Massachusetts, Elizabeth Stuart began writing stories as a child to entertain her siblings. Educated at the Mount Vernon School in Boston, she was taught by minister and author Jacob Abbott. Abbott published some of her articles under the pseudonym "H. Trusta," an anagram of Stuart. In 1842 Stuart married Austin Phelps, a Congregational minister and later professor at Andover Theological Seminary. After the birth of two children and seeing the success of a series of books for girls written by Abbott, Phelps wrote her own four-volume religious series for children called the Kitty Brown books. She also wrote semiautobiographical novels for adults. After Phelps's death, her daughter *Mary Ward took her mother's name and became a popular writer.

ANB; NoAW; Austin Phelps, "Memorial," in Elizabeth Stuart Phelps, *The Last Leaf from Sunny Side* (1853).

BEVERLY ZINK-SAWYER

Philadelphia 11 (29 July 1974). Women's ordinations in the Episcopal Church in the U.S.A. (ECUSA). Amid substantial controversy, eleven women were ordained to the priesthood on the feast of Saints Mary and Martha of Bethany. While granting women access to the diaconate in 1970, the General Convention rejected the ordination of women to the priesthood in 1973. Before the General Convention met again, three retired bishops ordained Merrill Bittner, Alla Bozarth-Campbell, Allison Cheek, Emily Hewitt, Carter Heyward, *Suzanne Hiatt, Marie Moorefield, *Jeannette Piccard, Betty Schiess, Katrina Swanson, and Nancy Wittig to the priesthood at the Church of the Advocate in North Philadelphia. Antonio Ramos, the bishop of Puerto Rico and the only nonretired bishop present, was a witness to the ordination. *Barbara Clementine Harris, at that time an active member of the Church of the Advocate (and later the first woman bishop in the ECUSA) was the crucifer for the service. Within two weeks of the ordination, the House of Bishops of the Episcopal Church met in emergency session, declared the ordinations invalid (later softened to "irregular"), and censured the three bishops—Robert L. Dewitt, Edward Welles, and Daniel Corrigan—who officiated at it. Two male priests who invited some of the women to celebrate the Holy Eucharist in their parishes were subject to ecclesiastical trials. Despite the negative consequences endured by many of the participants in the historic service, supporters of the Philadelphia 11, including sympathetic bishops and women called to the priesthood, would not be deterred. In 1975 four additional women were ordained to the priesthood in Washington, DC. The General Convention voted officially to approve the ordination of women to the priesthood in September 1976. The controversy, however, continued for some ECUSA members, and some chose to leave the church. Residual negative feelings over the Philadelphia 11 and the ordination of women to the priesthood intensified when Barbara Clementine Harris was elected suffragan bishop of the Diocese of Massachusetts. In 1977 the ordinations of the Philadelphia 11 to the priesthood were regularized.

EAWR; Pamela W. Darling, *New Wine: The Story of Women Transforming Leadership and Power in the Episcopal Church* (1994); Alla Bozarth-Campbell, *Womanpriest* (1978);

Carter Heyward, *A Priest Forever* (1976); Emily C. Hewitt and Suzanne R. Hiatt, *Woman Priests: Yes or No?* (1973); Related papers, Archives of Women in Theological Scholarship, Burke Library, Union Theological Seminary.

SHERYL A. KUJAWA-HOLBROOK

Piccard, Jeannette Ridlon (1895–1981). One of the *Philadelphia 11 in the Episcopal Church in the U.S.A. (ECUSA) and balloonist. Jeannette Ridlon wanted to be a priest from the age of 11. She attended Bryn Mawr College and the University of Chicago, and received a doctorate in education from the University of Minnesota. She married Swiss scientist Jean Felix Piccard in 1919. Piccard and her husband were balloonists. In 1934 she piloted the balloon that took them a record-breaking 57,579 feet into the stratosphere. An active Episcopalian, Piccard wrote a successful motion to allow women to serve as lay readers in 1967. She was ordained deacon in 1971 and "irregularly" to the priesthood in 1974. Her priestly ordination was regularized in 1977. She served St. Philip's Church and, before her death, was made an honorary canon of St. Mark's Cathedral, Minneapolis.

EAWR; Alla Bozarth-Campbell, *Womanpriest* (1978); Betsy Covington Smith, *Breakthrough: Women in Religion* (1978).

SHERYL A. KUJAWA-HOLBROOK

Picotte, Susan LaFlesche (1865–1915). Physician and humanitarian. Daughter of one of the last recognized Omaha chiefs, Susan LaFlesche was reared on the Omaha reservation but educated in the values of white, middle-class culture. Versed in both Anglo and Native worlds, LaFlesche wanted to become a doctor and help her tribe. She became the first Native American female physician in 1889. LaFlesche served as a doctor and missionary to the Omaha tribe. Despite marrying Henry Picotte, mothering two sons, and battling chronic illness, she worked tirelessly for the Omaha. She advocated for tribal rights, educated her tribe on the dangers of alcohol, and promoted the importance of sanitary measures. She served as a Presbyterian missionary to the Omaha, and participated in local and state medical societies. Her dream of building a hospital for the Omaha was realized in 1913, and she worked there until her death. Despite the drawbacks of LaFlesche Picotte's assimilationist philosophy, she earned the respect of the Omaha, both past and present.

ANB; NaAW; NoAW; Benson Tong, *Susan LaFlesche Picotte, M.D.* (1999); Valerie Sherer Mathes, "Dr. Susan LaFlesche Picotte," in *Indian Lives*, ed. L. G. Moses and Raymond Wilson (1985).

LYNN S. NEAL

Platz, Elizabeth Alvina (1941–). First Lutheran woman ordained in the U.S. After graduating from Chatham College in 1962, Elizabeth Platz applied to the Lutheran Theological Seminary in Gettysburg. While other women in the student body took courses in Christian education or music, Platz in 1965 became the first woman from the seminary to receive its bachelor of divinity. Since the Lutheran Church in America (LCA) did not yet ordain women, Platz served after graduation in the chaplain's office at the University of Maryland–College Park. When the LCA in 1970 changed its bylaws to allow the ordination of women, the president of the Maryland Synod, Robert Orso, asked Platz to become the first woman pastor in the LCA. The historic ordination service was held in November 1970. Platz has continued to serve as chaplain at the University of Maryland.

Archives, Evangelical Lutheran Church in America.

MARIA ERLING

Polier, Justine Wise (1903–87). Judge and child welfare advocate. Justine Wise Polier was the daughter of Stephen Wise, a prominent Reform rabbi known for his social activism. After completing college she spent a year organizing textile mill workers in New Jersey. In 1928, after completing Yale Law School, she joined the New York State Labor Department. In 1935 the mayor of New York City appointed Polier a judge in the Domestic Relations Court, a position she held for 38 years, interrupted by a one-year post (1941–42) as special counsel at the Office of Civil Defense under Eleanor Roosevelt. During her judgeship Polier challenged race discrimination and advocated children's rights. She remained involved in the Jewish community. Her dedication to social justice sculpted public policy in an era of political tumult in the U.S.

JWA; NoAWC; Joyce Antler, *The Journey Home: Jewish Women and the American Century* (1997).

LILA CORWIN BERMAN

Polyblank, Ellen Albertina ("Sister Albertina") (1840–1930). Anglican sister and educator. Ellen Polyblank was born in Devon, England. Little is known of her early life, except that she never enjoyed reading Scripture. Despite this aversion and an overall lack of religious discipline, she was clothed as a novice in 1867 and took the name Sister Albertina. She went to Honolulu with her mother superior and two other sisters, and in May 1867 they opened St. Andrew's Priory school, which offered girls of diverse racial backgrounds the best education available in the islands. Together with *Elizabeth Ann Rogers ("Sister Beatrice"), Sister Albertina managed the school after 1890 until their retirement in 1902. She never recovered from Sister Beatrice's death in 1921, and was said to have practiced Buddhism.

NoAW; Barbara H. Ching, *St. Andrew's Priory* (1955); Thomas Jay Williams, *Priscilla Lydia Sellon* (1950).

SHERYL A. KUJAWA-HOLBROOK

Pool, Tamar Hirschenson de Sola (1890–1981). Author and activist. Born in Jerusalem, Tamar Hirschenson's Orthodox parents spoke only Hebrew to their children even after settling in the U.S. in 1904. She studied and taught comparative literature at Hunter College. After marrying David de Sola Pool, rabbi of New York's Congregation Shearith Israel, she became an active *Hadassah member. She was involved with Youth Aliyah and served as Hadassah's president from 1939 to 1943. After the war she visited children in the Cyprus detention camps and organized the provision of textbooks and teachers for them. She and her husband edited a Passover Haggadah for use by Jews in the U.S. armed forces and cowrote two books: *An Old Faith in the New World* (1955), which traces the 300-year history of Shearith Israel, and *Is There an Answer?* (1966), which expounds on their faith in the face of Nazi genocide and other horrors.

JWA.

JOAN S. FRIEDMAN

Powers, Jessica (Sister Miriam of the Holy Spirit) (1905–88). Poet and Roman Catholic sister. Raised on a farm in central Wisconsin, Jessica Powers spent a few years in urban centers (Chicago, 1923–24; New York City, 1937–41), but lived most of her life surrounded by the lakes and woods of Wisconsin. She joined the *Carmelite community in Milwaukee in 1941 and remained there until her death. Her early poetry focused on the beauty of nature and life in the countryside; later, in New York, her poetry took a more spiritual turn. Powers produced poetry whose biblical themes and mystical imagery reflected her Carmelite tradition and connected deeply to the spirituality of many 20th-century Americans.

Jessica Powers, *Selected Poetry of Jessica Powers* (1999); Marcianne Kappes, *Track of the Mystic: The Spirituality of Jessica Powers* (1994); Delores Leckey, *Winter Music: A Life of Jessica Powers* (1992); Papers, Special Collections and Archives, Marquette University.

COLLEEN CARPENTER CULLINAN

Prentiss, Elizabeth Payson (1818–78). Author and hymn writer. Born in Portland, Maine, Elizabeth Payson was the daughter of a well-known Congregational minister. She came to express her evangelical faith and lifelong struggles with illness through writing popular novels, stories, poetry, and hymns. Payson married George Lewis Prentiss, a Congregational minister, in 1845 and moved with him as he served churches in the northeastern U.S. She wrote 20 books, including *Stepping Heavenward* (1869), an autobiographical novel recounting a young girl's emotional life. Many of her writings were intended for children and youth, including her first published work in *Youth's Companion* (1834). The popularity of her writings has been attributed to her ability to interpret the culture of evangelicalism prevalent in mid-19th-century America. She remains best known for her hymn "More Love to Thee, O Christ."

ANB; NoAW; George Lewis Prentiss, *The Life and Letters of Elizabeth Prentiss* (1882).

BEVERLY ZINK-SAWYER

Presentation Sisters (1775–). Roman Catholic religious order. The Presentation Sisters were founded in Cork, Ireland, in 1775. The founder, Nano (Honoria) Nagle, named the community Sisters of Charitable Instruction of the Sacred Heart of Jesus and invited women to join her in service to the poor, especially children, through education. The community's teaching apostolate included orphanages, day schools, and academies. In 1793 Pius VI recognized the community as a religious order, with a constitution adapted from the Augustinian rule. In 1805 Pius VII gave final approval, and the community became the Sisters of the Presentation of the Blessed Virgin Mary. Canonical authority resided in each convent's mother superior under the jurisdiction of the local bishop. The Presentation Sisters' first North American establishment was in Newfoundland (ca. 1829). In 1854 the order accepted the invitation of San Francisco's Bishop Alemany to establish schools, especially for poor children. Around 1874, 11 sisters went to St. Michael's, New York City, to staff a school. A group also went to the Dubuque diocese and expanded into Nebraska. Six years later they established a convent in Fargo, North Dakota. By 1900 they had also established communities in several New England dioceses. The Presentation Sisters have maintained a commitment to serving the poor, especially through education, health care, and other forms of pastoral ministry. They now have communities in China, Australia, Africa, Latin America, and the Philippines.

EACH; NCE; ROWUS; Susan Carol Peterson and Courtney Ann Vaughn-Roberson, *Women with Vision* (1988); T. J. Walsh, *Nano Nagle and the Presentation Sisters* (1959).

SANDRA YOCUM MIZE

Price, Eugenia (1916–96). Writer. Eugenia Price was born to Walter Wesley and Anna Davidson Price. She attended Ohio University and studied dentistry at Northwestern University before dropping out to pursue a writing career. Price began by writing for soap operas. After converting to Christianity she formed her own production company and later wrote, produced, and directed *Unshackled* for WGN, Chicago. She began writing inspirational books and had immediate success. In addition to her devotional writings, she wrote romantic fiction, much of it set on St. Simons Island, Georgia, where she resided from 1965 until her death. Her antebellum settings and religious themes brought her acclaim as a southern writer and frequently earned her a place on the *New York Times* bestseller list. At the time of her death more than 40 million of her books had been sold in 18 languages.

EE; RLA; Hugh Ruppersbury and John C. Inscoe, eds., *The New Georgian Encyclopedia Companion to Georgia Literature* (2007); Obituary, *New York Times* (30 May 1996); *Contemporary Authors: A Bio-Bibliographical Guide*, ed. Ann Evory (1981).

VALERIE REMPEL

Priesand, Sally Jane (1946–). First woman rabbi in the U.S. Sally Priesand became the first American woman ordained as a rabbi on 3 June, 1972. That Priesand succeeded when other women who had entered Reform Judaism's Hebrew Union College before her had not succeeded was due to her remarkable tenacity and also to her historical moment during the second wave of American feminism. After seven years as an assistant and associate rabbi at New York City's Stephen Wise Free Synagogue (1972–79), Preisand took several part-time positions before arriving in 1981 at Monmouth Reform Temple in Tinton Falls, New Jersey. She forged a creative partnership with this congregation and realized there her belief that a rabbi's primary task is to help Jews take responsibility for their Judaism.

EAWR; JWA; Pamela S. Nadell, *Women Who Would Be Rabbis* (1998); Sally Jane Priesand, *Judaism and the New Woman* (1975).

PAMELA S. NADELL

Prince, Rose (1915–49). Roman Catholic candidate for sainthood. Born of the Dakelh (Carrier) indigenous people at Fort St. John, northern British Columbia, Rose Prince attended Lejac Indian residential school, where she continued to live and work until the time of her death. In life she was humble, wise, and kind. She had a gentle sense of humor and was remarkable in her holiness. Two years after her death, when her grave was relocated, her body inexplicably had not decayed. Her people witnessed this as a miracle, and since then they have experienced miraculous healings that they attribute to her intercession. Large numbers of believers travel great distances in an annual pilgrimage to Lejac, where they seek healings and blessings in her name, and pray for the day Rose Prince will be canonized a saint in the Roman Catholic Church.

Ken Frith, prod., *Uncorrupted: The Story of Rose Prince* [VHS/DVD] (1998); Rose Prince, www.roseprincecatholic.net.

JANET SILMAN

Prior, Margaret Barrett Allen (1773–1842). Moral reform worker. At age 16 Margaret Barrett married William Allen of Baltimore. All but one of their children died young. When her husband perished at sea, she and her son moved to New York, and there she married William Prior, a merchant, in 1815. The following year she joined the Methodist Episcopal Church. Soon she began to do charitable work among the poor. The couple had children, but they also died young. After the death of their seventh child, Prior decided to be a "mother to the motherless"; she took several children into their home and adopted one. She felt particularly interested in the work of the New York Female Moral Reform Society. In 1834 she became a missionary for the society, working in the poorer parts of the city and visiting about 50 families a week until illness forced her to discontinue her activities.

NoAW.

MARILYN FÄRDIG WHITELEY

Prophet, Elizabeth Clare Wulf (1940–). Leader of the Church Universal and Triumphant. Elizabeth Clare Wulf was raised in Christian Science. She attended Boston University, where she met and married Mark L. Prophet. Mark Prophet dictated and published messages from ascended masters, such as Saint Germain. After her husband's death in 1973 Prophet took over his spiritual role. She incorporated her organization as the Church Universal and Triumphant; moved it to Malibu, California, in 1978; and then to a site near Yellowstone Park, Montana, in 1986. Known also as Guru Ma, Prophet claims to be the incarnation of the biblical Martha and conduit for the "lost" teachings of Jesus. Her apocalyptic predictions have provoked members to build bomb shelters and expect nuclear war. The organization claims 200 groups in the U.S. and representatives in 40 other countries.

ANB; EAWR; RLA; Bradley C. Whitsel, *The Church Universal and Triumphant* (2003).

GRAEME SHARROCK

Protten, Rebecca Freundlich (ca. 1718–80). Missionary and one of the first African American women ordained. Rebecca was born on the island of Antigua and sold as a slave on St. Thomas in the 1720s. She was freed as an adolescent, after she was baptized. In 1736 she initiated a relationship with Moravian evangelists serving on St. Thomas. Shortly after being converted by them, she began evangelizing among the enslaved and freed African population despite violent opposition from white planters. She married the German missionary Matthäus Freundlich in 1738, a rare instance of interracial marriage at the time. She was an effective evangelist and helped establish the Posaunenberg Moravian congregation (and plantation) on St. Thomas, one of the oldest African American churches in the U.S. (The Virgin Islands, Danish colonies from the end of the 17th century, were purchased by the U.S. in 1917.) After the death of her husband in 1741 Freundlich relocated to Germany. In 1746 she married Christian Protten, a Moravian from Africa, and shortly after she was ordained a deaconess in the Moravian Church, making her one of the first African American women to be ordained in any church. In 1765 the Prottens arrived as missionaries to the Gold Coast of Africa, where she had limited success as a teacher and evangelist.

Jon F. Sensbach, *Rebecca's Revival* (2005); C. G. A. Oldendorp, *History of the Mission of the Evangelical Brethren on the Caribbean Islands of St. Thomas, St. Croix, and St. John* (1987).

CRAIG D. ATWOOD

Pugh, Sarah (1800–1884). Unitarian abolitionist and women's rights advocate. Born into a Quaker home, Sarah Pugh became a Unitarian. She founded an elementary school in 1829, where she taught until 1840. In the 1830s Pugh became active in the abolition movement; she joined the Philadelphia Female Anti-Slavery Society and the American Anti-Slavery Society. The Anti-Slavery Convention of American Women used Pugh's school for discussions after a mob burned down the convention's meeting place in 1838. In the 1840s Pugh delivered antislavery petitions in neighborhoods and urged Congress and state legislatures to abolish slavery. Denied permission to participate at the World Anti-Slavery Convention in London in 1840 because of her gender, Pugh wrote a letter of protest on behalf of Pennsylvania delegates. After the Civil War she worked to improve the plight of women and of freed slaves. Pugh was reformer Florence Kelley's great-aunt.

ANB; EAWR; NoAW.

KEITH DURSO

Pupo-Ortiz, Yolanda (1937–). Methodist minister. Yolanda Pupo-Ortiz was the first Hispanic/Latina woman received in full (1983) into the former Southern New England Conference of the United Methodist Church (UMC). Pupo-Ortiz was raised in Cuba in a Quaker family. She converted to Methodism upon her marriage, and is known for her distinctive and prophetic contribution to Hispanic preaching. She holds degrees from Colegio Los Amigos and Seminario Evangélico de Teologia, in Cuba, and a master's degree from Emory University. She has served as a pastor and as the associate general secretary on the Religion and Race Commission for the UMC, and is currently the director of the course of study program for Spanish students at Garrett-Evangelical Theological Seminary.

Justo L. González and Pablo A. Jiménez, *Púlpito* (2005).

ELIZABETH HINSON-HASTY

Qoyawayma, Polingaysi (Elizabeth Q. White) (1892–1990). Teacher and potter. Polingaysi Qoyawayma was born on the Hopi reservation. She attended the local Bureau of Indian Affairs (BIA) school and the Sherman Institute in Riverside, California. She returned home after four years, and, inculcated with the notion of the superiority of European American culture, she refused marriage and was chastised by the elders. She left for the Bethel Academy (Kansas) and returned home as a missionary. She found herself at odds with traditional Hopi culture, however, and began to teach. Her pedagogy was innovative. She reclaimed the value of Hopi traditions and incorporated Hopi culture into the curriculum. After her retirement she became a renowned potter who employed traditional Hopi symbols in her work. She cofounded the Hopi Scholarship Foundation and received many honors.

EAWR; NaAW; NoAWC; Polingaysi Qoyawayma, *The Sun Girl* (1978); *No Turning Back* (1964).

LISA J. POIRIER

Rand, Caroline Amanda Sherfey (1828–1905). Philanthropist. Caroline Rand was married to Elbridge D. Rand, a wealthy businessman, who died in 1887. In 1891 George Herron became the assistant pastor at the congregational church in Burlington, Iowa, where his socialist ideas created conflict. He and Rand had become friends, and Rand gave $35,000 to Iowa College (now Grinnell) to endow a chair in Applied Christianity for Herron. When the Herrons moved to Grinnell, Rand and her daughter, *Carrie, moved also. In 1897 the Rands gave the E. D. Rand Women's Gymnasium to the college. Herron resigned in 1899, and he and the Rands took an eight-month trip to Europe. Herron's wife filed for divorce in 1900, and George Herron and Carrie Rand married in 1901. Rand and the Herrons moved to Italy in 1904. Part of Rand's estate was used to endow the Rand School of Social Science in New York City.

NoAW; George D. Herron papers, Grinnell College Archives.

LYNN JAPINGA

Randall, Claire (ca. 1916–2007). Presbyterian elder, educator, ecumenist. Claire Randall was the first woman general secretary of the National Council of the Churches of Christ in the USA (NCC). A native of San Antonio, Texas, Randall attended several institutions of higher education, including Scarritt College in Nashville, Tennessee, and the Presbyterian School of Christian Education in Richmond, Virginia. Randall brought her gifts of art, music, biblical scholarship, and theological understanding to the national staff of *Church Women United (CWU) as its associate executive from 1962 to 1973. Among many contributions, she organized some of the first women and theology conferences. Randall was the general secretary of the NCC from 1974 until 1984; in these difficult years of the ecumenical movement, she worked tirelessly for a more visible unity among the member communions of the NCC. Following her service at the NCC she became the 14th national president of CWU (1988–92). Randall was deeply committed to the struggles for civil and human rights in the U.S. and around the world.

Jerry L. Van Marter, "Noted Ecumenist Claire Randall, 91, Dies," Presbyterian News Service (9 December 2007); Susan M. Hartmann, "Women in Protestant Church Societies and Bureaucracies," in *Encyclopedia of Women and Religion in North America*, vol. 3, ed. Rosemary Skinner Keller et al. (2006).

LINDA B. BREBNER

Randolph, Florence Spearing (1866–1951). Minister and reformer. Florence Spearing was a graduate of Avery Normal Institute and moved to New Jersey in 1885, where she met and married Hugh Randolph (d. 1913). Florence Randolph served as an exhorter in the African Methodist Episcopal (AME) Zion Church by the mid-1890s. A controversial revival broke out under her leadership in 1896; the congregation made her its minister and forced the New Jersey conference to license her. The denomination began to permit women's ordination in 1898. Randolph served churches in New York and New Jersey until her 1946 retirement. She was president of the Women's Home and Foreign Missionary Society (1916–41). In 1915 she organized the New Jersey Federation of Colored Women's Clubs and served as president until 1927. She advocated an integrationist model of race relations and believed in the transforming power of democracy.

NBAW; Joan Burstyn, ed., *Past and Promise* (1997); New Jersey Historical Society Archives.

SCOTT D. SEAY

Ransom, Emma S. Connor (ca. 1866–1943). Churchwoman, clubwoman, and civil rights activist. Emma Ransom was among the 85 African American women who gathered in January 1905 to establish the Harlem *YWCA (Young Women's Christian Association). She was a leader in the women's missionary work of the African Methodist Episcopal (AME) Church, and worked closely with her minister husband, Cassius Ransom, who in 1924 was elected the 48th bishop in the AME Church. She was the cofounder of the Ohio Conference Branch Missionary Society and edited and published *Women's Light and Love for Heathen Africa*, the only AME missionary journal edited and published by women. Ransom made an important contribution to the ongoing missionary work of black churches and helped to build an institutional structure through which women could exert influence in the church.

NBAW; NWARC; Judith Weisenfeld, "The Harlem YWCA and the Secular City, 1904–1945," *Journal of Women's History* 6, no. 3 (1994).

ANGELA D. SIMS

Reed, Mary (1854–1943). Missionary. At age 30 Mary Reed decided to become a missionary. Supported by the Cincinnati branch of the Methodist Woman's Missionary Society she departed for India in November 1884. In the foothills of the Himalayas she observed the plight of lepers. After four years in India she returned to the U.S. on furlough. She discovered that she had contracted leprosy, but without sharing that knowledge with family or friends, she returned to India to work among lepers near Pithoragarh. In 1892 she took charge of a leprosy asylum and greatly improved living conditions there. Her health remained good and, with the help of Indian assistants, she continued to administer the asylum until 1938. She died at the age of 88 as the result of an accident, and was buried near the chapel of the asylum.

NoAW; John Jackson, *Mary Reed, Missionary to the Lepers* (2005) [1899].

MARILYN FÄRDIG WHITELEY

Regan, Agnes Gertrude (1869–1943). Roman Catholic social reformer. Agnes Regan graduated from San Francisco Normal School in 1887 and was a public elementary educator and administrator until 1919. She was elected the executive secretary of the *National Council of Catholic Women in 1920 and moved to Washington, DC. She helped found the Catholic Service School for Women in 1921 (later called the National Catholic School for Social Service). As the school's assistant director from 1925 until her death she brought a Catholic presence to the national movement of social welfare, and was a member of the White House Conference on Children and Democracy in 1939 and 1940. Her Catholic-inspired dedication to social reform was recognized in 1933 with the Holy See's Pro Ecclesia et Pontifice award.

EACH; EAWR; NCE; NoAW; RLA; L. R. Lawler, *Full Circle: The Story of the National Catholic School of Social Services* (1951).

SANDRA YOCUM MIZE

Re-Imagining Conference (1993). Ecumenical women's gathering. In November 1993 the World Council of Churches sponsored a Re-Imagining God conference in Minneapolis, Minnesota. Womanist and feminist theologians, including *Virginia Mollenkott, *Delores Williams, *Lois Wilson, Jose Hobday, Chung Hyung Kyung, and Elizabeth Bettenhausen, urged participants to reimagine God, ethics, and themselves. Liturgies were introduced that focused on feminine images of God, including Sophia (the wisdom of God). Controversy erupted following the conference. Even though few Christians would contend that God could be adequately understood as possessing only masculine attributes, many Christians felt their primary relationship with God as Father was threatened by exploring feminine attributes that might also be embodied by God. The Presbyterian and Methodist churches received thousands of complaints. Some organizations, including the American Family Association and the American Baptist Churches, denounced the conference. Officials from the United Church of Christ and the United Church of Canada were among its few vocal supporters.

Nancy J. Berneking and Pamela Carter Joern, eds., *Re-Membering and Re-Imagining* (1995).

LOUISE GRAVES

Religious Formation Conference (RFC) (1954–). National Roman Catholic organization. The RFC was formed by a committee of the National Catholic Education Association (NCEA) in the 1950s to address a concern regarding the adequate preparation of women religious for the ministries in which they were engaged. Its organization was initially approved as the Sister Formation Conference (SFC) by the NCEA. Ten years later the SFC, while maintaining ties with the NCEA, became a conference under the auspices of the Conference of Major Superiors of Women's Institutes, later renamed the *Leadership Conference of Women Religious (LCWR). In 1971 the SFC became an autonomous national conference. In 1976 it was renamed the Religious Formation Conference (RFC), when its membership was broadened to include male religious and religious from noncanonical groups. The RFC today provides intellectual and spiritual opportunities for ministers of initial and ongoing formation, as well as for persons in initial formation in religious institutes, through an annual national conference, regional workshops, a variety of publications, and its regular newsletter, *In-Formation*.

The Harper Collins Encyclopedia of Catholicism (1995); Mary L. Schneider, "American Sisters and the Roots of Change: The 1950s," *U.S. Catholic Historian* 7, no. 1 (Winter 1988).

EPHREM (RITA) HOLLERMANN, OSB

Religious of the Sacred Heart (Religieuses du Sacré de Jésus) (RSCJ) (1800–). Roman Catholic religious congregation. Founded in Paris by Madeleine Sophie Barat (1779–1865) with the aid of the Reverend Joseph Varin, the RSCJ was intended to parallel the then-suppressed Society of Jesus. The sisters aimed to revitalize Catholicism in postrevolutionary France as contemplatives in action. Their principal works included the education of girls in boarding schools, free instruction of poor children, spiritual retreats for persons of all classes, and the establishment of sodalities, the Children of Mary. Their comprehensive system of education for young women grew to be widely in demand. By 1865 the community had more than 3,500 members in 17 countries and grew to more than 6,500 members. The sisters' first mission in the U.S. opened in St. Charles, Missouri, in 1818 under the leadership of *Rose Philippine Duchesne (1769–1852). Recognized for their commitment to excellence in education, during the first decades of the 20th century they established 10 institutions of higher learning for women, in addition to their academies, orphanages, and other educational works. Responding to changes in the Roman Catholic Church following the Second Vatican Council, the congregation articulated a renewed purpose and vision. They also reorganized their schools into the Network of Sacred Heart Schools. There are currently 3,500 sisters in 45 countries, including 450 members in the U.S. province.

EACH; NCE; ROWUS; Louise Callan, *The Society of the Sacred Heart in North America* (1937).

JUDITH METZ, SC

Remond, Sarah Parker (1826–94). Abolitionist and physician. Sarah Remond was born to Nancy Lenox and John Remond, ardent abolitionists and influential African American citizens of Salem, Massachusetts. Sarah acquired a distinguished education despite New England schools' discriminatory practices. In 1853 Remond successfully sued employees of Boston's Howard Athenaeum for forcibly evicting her when she refused to sit in a segregated gallery. She joined her brother, Charles Lenox Remond, on the antislavery lecture circuit in 1856 and is best remembered for her 1859–61 speaking tour in Britain. Remond completed medical school in Florence, Italy, in 1871, and practiced medicine there for over 20 years, marrying Lazzaro Pintor in 1877. She is buried in the Protestant Cemetery in Rome.

BWA; NoAW; Sibyl Brownlee, *Out of the Abundance of the Heart: Sarah Ann Parker Remond's Quest for Freedom* (PhD diss., University of Massachusetts, 1997); Sarah Parker Remond, "A Colored Lady Lecturer," *English Woman's Journal* 7 (June 1861).

MARGARET MCMANUS

Repplier, Agnes (1855–1950). Essayist and biographer. Born and educated in Philadelphia, Agnes Repplier began her writing career at the age of 16. She wrote literary (often humorous) essays on a range of subjects, from war stories, to cats, to the benefits of drinking tea. Her first essay collection, *Books and Men* (1888), went into 20 editions. Repplier's essays in the *Atlantic Monthly* fostered friendships with other intellectuals, among them Oliver Wendell Holmes, Henry James, and Walt Whitman. A devout Roman Catholic who never married, her biographies focused on important figures in the Catholic Church. Repplier's charm was her quick mind, polished prose, and good humor. This thin, chain-smoking woman was not above mercilessly satirizing those who fell beneath her standards, however. Repplier was one of the first women offered membership in the National Institute of Arts and Letters.

ANB; EACH; NoAW; P. Carey, *The Roman Catholics* (1993); *American Women Writers*, vol. 2 (1983); *Dictionary of American Biography* (1974).

ELLEN WHELAN, OSF

Reyes, Rebecca (1951–). Minister, social worker, and activist. In 1979 Rebecca Reyes was the first Hispanic woman to be ordained in the Presbyterian Church in the U.S. (PCUS). She was born to Mexican American parents in San Bernardino, California, and raised in Texas. (Presbyterian missionaries, who had worked among her people for four generations, had impacted her family and ancestors.) Reyes graduated from Austin Presbyterian Theological Seminary in 1975 and was ordained by the Presbytery of Del Salvador in 1979. She served on the national staff of the PCUS in the areas of global ministries and national ministries (Youth and Young Adult Office). She also was a campus minister at the University of North Carolina at Chapel Hill, where she earned a master's degree in social work in 1993. Since 2001 she has served as the coordinator of the Latino Health Project at Duke University Hospital in Durham, North Carolina. In 2003 she received the Duke University Diversity Award, which honors a faculty or staff member who demonstrates a respect and value for various cultural backgrounds and points of view within the university and health system.

Rebecca Reyes, "Musings for the Soul," *Voices of Sophia* (2001); (no author given) "Haynes and Reyes Receive Diversity Award," *Inside* 12, no. 18 (Duke University Medical Center, 2003); El Pueblo Inc., "Board Profiles," www.elpueblo.org/english/about/board.html.

LINDA B. BREBNER

Rhodes, Mary (1782–1853). Founder of the *Sisters of Loretto. Born and educated in a comfortable Maryland family, Mary Rhodes journeyed to frontier Kentucky in 1811 to visit relatives. Shocked to discover her nieces growing up without educational opportunities, Rhodes started schooling them herself. As the number of pupils increased, Rhodes sought assistance from her sister, Anna, and three other young women. With the support of Father Charles Nerinckx, the tiny community became the Little Society of the Friends of Mary in 1812, later known as the Sisters of Loretto. They were the first American community of sisters not established as an extension of an existing European congregation. Rhodes was the second mother superior (her sister, Anna, the first, died of tuberculosis only a few months after her election) and led the congregation from 1812 to 1822.

EACH; ROWUS; Florence Wolff, *From Generation to Generation: The Sisters of Loretto* (1982).

COLLEEN CARPENTER CULLINAN

Richardson, Gertrude Twilley (1875–1946). Pacifist, writer, and social gospeler. Shaped by the Fabian socialism of her Leicester, England, birthplace, Gertrude Richardson was active in suffrage, socialist, and pacifist causes even before arriving in northern Manitoba in 1911. With the outbreak of World War I she became one of Canada's most ardent voices against war and conscription. She helped organize the Women's Peace Crusade in 1917. She used her freelance writings to proclaim the shared humanity of all peoples and to uplift the Golden Rule, which she believed was the aim of authentic religion. Richardson experienced periods of debilitating physical and mental illness, and, unfortunately, she was unable to engage in social reform activities during the last 25 years of her life.

Barbara Roberts, *A Reconstructed World: A Feminist Biography of Gertrude Richardson* (1996).

ELEANOR J. STEBNER

Richmond, Cora L. V. Scott (1840–1923). Spiritualist medium and pastor. Cora Scott had two major influences in her life: her birth to a Presbyterian mother and a father influenced by free thought and universalism, and her brief stay in Hopedale, a Spiritualist colony. Scott's gifts as a healing medium emerged in 1851, and she became a famous child trance lecturer on the national Spiritualist circuit. She married an older, exploitive man, and then survived the scandal of divorce from him. She continued her career, speaking through spirit inspiration on religious, scientific, and political subjects. Henry James used her as the model for Verna Tarrant in his novel *The Bostonians*. She delivered "Presentation of Spiritualism" at the 1893 World's Parliament of Religions and served a five-year term as vice president of the National Spiritualist Association. She was pastor at the First Spiritualist Society of Chicago for 50 years.

ANB; EAWR; RLA; WBC; Ann Braude, *Radical Spirits* (1995); Harrison D. Barrett, *Life Work of Mrs. Cora L. V. Richmond* (1895).

MARY FARRELL BEDNAROWSKI

Riepp, Benedicta (Sybilla) (1825–62). Founder of *Benedictine women in North America. Born in Waal, Bavaria, Sybilla Riepp entered the Benedictine monastery in Eichstätt in 1844. In 1852 she volunteered to go to the U.S. to teach the children of German immigrants who had settled in St. Marys, Pennsylvania, where she established the country's first monastery of Benedictine sisters. Her years were plagued with physical hardships and misunderstandings with local churchmen. Riepp resisted male interference in the internal matters of her communities and repeated attempts to thwart her authority as the legitimate superior of the monasteries she went on to establish. In 1857 she returned to Europe to appeal to Pius IX relative to the issues of authority and autonomy. Failing to gain access to him, Riepp returned to the U.S. in 1858, where she took up residence in St. Cloud, Minnesota, until her death from tuberculosis. Riepp founded six Benedictine monasteries in five different states during her 10 years in the U.S.

EACH; NoAW; William M. Johnston, ed., *Encyclopedia of Monasticism* (2000); Ephrem Hollermann, *The Reshaping of a Tradition* (1994).

EPHREM (RITA) HOLLERMANN, OSB

Ripley, Sophia Willard Dana (1803–61). Transcendentalist, intellectual, reformer, and Roman Catholic. Born into a prominent Boston family, Sophia Ripley became a member of the Transcendentalist Club and a core participant in *Margaret Fuller's conversations in the early 1840s. In 1841 she published her essay "Woman" in the Transcendentalist periodical the *Dial*. The same year, she and her husband, George Ripley, founded the Brook Farm utopian community in Massachusetts. She tirelessly promoted Brook Farm, despite growing disagreement with some of its components, until its collapse in 1847. She privately converted to

Roman Catholicism in 1846. Increasing religious and ideological differences between the Ripleys, compounded by the emotionally and financially draining failure of Brook Farm, led to strains in their marriage. Ripley died prior to her husband's success as a journalist.

ANB; NoAW; Joel Myerson, ed., *The Brook Farm Book* (1984); Henry L. Golemba, *George Ripley* (1977).

AMY BLACK VOORHEES

Rivera, Alicia ("Sister Cristina") (1933–96). Episcopal religious and missionary. Born to a Baptist family in Ponce, Puerto Rico, Alicia Rivera became an Episcopalian in 1945. After a move to New York City to work as a laboratory technician and hematologist, she entered the Order of Saint Helena (OSH) as a postulant in 1959 and was life professed in 1964. Following ministries in Africa and in Georgia, Sister Cristina returned to New York City, where she was a founder and pastor of the San Juan Bautista Mission in the South Bronx. Rivera was a member of the Hispanic Commission of the Diocese of New York, the National Hispanic Commission, the Episcopal Urban Caucus, and the Coalition of Human Need. She was awarded the Bishop's Cross for her contributions to Hispanic ministry.

Sheryl A. Kujawa-Holbrook, *Freedom Is a Dream* (2002); Official biography, Convent of St. Helena (Vails Gate, New York).

SHERYL A. KUJAWA-HOLBROOK

Roback, Léa (1903–2000). Feminist, social activist, and union organizer. Born in Montreal to Jewish immigrants from Poland, Léa Roback became a freethinking political activist and champion of women's rights. She studied at the University of Grenoble (France) and traveled to England and Germany, where she developed her strong commitment to communism. She returned to Canada in the 1930s and became involved in women's labor movements. She helped to organize a garment workers' strike, which led to the signing of Montreal's first collective agreement with the International Ladies Garment Workers' Union in 1937. In 1943 she helped to secure the first union contract for over 4,000 workers at an RCA Victor munitions plant. She worked tirelessly to improve living conditions for women and families. Roback was also active in the Quebec provincial suffrage movement, worked as a peace activist within the Voice of Women organization (founded 1960), and participated in struggles against the Vietnam War and racism. She worked for access to housing, education, wage equity, and the right to free abortion. She was made a member of the Order of Quebec in 2000.

Library and Archives Canada, www.collectionscanada.gc.ca/women/002026-308-e.html; Lea Roback Fondation/Foundation, www.fondationlearoback.org.

TRUDY FLYNN

Robertson, Ann Eliza Worcester (1826–1905). Missionary and biblical translator. Ann Worcester was the daughter of missionaries to the Cherokee Nation. Her father was an ordained Congregational minister who opposed attempts to relocate the Cherokee from Georgia to Oklahoma. In 1849 Worcester was appointed to the Tullahasse Manual Labor Boarding School, operated by the Creek Nation and the Presbyterian Board of Foreign Missions. In 1850 she married William Schenck Robertson, the school principal and a Presbyterian minister, and joined the Presbyterian Church. She continued to teach and work on translations in the Creek language. In 1887 she completed a Creek New Testament. She also produced translations of Genesis and Psalms and wrote an original Creek hymnal. In 1892 she received an honorary doctorate from the College of Wooster in Ohio.

EAWR; EE; NoAW; RLA; J. Gordon Melton, *Religious Leaders of America* (1991).

JUDITH L. GIBBARD

Robins, Margaret Dreier (1868–1945). Labor reformer. Descended from German immigrants, Margaret Dreier was born and raised in New York. Upon completing her private school education, she joined the new Women's Trade Union League (WTUL), which sought to organize working women and secure legislation bettering their working conditions, wages, and hours. Her marriage to Raymond Robins took her to Chicago, where she became president of the Chicago branch of the WTUL and the national WTUL. Her religious convictions as a Congregationalist inflamed her sense of outrage at injustice and exploitation. She believed in free enterprise, but her experience taught her that the government must step in to support the weak. Robins was instrumental in founding the International Federation of Working Women, the outgrowth of two international congresses of working women that she convened in 1919 and 1921.

NoAW; Mary Dreier, *Margaret Dreier Robins* (1950); Papers, Special and Area Studies Collections, George A. Smathers Libraries, University of Florida (Gainesville).

BETH SPAULDING

Robinson, Ida Bell (1891–1946). Founder and bishop of the Mount Sinai Holy Church of America. Ida Bell grew up in Pensacola, Florida, the seventh of 12 children born to Robert and Annie Bell. After her conversion as a teenager at an evangelistic street meeting, she led prayer services in homes. In 1909 she married Oliver Robinson, and they soon relocated to Philadelphia for better employment opportunities. She did street evangelism in Philadelphia under the auspices of the United Holy Church of America. In 1919 the church ordained her and appointed her to a small mission church, but she increasingly felt that prospects for women within the denomination were dwindling. After a period of fasting and prayer she founded a new denomination, the Mount Sinai Holy Church of America. It spread rapidly along the eastern seaboard, largely due to Robinson's evangelistic work and church planting. She was consecrated as bishop in 1925. When she died the denomination consisted of 84 churches, more than 160 ordained ministers, an accredited school in Philadelphia, mission work in Cuba and Guyana, and a farm in New Jersey that provided a safe haven away from the city for church members.

BWA; EAWR.

PRISCILLA POPE-LEVISON

Robinson, Jane Marie Bancroft (1847–1932). Leader in Methodist deaconess movement and educator. Jane Bancroft was highly educated for a woman of her time, receiving a doctorate from Syracuse University in 1884. She was dean of women and professor of French at Northwestern University from 1877 to 1885. During an educational sojourn in Europe she studied the developing deaconess movement and returned home to launch a deaconess program for the Woman's Home Missionary Society (WHMS) of the Methodist Episcopal Church. Under her leadership, the WHMS established numerous deaconess homes, schools, and hospitals throughout the northern U.S. Robinson served as president of the WHMS from 1908 to 1913. Concerned for the care of elderly deaconesses and ministers, she bequeathed her home in California as a retirement home for them.

ANB; NoAW; Mary Agnes Dougherty, *My Calling to Fulfill: Deaconess in the United Methodist Tradition* (1997); Jane Bancroft

Robinson, *Deaconesses in Europe and Their Lessons for America* (1889).

CAROLYN DESWARTE GIFFORD

Robinson, Lizzie Woods ("Mother") (1860–1945). Pastor and leader in the Church of God in Christ (COGIC). In 1906 Lizzie Woods experienced a "baptism of the Holy Ghost" after meeting Bishop Charles Mason, founder of the COGIC. Woods, chosen as the general mother of all the women in COGIC, immediately brought structure to women's activities in the movement, and her career highlighted Mason's attempts to promote gender equity within his church. Under her leadership, women prayed, studied the Bible, taught Scripture to others, sewed clothes for the needy, and assisted in the planting of new churches. Through the women's ministry, she directed several successful fund-raising efforts. The money raised allowed for the construction of a COGIC headquarters to direct national efforts. Robinson also played a key role in the creation of a foreign missions board in COGIC. After she married Edward Robinson, the two traveled together founding churches in several states. They later settled in Nebraska where Ida Baker, Robinson's only child, lived. (In some sources, Robinson is referred to as Roberson.)

EAWR; Anthea Butler, *Women in the Church of God in Christ* (2007); Elijah L. Hill, *Women Come Alive: Biography of Mother Lizzie Robinson* (2005).

LORETTA LONG HUNNICUTT

Rodgers, Elizabeth Flynn (1847–1939). Union organizer and social reformer. Elizabeth Flynn was born in Ireland. She immigrated with her family in 1854 to New York City and then London, Ontario, where she received a Catholic education until she was age 14. She was employed as a tailor and, at the age of 17, married George Rodgers, a labor organizer, social reformer, and women's rights advocate. They had 12 children, and lived in Detroit and then in Chicago, where Rodgers organized working women. She became a Knights of Labor leader and supported the Haymarket Eight, using Knights' funds for their defense. She left the failing Knights and joined the Catholic Order of Foresters after Leo XIII's 1891 *Rerum Novarum* relaxed prohibitions against such organizations. Rodgers established a parallel Order of Foresters that granted women death benefits and insurance premiums. She left public life in 1908.

WBC; Susan Levine, *Labor's True Woman* (1984).

SANDRA YOCUM MIZE

Rogers, Aurelia Spencer (1834–1922). Advocate for Mormon children. Aurelia Spencer was born in Connecticut, the daughter of a Protestant minister. Her parents joined the Church of Jesus Christ of Latter-day Saints when she was six and moved the family to Nauvoo, Illinois, and then to Utah. Spencer married at age 17 and gave birth to 12 children, only seven of whom survived infancy. Her devotion to children led her to establish the Primary organization to provide recreation and religious instruction, one of several such female-run organizations in Utah. In 1878 she opened the first Primary at Farmington, Utah, taking charge of the settlement's children with the permission of the presiding bishop. Rogers was also active in the suffrage movement, serving as a delegate to the 1894–95 Woman's Suffrage Convention in Georgia.

Daniel H. Ludlow, ed., *Encyclopedia of Mormonism* (1992); Aurelia Spencer Rogers, *Life Sketches of Orson Spencer and Others and History of Primary Works* (1898).

ANDREW H. STERN

Rogers, Elizabeth Ann ("Sister Beatrice") (1829–1921). Anglican sister and educator. Elizabeth Rogers was born in Cornwall, England, and showed an early inclination for the religious life. In 1865, while visiting one of the houses of the Congregation of the Religious of the Most Holy Trinity, she met Queen Emma of Hawaii, an Anglican interested in securing teachers for a school for Hawaiian girls. In 1867 Rogers, now called Sister Beatrice, was clothed as a novice and landed in Honolulu with her mother superior and two other sisters. Together with *Ellen Albertina Polyblank (Sister Albertina), Sister Beatrice ran the St. Andrew's Priory school in Hawaii, which opened in 1867 and offered girls of diverse racial backgrounds the best education available in the islands. Sisters Beatrice and Albertina managed the school on their own after 1890 until their retirement in 1902.

NoAW; Barbara H. Ching, *St. Andrew's Priory: Historical Sketch* (1955); Thomas Jay Williams, *Priscilla Lydia Sellon* (1950).

SHERYL A. KUJAWA-HOLBROOK

Rogers, Mary Josephine ("Mother Mary Joseph") (1882–1955). Founder of the *Maryknoll Sisters. Mary Rogers was a graduate of Smith College, where she later became an assistant in the biology department. She was a public school teacher in Boston from 1908 to 1912. While at college, Rogers organized a mission study club in an attempt to interest Roman Catholic women in foreign missions. In 1912 Rogers enlisted some women to work as secretaries and housekeepers at the Catholic Foreign Mission Society of America (now the Maryknoll Fathers and Brothers) in Hawthorne, New York. The women also worked on *The Field Afar*, a missionary journal. After convincing Catholic leaders that women could be foreign missionaries, Rogers founded the Foreign Mission Sisters of St. Dominic in 1920, which was renamed the Maryknoll Sisters of St. Dominic in 1954. She was elected mother general of the order every year from 1925 to 1946. At Rogers's retirement in 1946 the order had 733 members in Asia, Latin America, and the U.S.

DARB; EACH; EAWR; NCE; NoAWMP; RLA; J. M. Lyons and C. Kennedy, "Rogers, Mary Joseph, Mother," *New Catholic Encyclopedia*, vol. 12, 2nd ed. (2003) [1967]; Susan Hill Lindley, *"You Have Stept Out of Your Place"* (1996); Jeanne Marie Lyons, *Maryknoll's First Lady* (1964).

KEITH DURSO

Rohrbough, Faith Elizabeth (Burgess) (1935–). First woman dean and first woman president of a Lutheran seminary in North America. Faith Rohrbough was born in Boston to parents who were both teachers. She received her doctoral degree from the University of Basel in 1968. In 1978 she was named academic dean and vice president and professor of church history at the Lutheran Theological Seminary at Philadelphia (LTSP). While at LTSP she established the Urban Theological Institute and introduced a globalization emphasis. In 1996 Rohrbough became the president of the Lutheran Theological Seminary at Saskatoon (LTS), a post she held until her retirement in 2004. Under her leadership LTS developed emphases on cross-cultural and pastoral formation. Rohrbough was ordained in the Evangelical Lutheran Church in America (ELCA) in 1996. She has been active in the Association of Theological Schools (ATS) and has received honors from several universities in the U.S.

Faith E. Rohrbough, "Patience, Common Sense and Learning," in "A President's Voyage," *In Trust* 16 (Summer 2005); Clifford Reinhardt, "Foreword," *Consensus: A Canadian Lutheran Journal of Theology* 30, no. 2 (Fall 2005).

SANDRA L. BEARDSALL

Rose, Ernestine Susmond Potowski (1810–92). Jewish activist and freethinker. The daughter of a Polish rabbi,

Ernestine Potowski reportedly nullified an arranged marriage before immigrating to Berlin and then England. In the 1830s she became a disciple of utopian socialist Robert Owen, lectured with him, and married his associate, William Ella Rose. The Roses moved to New York in 1836, where Ernestine advocated reform and Free Thought causes, particularly antislavery and women's rights. Identified as a foremother by *Susan B. Anthony, Rose was an exceptional speaker known as the "Queen of the Platform." The extent of her rejection of Judaism is debated, but whatever her personal views, she deplored anti-Semitism, as she did other forms of prejudice that restricted human rights. She and her husband, who were unusually close for that era, moved to England in 1869.

ANB; EAWR; JWA; NoAW; Carol A. Kolmerten, *The American Life of Ernestine L. Rose* (1998); Yuri Suhl, *Ernestine L. Rose*, rev. ed. (1990) [1959]; Elinor Lerner, "Jewish Involvement in the New York City Woman Suffrage Movement," *American Jewish History* 70, no. 4 (1981); Speeches in Elizabeth Cady Stanton et al., eds., *History of Woman Suffrage*, vol. 1 (1887).

AMY BLACK VOORHEES

Rosensohn, Henrietta ("Etta") Lasker (1885–1966). Social worker and Zionist leader. Born and bred in Galveston, Texas, to a German Jewish family, Etta Lasker Rosensohn grew to become a major activist and philanthropist, especially on behalf of Jewish and Zionist causes. A trained social worker she was professionally and personally committed to her causes, including the *National Council of Jewish Women, American Red Cross, and Travelers Aid Society. Her tenure on the national board of *Hadassah, including the presidency from 1952 to 1953, represented her most ardent commitment. Rosensohn's first trip to Israel in 1914 did not immediately seal her fate as a Zionist, although she claimed that the journey ignited the emotional spark that would ultimately become fire. Rosensohn was particularly committed to Hadassah's medical work, as evidenced by her founding role in the Hebrew University–Hadassah Medical School in Jerusalem.

JWA; Obituary, *New York Times* (21 September 1966); *Who's Who in American Jewry* (1927).

DEBORAH SKOLNICK EINHORN

Rotenberg, Mattie Levi (1897–1989). Broadcaster, physicist, and community organizer. Mattie Levi Rotenberg was awarded a BA in 1921 and a PhD in 1926, the first woman and the first Jew to receive a doctorate in physics from the University of Toronto. In 1929 she helped found the Hillcrest Progressive Day School, the first Jewish day school in Toronto. She worked as a demonstrator in the physics department from 1941 to 1968. Rotenberg also pursued a career in journalism. She was the editor of the women's department of the *Jewish Standard* from 1930 to 1931 and a broadcaster on women's issues for the Canadian Broadcasting Corporation from 1940 to 1960. In 1945 Rotenberg won the Canadian Women's Press Club Award for best broadcast for *The Post-War Woman*.

Edmond Lipsitz, ed., *Canadian Jewish Women of Today* (1983); Nessa Rapoport, "Recollections of Mattie Levi Rotenberg," Jewish Women's Archive, www.jwa.org/discover/recollections; Fonds, Archives of Canada.

TRUDY FLYNN

Ruether, Rosemary Radford (1936–). Feminist theologian and social justice advocate. Rosemary Radford Ruether is a prolific and influential writer in the contemporary feminist movement, having published over 30 books and hundreds of articles. Ruether graduated from Scripps College (1958) and holds a PhD in classics and patristics from Claremont Graduate School (1965). She spent the summer of 1965 working for racial justice in Mississippi with the Delta Ministry. Ruether taught at Howard University (1966–76), Garrett-Evangelical Theological Seminary (1976–2000), and in retirement at the Pacific School of Religion (2000–2005). She married Herman Ruether in 1957, and they have three children. Ruether has remained connected with, although critical of, the Roman Catholic Church. Many of her books deal with women in religious history and document patriarchal attitudes toward women. She has edited several books with Rosemary Skinner Keller about women in contemporary American religion. One of her most influential books is *Sexism and God-Talk* (1983), a systematic feminist theology. Ruether has written extensively about Christian anti-Semitism, politics, racial justice, and the environment. She insists that racism, classism, sexism, anti-Semitism, and other forms of oppression are linked and serve as ways in which the powerful maintain power. She has spent her life identifying and explaining the many modes of oppression, and has encouraged women throughout the world to develop their own feminist theological perspectives.

EACH; EAWR; Rosalind Hinton, "A Legacy of Inclusion: An Interview with Rosemary Radford Ruether," *Cross Currents* 52, no. 1 (Spring 2002); Rosemary Radford Ruether, *Disputed Questions*, rev. ed. (1989).

LYNN JAPINGA

Ruffin, Josephine St. Pierre (1842–1924). Race reformer, editor, and clubwoman. The youngest child of a Bostonian mixed-race couple, Josephine St. Pierre married George Ruffin in 1858. Her husband's prominence in black Boston and his status as a judge gave Ruffin the access and time to live out her Episcopal faith through service in civic groups. She first took on a leading role in the Sanitary Commission during the Civil War. In 1879 she organized support for Boston blacks homesteading in Kansas. She founded and edited (1890–97) the *Woman's Era,* a weekly paper dedicated to advancement of black women, becoming the first black woman editor of a newspaper for women. In 1894 she and her daughter formed a club by the same name. She was also instrumental in organizing the *National Association of Colored Women (NACW) and the Boston chapter of the National Association for the Advancement of Colored People (NAACP).

ANBO; BWA; NBAW; NoAW; Rodger Streitmatter, *Raising Her Voice* (1994).

JOAN R. GUNDERSEN

Ruskay, Esther Jane (1857–1910). Author and speaker. A second-generation American Jew, Esther Ruskay sought to improve Jewish women's lives and defended the vitality of traditional Judaism in the modern period. A member of the first graduating class of Normal (now Hunter) College in 1875 and a public school teacher by profession, Ruskay was active in founding the New York branches of the *National Council of Jewish Women (1894), the Young Women's Hebrew Association (YWHA), the Educational Alliance, and the Vacation Home for Girls. Her *Hearth and Home Essays* was published in 1902. A passionate supporter of traditional Judaism when many Jews championed other movements, Ruskay advocated examining Judaism itself to find ethical and moral instruction, encouraged the use of Hebrew as the language of prayer, and resisted calls to change observance of the Jewish Sabbath to Sunday.

JWA; *American Jewish Yearbook* (1904–05); Jewish Women's Archive, www.jwa.org.

MICHAEL A. SINGER

Russell, Ida Evelyn ("Mrs. Alexander Russell") (1862–1917). Early patron of Japanese Zen Buddhism. Ida Evelyn Conner was born in Bangor, Maine. She married Alexander Russell, a businessman, and they lived in San Francisco. Russell had already traveled in Asia and developed an intense interest in Asian religions when she hosted for nine months the Japanese Zen teacher, Soyen Shaku, in 1905. Soyen Shaku had attended the 1893 World's Parliament of Religions and returned to the U.S. as the personal guest of the Russells. Mrs. Russell's home became the first Zen center in America, and she became the first American to study Zen koans in the U.S. She not only hosted Soyen Shaku, but also the Japanese Zen monk Nyogen Senzaki.

Rick Fields, *How the Swans Came to the Lake: A Narrative History of Buddhism in America*, 3rd rev. ed. (1992) [1981].

BARBARA E. REED

Russell, Katherine ("Mother Mary Baptist") (1829–98). Mother superior of *Sisters of Mercy in San Francisco. Born Katherine Russell in Ireland, she entered the Sisters of Mercy in 1848 and made final profession as Mary Baptist in 1851. She became mother superior to seven other sisters and arrived in San Francisco in 1854, in time to care for the poor during the 1855 cholera epidemic. That same year Russell founded the House of Mercy for destitute women. She established Saint Mary's Hospital (1857) and Magdalene Asylum (1861), and organized the Sodality of Our Lady (1859) to finance the sisters' works of mercy. She oversaw the founding of many elementary schools and convened an 1894 meeting of Catholic schoolteachers throughout San Francisco's archdiocese. Her funeral drew huge crowds, a testament to her life of charitable works.

EACH; NCE; NoAW; ROWUS; Mary K. Doyle, *Like a Tree by Running Water* (2004); M. Aurelia McArdle, *California's Pioneer Sister of Mercy* (1954).

SANDRA YOCUM MIZE

Russell, Letty Mandeville (1929–2007). Christian theologian, writer, and ecumenist. Letty Russell was born in Westfield, New Jersey. She received a BA (1951) from Wellesley College, an STB from Harvard Divinity School, and an STM and ThD from Union Theological Seminary (New York). One of the first women ordained in the United Presbyterian Church, she served in the East Harlem Protestant Parish from 1952 to 1968. From 1974 until 2001 she taught at Yale Divinity School, where she pioneered in feminist liberation theology and ecclesiology. A prolific writer and editor of more than 17 books, she and her life partner, Shannon Clarkson, also coedited the *Dictionary of Feminist Theologies* (1996). A leader in the ecumenical movement Russell participated in the World Council of Churches and U.S. National Council of Churches. She was devoted to nurturing a global network of women scholars and founded international doctoral programs and theological education travel funds.

"In Memoriam," *Yale Bulletin and Calendar* 36, vol. 1 (31 August 2007); Letty Russell, "Outsiders Within: Women in Ministry," in *Celebrating Our Call: Ordination Stories of Presbyterian Women*, ed. Patricia Lloyd-Sidle (2006); NCC News Service, "Letty Russell Dies at 77," www.ncccusa.org/news/070716lettyrussell.html.

JANET SILMAN

Sacred White Buffalo (Josephine Crowfeather) ("Mother Mary Catherine") (1867–93). Native American Roman Catholic sister. Josephine Crowfeather was born to Joseph Crowfeather, a chief of the Hunkpapa Sioux in the Dakota Territory. She received her Indian name, Sacred White Buffalo (Ptesanwanyakapi), shortly after her birth, when her father carried her into a battle and both returned unharmed. From then on, her people considered her to be a sacred virgin. Sacred White Buffalo attended the *Benedictine Sisters' school at Fort Yates, North Dakota. She took her vows in 1890, fulfilling one childhood dream. She established the Congregation of American Sisters, fulfilling another lifelong dream. She was elected as the first prioress and took the name Mother Mary Catherine. The congregation followed the Benedictine discipline. Her community reached a membership of 12 before disbanding in 1900, seven years after her death.

NaAW; Christianity in Native North America, Special Collections and Archives, Marquette University.

KEITH DURSO

Saddler, Juanita Jane (1892–1970). *YWCA worker and civil rights advocate. Born in Guthrie, Oklahoma, Juanita Saddler graduated from Fisk University in 1915 and earned a master's degree from Teachers College at Columbia University in 1935. She was branch secretary for interracial education with the national YWCA (1920–33), and drafted policy statements regarding racial integration within the organization; her work provided a foundation for the YWCA's 1946 interracial charter. She was dean of women at Fisk (1933–35), and worked under *Mary McLeod Bethune in the division of Negro affairs (1935–36). In later life she worked to integrate welfare-funded programs for youth in Washington, DC, and established initiatives in Boston to assist African American girls. She also organized interracial and ecumenical activities among the churches of New York City through Riverside Church and *Church Women United.

BWA; BWARC; B. Joyce Ross, "Mary McLeod Bethune and the National Youth Administration," *Journal of Negro History* 60, no. 1 (January 1975).

SCOTT D. SEAY

Sadlier, Mary Ann Madden (1820–1903). Author. Mary Anne Madden emigrated from Ireland to Montreal in 1844. Soon after her arrival she married James Sadlier, cofounder of D. & J. Sadlier publishing company, with whom she had six children. Mary Ann Sadlier's novels offered a Roman Catholic counterpart to the Protestant sentimental fiction. Written amid the nativist crusades and the rise of the Know-Nothing Party, her novels depict the ultimate success of Irish Catholic immigrants who advocated for separate schools and challenged the notion that ultimate authority could be found in the individual over those who sought to assimilate. She wrote more than 30 novels and plays.

EACH; NCE; NoAW; Marjorie Elizabeth Howes, "Discipline, Sentiment, and the Irish-American Public: Mary Ann Sadlier's Popular Fiction," *Eire-Ireland* 40, nos. 1 and 2 (Spring–Summer 2005); W. H. New, ed., *Dictionary of Literary Biography*, vol. 99 (2000); Maureen E. O'Reilly, "Mary Ann Sadlier," Christian Educators of the 20th Century, www.talbot.edu/ce20.

SUSAN B. RIDGELY

Safford, Mary Augusta (1851–1927). Unitarian minister. Mary Safford was born in Hamilton, Illinois, and received her early education from her parents. After studying for a year at Iowa State University she returned home and became a teacher. In 1871 she and her childhood friend *Eleanor Gordon founded the Hawthorne Literary Society. In 1880, with the approval of the local Unitarian clergy, the two women were ordained and assumed leadership of the Christian Unity Church in Humboldt, Iowa. For 30 years, Safford served established Unitarian churches in Iowa and helped found new ones as the executive secretary of the Iowa Unitarian Association. After retiring in 1910 she moved to Florida to help found the Unitarian Church in Orlando, serving as its minister until her death.

DUUB; UU; UUWM; Sarah Oelberg, "Mary Safford," in *Standing before Us*, ed. Dorothy M. Emerson et al. (1999); Cynthia Tucker, *Prophetic Sisterhood* (1990); Catharine Hitchings, "Universalist and Unitarian Women Ministers," *Journal of the Unitarian Historical Society* 10 (1975).

SCOTT D. SEAY

Sampter, Jessie Ethel (1883–1938). Zionist, poet, activist, and educator. Jessie Sampter organized the *Hadassah's School of Zionism, mentoring young Zionist leaders in the U.S. during World War I. Largely educated at home due to polio, Sampter later flourished under the guidance of a close network of friends, including Mordecai Kaplan and *Henrietta Szold, who contributed greatly to Sampter's understanding of Jewish identity. Amid controversy relating to her pacifist beliefs, Sampter withdrew from a pacifist organization following the entrance of the U.S. into World War I. Sampter's poetry and political work reflected a vision for peace between Arabs and Jews. After settling in Palestine in 1919 Sampter joined Kibbutz Givat Brenner and later constructed a home for convalescents. Sampter is also known for her advocacy for Yemenite Jews.

JWA; Erica Simmons, "Playgrounds and Penny Lunches in Palestine: American Social Welfare in the Yishuv," *American Jewish History* 92, no. 3 (2004).

KAREN-MARIE WOODS

Sanapia ("Memory Woman," "Sticky Mother") (Mary Poafpybitty) (1895–1984). Comanche eagle doctor. Born to a Christian father and a traditionalist Comanche mother, Sanapia was reared among her mother's people. An uncle who healed her of influenza named her in an effort to influence her to seek medical training when she came of age. At age 13 she agreed to receive training from her mother (an eagle doctor) and other relatives, even though she was not able to practice medicine until menopause, according to tribal practices. She later rejected her vocation in grief after her second husband died. A few years passed before she remarried and began practicing medicine. Fearing that she could not pass on her training, she worked with anthropologist David Jones on an account of her life and medical training. It became the most complete description of an eagle doctor's methods and pharmacopoeia.

EAWR; NaAW; *Encyclopedia of the Great Plains Indians* (2007); David E. Jones, *Sanapia* (1984).

LORETTA LONG HUNNICUTT

Sanghamitta, Sister (Marie de Souza Canavarro) (1849–1933). First European American woman convert to Buddhism. Marie Canavarro publicly converted to Buddhism in New York City in 1897 with the guidance of Sinhalese Buddhist Anagarika Dharmapala. Raised as a Roman Catholic, Marie Canavarro explored not only Buddhism, but also Hinduism, Theosophy, and Bahá'i. In 1900 and 1901 she lectured about Buddhism in several U.S. cities, attracting great media coverage.

Tessa Bartholomueusz, "Real Life and Romance: The Life of Miranda de Souza Canavarro," *Journal of Feminist Studies in Religion* 10, no. 2 (Fall 1994).

BARBARA E. REED

Sasaki, Ruth Fuller Everett (1883–1967). Japanese Zen Buddhist practitioner and writer. Ruth Everett first traveled to Japan in 1930 with her attorney husband, Charles, and then she practiced meditation with the Zen monks at Nanzenji (Kyoto) in 1932. In 1938 she became a primary supporter of Sokei-an Sasaki's Buddhist Society of America (New York) and edited the society's journal, *Cat's Yawn*. After becoming a widow she married Sokei-an Sasaki in 1944. Before her second husband died in 1945 he had asked Ruth Sasaki to find a Zen teacher to replace him at the society and to complete his translation of the *Rinzia-roku*. Sasaki returned to Japan to accomplish these tasks, to study, and to be ordained as a Zen priest at Daitokuji. She published numerous books in the 1950s and 1960s.

EAWR; RLA; Isabel Stirling, *Zen Pioneer* (2006); Rick Fields, *How the Swans Came to the Lake*, 3rd rev. ed. (1992) [1981].

BARBARA E. REED

Sasso, Sandy Eisenberg (1947–). Rabbi and children's author. The first woman ordained a rabbi by the Reconstructionist Rabbinical College in 1974, Sandy Sasso and her husband, Dennis, have served as the rabbis of Congregation Beth-El Zedeck (Cons./Recon.) in Indianapolis since 1977. Sasso is interested in women's spirituality and the discovery of the religious imagination in children. She has written 12 highly regarded children's books, including *God's Paintbrush* (1992), *In God's Name* (1994), and *Adam and Eve's First Sunset* (2003). She also coedited *Nurturing Child and Adolescent Spirituality: Perspectives from the World's Religious Traditions* (2006). Sasso holds a doctor of ministry degree from Christian Theological Seminary as well as numerous honorary degrees. She is a past president of the Reconstructionist Rabbinical Association and was named a Sagamore of the Wabash in 1995 by the governor of Indiana.

EAWR; JWA; Congregation Beth-El Zedeck, www.bez613.org.

JOAN S. FRIEDMAN

Saulteaux, Jessie Prettyshield (1912–95). Assiniboine elder and leader in aboriginal theological education. Jessie Saulteaux was born into a Plains Indian tribe that settled in Canada in the 1870s. Barred from becoming a nurse because of her race, she committed her leadership gifts to her community of Carry-the-Kettle First Nation and to her church. She was one of the first woman Indian chiefs elected in the province of Saskatchewan and believed in her own people becoming church ministers and governing their own church affairs. To realize this vision she participated in the foundation of the All Native Circle Conference, a self-governing body of the United Church of Canada, and in the establishment of an indigenous theological college. St. Andrew's College, Saskatoon, honored Jessie Saulteaux in 1983 with a doctor of divinity degree. In 1984 the Dr. Jessie Saulteaux Resource Center, the theological center of which she had dreamed, was named after her. A practitioner of Assiniboine traditions and the Christian faith, her life inspired those seeking to walk the two spiritual traditions.

Joyce Carlson and Alf Dumont, eds., *Bridges in Spirituality* (1997); Joyce Carlson, ed., *The Journey* (1991); John McFarlane, "Dr. Jessie Saulteaux: The Faith Goes On," *Touchstone: Heritage and Theology in a New Age* 9, no. 1 (January 1991).

JANET SILMAN

Schechter, Mathilde Roth (1857–1924). Jewish leader. Mathilde Roth was an orphan who was raised in a children's home in Breslau (now Wroclaw, Poland). Her intellect led to her receiving a strong education. Roth graduated from the Breslau Teacher's Seminary and became a teacher. She then attended Queen's College in England, where she met and married Solomon Schechter, a scholar and communal leader. She assisted her husband in his scholarship while raising their three children. After arriving in the U.S. in 1902, her husband became president of the Conservative movement's Jewish Theological Seminary, while Schechter founded a vocational school for Jewish girls and the *Women's League for Conservative Judaism (WLCJ). The WLCJ helped unify local Jewish women's synagogue groups into a national organization. While positioning herself as a helpmate to her husband, Schechter carved out an important niche for herself in the Jewish public sphere.

ANB; EAWR; JWA; Shuly Rubin Schwartz, *The Rabbi's Wife* (2006).

SHIRA M. KOHN

Schellenberg, Katharina (1870–1945). Medical missionary. Katharina Schellenberg was born to Abraham and Katharina Lohrenz Schellenberg in Tiegerweide, South Russia. They immigrated to Kansas in 1879. She trained at the Deaconess Hospital in Cleveland, Ohio, and later at the Medical Institute of Homeopathic Medicine in Kansas City, Kansas. Schellenberg was the first female doctor among North American Mennonite Brethren. She served as the denomination's first medical missionary to India from 1907 until her death. In India she trained her own nurses and helped establish several hospitals.

Esther Jost, "Free to Serve," in *Women among the Brethren*, ed. Katie Funk Wiebe (1979); *Global Anabaptist Mennonite Encyclopedia Online*, www.gameo.org.

VALERIE REMPEL

Schlafly, Phyllis Stewart (1924–). Conservative activist. In the 1970s Phyllis Schlafly, a devout Catholic and mother of six, mobilized thousands to fight the Equal Rights Amendment (ERA). Her "Stop ERA" campaign may have been responsible for the amendment's failure. An expert organizer, effective writer, and unflappable speaker, Schlafly ran for Congress twice, worked in anticommunist campaigns, and lobbied against the SALT treaties. She also served as president of the Illinois Federation of Republican Women and was vice president of the National Federation of Republican Women. As a result, Schlafly, a known leader and organizer, was able to call upon an already existing network of women to join her in her anti-ERA compaign. Schlafly's activism continues through her radio commentaries, syndicated columns, and monthly newsletter, the *Phyllis Schlafly Report*.

EAWR; Donald T. Critchlow, *Phyllis Schlafly and Grassroots Conservatism* (2005); Carol Felsenthal, *The Sweetheart of the Silent Majority* (1981).

LYNN S. NEAL

Schneiderman, Rose (1882–1972). Labor organizer and activist. In 1890 Rose Schneiderman traveled with her family from their home in Saven, Poland, to New York City. After her father's death, Schneiderman became the family's primary wage earner, working first in a department store and then in a garment factory. She helped unionize her fellow female capmakers, and in 1908 she became an organizer for the Women's Trade Union League (WTUL). Her commitment to unionism was recognized in 1926 when she was elected president of the national WTUL. Schneiderman also participated in the suffrage movement. In 1933 she was the only woman to be appointed to Roosevelt's National Recovery Administration advisory board. She served as secretary of labor for New York state from 1937 to 1943. She dedicated her life to protecting workers, especially women.

ANB; JWA; NBAW; NoAW; Annelise Orleck, *Common Sense and a Little Fire* (1995); Rose Schneiderman, *All for One* (1967).

LILA CORWIN BERMAN

Schofield, Martha (1839–1916). Educator. Born into a family of Hicksite Quakers, Martha Schofield was educated in a private school conducted by her uncle. She taught school in Philadelphia and upstate New York, and during the Civil War volunteered with the Pennsylvania Freedman's Relief Association. She taught in a number of schools for freedmen on the Sea Islands before settling in Aiken, South Carolina, in 1868. After the collapse of the Freedman's Bureau she assumed leadership of the school; she secured its financial support and embarked on an ambitious building program. The school was incorporated as the Schofield Normal and Industrial School by 1886. Scholfield advocated a Bookerite philosophy of education, training freedmen in trades and homemaking. Schofield Normal was absorbed into the South Carolina public school system in 1952.

ANB; NoAW; Katherine Smedley, *Martha Schofield and the Re-education of the South* (1987); Papers, Friends Historical Library, Swarthmore College.

SCOTT D. SEAY

Schwager, H. Vardis Brown (1904–2006). Minister's wife, ecumenist, and lay pastor. Vardis Brown, a Quaker by birth, received her bachelor of divinity degree in 1928 and her doctor of philosophy degree in theology in 1931 from Hartford Theological Seminary. While studying on a scholarship in Marburg, Germany, she met Joseph Schwager, a Moravian minister. They married in 1931 and served various congregations in Wisconsin, North Dakota, and Pennsylvania. Vardis Schwager worked as the executive director of the women's department of the Philadelphia Council of Churches and was active in *Church Women United. In the 1970s she was appointed a lay pastor in North Dakota and worked as a congregational Christian education director in Wisconsin. Moravian Theological Seminary awarded her a doctor of divinity degree in 1977.

Nora I. Adam, comp., *Moravian Women of Faith Today: Autobiographies of Contemporary Women*, book 2 (1990?).

ELEANOR J. STEBNER

Scudder, Ida Sophia (1870–1960). Missionary doctor. Ida Scudder was born in India, where her father and grandfather, along with other relatives, were medical missionaries. She did not want to be a missionary but returned to India from the U.S. (where she was studying) when she was about 20 to care for her sick mother. One night three men asked her to help their wives in childbirth because they refused to have a male doctor. By morning the women had died and Scudder felt called to become a doctor. She attended the Woman's Medical College of Pennsylvania and finished her training at Cornell Medical College. She returned to India as a missionary for the Reformed Church in America, but received support from people of many denominations. Scudder built a hospital in Vellore, cared for people in rural roadside clinics, and started a nursing school (1909) and the Vellore Medical College for Women (1918). She was so well known that a letter addressed to "Dr. Ida, India," was delivered to her. She stayed in India until her death.

ANB; NoAWMP; R. Pierce Beaver, *American Protestant Women in World Mission*, rev. ed. (1980) [1968]; Dorothy C. Wilson, *Dr. Ida* (1959); Pauline Jeffery, *Ida S. Scudder of Vellore* (1951); Papers, Schlesinger Library, Radcliffe Institute, Harvard University.

LYNN JAPINGA

Scudder, Vida Dutton (1861–1954). Episcopal educator, activist, and social gospel leader. Vida Scudder was born to Congregationalist missionaries in India but returned to the U.S. after her father's death. After studying English literature at

Smith College and Oxford University, Scudder began teaching at Wellesley College. Her love of scholarship was matched by her social conscience and deep spirituality. As a young woman, Scudder began the College Settlements Association, joined the Society of Christian Socialists, and began her long association with the *Society of the Companions of the Holy Cross. In 1893 she took a leave of absence from Wellesley to work with *Helena Stuart Dudley to found Denison House in Boston. Scudder experienced a breakdown in 1901, due to the stress of teaching and activism. After two years of recuperation in Italy she returned renewed and became more active in church and socialist groups; she started a group for Italian immigrants at Denison House and took an active part in organizing the Women's Trade Union League. In 1911 Scudder founded the Episcopal Church Socialist League and formally joined the Socialist Party. Her support of striking textile workers in Lawrence, Massachusetts, in 1912 drew significant criticism and threatened her teaching position. Although she initially supported World War I, by the 1930s she was a pacifist. Scudder's primary support network throughout her life was with women; her closest companion was *Florence Converse, who shared her religious faith and political ideals. After retirement, Scudder authored 16 books on religious and political subjects, combining her intense activism with an equally vibrant Anglo-Catholic spirituality.

ANB; EAWR; NoAWMP; Elizabeth L. Hinson-Hasty, *Beyond the Social Maze* (2006); Sheryl A. Kujawa-Holbrook, *Freedom Is a Dream* (2002); Allen F. Davis, *Spearheads for Reform*, 2nd ed. (1984) [1967]; Theresa Corcoran, *Vida Dutton Scudder* (1982); Vida Scudder, *On Journey* (1937).

SHERYL A. KUJAWA-HOLBROOK

Segale, Rosa Maria ("Sister Blandina") (1850–1941). Catholic sister, missionary, and social activist. Born in Cicagna, Italy, Rose Segale entered the *Sisters of Charity of Cincinnati in 1866 and became known as Sister Blandina. She spent more than 20 years (1872–93) on the frontier in southern Colorado and the New Mexico Territory, building schools, visiting jails, working among the poor, seeing to the burial of the homeless, and providing nursing care. Her colorful journal is published as *At the End of the Santa Fe Trail* (1932). Beginning in 1897 Segale founded the Santa Maria Italian Educational and Institutional Home in Cincinnati, one of the first Catholic settlement houses in the country. She worked 36 years among Italian immigrants, campaigned against white slavery, and was appointed a probation officer in the newly organized juvenile court.

EAWR; M. Christine Anderson, "Catholic Nuns and the Invention of Social Work," *Journal of Women's History* 12, no. 1 (Spring 2000); Anna Minogue, *The Story of the Santa Maria Institute* (1922).

JUDITH METZ, SC

Seton, Elizabeth Ann Bayley ("Mother Seton") (1774–1821). First Catholic saint born in the U.S. and founder of the *Sisters of Charity (SC) in North America. Elizabeth Bayley was a devout and socially sensitive Episcopalian as a child. As a young woman, she married businessman William Seton and had five children. When the children were young, her husband took ill; the couple and their eldest child traveled to Italy in hopes of his recovery, but he died in 1802. Seton studied the Catholic faith while in Italy. Upon her return to the U.S., and against the wishes of many family members, she was received into the church on Ash Wednesday, 1805. Initially she ran a boardinghouse for boys, but soon thereafter she formed a school for girls in Baltimore. While there, she felt called to the religious life. She received permission to found a new religious order and was named superior of it in 1809. The community adopted a modified version of the rule of St. Vincent de Paul's *Daughters of Charity. Located in Emmitsburg (Maryland), the community educated girls and expanded its ministry to the area's poor and orphaned children. Sisters later founded orphanages in Philadelphia and New York. Seton taught and administered her community and left numerous writings that underscore a mystical spirituality focused upon Christ's cross. She was beatified in 1963 and canonized in 1975.

ANB; DARB; EACH; EAWR; NCE; NoAW; Ellin M. Kelly et al., *Elizabeth Seton, Selected Writings* (1986); Joseph I. Dirvin, *Mrs. Seton* (1975) [1962].

OSCAR COLE-ARNAL

Severance, Caroline Maria Seymour (1820–1914). Clubwoman and reformer. Caroline Seymour was born in Canadaigua, New York, and married in 1840. She chaired the first annual meeting of the Ohio Woman's Rights Association in 1853, and she and *Lucy Stone began the American Woman Suffrage Association in 1869. In Boston, she was a Free Religious Association founder and the first woman Parker Fraternity lecturer. As the founding president of the New England woman's club in 1868 she established a pattern of cultural expression that sought reforms. This progressive model of regular association was emulated nationally and internationally. In 1875 she began the first Unitarian congregation in Los Angeles and campaigned for free kindergartens and juvenile courts. She was president of the Los Angeles Woman Suffrage League from 1900 to 1904. As she aged Severance held weekly discussions in her home, exploring current movements.

DUUB; NoAW; Ella G. Ruddy, ed., *The Mother of Clubs* (1906).

IRENE BAROS-JOHNSON

Shaw, Anna Howard (1847–1919). Women's ordination and suffrage advocate. Born in England, Anna Shaw was raised in primitive surroundings in Michigan. She preached her first sermon in 1870, and in 1871 she was licensed to preach in the Methodist Episcopal (ME) Church. She entered Albion College in 1873 and went to Boston University in 1876 for ministerial training. Shaw graduated in 1878, the only woman in her class. Appointed to local parishes in Massachusetts, Shaw applied to the New England Annual Conference (ME Church) for permission to administer the sacraments but was denied. After a failed appeal she applied to the Methodist Protestant Church. After much debate Shaw was ordained in 1880 by the Methodist Protestants, becoming one of the first ordained Methodist women. After completing an MD at Boston University in 1886, Shaw realized that social and ecclesiastical limitations upon women would persist without their right to vote. Also involved with the *Woman's Christian Temperance Union, Shaw lectured widely on suffrage and temperance. She was president of the National American Woman Suffrage Association from 1904 to 1915.

ANB; EAWR; EE; NoAW; Beverly Zink-Sawyer, *From Preachers to Suffragists* (2003); Mary D. Pellauer, *Toward a Tradition of Feminist Theology* (1991); Anna Howard Shaw, *Story of a Pioneer* (1915); Papers, Women's Rights Collection, Schlesinger Library, Radcliffe Institute, Harvard University.

LACEYE C. WARNER

Sheffield, Mary Telfer Forster (1846–1937). Founder of a city mission. Mary Sheffield moved to Toronto following the death of her husband in 1872 and worked as a stenographer. She opened a Sunday school in 1886 for the poor children in her neighborhood and it quickly grew to include meetings for adults. In 1887 the mission came under the supervision of the Metropolitan Methodist Church, and she was named superintendent. As the role of the church increased, that of Sheffield narrowed. In 1894, when what is now the Fred Victor Mission moved into its own building, Sheffield had little role in the institution she had founded.

Cary Fagan, *The Fred Victor Mission Story* (1993).

MARILYN FÄRDIG WHITELEY

Shirley Symmonds Paulig, Eliza (1863–1932). Salvation Army leader and Baptist pastor. Born in Coventry, England, into a working-class family, Eliza Shirley joined the Salvation Army in 1878. Shirley and her parents moved to Philadelphia, where she opened the first corps of the Salvation Army in the U.S. in 1879. Shirley was recalled to England and married Captain Philip Symmonds in 1882. In 1885 the couple returned to Philadelphia, but her husband was dismissed from his office in 1890 because of financial irregularities in his command. They moved with their children to Green Bay, Wisconsin, and began to minister in a Baptist church. When her husband died in 1894 Shirley became pastor and served the church for the next 10 years. She rejoined the army in 1905 and undertook corps appointments throughout the Midwest. Failing health forced her to retire in 1920, but she continued limited work with the army until her death. An emergency shelter for women and children is named after her in Philadelphia.

Beverly C. Davison, "Eliza Shirley Symmonds Paulig, Wisconsin's First American Baptist Pastor," *American Baptist Quarterly* 24, no. 3 (2005); Lillian Taiz, *Hallelujah Lads and Lasses* (2001); Edward McKinley, *Marching to Glory: The History of the Salvation Army in the United States*, 2nd ed. (1995) [1980].

SCOTT D. SEAY

Simkhovitch, Mary Kingsbury (1867–1951). Settlement house leader and reformer. Born to prosperous parents, Mary Kingsbury attended Newton schools and graduated in 1890 from Boston University. After graduate work at Radcliffe, she attended the University of Berlin and became engaged to Vladimir Simkhovitch; they married in 1899 and had two children. Simkhovitch worked at the College Settlement House and then the Friendly Aid House before she and her husband opened Greenwich House in 1902. Mary Simkhovitch was its director until 1946. She established a music school, a neighborhood theater, and a pottery studio. Her husband, who taught at Columbia University, encouraged student researchers to live at the house. (*Frances Perkins was one such resident.) Mary Simkhovitch lobbied for public school reform, recreational facilities, and labor regulation. She was appointed to the New York City Public Housing Authority in 1934. As vice chair until 1948 she helped build the city's first housing projects. Religious convictions guided her work, even though the house was nonsectarian. An Episcopalian, Simkhovitch served on the diocesan and national social service commissions, was active in the *Society of the Companions of the Holy Cross, and helped found the Episcopal Woman's Suffrage Association. She wrote several books and lectured widely.

NoAWMP; Sheryl Kujawa-Holbrook and Fredrica Harris Thompsett, eds., *Deeper Joy: Lay Women and Vocation in the 20th Century* (2005); Richard L. Edwards, ed., *Encyclopedia of Social Work*, 19th ed. (1995) [1965]); Papers, Schlesinger Library, Radcliffe Institute, Harvard University.

MARY SUDMAN DONOVAN

Simms, Daisy Florence (1873–1923). Leader in the *YWCA (Young Women's Christian Association). Born and educated in Indiana, Daisy Simms graduated from Depauw University in 1895. She was deeply religious and a strong believer in the causes of temperance and women's rights. After working as a national secretary in the college department of the YWCA, Simms moved to

New York City and became the director of the YWCA's newly founded industrial department. During World War I Simms's position gave her the opportunity to cooperate with union leaders to begin the process of achieving international labor standards for women. In spite of the prevailing conservative atmosphere in the postwar period, Simms continued to embrace the social gospel. She joined the Federal Council of Churches of Christ and assisted in bringing about the adoption of a 16-point program, "The Social Ideals of the Churches."

NoAW; Marion O. Robinson, *Eight Women of the YWCA* (1966); Richard Roberts, *Florence Simms* (1926).

BETH SPAULDING

Simon, Carrie Obendorfer (1872–1961). Founder of the National Federation of Temple Sisterhoods (NFTS) [see *Women of Reform Judaism]. Carrie Obendorfer was raised in Cincinnati, was a graduate of the Cincinnati Conservatory of Music, and was active in the local chapter of the *National Council of Jewish Women (NCJW). In 1896 she married Rabbi Abram Simon, a graduate of the Hebrew Union College, and in 1904 her husband became rabbi of the Washington, [DC], Hebrew Congregation. Simon shared her husband's desire to strengthen Jewish religious life, but concluded that the NCJW, which focused on social service, was not the best vehicle for it. Instead, she deepened her involvement with the temple's sisterhood. In 1913 she organized Reform congregations' sisterhoods into NFTS and served as its president until 1919. Simon wanted NFTS to deepen the religious spirit of Reform Judaism. She focused its efforts on increasing synagogue attendance, enhancing holiday celebrations, raising the quality of religious school instruction, and providing financial support for the Hebrew Union College. In her role as president, she also pressured member synagogues of the Union of American Hebrew Congregations (now the Union for Reform Judaism) to include more women on synagogue boards and to welcome intermarried couples into the synagogue.

JWA.

JOAN S. FRIEDMAN

Sisters of the Blessed Sacrament for Indians and Colored People (SBS) (1891–). Roman Catholic religious congregation. The SBS was formed by Philadelphia heiress *Katherine Drexel and a small group of women who shared her vision of alleviating the conditions of poverty and neglect suffered by Indians on government-administered reservations and recently freed African Americans. The SBS remains the only order of nuns dedicated specifically to both these populations. Inspired by a belief that full emancipation of African American and Native American peoples depended not only on improvement in material well-being but also, and most importantly, on equal education and coming to know of God's love, the SBS took education as their primary work. The SBS are responsible for founding 145 missions, 12 schools for Native Americans, and 50 schools for African Americans. They founded Xavier University in New Orleans in 1915. It was revolutionary in its time, in that it was a coeducational and nonsectarian institution of higher learning for African Americans. The university multiplied the educational impact of the SBS by graduating thousands of teachers and other professionals. The congregation today numbers some 200 women serving in 14 states, the District of Columbia, Haiti, and Guatemala. Its central offices are in Bensalem, Pennsylvania.

EACH; NCE; Patricia Lynch, *Sharing the Bread in Service: Sisters of the Blessed Sacrament*, 2 vols. (1998); Mary J. Oates, *The Catholic Philanthropic Tradition in America* (1995).

KAREN M. KENNELLY, CSJ

Sisters of Charity (SC) (1809–). Roman Catholic religious congregation. Founded by *Elizabeth Ann Bayley Seton at Emmitsburg, Maryland, the SC modeled their congregation on the French *Daughters of Charity and adopted a modified version of their rule. They operated academies and orphanages and established the first free Catholic school staffed by sisters in the U.S. By the 1820s they began their ministry in health care. In 1845, when superiors decided that institutional ministries would not include boys, over 30 sisters in the Archdiocese of New York withdrew to form an independent diocesan congregation, the Sisters of Charity of St. Vincent de Paul of New York. When Emmitsburg superiors united this congregation with the Daughters of Charity in 1850, seven sisters from the Cincinnati mission withdrew and formed the independent diocesan congregation, Sisters of Charity of Cincinnati. From the New York and Cincinnati foundations, three congregations were founded: Sisters of Charity of Halifax, Nova Scotia (1856); Sisters of Charity of St. Elizabeth in Convent Station, New Jersey (1859); and the Sisters of Charity of Seton Hill in Greensburg, Pennsylvania (1870). Other SC congregations received copies of the rule adopted by Seton's community: Sisters of Charity of Nazareth, Kentucky (1812); Sisters of Charity of Our Lady of Mercy from Charleston, South Carolina (1829); and the Sisters of Charity of Leavenworth, Kansas (1858), who developed from a mission of the Sisters of Charity of Nazareth. Several Canadian and European congregations using an adapted rule of the Daughters of Charity also minister in the U.S. Thirteen of these congregations form a Sisters of Charity federation of approximately 7,000 sisters and more than 1,500 lay associates. Foreign missions in Korea and India have swelled these numbers.

DARB; EAWR; NCE; RLA; ROWUS; Regina Bechtle and Judith Metz, eds., *Elizabeth Bayley Seton: Collected Writings*, 3 vols. (2000–2006); Geraldine Anthony, *A Vision of Service* (1997).

JUDITH METZ, SC

Sisters of Charity of the Blessed Virgin Mary (BVM) (1833–). Roman Catholic religious congregation. Founded by *Mary Frances Clarke and four companions in Philadelphia, the BVM's roots reach to Dublin, Ireland, where the women met. They formed a community to live and pray together in 1831 and founded Miss Clarke's Seminary in 1832 to teach Catholic children. An Irish priest invited the women to Philadelphia (where anti-Catholic attitudes prevailed) to teach Irish immigrants. When he failed to meet them in 1833, another Irish priest, Terence James Donaghoe, assisted in formalizing their religious order. In 1843 Mathias Loras, bishop of Dubuque, invited the sisters to his diocese. They opened schools in Iowa, Wisconsin, Illinois, Missouri, Kansas, and California under Clarke's leadership. She was clear that the sisters would serve wherever there was need. As their numbers grew—approximately 4,900 women have become BVMs—so did their number of schools. BVMs have served in 43 states in the U.S. Today, over 600 BVMs minister in 24 U.S. states and in Ecuador, Guatemala, and Ghana. BVM sisters serve as educators and parish ministers; they serve in prisons and in health and retirement care. Retired sisters support the congregation through volunteer work and prayer. The BVM mission is "to be freed and help others enjoy freedom in God's steadfast love."

EACH; NCE; ROWUS; Ann M. Harrington, *Creating Community* (2004); Kathryn Lawlor, ed., *Your Affectionate: Commentary on Mary Frances Clarke's Writings* (2003); Jane Coogan, *The Price of Our Heritage: History of the Sisters of Charity of the Blessed Virgin Mary*, 2 vols. (1975, 1978).

ANN M. HARRINGTON, BVM

Sisters of the Holy Cross (CSC) (1841–). Roman Catholic religious congregation. Founded as Marianites of the Holy Cross by Father Basil Moreau in Le Mans, France, the women developed their own apostolates in North America and eventually became three congregations. One group is based in Le Mans and New Orleans, and retains the original name. A second group, comprising Marianites who went to Canada in 1847 and to New England in 1881, became the Sisters of Holy Cross based in Montreal. A third group went to South Bend, Indiana, in 1843 to assist at Notre Dame College and soon founded a school for girls in Bertrand, Michigan, which was moved in 1855 to Saint Mary's, Notre Dame; in 1869 this group became independent as Sisters of the Holy Cross, and by 1882 they had founded 45 schools in the U.S. In 1943 Saint Mary's College became the first Catholic institution to offer women graduate theological education. Having gained nursing experience during the Civil War, the congregation also established hospitals and nursing schools. In 1979 eight hospitals became the Holy Cross Health System, which merged in 2000 with the *Sisters of Mercy Detroit Regional Health System to form Trinity Health.

EACH; NCE; ROWUS; M. Georgia Costin, *Priceless Spirit: A History of the Sisters of the Holy Cross* (1994), and *Fruits of the Tree: Sesquicentennial Chronicles, Sisters of the Holy Cross*, 3 vols. (1991); "The Journey Continues . . . A History of the Sisters of the Holy Cross," www.cscsisters.org/publications/publications_home.asp.

ANNE E. PATRICK, SNJM

Sisters of the Holy Family (SHF) (1842–). Roman Catholic religious congregation. Founded in New Orleans by *Henriette Delille (1813–62), the SHF is one of two U.S. Catholic religious congregations of African American women. From her youth, Delille, a free woman of color, served the black community of New Orleans through teaching and social outreach. In 1836 a group of white and Creole women organized the Confraternity of the Sisters of the Presentation but had to disband because of segregation laws. In 1842 Delille and Juliette Gaudin formed the SHF, and in 1843 they were joined by Josephine Charles. Needing legal, moral, and financial support they formed the Association of the Holy Family, and, with the assistance of Frenchwoman Jean Marie Aliquot, built a hospice. In 1852 they made religious vows. At Delille's death their community included 12 Creole women of color. After the Civil War the congregation was permitted to accept former slaves. Facing animosity and hardship these women expanded their earlier work. In 1869 they adopted a formal rule, and in 1872 they were permitted to wear religious habits. By 1900 the community of nearly 100 members was engaged in schools, orphanages, and homes for the aged in New Orleans and elsewhere in Louisiana. By the 1950s membership reached about 400, but has dwindled in recent years. Today they serve in the U.S., Belize, and Nigeria.

BWARC; EACH; Dorothy Dawes and Charles Nolan, *Religious Pioneers* (2004); Cyprian Davis, *The History of Black Catholics in the United States* (1990).

JUDITH METZ, SC

Sisters of the Holy Names of Jesus and Mary (SNJM) (1843–). Roman Catholic religious congregation. Founded by *Eulalie (Mother Marie-Rose) Durocher near Montreal, this community established schools and colleges in Canada and the U.S., and missions in Lesotho, Japan, Brazil, Peru, and Haiti. Canadian foundations centered in the provinces of Quebec (Longueuil, 1843), Ontario (Windsor, 1864), and Manitoba (Winnipeg, 1874). Early U.S. establishments included Portland, Oregon (1859); Oakland, California (1868); Schenectady, New York (1865); and Key West, Florida

(1865). Holy Names University, founded in 1868 in California, and Marylhurst University, founded in 1893 in Oregon, continue today as vibrant centers of higher education. Despite opposition from the Ku Klux Klan, the sisters pioneered in educating African Americans in Florida. They also opposed an Oregon law threatening the existence of private and parochial schools, which the U.S. Supreme Court declared unconstitutional in 1925 (*Pierce v. Society of Sisters*). In the 1980s the sisters established new health and educational ministries in the Mississippi Delta and the Yakima Valley, including the independent Heritage University in Toppenish, Washington. In 1960 there were 4,000 sisters teaching over 100,000 students; in 2005 there were 1,385 sisters and 561 associates continuing the congregation's mission in diverse educational, pastoral, and social justice ministries.

NCE; ROWUS; Christl Dabu, "Sisters Working for 'Education and Action' on Behalf of Women, Children and Poor," *Catholic New Times* (6 March 2005); Eleanor J. Stebner, *GEM: The Life of Sister Mac* (2001); M. F. Dunn, *Gleanings of Fifty Years* (1909).

ANNE E. PATRICK, SNJM

Sisters of Loretto (SL) (Loretto Community) (1812–). Roman Catholic religious order. *Mary Rhodes began providing education for fellow Catholics migrating from Maryland to Kentucky. Other women soon joined her, and, encouraged by Father Charles Nerinckx's spiritual leadership, the Loretto Community flourished despite the harshness of frontier life, reporting in 1823 a membership of 130. In 1834 the sisters opened a "proper academy" for girls, and in 1852 established a mission to Spanish-speaking children in Santa Fe, New Mexico. Over the course of its history, the Loretto Community established premier educational institutions in 16 U.S. states and five foreign countries, becoming one of the most influential of U.S. Catholic women's religious orders. In response to Vatican II's call for a renewed vision of religious life in the modern world, the Loretto Community, with extraordinary leadership from Mary Luke Tobin (1958–70) and Helen Sanders (1970–78), transformed the community's structures and lifestyle, ventured into diverse fields of ministry, and came to characterize themselves as working for justice and acting for peace. Widely respected for taking public stands on justice issues, the SL in December 2000 joined with two other Kentucky religious orders in seeking forgiveness from the local African American community for their ownership of slaves during the 19th century.

Barbara Misner, *"Highly Respected and Accomplished Ladies": Catholic Women Religious in America* (1988); Helen Sanders, *More Than a Renewal: Loretto before and after Vatican II* (1982).

MARGARET MCMANUS

Sisters of Mercy of the Americas (1831–). Roman Catholic religious congregation. Incorporating Sisters of Mercy from North, Central, and South America, as well as Guam, the Philippines, and the Caribbean, the Sisters of Mercy of the Americas are historically rooted in the Sisters of Mercy founded in Ireland by Catherine McAuley in 1831. The first Sisters of Mercy to serve in the U.S. arrived in Pittsburgh in 1843; within a decade there were sisters in New York, San Francisco, and many points in between. Their work has always included the founding and operation of schools and hospitals, but since Vatican II the sisters have begun working in other ministries, including peacemaking, antiracism work, ecology, housing services for the poor, and advocacy for immigrants.

EACH; ROWUS; Mary Daigler, *Through the Windows: A History of the Sisters of Mercy of the Americas* (2005); Kathleen Healy, ed., *Sisters of Mercy* (2002).

COLLEEN CARPENTER CULLINAN

Sisters of Notre Dame de Namur (SND) (1804–). Roman Catholic religious congregation. Founded by Julie Billiart and Francoise Blin de Bourbon in Amiens, France, in the aftermath of the revolution, their vision was the education of poor girls. In 1809 the sisters moved their motherhouse to Namur, Belgium. Eight sisters established the first house of the SND outside of Europe in Cincinnati, Ohio, in 1840. Their school had three divisions: a boarding academy, a day school, and a free (poor) school. Soon the sisters established academies and parish schools in other parts of Ohio. By the late 1840s they began to accept schools in cities in Massachusetts, Pennsylvania, and Maryland. A separate foundation from Namur settled in the Oregon Territory in 1844 to labor among Native Americans; this group later moved to California. Besides conducting schools the SND engaged in social service work and encouraged their alumnae to do the same through their Sunday sodalities. They also conducted night schools, engaged in deaf education, and did foreign mission work. In 1897 they established Trinity College in Washington, DC, one of the first Catholic women's colleges in the U.S. In the 1960s the congregation broadened its activities. Today more than 1,800 SNDs, including 1,100 in the U.S., minister on five continents.

EACH; NCE; RLA; ROWUS; Roger Fortin, *Faith and Action* (2002); Takako Frances Takagi, *A History of the Sisters of Notre Dame de Namur in Japan* (1987); SND, comp., *The American Foundations of the Sisters of Notre Dame de Namur* (1928).

JUDITH METZ, SC

Sisters of Providence of St. Mary-of-the-Wood (SP) (1806–). Roman Catholic religious congregation. Tracing their origins to a foundation in the Diocese of LeMans, France, the purpose of the SP was to give religious instruction to Catholic children and to visit the sick poor in their homes. In 1839 the congregation was invited to send sisters to the missionary diocese of Vincennes, Indiana. Six sisters, led by *Mother Theodore (Anne-Therese) Guérin, settled near Terre Haute, where they opened a school. In 1843 the foundation in the U.S. became an autonomous congregation. Despite ignorance of the English language, extreme poverty, and anti-Catholicism, the sisters expanded their ministries in Indiana, Illinois, and Michigan. They operated academies and parish schools. During the Civil War they served in military hospitals. By the 20th century the sisters spread to additional U.S. states. They became in 1920 the first congregation in the U.S. to establish a mission in China. An outgrowth of this mission was a foundation of Chinese women, Providence Sister Catechists, which became an autonomous congregation in Taiwan in 1962. The SP of Holyoke (Massachusetts) began their work of serving immigrants and mill workers in 1873 as a mission of the SP from Kingston, Ontario. Thirty sisters formed a diocesan congregation in 1892, and their work came to include hospitals, nursing schools, orphanages, nursing homes, and other social services. The SP adjusted their ministries in the 1960s in response to the changing needs of the world.

EACH; NCE; ROWUS; Katherine Burton, *The Eighth American Saint: The Story of Saint Mother Theodore Guerin* (2006) [1959].

JUDITH METZ, SC

Sisters of St. Joseph of Carondelet (CSJ) (1650–). Roman Catholic religious congregation. Founded in France, the first sisters immigrated to North America in 1836, when a small group went to Carondelet, Missouri, to teach the deaf. From there the sisters founded missions that became centers for provinces united under Carondelet central government or autonomous congregations. In Canada, congregations were established in Hamilton, London, Pembroke, Peterborough, Sault Ste. Marie, and Toronto. In the U.S., congregations were established in Albany, Baden, Boston, Brentwood, Buffalo, Cleveland, Concordia, Erie, LaGrange, Los Angeles, Nazareth, Orange, Philadelphia, Rochester, Springfield, St. Paul, Tipton, Watertown, Wheeling, and Wichita. Additional groups were founded later directly from France: Medaille, St. Augustine, West Hartford, and Winslow. Among the earliest of numerous European-based congregations to send members to present-day U.S. territory and English-speaking Canada, the CSJ soon earned a reputation for adapting quickly to local language and customs. They took up a variety of works in education, health care, and social welfare. Their role, along with a number of other congregations, in nursing Civil War wounded is credited with alleviating anti-Catholic prejudice, while their parochial schools, academies, orphanages, hospitals, colleges, and schools of nursing made significant contributions to American life and culture. Federations formed in the 1950s in the U.S. and Canada which united the over 7,000 sisters in common endeavors relating to the education of new members and to works of historical research, advocacy, and social justice. Missionary outreach, beginning with the China mission of the Baden congregation in the 1920s, resulted in sisters forming communities in other Asian countries as well as in Africa and Latin America.

EACH; NCE; Carol K. Coburn and Martha Smith, *Spirited Lives* (1999); Patricia Byrne, "Sisters of St. Joseph: The Americanization of a French Tradition," *U.S. Catholic Historian* 5, nos. 3 and 4 (Summer–Fall 1986).

KAREN M. KENNELLY, CSJ

Small, Mary Julia (1850–1945). Minister and missionary society worker. In 1873 Mary Small married a minister, John Bryan Small, who later became a bishop in the African Methodist Episcopal (AME) Zion Church. Three days after her wedding she was converted. She felt called to become a preacher, and in 1892 the presiding elder of the Philadelphia and Baltimore Conference of the AME Zion Church licensed her to preach. Later she was ordained as deacon, and in May 1898 she was ordained an elder, the first woman to attain that status in the Methodist Church. Although there is no evidence that she pastored a church, she worked with her husband until his death. She was active in her denomination's Women's Home and Foreign Missionary Society, serving as president from 1912 to 1916. She also participated actively in the *Woman's Christian Temperance Union.

NBAW; Bettye Collier-Thomas, *Daughters of Thunder: Black Women Preachers and Their Sermons* (1998).

MARILYN FÄRDIG WHITELEY

Smith, Amanda Berry (1837–1915). Evangelist and missionary. Born into slavery in Maryland, Amanda Berry was freed when her father purchased release for his family and moved them to Pennsylvania. Despite her freedom, her early life was difficult. Berry received little formal schooling, worked as a maid and washerwoman, married at the age of 17, and eventually lost all of her children. When her first husband never returned from the Civil War she married James Smith. A religious conversion in 1856 and her subsequent reception of the second blessing in 1868 provided strength to help her endure her unhappiness. When her second husband died Smith conducted revivals in African Methodist Episcopal (AME) churches in New Jersey and New York, even if her early audiences were reluctant to hear a woman. She attended her first Holiness camp meeting in 1870, quickly earning a name for herself as an evangelist and speaking to large audiences of blacks and whites. Beginning in 1878 Smith spent 11 years abroad, participating in Holiness meetings in England, speaking to large audiences in India, and serving as a missionary in Liberia. She returned to the U.S. in 1890. She preached for a few years in the East before moving to Chicago, where she participated in the temperance movement, published her memoirs, and opened an orphanage for African American children.

BWARC; DARB; EAWR; NoAW; WBC; Amanda Berry Smith, *An Autobiography* (1893).

MANDY E. MCMICHAEL

Smith, Emma Hale (1804–79). Leader and dissenter in the Church of Jesus Christ of Latter-day Saints (Mormon). As wife of Joseph Smith, Emma Smith played a pivotal role in building Mormonism. A revelation of Joseph Smith named her an "Elect Lady" and instructed her to exhort the church and compile a hymnal. In compliance, she published a hymnal, helped administer church finances, defended Mormonism to the governor of Illinois, and became the first president of the Female Relief Society. Smith supported her husband's ministry until his revelation on plural marriage. She sometimes fought against the doctrine; at other times she reluctantly accepted it; in her later years she denied that her husband ever practiced it. Her opposition led Brigham Young to condemn her. Until recently her role in Mormon history was downplayed. Smith remained tied to the movement, however, through her sons and their descendants. They rejected plural marriage and eventually led the Reorganized Church of Jesus Christ of Latter-day Saints.

ANB; NoAW; Mary D. Poulter, "Doctrines of Faith and Hope Found in Emma Smith's 1835 Hymnbook," *BYU Studies* 37, no. 2 (1998); Linda King Newell and Valeen Tippetts Avery, *Mormon Enigma*, 2nd ed. (1994) [1984]; Valeen Tippetts Avery, "Emma Smith through Her Writings," *Dialogue* 17, no. 3 (Autumn 1984).

LYNN S. NEAL

Smith, Hannah Whitall (1832–1911). Bible teacher, preacher, and writer in the Higher Life movement. Raised and educated in a Quaker environment Hannah Whitall married a Quaker, Robert Pearsall Smith, in 1851, and they had seven children. They immersed themselves in the emerging Holiness movement, preaching at camp meetings and editing a periodical, *Christian's Pathway to Power*. When her husband suffered a nervous breakdown they moved to England, where they became well-known preachers in the Higher Life movement. Smith was involved in women's issues as a founder of the *Woman's Christian Temperance Union (WCTU) and an advocate for women's suffrage and women's higher education. She was the author of a classic on Protestant spirituality, *The Christian's Secret of a Happy Life*.

ANB; BWA; EAWR; EE; NoAW; RLA; Hannah Whitall Smith, *The Unselfishness of God and How I Discovered It* (1903), *Everyday Religion; or, the Common-Sense Teaching of the Bible* (1893), and *The Christian's Secret of a Happy Life* (1875).

PRISCILLA POPE-LEVISON

Smith, Virginia Thrall (1836–1903). City missionary and children's advocate. Born in Connecticut and educated at the Mount Holyoke Seminary, Virginia Smith settled in Hartford with her new husband, William, in 1857. In 1876 her interests in church and private charity led to her selection as city missionary, the administrative head of the Hartford City Mission. The mission was a joint enterprise of the city's six Congregational churches. Smith expanded its program and added a volunteer corps. Her particular concern was with children, however. Her appointment to the State Board of Charities in 1882 allowed her to develop a program to place unwanted children in adoptive homes and establish a free kindergarten program that eventually led to the state authorizing kindergarten programs in public schools.

NoAW; Andrew H. Walsh, *Virginia Thrall Smith* (1993); Mary K. O. Eagle, ed., *The Congress of Women* (1894).

BETH SPAULDING

Smith, Willie Mae Ford (1904–94). Gospel singer and evangelist. Described as a "gospel legend," Willie Mae Smith sang from her youth. A chance meeting with Thomas Dorsey in 1931 led "Mother," as she became known, to join with him and Sallie Martin to organize the National Convention of Gospel Choirs and Choruses. She was among the first gospel singers to tour widely, creating great excitement with her contralto voice and distinct style. She made few recordings; instead, she mentored other singers, in particular Joe May. Raised a Baptist she joined the Church of God Apostolic in 1939, and her music reflected the new rhythmic character of her Sanctified tradition. She introduced the "song and sermonette" into gospel music performances, spending her last years as an evangelist who interspersed short sermons with her songs.

BWA; Horace Boyer, *How Sweet the Sound* (1995); Tony Heilbut, *The Gospel Sound: Good News and Bad Times* (1971).

JANE HARRIS

Smith Davis, Holly Haile (1960–). Presbyterian minister, teacher, and folk singer. Holly Haile Smith was the first Native American woman ordained as a Minister of Word and Sacrament in the Presbyterian Church (U.S.A.). She was born into the Shinnecock Nation, most of whose members are Presbyterians connected with the First Presbyterian Church in Southampton, New York. (The congregation was organized in the 1600s.) She is a granddaughter of Chief Thunder Bird. After attending Cook College and Theological School and the University of Dubuque Theological Seminary, Smith was ordained by the Presbytery of Western Colorado in 1986. Among other positions she served as pastor of Ute Mountain Presbyterian Church in Towaoc, Colorado, and as temporary supply pastor of First Presbyterian Church (better known as the Old Whalers Church) in Sag Harbor, New York. In addition to her work within the church, she has taught in public schools. Davis and two of her cousins perform as the Thunder Bird Sisters, a singing group that won the Native American Music Award (Nammy) as the Best Folk Group in 2000 for their compact disc *Still Singin'*. This group has related music to its political activism for 25 years. She is the mother of one son, Canku Smith.

Jim Adams, "Thunder Bird Sisters Are the 'Benefit Sisters,'" *Indian Country Today* (*Lakota Times*) (21 March 2001); "Presbyterians in America, A Timeline," Presbyterian Historical Society [online]; Shinnecock Indian Nation, www.shinnecocknation.com.

LINDA B. BREBNER

Snow Smith Young, Eliza Roxey (1804–87). Leader and poet in the Church of Jesus Christ of Latter-day Saints (Mormon). Eliza Snow is one of the most important women in Mormon history. Baptized into the church in 1835 Snow composed many religious poems, served as secretary to the Female Relief Society in Nauvoo, and became a plural wife to Joseph Smith in 1841. After Joseph Smith's murder, she married Brigham Young and rose to unparalleled prominence in the church. While contemporary historians debate her feminism, Snow was a leader of Mormon women. She wrote the hymn "O My Father," which promotes the belief in a Heavenly Mother (as well as a Heavenly Father). When in the Endowment House, she performed religious rites for other women. In 1866 she led the reorganization of the Female Relief Society and served as president until her death. Snow also worked with the Mutual Improvement Association and the Primary Association, groups designed to inculcate religious values in Mormon women and youth. In 1872 she helped establish the *Woman's Exponent*, the second women's periodical in the trans-Mississippi West, as the voice of the relief society. Throughout her life Snow advocated for polygamy, evangelized for Mormonism, and attained an influence that was unmatched among Mormon women and many Mormon men.

ANB; EAWR; NoAW; RLA; Maureen Ursenbach Beecher, ed., *The Personal Writings of Eliza Roxey Snow* (2000); Claudia L. Bushman, ed., *Mormon Sisters* (1997); Maureen Ursenbach Beecher, *Eliza and Her Sisters* (1991); Vicky Burgess-Olson, ed., *Sister Saints* (1978).

LYNN S. NEAL

Society of the Companions of the Holy Cross (SCHC) (1884–). Organization for women in the Episcopal Church. Founded as a women's devotional organization by *Emily Malbone Morgan and Harriet Hastings, the SCHC became one of the most effective social justice and reform organizations for Episcopal laywomen in the social gospel era. From its start, the society supported working women, the settlement house movement, world peace, church unity, and other humanitarian causes. Members of the society are united through a rule of life, belief in intercessory prayer, and a commitment to social justice. Originally founded in New England, chapters quickly spread throughout the worldwide Anglican Communion. Notable "companions" included *Vida Scudder, *Helena Dudley, and *Florence Converse. The SCHC owns and operates Adelynrood Retreat and Conference Center in Byfield, Massachusetts.

EAWR; Mary Sudman Donovan, *A Different Call: Women's Ministries in the Episcopal Church* (1986); Emily Malbone Morgan, *Letters to Her Companions* (1944).

SHERYL A. KUJAWA-HOLBROOK

Solares, Maria (ca. 1842–1922). Cultural informant. In the early 20th century, Maria Solares worked extensively with an anthropologist named John Peabody Harrington (1884–1961), whose work focused on recording the languages of California, including the Chumash language of the Santa Ynez Valley. Little is known of Solares's life because Harrington closely guarded the privacy of his informants. It is known, however, that Solares was born at Mission Santa Ynez and lived in the area most of her life. She was Harrington's primary source for information on the language, beliefs, culture, and customs of the Inezeño people. Much of what is known of Inezeño mythology is due to Solares's preservation and to her collaboration with Harrington.

Brian D. Haley and Larry R. Wilcoxon, "Anthropology and the Making of Chumash Tradition," *Current Anthropology* 38 (1997); Thomas C. Blackburn, *December's Child: A Book of Chumash Oral Narratives* (1975).

ANDREW H. STERN

Solis-Cohen, Emily (1886 or 1890–1966) Author, communal activist, and historian. Scion of a prominent Portuguese Jewish family of Philadelphia, Emily Solis-Cohen devoted her entire professional career to the Jews of that city. Educated at the University of Pennsylvania, she authored children's literature, including an abridged Hebrew Bible (1931), a collection of poems (1922), and biblically themed plays. A champion of Jewish women's physical and educational improvement, Solis-Cohen organized Young Women's Hebrew Associations (YMHA) in the U.S., worked in the department of women's activities at the Philadelphia Jewish Welfare Board, and wrote essays on women's roles in Judaism and religion. Solis-Cohen revolutionized research into American Jewish history with her unfinished biography of distinguished Philadelphia rabbi and thinker Isaac Leeser. Never married, Solis-Cohen's independence, prolific literary output, and strong commitment to Jewish women's advancement remain a model for 21st-century American Jewish women.

JWA; Fred Skolnic, ed., *Encyclopedia Judaica*, 2nd ed. (2007); Papers of the Solis-Cohen Family, American Jewish Historical Society; Jewish Women's Archive, www.jwa.org.

MICHAEL A. SINGER

Solomon, Hannah Greenebaum (1858–1942). Clubwoman and social reformer. Born into a wealthy and prominent Reform Jewish family in Chicago, Hannah Greenebaum and her sister became the first Jewish members of the Chicago Woman's Club in 1876. She married Henry Solomon in 1879, and the couple had three children. Solomon chaired the Jewish women's committee at the 1893 World's Columbian Exposition, where delegates founded the *National Council of Jewish Women (NCJW), the first national Jewish women's organization. Elected president, she served from 1893 to 1905. Pioneering in Jewish philanthropy and immigrant aid, the NCJW also worked on a number of social and family issues. NCJW joined non-Jewish women in supporting the idea that women were responsible for promoting religion in the home. Solomon established herself as one of the premier community leaders of Chicago. She maintained close ties with several settlement houses (including Hull House) and the Chicago Civic Federation. In 1905 she began working for the Illinois Industrial School for Girls, served on a number of boards, and was a prominent civic reformer. She was fluent in English, French, and German.

JWA; WBC; Elinor Slater and Robert Slater, *Great Jewish Women* (1994); Jewish Women's Archive, www.jwa.org.

JUDITH METZ, SC

Sonneschein, Rosa Fassel (1847–1932). Zionist, journalist, and clubwoman. Born in Austria, Rosa Fassel enjoyed an educated childhood through her teenage years. She married Solomon Hirsch Sonneschein, a Reform rabbi, and they immigrated to the U.S. and eventually settled in St. Louis in 1869. While mothering their four children, Sonneschein became active in the city's Jewish community. She created choral societies at her synagogue and formed the Pioneers, a literary discussion club. She published articles in Jewish periodicals and eventually for a German-language press. She and her husband divorced in 1893. To support herself Sonneschein turned to writing and created the *American Jewess*, published between 1895 and 1899. The journal was written in English; it advocated for Jewish women's increased involvement in religious and communal life, and called for Jewish women's organizations to embrace Zionism.

ANBO; JWA; Jack Nusan Porter, "Rosa Sonnenschein and the *American Jewess*," *American Jewish History* 67 (September 1978).

SHIRA M. KOHN

Soule, Caroline Augusta White (1824–1903). Universalist minister, missionary, and author. Born to a Dutch Reformed mother and a Universalist father, Caroline White was educated at the Albany Female Academy and became principal at the Universalists' Clinton Liberal Institute. She married Universalist minister Henry Soule in 1843. After her husband died in 1852 Soule provided for their five children by writing, teaching, and editing. While she was the assistant editor of *Ladies' Repository* she lived in Iowa and New York. In 1869 she helped organize the Woman's Centenary Aid Association, which grew to 13,000 members. Renamed the Woman's Centenary Association, Soule served as its first president from 1873 to

1880. Soule first preached in 1874, while she was a missionary to Scotland. She was ordained by the Scottish Universalist Convention in 1880, the first woman ordained in Britain.

ANB; DUUB; NoAW; UU; UUWM; E. R. Hanson, *Our Woman Workers* (1884); Papers, Manuscripts, and Archives, New York Public Library.

BARBARA COEYMAN

Soule, Ida Whittemore (1849–1944). Founder of the United Thank Offering (UTO). Although born, raised, and buried in Boston, Ida Whittemore's marriage to Richard Soule, a railroad builder, took her all over the U.S. Soule first attended a national meeting (triennial) of the Episcopal Church's women's auxiliary in 1877. Soule was committed to its work and was active in the auxiliary in each place she lived. She was also a longtime friend of the auxiliary president, *Julia Emery. At the 1886 triennial Soule proposed that the auxiliary create a special offering over which it would have control; President Emery announced the first UTO at the 1889 triennial. Soule's proposal was part of a strategy to support women's mission work, including that conducted by deaconesses. By 1899 the UTO campaign brought in over $1 million each year.

Mary Sudman Donovan, *A Different Call: Women's Ministries in the Episcopal Church* (1986); Frances M. Young, *Thankfulness Unites* (1979).

JOAN R. GUNDERSEN

Spaeth, Harriet Reynolds Krauth (1845–1925). Hymn translator and author. Harriet Krauth's work as a translator and musician began when she was in her 20s; she served also as an organist during these years at St. Stephen's Church in West Philadelphia. In 1880 she married the Reverend Adolph Spaeth, a professor at the Lutheran Theological Seminary at Philadelphia and the president of the Lutheran General Council. Harriet Spaeth mothered several stepchildren as well as five of her own. In addition to her multiple hymn translations and liturgical compositions she translated two books, *The Deaconess and Her Works* and *Pictures from the Life of Hans Sachs*; was a coauthor (uncredited) of a two-volume biography of her father, Charles Krauth, and wrote a biography of her husband. Spaeth's many articles in the *Lutheran* assisted greatly in introducing and aiding the use of the Common Service. She also supported the social work of the church, especially the deaconess movement.

The Cyber Hymnal, Harriet Reynolds Krauth Spaeth, www.cyberhymnal.org/bio/s/p/spaeth hrk.htm.

MARIA ERLING

Spalding, Catherine ("Mother Spalding") (1793–1858). Roman Catholic religious and social worker. Born in Charles County, Maryland, Catherine Spalding migrated to Nelson County, Kentucky, with her family. In January 1813 she was one of the first three women to join the newly established *Sisters of Charity of Nazareth (SCN), a congregation intended to serve the frontier South. Spalding was elected its first superior and was elected for four more six-year terms during her life. Following the rule of St. Vincent de Paul, the SCN engaged in serving the educational, social, and health needs of the people. Mother Spalding was known for her leadership and business acumen. She was instrumental in founding academies and orphanages, including the St. Vincent Orphanage in Louisville, and established the motherhouse near Bardstown, Kentucky. Spalding University in Louisville is named after her.

EACH; NoAW; James Maria Spillane, *Kentucky Spring* (1968); Anna Blanche McGill, *The Sisters of Charity of Nazareth* (1917).

JUDITH METZ, SC

Spalding, Eliza Hart (1807–51). Missionary, teacher, and artist. Born in Berlin, Connecticut, Eliza Hart was a bright and religious young woman. In 1833 she married fellow Presbyterian Henry Spalding. They had four children. In 1836 the Spaldings joined Marcus and *Narcissa Whitman on a difficult missionary expedition westward, marking the first passage of white women across the Rocky Mountains. The Spaldings settled with the Nez Perce Indians in present-day Idaho, where Eliza opened a school. After a decade their life's work unraveled. Fighting between Henry Spalding and Narcissa Whitman almost led to the Spaldings' termination, and disease and encroaching white settlement caused tribes to reconsider their friendly coexistence. In 1847 the Whitmans and 12 others were killed by members of the tribe they sought to convert. The massacre ended both missions. Spalding is buried near the mission home she loved.

ANB; Narcissa Whitman and Eliza Spalding, *Where Wagons Could Go* (1963); Eliza Spalding Warren, *Memoirs of the West* (1916).

CATHERINE BOWLER

Sparling, Olive Dora (1910–94). Deaconess and Christian educator. Having earned tuition fees during the 1930s Depression era, Olive Sparling graduated from the United Church Training School (Toronto) in 1937. Her ministry began with Montreal's Church of All Nations, which inspired her pursuit of two degrees in religious education. Sparling then assumed responsibilities for curriculum development with the United Church of Canada's board of Christian education; she brought passion for experiential learning and lay leadership development. Convinced that informed leadership inspired effective education, Sparling resisted the norm of implementing new curriculums from the youngest upward. This belief inspired Sparling's Observation Practice Schools, a leadership training program that motivated thousands of Sunday school teachers throughout Canada in the 1960s.

Peter Gordon White, "To Seek Truth, Know God, and Serve Others: The Olive Sparling Story," *Touchstone: Heritage and Theology in a New Age* 14, no. 1 (January 1996); Association of Professional Church Workers, "The Newsletter: Historical Issue" (1988); United Church of Canada Archives, Victoria University (Toronto).

SARAH BRUER

Speer, Margaret Bailey (1900–1997). Educator. The oldest daughter of the great Presbyterian missionary leader Robert E. Speer, Margaret Speer committed herself to foreign missions at a Student Volunteer Movement convention in 1920, during her sophomore year at Bryn Mawr College. Before her arrival in China in 1925 she gained experience at Sweet Briar College and Bryn Mawr College. As a member of the Presbyterians' North China mission Speer taught Western languages at Yenching Women's College (YWC), where she advanced from faculty leader to dean. Between 1934 and 1941 Speer administered YWC during a period of student unrest and political upheavals, which culminated in Japanese troops detaining Speer from December 1941 until March 1943. After her repatriation she served as the headmistress of the Shipley School, a private girls' school in Bryn Mawr, Pennsylvania, from 1944 until her retirement in 1965.

Trina Vaux, *Recollection of Miss Speer* (1990); Dwight Edwards, *Yenching University* (1968).

JANE HARRIS

Spencer, Anna Carpenter Garlin (1851–1931). Minister, author, and social reformer. Anna Garlin was born into a socially active family and married a Unitarian minister, William Spencer, in 1878. Spencer had a varied career. She taught school, served as minister in the Bell Street Chapel (a nondenominational church in Providence, Rhode Island), wrote 70 articles, and taught at Meadville (Pennsylvania) Theological School and at Teachers College, Columbia University. She was the first woman ordained in Rhode Island. She was active in the *Woman's Christian Temperance Union, Woman's Peace Party, and suffrage movement. In her book *Woman's Share in Social Culture* (1913), she argued that women were fully capable of achievements in science, music, and literature, but that their duties as homemakers and mothers usually did not allow gifted women the time required for such pursuits.

ANB; NoAW; Anna Garlin Spencer, *The Family and Its Members* (1923); Papers, Swarthmore College Peace Collection.

LYNN JAPINGA

Spicer, Sirilda Belva (1894–?). Educator and minister. Born in Iowa and raised in Nebraska, Belva Spicer received a degree in education at the University of Nebraska. Because positions for black teachers in Nebraska were scarce, she moved to Kansas City, Kansas. While living there, she experienced a call to ministry. In 1941 she returned to Nebraska and became a lay preacher in the African Methodist Episcopal (AME) Church. In 1948, at the age of 54, she was ordained as an AME minister in Omaha. *Perspectives: Women in Nebraska History* states that she was the first woman ordained in the AME Church, while other sources (Dodson, *Engendering Church*; Hill, Lippy, and Wilson, *Encyclopedia of Religion in the South*) award that distinction to Rebecca Glover. After serving several churches in Nebraska, Spicer returned to teaching. She was awarded a Medal of Honor from the Bureau of Indian Affairs for her fourteen years of work with Native American children in South Dakota upon her retirement in 1970.

Susan Pierce, ed., *Perspectives: Women in Nebraska History* (1984).

ANNIE RUSSELL

Sponland, Ingeborg (1860–1951). Lutheran deaconess. From a pious family in rural Norway, Ingeborg Sponland committed herself to Christianity in her teens and began deaconess training in 1881 at the Oslo motherhouse. Following consecration and some years of nursing, she came to the U.S. in 1891 to visit her parents and siblings. During her furlough she agreed to give leadership to the Minneapolis Norwegian Lutheran deaconesses. Sponland supervised hospital work and oversaw expansion throughout the upper Midwest, which included homes for children and the elderly. In 1906 she assumed similar responsibilities in Chicago. Sponland worked with leaders from several branches of Norwegian American Lutheranism and with their women's organizations. Although deeply connected to these communities she insisted that deaconesses provide medical care to anyone who was ill, not only to their country folk or church family.

Frederick S. Weiser, comp., *Pioneers of God's Future* (1991); Ingeborg Sponland, *My Reasonable Service* (1938).

L. DEANE LAGERQUIST

Squire, Anne Marguerite (1921–). First laywoman elected moderator of the United Church of Canada (UCC). While teaching religion at Carleton University between 1975 and 1982, Anne Squire discovered feminism and applied it to theology. She believed in all forms of ministry, including that done by women and laypeople, and worked to make theological education more accessible to everyone. Squire was moderator of the UCC between 1986 and 1988, when the divisive issue of sexual orientation emerged. Squire argued that sexual orientation was not in itself a barrier to either church membership or eligibility for ordered ministry. Her position attracted both attack and admiration. Squire continues to be involved in interfaith dialogue and peace and justice issues.

Michael W. Higgins, ed., "Women and the Church, Special Issues," *Grail* 4, no. 2 (June 1988); Anne Squire, "Women and the Church," *Christian* 6, no. 4 (1981); "Envisioning Ministry," MP&E (Ministry Personnel & Education) Paper 10 (1985).

TRACY J. TROTHEN

Stair, Lois Harkrider (1923–82). First woman moderator of the General Assembly in the United Presbyterian Church, U.S.A. (UPCUSA). Lois Harkrider Stair was born in Waukesha, Wisconsin, and graduated from Smith College. After years of service at all levels of the UPCUSA she was elected to moderate the General Assembly in 1971. In the process of carrying out the moderator's responsibilities, she challenged many stereotypes about women in leadership. Stair was committed to ecumenism and served as the vice chair of the Consultation on Church Union (COCU). Her service as the chair of the Major Mission Fund for the denomination reflected her concern for Presbyterian mission programs throughout the world.

Ellen D. Langill, "Lois Stair: General Assembly Moderator and Reconciler," *American Presbyterians* 68, no. 4 (Winter 1990); Elizabeth Howell Verdesi and Sylvia Thorson-Smith, *A Sampler of Saints* (1988); Jean Coffey Lyles, "Dauntless Lois," *Christian Century* 98, no. 25 (12–19 August 1981).

LINDA B. BREBNER

Stanley, Sara G. (1836–1918). Activist, writer, and teacher. Freeborn to parents who ran a school for free African American children in New Bern, North Carolina, Sara Stanley, a Presbyterian, attended Oberlin College and then taught in Ohio public schools. She was active in the abolitionist movement before the Civil War, and one of her speeches was published as an antislavery tract. Stanley taught for the American Missionary Association (AMA) in several southern states from 1864 to 1868. She left the AMA when her 1868 marriage to a white Civil War veteran led to conflict with a white AMA worker. In her teaching, speaking, and writing, Stanley employed her Christian ideals to challenge the racism and paternalism she encountered even within the AMA.

ANB; BWA; EE; Judith Weisenfeld, "'Who Is Sufficient for These Things?' Sara G. Stanley and the American Missionary Association," in *This Far by Faith*, ed. Judith Weisenfeld and Richard Newman (1995).

SANDRA L. BEARDSALL

Stanton, Elizabeth Cady (1815–1902). Women's rights activist. Elizabeth Cady Stanton experienced firsthand the daily drudgery of women's work as a housewife and mother of seven children. She and *Lucretia Mott planned the first convention on women's rights held in Seneca Falls, New York, in 1848. Modeled on the Declaration of Independence, the Seneca Falls Declaration included a resolution on female suffrage inserted by Stanton. Stanton was president of the National Woman Suffrage Association (NWSA) in the 1890s. She also worked to pass the Married Women's Property Act, for which she gave several speeches before the New York state legislature. Believing that religion was the supreme impediment to women's advancement she organized the publication of *The Woman's Bible*, for which she recruited women scholars to write commentaries on every biblical reference about women. Stanton assumed that biblical texts were written and edited by men, not by God, and were therefore open to interpretation, criticism, and even rejection. Volume 1 (1895) of *The Woman's Bible* covered the first five books of the Old Testament, while volume 2 (1898) dealt with the rest of the Old Testament and the New Testament. Reaction against *The Woman's Bible* arose from many arenas, including the NWSA, which passed a resolution denouncing it. Stanton was the leading intellectual of the first wave of feminism in the U.S.

ANB; DARB; EAWR; NoAW; Kathi Kern, *Mrs. Stanton's Bible* (2001); Elisabeth Griffith, *In Her Own Right* (1984); Lois W. Banner, *Elizabeth Cady Stanton* (1980); Elizabeth Cady Stanton, Susan B. Anthony, and Matilda Joslyn Gage, eds., *History of Woman Suffrage*, vol. 1 (1881).

PRISCILLA POPE-LEVISON

Starbuck, Mary Coffyn (Coffin) (ca. 1644–1717). Quaker preacher. Mary Coffyn was born to a prominent Haverhill, Massachusetts, family and reared in Puritanism. She moved with her family to Nantucket Island in 1660 or 1661, where her father became the settlement's first magistrate. Shortly after their move Coffyn married a prominent landowner named Nathaniel Starbuck, with whom she raised 10 children; he later succeeded her father as magistrate of the island. Between 1701 and 1704 Starbuck became convinced of the truth of Quaker doctrine. With her oldest son, she helped found the first recognized Quaker meeting in Nantucket, which was approved by the New England Yearly Meeting in 1708. Little is known about her life and ministry over the next decade, but the Nantucket meeting became the most influential religious organization on the island in the early years of the 18th century.

ANB; NoAW.

SCOTT D. SEAY

Starhawk (Miriam Simos) (1951–). Wiccan, author, and activist. Born Miriam Simos and raised Jewish, Starhawk first explored witchcraft in her late teens. In 1979 she wrote *The Spiral Dance: A Rebirth of the Religion of the Great Goddess.* Her book spurred the creation of the contemporary Wiccan movement. It included instructions on how to form one's own coven, cast a circle, and enact initiation rites. Starhawk advocates an interpretation of Wicca that combines ecofeminism and political action. She emphasizes the interconnectedness of all things, an earth-based spirituality. Starhawk has also begun to chart a path for the nurturing of witchlings with the coauthoring of *Circle Round: Raising of Children in the Goddess Tradition* in 1998. In her 1993 novel, *The Fifth Sacred Thing,* Starhawk depicts a world that is governed by the inclusive principles of feminist Wicca. She speaks and writes about environmental activism, paganism, tolerance, and healing. She is featured in the Canadian-produced documentaries *Goddess Remembered* (1989) and *Burning Times* (1990).

EAWR; RLA; Wade Clark Roof, ed., *Contemporary American Religion,* vol. 2 (1999); Rosemary Radford Ruether, "The Way of Wicca," *Christian Century* 97, no. 6 (February 1980).

SUSAN B. RIDGELY

Starr, Eliza Allen (1824–1901). Artist, educator, and author. Eliza Starr was an accomplished student of artist Caroline Negus Hildreth. She opened a studio and taught in Boston, Brooklyn, Philadelphia, and Natchez (Mississippi). After a nine-year struggle, she converted from Unitarianism to Roman Catholicism in 1854. She moved to Chicago in 1856, opened a studio, and integrated her art and religious convictions. In 1871 she founded the art department at Saint Mary's Academy (renamed St. Mary's College) in South Bend, Indiana. She published articles in periodicals, such as *Catholic World*, and books with Catholic themes. She spoke at the 1893 Columbian Catholic Congress in Chicago. Starr received Notre Dame's first Laetare Medal (1885) and a medallion from Leo XIII in recognition of *The Three Archangels and the Guardian Angel in Art* (1899).

NoAW; RLA; WBC; James J. McGovern, ed., *The Life and Letters of Eliza Allen Starr* (2007) [1905].

SANDRA YOCUM MIZE

Starr, Ellen Gates (1859–1940). Settlement house founder and labor activist. Ellen Starr cofounded the Hull House settlement in Chicago with her friend and former classmate at Rockford Female Seminary, *Jane Addams, in 1889. Starr taught art classes and bookbinding at Hull House and decorated its interior with fine art reproductions. After becoming an Episcopalian in 1884 Starr came into contact with the Episcopal monk and labor organizer James Otis Sargent Huntington. Her friendship with Huntington and *Vida Dutton Scudder drew her deeply into radical Christian socialist activism, which included involvement with the National Women's Trade Union League and marching on picket lines. In 1916 she ran unsuccessfully for alderman in Chicago. After several years of prayer and consideration she converted to Roman Catholicism in 1920. She then spent her time writing and speaking on art, worship, and her conversion experience. An operation in 1929 left Starr paralyzed from the waist down, and she spent her remaining years at a convent in Suffern, New York.

ANB; DARB; EACH; EAWR; NoAW; RLA; WBC; Ellen Gates Starr, *On Art, Labor and Religion*, ed. Mary Jo Deegan and Ana-Maria Wahl (2003); Eleanor J. Stebner, *The Women of Hull House* (1997); Papers, Sophia Smith Collection, Smith College.

ANNIE RUSSELL

Stetson, Augusta Emma Simmons (1842–1928). Christian Science practitioner and teacher. A native of Maine and a Methodist in her youth, Augusta Stetson lived in Europe and Asia until her husband's ill health compelled their return to Boston. She began education in public speaking in 1882, and after meeting *Mary Baker Eddy in 1884 she sought training as a Christian Science practitioner. She achieved immediate success as a healer and entered a long but conflicted friendship with Eddy. Their relationship lasted 25 years, during which time Stetson founded the First Church of Christ, Scientist, in Manhattan, acquired a large following of practitioners, and built an elaborate church (with a mansion next door for herself). Stetson was dismissed from church membership in 1909, a result of longtime tensions over issues of rival leadership and questions of doctrine (such as Stetson's denigration of sexuality and her semi-deification of Eddy). Stetson died professing loyalty to Eddy but still teaching her own version of Christian Science, which included an emphasis on wealth and promotion of Nordic supremacy.

ANB; DARB; EAWR; NoAW; Gillian Gill, *Mary Baker Eddy* (1998); *Letters of Mary Baker Eddy to Augusta E. Stetson*, ed. Gail M. Weatherbe (1990); Augusta E. Stetson, *Reminiscences, Sermons and Correspondence* (1913).

MARY FARRELL BEDNAROWSKI

Stevens, Georgia Lydia (1870–1946). Musician, Roman Catholic sister, and educator. Born into a prominent Episcopalian family in Boston, Georgia Stevens began playing the violin at the age of seven. At age 18 she traveled to Germany to continue her violin studies. Later, in the U.S., she was tutored by Charles Loeffler of the Boston Symphony Orchestra. She performed and taught music as a career. At age 24 she converted to Roman Catholicism, and in 1906 she joined the Sisters of the Sacred Heart. As part of the early-20th-century Catholic movement to reclaim traditional liturgical music, including Gregorian chant, Stevens cofounded the Pius X School of Liturgical Music at Manhattanville College, New York (with Justine Bayard Ward). She also wrote the *Tone and Rhythm Series* of books for teaching music to children.

NoAW; Georgia Stevens, "Gregorian Chant," *Musical Quarterly* 30, no. 2 (April 1944).

COLLEEN CARPENTER CULLINAN

Stewart, Maria W. Miller (1803–79). Orator, educator, and reformer. Maria Miller was orphaned as a child, received little formal education, and married James W. Stewart in 1826. After his death in 1829 Stewart underwent a conversion and settled in the Episcopal Church. The first African American woman to speak publicly on behalf of women's rights, Stewart opposed slavery, the oppression of women, and all exploitation. Her addresses were given in Boston during a time when women and African Americans did not speak in public. She was condemned for her speaking but still believed that God spoke through women. In her retirement Stewart held prayer meetings in her home since she was denied funding for her Sunday school from the Episcopal Church (because she was black) and from black churches (because she was Episcopalian).

ANB; BWA; EAWR; NBAW; NoAW; Sheryl A. Kujawa-Holbrook, *Freedom Is a Dream* (2002); Marilyn Richardson, ed., *Maria W. Stewart* (1987).

SHERYL A. KUJAWA-HOLBROOK

Stokes, Olivia Egleston Phelps (1847–1927), and **Caroline Phelps Stokes** (1854–1909). Philanthropists. The Stokes sisters were born in New York City and raised Presbyterian. They later joined the Episcopal Church. Neither of them chose to marry. Philanthropic work was a legacy of their family; their grandparents, Thomas Stokes and Anson Green Phelps, helped to establish and direct significant 19th-century benevolent organizations, such as the American Bible Society. The Stokeses gave generously to build St. Paul's Chapel at Columbia University in New York and a chapel at Berea College in Berea, Kentucky. Olivia Stokes authored several books, including *Pine and Cedar: Bible Verses* (1885), *Forward in the Better Life* (1915), and *Saturday Nights in Lent* (1922). Funds from Caroline Stokes's will established the Phelps-Stokes Fund to improve race relations and for African American educational facilities.

NoAW; Papers, Schlesinger Library, Radcliffe College, Harvard University.

ELIZABETH HINSON-HASTY

Stone, Lucy (1818–93). Lecturer and women's rights activist. Lucy Stone was the fifth of eight children born to Francis and Hannah Stone in West Brookfield, Massachusetts. The Stones provided primary schooling for their children but sent only boys to college. Stone saved for 10 years to enter Oberlin College and received a degree in 1847, the first Massachusetts woman to do so. She gained recognition for public speaking and lectured for the Massachusetts Anti-Slavery Society (1848–51), and taught school to slaves and fugitives. Stone inspired the 1850 National Woman's Rights Convention (Worcester) and helped organize the second convention in 1851, beginning her association with *Susan B. Anthony and *Elizabeth Cady Stanton. Stone converted to Unitarianism in 1851. During the 1850s she lectured widely. In 1855 she married Henry Blackwell. While they agreed on a marriage of equal partnership, the birth of their daughter in 1857 required Stone to curtail her public speaking for several years. Following the Civil War, Stone broke ranks with Anthony and Stanton because she supported suffrage for blacks. In 1869 Stone organized the American Woman Suffrage Association, a rival to their National Woman Suffrage Association. She founded *Woman's Journal*, which she and her husband edited for many years. After she died in Dorchester, Massachusetts, over 1,100 people attended her funeral.

ANB; DUUB; NoAW; Joelle Million, *Woman's Voice, Woman's Place: Lucy Stone and the Birth of the Woman's Rights Movement* (2003); Dorothy Emerson, ed., *Standing before Us* (2000); Andrea Moore Kerr, *Lucy Stone* (1992); Alice Stone Blackwell, *Lucy Stone, Pioneer of Woman's Rights* (1930).

BARBARA COEYMAN

Stoughton, Judith Mary Mansfield (1917–91). Artist, art historian, author, and teacher. Educated by the *Sisters of St. Joseph of Carondelet (CSJ) in St. Paul, Minnesota, through her undergraduate years Mary Stoughton joined that congregation in 1939. She received her master's degree from the California College of Arts and Crafts. Sister Judith was a longtime faculty member at the College of St. Catherine, where she introduced a Women in Art program in the 1970s. She was an editor and writer for *Sacred Signs* and *Catholic Art Quarterly*, art editor (1961–64) for the 15-volume *New Catholic Encyclopedia*, and author of the biography *Proud Donkey of Schaerbeck: Ade Bethune, Catholic Writer, Artist* (1988).

CSJ, *Eyes Open on a World* (2001); Rosalie Ryan and John Christine Wolkerstorfer, *More Than a Dream, Eighty-five Years at the College of St. Catherine* (1992); Archives, Sisters of St. Joseph of Carondelet, St. Paul Province.

KAREN M. KENNELLY, CSJ

Stowe, Emily Howard Jennings (1831–1903). Physician and suffragist. Born in Ontario into a Quaker family, Emily Jennings was educated by her mother. She taught in local schools for 17 years while raising three children with her husband, John Stowe, whom she had married in 1856. Denied admission to Canadian medical schools, she attended the New York Medical College and graduated in 1867. After she returned to Toronto, the Canadian Council of Physicians refused to grant her a medical license, so she began practicing homeopathic medicine and lecturing on women's health. She finally received her license in 1880. Inspired by *Elizabeth Cady Stanton and *Susan B. Anthony she founded the Canadian Woman's Suffrage Association in 1876. Throughout the 1880s and early 1890s, she collaborated with influential leaders in the U.S. and successfully lobbied to expand educational opportunities for women. A member of a Unitarian church and of the first Canadian branch of the Theosophical Society, Stowe came to reject all religious creeds. Stowe retired from medicine and slowed her work in the suffrage movement after breaking her hip at the 1893 Chicago World's Fair. She spent her last years in Toronto with her family.

DCB; DUUB; Mary Beacock Fryer, *Emily Stowe* (1990).

SCOTT D. SEAY

Stowe, Harriet Beecher (1811–96). Author. Harriet Beecher was born in Litchfield, Connecticut, the seventh child of prominent clergyman Lyman Beecher. She attended and later taught at the Hartford Female Seminary, founded by her sisters, where her literary gifts were first recognized. The Beechers moved to Cincinnati in 1832, where she and her sister *Catharine Beecher founded the Western Female Institute. In 1836 she married Calvin Stowe, a professor at Lane Seminary, with whom she raised seven children. While in Cincinnati, Stowe became aware of the devastations of slavery through her reading and her awareness of the Underground Railroad that passed through the city. She began writing for local and religious periodicals to support her family. Among her writings was a serialized story of a runaway slave inspired by the passage of the Fugitive Slave Act (1850) and written for the *National Era*, an antislavery weekly. The serial was published in 1852 as a two-volume novel entitled *Uncle Tom's Cabin.* A moral and religious indictment of a sinful system and a call for national repentance, the novel earned her international acclaim and, some believe, heightened the tensions that led to the Civil War. In 1862 she was invited to the White House to meet President Lincoln, who reportedly greeted her as the "little woman who wrote the book that started this Great War." Stowe wrote 30 books, including novels and works on homemaking, child rearing, and religion.

ANB; DARB; EE; NoAW; Joan D. Hedrick, *Harriet Beecher Stowe* (1994); Charles Edward Stowe, *Life of Harriet Beecher Stowe* (1889).

BEVERLY ZINK-SAWYER

Sunday, Helen Amelia Thompson (1868–1957). Wife, administrator, and evangelist. Helen Thompson married Billy Sunday when he was still a professional baseball player. Billy Sunday soon became one of the century's greatest evangelists, and Helen Sunday became the general manager of his campaigns. After her husband's death, Sunday embarked on her own 22-year preaching ministry, sharing the platform with evangelists such as Billy Graham.

WBC; Helen Sunday, *"Ma" Sunday Still Speaks* (1957); Papers, Archives, Billy Graham Center.

PRISCILLA POPE-LEVISON

Sunderland, Eliza Jane Read (1839–1910). Educator and lecturer. Born in Huntsville, Illinois, Eliza Read began teaching school at the age of 15. She graduated from Mount Holyoke in 1865 and became a high school principal in Aurora, Illinois. She married Baptist minister Jabez Sunderland in 1871, and they became Unitarians in 1872. The Sunderlands had three children. Sunderland earned a PhD at the University of Michigan in 1892 and taught a Bible class at the university for 17 years, even though women were denied faculty appointment. She fostered religious education and preached from many pulpits. During the Western Unitarian controversy of the 1880s she conservatively called for explicit theism. She addressed the 1893 World Congress of Religions, made numerous women's suffrage and temperance speeches, and was active in various women's organizations.

DUUB; Charles H. Lyttle, *Freedom Moves West* (1952); Papers, Bentley Historical Library, University of Michigan.

IRENE BAROS-JOHNSON

Swain, Clara A. (1834–1910). Medical doctor and foreign missionary. Upon graduation from the Woman's Medical College in Philadelphia in 1869 with an MD, Clara Swain agreed to serve an orphanage and attend to women in secluded zenanas in Barielly, India. Swain and *Isabella Thoburn represented the newly formed Woman's Foreign Missionary Society of the Methodist Episcopal Church as its first single female missionaries. In 1871 a local prince more than fulfilled Swain's request for property with enough land to build a dispensary, a hospital, and accommodations for families. By June 1873 she was offering medical training to young women, treating patients, running the dispensary and hospital, as well as teaching Sunday school, training Bible women, and evangelizing in zenanas. After 15 years Swain became the personal physician to the rajah of Khetri, which led to further opportunities for medical care, training, and evangelism.

ANB; NoAW; Maina Chawla Singh, "Women, Mission, and Medicine: Clara Swain, Anna Kugler, and Early Medical Endeavors in Colonial India," *International Bulletin of Missionary Research* 29, no. 3 (July 2005); Dana Robert, *American Women in Mission* (1997); Dorothy Clark Wilson, *Palace of Healing: The Story of Dr. Clara Swain* (1968).

LACEYE C. WARNER

Swensson, Alma Lind (1859–1939). Lutheran musician and churchwoman. Born in Sweden, Alma Lind immigrated in 1863 with her family to Moline, Illinois. She became a church organist when she was only 12 years old. When she was 20 she married Carl Aaron Swensson and moved to Lindsborg, Kansas, where her husband became the pastor of Bethany Lutheran Church and she became the organist. The position at Bethany included the responsibility of founding Bethany College. In the fall of 1881 the Swenssons proposed that the college and church community put on a production of Handel's *Messiah* the next spring. Swensson taught the music by rote to untrained Kansas farmers and merchants; the college's annual Messiah Festival grew out of these beginnings. Swensson also worked with other women to found the Augustana Synod Woman's Foreign Missionary Society. She became the editor of the *Missions Tidning*, which began in 1906, and continued as its Swedish language editor until her death.

Emory Lindquist, *Bethany in Kansas: The History of a College* (1975); Alfred Bergin, "Life Sketch, Alma Christina Swensson," *Korsbaneret* (1941).

MARIA ERLING

Syrkin, Marie (1899–1989). Author, educator, and advocate for the state of Israel. Marie Syrkin was the daughter of Socialist Zionist theoretician Nachman Syrkin. She was educated at Cornell University and joined the staff of the Labor Zionist *Jewish Frontier* in 1934. Her first marriage ended over her desire to pursue her own career, and in 1930 she married poet Charles Reznikoff. During World War II she advocated for European Jewry and wrote speeches for Chaim Weizmann and Golda Meir. After the war she researched and wrote *Blessed Is the Match: The Story of Jewish Resistance* (1947), visited displaced persons' camps to select recipients of college scholarships, investigated treatment of Muslim holy sites by the new state of Israel for Israel's report to the United Nations, and wrote several essays on Palestinian refugees and nationalism. In 1950 she was named professor of English at Brandeis University, where she taught the first courses on Holocaust literature and American Jewish literature. She continued her journalistic and editorial activities. Her works include *Your School, Your Children* (1944), *Nachman Syrkin: Socialist Zionist* (1960), *Hayim Greenberg Anthology* (1968), *Golda Meir: Israel's Leader* (1970), and *The State of the Jews* (1980).

ANBO; JWA; Papers, Jacob Rader Marcus Center, American Jewish Archives.

JOAN S. FRIEDMAN

Szold, Henrietta (1860–1945). Zionist and founder of *Hadassah. Born in Baltimore to Central European immigrant parents, Henrietta Szold became an intellectual disciple of her rabbi father. She used her language skills and Judaic knowledge to establish a night school for Russian Jewish immigrants. Soon after, the newly formed Jewish Publication Society (JPS), which translated and published works of Jewish studies and history, asked Szold to join its board as the only female member. In 1902 Szold enrolled at the Jewish Theological Seminary. The contacts she made during these years led to her organizing

Hadassah, the first national Jewish women's Zionist organization.

ANBO; DARB; EAWR; JWA; RLA; Allon Gal, "The Zionist Vision of Henrietta Szold," in *American Jewish Women and the Zionist Enterprise*, ed. Shulamith Reinharz and Mark Raider (2005); Joyce Antler, "Zion in Our Hearts: Henrietta Szold and the American Jewish Women's Movement," in *American Jewish Women's History*, ed. Pamela Nadell (2003).

SHIRA M. KOHN

Talcott, Eliza (1836–1911). Missionary teacher and nurse. Descended from the first settlers of Connecticut, Eliza Talcott attended Porter School and became a teacher in the public schools of New Britain. A devout Congregationalist, Talcott involved herself with the American Board of Commissioners for Foreign Missions (ABCFM) and volunteered in 1873 to go to Kobe, Japan. She and her traveling partner, Julia E. Dudley, were the first single women sent to Japan by the ABCFM. The two held classes for girls in English, sewing, Bible, and singing. Kobe College was officially founded in 1894. Talcott blended her training in education and nursing with her faith throughout her life. She went to Kyoto in 1885 as house mother and head of the nurses' training school at Doshisha University. During the Sino-Japanese War (1894–95) her services in the military hospitals at Hiroshima earned her the title "The Florence Nightingale of Japan."

NoAW; Charlotte B. DeForest, *The History of Kobe College* (1950).

BETH SPAULDING

Tate, Mary Magdalena Lewis (1871–1930). Founder of a Pentecostal denomination. Mary Lewis was born in Vanleer, Tennessee. After a brief marriage and the birth of two sons, Tate felt called to ministry. Her early itinerant evangelizing throughout the South gained her hundreds of followers, whom she organized into groups called "Do Righters." She adopted the saint name Magdalena for her role as a preacher to men. In 1908 she experienced a dramatic healing and speaking in tongues, making her a devout Pentecostal. Founder and president of the Church of the Living God, the Pillar and Ground of the Truth, she led one of the earliest black Pentecostal denominations. The denomination spread to more than 20 states. A larger-than-life preacher, "Mother Tate" was an early leader in Pentecostalism.

EAWR; Mary Tate, *Mary Lena Lewis Tate* (2003); Kelly Willis Mendiola, *The Hand of a Woman* (2002).

CATHERINE BOWLER

Tekakwitha, Kateri (Catherine, Lily of the Mohawks) (1656–80). "Indian Saint" revered by Roman Catholic Native Americans. Born to a Mohawk father and Algonquin Christian mother, Kateri Tekakwitha was orphaned at the age of four by a smallpox epidemic that left her partially blind and her face scarred. In her village near present-day Fonda, New York, she was evangelized by Jesuit missionaries and, brooking strong family and community opposition, was baptized on Easter Sunday 1676. She refused marriage, vowing to remain a virgin. Persecuted, the young convert fled north to the Mohawk village of Kahnawake on the St. Lawrence River. Tekakwitha's extraordinary devotion, humility, and charity and her intense purgations soon were acclaimed. After an early death her fame spread with reports of miraculous cures and apparitions. Native Americans continue to venerate her, with multitudes visiting her shrines. The Tekakwitha Conference and Kateri movements, both named after her, are active Native American expressions of Roman Catholicism. Tekakwitha was declared venerable in

1943 and beatified in 1980, two steps on the way to sainthood. Her feast day is July 14.

DARB; EAWR; NaAW; NoAW; Allan Greer, *Mohawk Saint* (2005); Paula Elizabeth Holmes, "The Narrative Repatriation of Blessed Kateri Tekakwitha," *Anthropologica* 43, no. 1 (2001); Nancy Shoemaker, "Kateri Tekakwitha's Tortuous Path to Sainthood," in *Negotiators of Change*, ed. Nancy Shoemaker (1995); David Blanchard, ". . . to the Other Side of the Sky: Catholicism at Kahnawake," *Anthropologica* 24 (1982).

JANET SILMAN

ten Boom, Corrie (1892–1983). Speaker and author. Corrie ten Boom was born to Casper and Cor ten Boom in Haarlem, the Netherlands. She trained as a watchmaker. After the occupation of Holland by the Nazis she and her family became involved in the Dutch underground. When she and her family were discovered aiding Jews they were arrested and eventually interred at the Ravensbruck concentration camp. In memory of her sister, Betsie, who died in the camp, ten Boom opened a home for refugees on the site of a former concentration camp after the war. A tireless speaker, she traveled the world as an evangelist. She worked with the Billy Graham crusades and through her own organization, Christians Inc. The story of her imprisonment was told in her book, *The Hiding Place*, which also became a feature film.

EE; "Corrie ten Boom Dies at Age 91," *Christianity Today* 27, no. 9 (1983); Carole C. Carlson, *Corrie ten Boom: Her Life, Her Faith* (1983).

VALERIE REMPEL

Terrell, Mary Eliza Church (1863–1954). Civil rights activist. Born in Memphis, Tennessee, to former slaves, Mary Eliza Church graduated from Oberlin College with a bachelor's degree in 1884 and a master's degree in 1888. She married Robert Terrell, a prominent lawyer, in the early 1890s and relocated to Washington, DC. In 1896 she established the *National Association of Colored Women (NACW) and served as its president. She published essays on lynching, convict leasing, and other forms of institutionalized racism. She became more militant in the 1940s and 1950s, as she lectured widely against discrimination, led public demonstrations, and was the driving force behind *District of Columbia v. John Thompson* (1953), the case that ended segregation in Washington restaurants and hotels. Her efforts were recognized with honorary doctorates from Howard University and Oberlin College.

ANB; BWA; NBAW; Mary Church Terrell, *A Colored Woman in a White World* (2005) [1940]; Beverly Washington Jones, *Quest for Equality: The Life and Writings of Mary Eliza Church Terrell* (1990).

SCOTT D. SEAY

Thoburn, Isabella (1840–1901). Educator and foreign missionary. In 1869 Isabella Thoburn and Dr. *Clara Swain represented the newly formed Woman's Foreign Missionary Society of the Methodist Episcopal Church as its first single female missionaries. Thoburn served in Lucknow, India, where her brother, Bishop James Thoburn, was newly appointed. In her first two terms Thoburn established a boarding school for girls in Lucknow and served as principal of a girl's school in Cawnpore; she also worked among Lucknow's poor, teaching Sunday school and training "Bible reader" evangelists. During a furlough Thoburn was recruited by *Lucy Rider Meyer to supervise the first deaconess home in Chicago in 1887 and then another deaconess home and a hospital in Cincinnati. After returning to India, Thoburn continued to expand educational opportunities for women. She received a government charter in 1895 for her existing woman's college that would later become part of Lucknow University.

NoAW; Dana Robert, *American Women in Mission* (1997); Carolyn DeSwarte Gifford, "Isabella Thoburn," in *Something More Than Human: Biographies of Leaders in American Methodist Higher Education*, ed. Charles E. Cole (1986); James Mills Thoburn, *Life of Isabella Thoburn* (1903).

LACEYE C. WARNER

Thomas, Cora Ann Pair (1875–1952). Educator and missionary. Born in Knightdale, North Carolina, Cora Pair graduated from the Baptist-affiliated Shaw University in 1895. She continued her education with missionary training courses at Fisk University and then served as principal of an orphanage for black children in Oxford, North Carolina. She married William Henry Thomas in 1908, and they arrived at their mission station in Brewerville, Liberia, in early 1909. Once there, she convinced the Lott Carey Baptist mission board to establish a school where she taught hundreds of children. After her husband's death in 1942 Thomas was designated the superintendent of the mission, a position she filled until 1946 when poor health forced her to leave. She died of malaria while on a pilgrimage back to Liberia.

BWARC; Darlene Clark Hine, ed., *Facts on File Encyclopedia of Black Women in America: Religion and Community* (1997).

MANDY E. MCMICHAEL

Thurman, Sue Bailey (1904–96). African American author and historian. The youngest of 10 children born to prominent religious leaders the Reverend Issac and Susie Bailey, Sue Bailey attended Spelman Seminary (now Spelman College) and earned bachelor's degrees in music and liberal arts from Oberlin College in 1926. In 1928 she joined the *YWCA (Young Women's Christian Association) as a national secretary for colleges in the South. In 1932 she married Howard Thurman. The founder and editor of the *Aframerican Women's Journal*, Thurman served as founder and first chairperson of the *National Council of Negro Women's National Library, Archives, and Museum. In 1944 Thurman helped her husband and Alfred G. Fisk establish the Church for the Fellowship of All Peoples in San Francisco, an interreligious and interracial church. Thurman authored several books, including *Pioneers of Negro Origin in California* (1949) and *The Historical Cookbook of the American Negro* (1958).

Obituary, "Sue Bailey Thurman, Pioneering Activist, Dies at 93," *Jet* (20 January 1997); Bailey and Thurman Family Papers, Emory University.

LOUISE GRAVES

Thurston, Matilda Smyrell Calder (1875–1958). Missionary and college founder. Matilda Calder was reared in a Presbyterian family and was a 1896 graduate of Mount Holyoke College. In 1902 she married Lawrence Thurston, and they founded the Yale-in-China mission in Peking. They left after only a few months, owing to Lawrence's declining health; he died of tuberculosis in 1904. Thurston returned to China, and in 1915 she became the founder and president of Ginling College. In 1928 Thurston resigned her presidency to Wu Yifang, one of Ginling's first graduates, in the face of growing nationalist sentiments. She worked with the college and relief agencies in China until World War II, when the Japanese interned her for the duration of the war. In 1955 she published *Ginling College*, a history of the school.

ANB; Reuben Holden, *Yale in China* (1964); Henry B. Wright, *A Life with a Purpose* (1908).

CATHERINE BOWLER

Tibbles, Susette LaFlesche (1854–1903). Intercultural mediator, activist, and author. Susette LaFlesche, daughter of an Omaha chief, was educated at the Omaha Nation's Presbyterian mission school and at the Elizabeth Institute for Young Ladies (New Jersey). She then taught at the Omaha Indian school and witnessed the forced removal of the Ponca Nation. When Standing Bear was imprisoned, a local journalist, Thomas Tibbles, became his advocate. LaFlesche wrote to Tibbles and became involved with the case. After Standing Bear's trial resulted in the landmark 1879 ruling that Native People were "persons" under the U.S. Constitution, LaFlesche continued her activism, toured and lectured against removal, spoke before Congress, and traveled to England and Scotland. She married Tibbles in 1881 and wrote the introductions to several of his publications, as well as numerous articles and children's stories.

NoAW; Karen Kilcup, ed., *Native American Women's Writing* (2000); Dorothy Clarke Wilson, *Bright Eyes* (1974).

LISA J. POIRIER

Tillman, Alberta Ruth (1913–78). United Church of Canada deaconess. Raised amid an inactive church family, Ruth Tillman's church involvement began after her sister's suicide during their teen years. Involvement with the church's Young People's Union inspired Tillman's call to ministry. After graduating from the United Church Training School (Toronto) in 1947, Tillman spent one year in ministry at Stella Mission (Winnipeg). Tillman was then designated as a deaconess and began 12 years of Christian education work in Newfoundland. After a sabbatical to study theology in Scotland, Tillman spent her remaining years in ministry with the Canadian Council of Churches. A common element of Tillman's varied ministries was her involvement with church camping, through which she became a mentor to countless young women in Canada.

Association of Professional Church Workers, "The Newsletter: Historical Issue" (1988); Shirley Davy, *Women, Work, and Worship* (1983); United Church of Canada/Victoria University Archives.

SARAH BRUER

Tilly, Dorothy Eugenia Rogers (1883–1970). Civil rights activist. A descendant of Virginia gentry and daughter of a Methodist minister, Dorothy Rogers was reared in a religious, middle-class household that prized education and social responsibility. She married Milton Tilly in 1903. Tilly worked with the Women's Missionary Society, promoted improved race relations with the Commission on Interracial Cooperation, and crusaded against lynching. Tilly's work through the Southern Regional Council and the President's Committee on Civil Rights had made her a national civil rights leader by the 1940s. In 1949 she founded the Fellowship of the Concerned (FOC), which mobilized southern women to seek fair trials, safe voting registration, and integrated schools for African Americans. As desegregation approached, the FOC prepared women to reeducate their own families to accept integration.

ANB; Edith Holbrook Riehm, *Throwing Off the Cloak of Privilege: White Southern Women Activists in the Civil Rights Era* (2004); Alice G. Knotts, *Fellowship of Love: Methodist Women Changing American Racial Attitudes* (1996).

CATHERINE BOWLER

Tingley, Katherine Augusta Westcott (1847–1929). Theosophical leader. Katherine Tingley was a native of Newbury, Massachusetts. By the 1880s she lived in New York City and was active in philanthropic works; she founded an organization for prison and hospital visitations and the Do-Good Mission. Tingley emerged as a leader in the Theosophical Society in America after 1896. By 1900 she established the Point Loma Community (near San Diego), a center for the arts and social reform, and the location for the Raja Yoga school and college. Tingley's strong personality sometimes alienated her subordinates, which may explain why Point Loma struggled financially in spite of other successes. Tingley did not succeed in her desire to found other similar communities.

ANB; NoAW; W. Michael Ashcroft, *The Dawn of the New Cycle: Point Loma Theosophists and American Culture* (2002); Grace F. Knoche, "Katherine Tingley: A Biographical Sketch," *Sunrise: Theosophic Perspectives* (April/May 1998); Katherine Tingley and Point Loma, www.theosophy-nw.org/theosnw/theos/kt-selec.htm.

MARY FARRELL BEDNAROWSKI

Towne, Elizabeth Lois Jones (1865–1961). New Thought lecturer, author, and editor. Elizabeth Lois Jones moved from Portland, Oregon, to Holyoke, Massachusetts, after a failed early marriage. A former Methodist, she had become a successful New Thought healer but gave up this career to become a lecturer and writer. In 1900 she married William E. Towne, and together they built a profitable business in New Thought publishing. In 1898 Towne founded *Nautilus* magazine, in publication for more than 50 years. She was the author of numerous magazine articles and 13 books, among them *Joy Philosophy* (1903) and *How to Use New Thought in Home Life* (1915). In 1924 she was elected president of the International New Thought Alliance. Well known beyond the New Thought community, Towne served as a director of the Massachusetts Federation of Women's Clubs.

EAWR; Charles S. Braden, *Spirits in Rebellion: The Rise and Development of New Thought* (1963); Elizabeth Towne, *Experiences in Self-Healing* (1905).

MARY FARRELL BEDNAROWSKI

Towner, Margaret Ellen (1925–). First woman ordained in the Presbyterian Church in the U.S.A. (PCUSA). The daughter of a Presbyterian minister, Margaret Towner was born in Columbia, Missouri, but grew up in cities throughout the Midwest. She pursued an education in music and a career in photography. She settled in Syracuse, New York, in 1949 to open a photography studio. Through her volunteer work with church music and education programs she sensed a call to ministry and obtained a divinity degree at Union Theological Seminary. She served as an educator in churches in Tacoma Park, Maryland, and Allentown, Pennsylvania. The PCUSA approved the ordination of women in 1956, and Towner was ordained on October 24, 1956, the first woman ordained in the denomination. She served churches in Michigan, Indiana, and Wisconsin until her retirement in 1990.

John D. Krugler and David Weinberg-Kinsey, "Equality of Leadership: The Ordinations of Sarah E. Dickson and Margaret E. Towner in the Presbyterian Church in the USA," *American Presbyterians* 68, no. 4 (Winter 1990).

BEVERLY A. ZINK-SAWYER

Traxler, Margaret Ellen (1924–2002). Activist and cofounder of the *National Coalition of American Nuns (NCAN). Margaret Ellen Traxler, SSND (School Sisters of Notre Dame), taught for two decades as "Sister Mary Peter" before she found her calling as an activist after marching with Martin Luther King Jr. in 1965. In 1969 she was central in founding NCAN. For the next 30 years Traxler consistently (and often controversially) challenged the church to seek social justice. Traxler was arrested in St. Peter's

Square for protesting the exclusion of women religious from the worldwide 1994 Bishops' Synod. Traxler worked in Chicago in prison ministries and founded two homeless shelters for women. A dynamic and prayerful individual, she was beloved for her outspokenness and admired for her dedication.

NCAN, *If Anyone Can NCAN: Twenty Years of Speaking Out* (1989); Papers, Special Collections and University Archives, Marquette University.

MARY J. HENOLD

Truth, Sojourner (Isabella Baumfree) (ca. 1791–1883). Itinerant evangelist, abolitionist, and women's rights activist. Isabella Baumfree (or Bomefree) was bought and sold several times in New York while she was still a child. She married a slave named Thomas, and they had five children. After the 1827 State of New York Emancipation Act, Baumfree moved with her son to New York City, where she worked as a live-in domestic. She became involved in a religious cult known as the Kingdom, whose leader, Matthias, beat her and assigned her the heaviest workload. The turning point in her life came on June 1, 1843, when she adopted a new name, Sojourner Truth, and headed east. She preached at camp meetings, lived in a utopian community (in Massachusetts), and spoke on abolition and women's rights. In 1851 she gave her famous "Ain't I a Woman" speech at a women's rights convention in Akron, Ohio. She came to champion the idea of establishing a colony for freed slaves in the West, where they would be self-supportive and self-reliant.

ANB; BWA; DARB; EAWR; EE; NBAW; NoAW; Nell Irvin Painter, *Sojourner Truth: A Life, a Symbol* (1996); Carleton Mabee, *Sojourner Truth: Slave, Prophet, Legend* (1993); Olive Gilbert and Frances Titus, *Narrative of Sojourner Truth* (1875).

PRISCILLA POPE-LEVISON

Tubman, Harriet Ross (ca. 1820–1913). Leader in the Underground Railroad. Born a slave in Maryland, Harriet Tubman escaped to Philadelphia in 1849. She then became a "conductor" on the Underground Railroad, an organization in the border states that helped slaves escape to New York and Canada. From 1850 to 1860 Tubman made 19 trips into the South to lead approximately 300 slaves to freedom. She always carried a pistol with her so that she could give slaves who did not want to continue the choice of continuing or dying. She drugged infants, to keep them quiet, and carried them in sacks. Slave owners placed a $40,000 bounty for her capture or death. In 1858 she plotted with John Brown the unsuccessful raid on Harper's Ferry, but illness prevented her participation in the raid. During the Civil War, Tubman was a nurse, scout, spy, military guide, and officer. Her help in freeing slaves earned her the admiration of slaves who passed on military information they had overheard. Tubman helped plan and lead a group of black soldiers into South Carolina to disable a Confederate supply line. After the war Tubman worked for women's suffrage and founded a home for the elderly and the poor.

ANB; BWA; EAWR; NBAW; NoAW; Michael Martin, *Harriet Tubman and the Underground Railroad* (2005); Catherine Clinton, *Harriet Tubman* (2004); Kate Clifford Larson, *Bound for the Promised Land* (2004); Carol Hymowitz and Michaele Weissman, *A History of Women in America* (1978).

KEITH DURSO

Tucker, Helen Boonn (1905–97). Activist. Helen Boonn studied at universities in Michigan and Bordeaux, France. She married and moved to Toronto. Tucker was a founder of the Voices of Women (VOW) in 1960. She presided over the St. Lawrence Unitarian Universalist District, pushed for the Royal

Commission on the Status of Women, and founded the Canadian chapter of World Citizens.

Irene Baros-Johnson and Mary Lu MacDonald, *Concise Portraits of Canadian Unitarian and Universalist Women* (2006).

IRENE BAROS-JOHNSON

Tuite, Marjorie (1922–86). Educator, activist, and organizer. Born in New York City, Marjorie Tuite made vows in 1942 as a *Dominican Sister of St. Mary of the Springs (Columbus, Ohio), taught in U.S. Catholic schools, and held a faculty position at the Jesuit School of Theology in Chicago (1973–81). Linking educational work with social justice advocacy, Tuite was an influential leader in *NETWORK (a Catholic social justice lobby), the *National Assembly of Women Religious, and *Church Women United. Tuite's stance was consistently radical. In 1982 she founded Women's Coalition to Stop Intervention in Central America, and in 1984 she signed the *New York Times* advertisement calling U.S. Catholic bishops to dialogue on abortion. She is buried in Managua alongside others who worked for justice in Nicaragua.

Papers, Women and Leadership Archives, Loyola University Chicago.

MARGARET MCMANUS

Tuttle, Annie Leake (1839–1934). Methodist teacher and missionary. Annie Leake was born near Crossroads, Nova Scotia, and received training at the provincial normal school in Truro. She taught there and at the Methodist normal school in St. John's, Newfoundland, where she was a charter member of a Methodist Woman's Missionary Society (WMS) auxiliary. In 1887 she became the first matron of the WMS Chinese Rescue Home in Victoria, British Columbia. The mission provided a home for prostitutes and "slave girls" who appeared to be doomed to prostitution. Returning to Nova Scotia she married Milledge Tuttle in 1895. She retained her commitment to missions, becoming a district organizer for the WMS both during her marriage and after her husband's death.

Marilyn Färdig Whiteley, ed., *The Life and Letters of Annie Leake Tuttle* (1999).

MARILYN FÄRDIG WHITELEY

Tyler, Adeline Blanchard (1805–75) Deaconess and nurse. Adeline Blanchard was raised a Congregationalist in Massachusetts, but became an Episcopalian after her marriage. She was set apart as a deaconess shortly after her husband's death in 1853. After studying nursing at the deaconess institute in Kaiserwerth, Germany, she was invited to establish St. Andrew's Infirmary for the destitute in Baltimore. Tyler resigned her post as head deaconess of the infirmary after a man was hired as business manager, and she opened a deaconess house in the same city. After the outbreak of the Civil War she treated wounded on both sides of the conflict. She later served as superintendent of military hospitals in Baltimore, Chester, and Annapolis. In 1869 Tyler became the superintendent of the new Children's Hospital in Boston. In recognition of her work she was elected an associate of the Sisters of St. Margaret, Boston.

NoAW; David Hein and Gardiner H. Shattuck Jr., *The Episcopalians* (2003); Theresa McDevitt, *Women and the American Civil War* (2003); Joan E. Lynaugh, editorial, *Nursing History Review* 1 (1993); Papers, Children's Hospital (Boston) Archival Collections.

SHERYL A. KUJAWA-HOLBROOK

Tzu Chi (Ciji) Foundation (Buddhist Compassion Relief) (1966–). International relief organization. The Tzu Chi Compassionate Relief Association was founded by a 29-year-old Buddhist nun, Venerable Cheng Yen (Pinyin:

Zhengyan), in Taiwan with the support of 30 Taiwanese housewives. In the U.S., it had developed six chapters, 49 offices, and 12 weekend schools by the year 2004. Tzu Chi was established in Vancouver in 1992 and has members across Canada. Membership consists primarily of Chinese immigrant women from Taiwan. Members engage in local and international charity; support medical, educational, and cultural endeavors; and promote humanity.

Richard Madsen, *Democracy's Dharma* (2007); Cheng Yen, *Still Thoughts*, 2 vols. (1993, 1995); S. J. Chen, "Understanding the Buddhist Tzu-Chi Association: A Cultural Approach" (PhD diss., University of Southern California, 1990); Charles Prebish, *American Buddhism* (1979).

BARBARA E. REED

Underwood, Lillias Stirling Horton (1851–1921). Presbyterian missionary doctor. Lillias Sterling Horton began her mission career in 1888. With a medical degree from Woman's Medical College (Chicago) she was sent to serve as a physician primarily to the women and children of the Land of the Morning Calm. Upon her arrival in Seoul she was appointed as physician to Queen Min, with whom she developed a trusting friendship. In 1889 Horton married Horace Underwood, the first ordained Protestant missionary to enter Korea. Despite the suspicion Koreans at the time held for Western medicine, Underwood provided exceptional medical care during the cholera epidemic of 1895. The Underwoods worked together to expand the Presbyterian Church in Korea and to build hospitals. Underwood recorded her experiences in Korea and her relationship with the queen in her book, *Fifteen Years among the Top Knots* (1904).

NoAW; James H. Smylie et al., *Go Therefore: 150 Years of Presbyterian Global Missions* (1987).

ELIZABETH HINSON-HASTY

Union of Orthodox Jewish Congregations of America (UOJCA), Women's Branch (Women's Branch of the Orthodox Union) (1923–). Organization of Orthodox Synagogue Sisterhoods. In 1902 the UO undertook efforts to unify modern Orthodox congregations across the U.S. and to implement national initiatives. Following pressure from an initial group of women from synagogue sisterhood organizations in New York (among them noted rabbis' wives), the women's branch was formed. The women's branch has participated in a variety of influential activities. It played a key role in the establishment of the Kashruth Division of the UO (kosher supervision), fund raising for Yeshiva College (now Yeshiva University), and the establishment of Hebrew Teachers Training Institute for Girls (later renamed the Teachers Institute for Women and integrated into Yeshiva University).

Blu Greenberg, "Orthdox Jewish Women in America: Diversity, Challenges, and Coming of Age," in *Encyclopedia of Women and Religion in North America*, vol. 2, ed. Rosemary Skinner Keller et al. (2006).

KAREN-MARIE WOODS

Ursuline Sisters (Ursulines of the Roman Union) (OSU) (1535–). First Roman Catholic women's congregation in North America. Originally a lay community of 28 companions named the Company of St. Ursula (after the patron saint of education), the order was founded by Angela Merici in 1535 in Brescia, Italy. The congregation grew rapidly throughout Italy and beyond, especially to France, where by the 17th century the sisters had become a religious order and made the education of young women a prominent feature of their mission. From France missionary outposts were established in North America. They began with Quebec, where in 1638 they were the first to teach young women in the New World. In 1727 they established the first school for girls in New Orleans. They bore the brunt of antipopery sentiment, because they were visibly Catholic in dress and because of their independence, which violated then-prevalent social norms for women. The most tragic episode was the burning of their convent in Charlestown, Massachusetts, in 1834. After a relentless anti-Catholic campaign in New England, in which the nuns were accused of the most lurid and outlandish deeds and Catholics were said to be using parochial schools to take over the country (a campaign fueled in part by prominent Protestant clergyman Lyman Beecher), an angry mob burned the convent to the ground. Despite this setback the Ursulines regrouped elsewhere and established convents throughout the U.S. By 2000 there were 3,600 members of the order in the U.S.

DARB; EACH; NCE; ROWUS; Nancy Lusignan Schultz, *Fire and Roses: The Burning of the Charlestown Convent* (2002); George C. Stewart Jr., *Marvels of Charity: History of American Sisters and Nuns* (1994).

MARY JANE O'DONNELL

Utley, Uldine (1912–95). Child evangelist. At the age of nine, Uldine Utley was converted at an *Aimee Semple McPherson evangelistic meeting. Within two years Utley began to preach throughout the U.S. and Canada. In 1926 she preached to 14,000 people at Madison Square Garden. Her popularity waned in her adulthood. A brief marriage was annulled when she collapsed mentally, and she spent her remaining 57 years in mental institutions.

EE; Uldine Utley, *Why I Am a Preacher* (1931).

PRISCILLA POPE-LEVISON

Van Cott, Margaret Ann ("Maggie") Newton (1830–1914). Evangelist and social reformer. After the death of her husband in 1866 Van Cott joined the Methodist Episcopal (ME) Church and began to lead prayer meetings and Bible studies at the Five Points Mission in New York City. Although she was initially reluctant to preach, her effective work at the mission led to numerous preaching invitations. After receiving an exhorter's license in 1868 she was granted a local preacher's license in 1869, most likely the first woman in the MEC credentialed in this way. In 1870 Van Cott was asked to serve as an interim pastor in a prominent congregation where the New England Annual Conference met, resulting in her preaching to the gathering. Van Cott traveled as an evangelist between 3,000 and 7,000 miles a year for more than 30 years. Although she was recommended for ordination in California, the presiding bishop refused to consider her. Despite her effectiveness as a preacher, all local preacher's licenses granted to ME women were revoked in 1880. Van Cott retired in 1902, credited with the conversion of some 75,000 persons.

ANB; EAWR; EE; NoAW; Nancy Hardesty, *Women Called to Witness*, 2nd ed. (1999) [1984].

LACEYE C. WARNER

Vautrin, Minnie (1886–1941). Missionary educator. Born of French immigrants in Illinois, Minnie Vautrin taught mathematics for several years before receiving her BA in science from the University of Illinois. Upon her graduation in 1912 she moved to China to become principal of a girl's school in Luchow that was operated by the Disciples of Christ. She devoted her furloughs to advanced study and received an MA from Teachers College at Columbia University. Vautrin is best known for her protection and care of refugees during the capture and sack of Nanking by the Japanese army in 1937, when she headed the education department at Ginling College. Women and children poured into the college, where Vautrin was left with three teachers. She refused to abandon her charges. At the end of the war Vautrin was awarded the Emblem of the Blue Jade, the highest honor the Chinese government could bestow at that time.

NoAW; United Christian Missionary Society, *They Went to China* (1948).

BETH SPAULDING

Vennard, Iva Durham (1871–1945). Methodist holiness deaconess, evangelist, and educator. After experiencing conversion and sanctification, Iva Vennard worked as a deaconess evangelist and founded a deaconess training school in St. Louis. In 1910 she founded Chicago Evangelistic Institute and was its principal until her death. The school continues as Vennard College (Iowa). She was on the executive board of the Association of Women Preachers.

Mary Ella Bowie, *Alabaster and Spikenard* (1947).

PRISCILLA POPE-LEVISON

Visitation Sisters (Order of the Visitation of Holy Mary) (VHM) (1610–). Roman Catholic women's congregation. Founded in 1610 by Jane Frances de Chantal and Francis de Sales as a community of laywomen who sought a life of prayer and service in the world, the Visitations (Visitandines) were soon forced into the cloister as a result of the restrictive attitudes toward women in 17th-century France. In addition to its founders, the most prominent Visitandine has been Margaret Mary Alcacoque, whose devotion to the Sacred Heart was prompted by her continual visions of the suffering Christ. The Visitation Sisters were established in the U.S. by Jesuit Leonard Neale, president of Georgetown College and bishop (later archbishop of Baltimore), and Teresa (Alice) Lalor, an Irish immigrant. Working with a small group of laywomen known as the Pious Ladies, they established a school on the grounds of what would become the Georgetown Visitation Convent in 1799. This was the first school for girls established in the original 13 states. By 1816 the women were granted entry into the Order of the Visitation, and a convent was established that continues to this day, as do the congregations which it spawned throughout the U.S. Although the nuns have continued to operate schools in the U.S., they have also established strictly contemplative convents where they live in seclusion and prayer.

NCE; ROWUS; *The Official Catholic Directory*; George C. Steward Jr., *Marvels of Charity: History of American Sisters and Nuns* (1994); G. P. and R. H. Lathrop, *A Study of Courage: Annals of the Georgetown Convent of the Visitation* (1895).

MARY JANE O'DONNELL

Voth, Martha Moser (1862–1901). Missionary. Martha Moser was born in Dalton, Ohio. She married Heinrich R. Voth in 1892, and together they created a significant archival source of photographs and diaries that document life in the Hopi pueblo of Oraibi (Arizona) at the turn of the 20th century. Sent as Mennonite missionaries the Voths recorded religious rituals, daily life, and especially the disruptions to their society brought about by U.S. government policy. Voth's husband sold the collection of photographs, artifacts, and documents to the Field Museum in Chicago.

Cathy Ann Trotta, "Mennonite Missionary Martha Moser Voth in the Hopi Pueblos, 1893–1910," in *Strangers at Home*, ed. Kimberly D. Schmidt et al. (2002); Lois Barrett, *The Vision and the Reality: The Story of Home Missions in the General Conference Mennonite Church* (1983).

VALERIE REMPEL

Wallace, Elsie May Marble (1868–1946). Pastor and district superintendent. The leading pastor of the Church of the Nazarene's early Northwest District (encompassing Washington and Oregon), Elsie Wallace was ordained in 1902 by Phineas Bresee, the church's leading founder. Wallace founded and led Spokane (Washington) First Church of the Nazarene and was pastor of two other large and influential Nazarene congregations: Seattle First Church and Walla Walla First Church. She was also a pastor in California and helped establish congregations in Oregon and Idaho. Wallace served 45 years in active ministry. She was a clergy member on various denominational boards and committees, beginning in 1908 as a member of the denomination's first General Missionary Board. In 1920 she was appointed to lead the Northwest District, the first woman to be a Nazarene district superintendent and the only one until 1988 to hold that office within her church.

Rebecca Laird, *Ordained Women in the Church of the Nazarene* (1993); Stan Ingersol, "Nazarene Women in Ordained Ministry: A Historical Roadmap," *Grow* 3, no. 2 (Summer 1992); Obituary, *Herald of Holiness* (25 March 1946).

ANNIE RUSSELL

Ward, Kay Lynaugh (1942–). First woman bishop in the Moravian Church. An educator by initial training and disposition, Kay Ward was ordained a Moravian minister in 1979. She pastored several congregations (sometimes with her husband, Aden) and was director of continuing education at the Moravian Theological Seminary when she was elected a bishop by the Northern Province of the Moravian Church in 1998. She thereby became the first woman bishop in the worldwide Moravian Unity. (Moravian bishops serve lifelong terms and are considered spiritual leaders, not administrators.)

Nora I. Adam, comp., *Moravian Women of Faith Today: Autobiographies of Contemporary Women*, book 2 (1990?); Gustav Niebuhr, "Women Smash Yet Another Barrier," *New York Times*, 15 August 1998.

ELEANOR J. STEBNER

Ward, Margaret Mae Yoho (1900–1983). Christian Church (Disciples of Christ) missionary and executive. Born and raised in West Virginia, Margaret Mae Yoho graduated from Bethany College in 1923. Denied admission to the all-male Yale Divinity School she received a graduate degree from their School of Education in 1926. Shortly afterward she married a Stone-Campbell Movement preacher, Norman Ward, and they spent six years as missionaries in Argentina. Between 1941 and 1967 she held a variety of executive positions in the United Christian Missionary Society (UCMS). She was called out of retirement in 1969 to join the staff of the Board of Higher Education of the Christian Church, serving until 1976. In addition to her work with the UCMS, Ward served on the National Council of Churches and was a speaker in high demand on subjects like civil rights, foreign missions, and the rights of immigrant farm workers.

ES-CM.

SCOTT D. SEAY

Ward, Mary Gray Phelps ("Elizabeth Stuart Phelps") (1844–1911). Author. Mary Gray Phelps was born in Massachusetts to a well-known mother, *Elizabeth Stuart Phelps, who was an author, and a father who was a professor of homiletics at Andover Theological Seminary. Elizabeth Phelps died when Mary was just eight years old, and Mary eventually adopted and published under her deceased mother's name. Mary Phelps married journalist Herbert Ward in 1888. Beginning with Sunday school literature, Ward (as Elizabeth Stuart Phelps) published in various genres, but she became best known for her spiritualist trilogy: *The Gates Ajar* (1868), *Beyond the Gates* (1883), and *The Gates Between*

(1887). These novels depicted grief, unfinished earthly lives, and spirit visitations, along with vivid portraits of a comfortable material afterlife. Although typical of the "consolation" literature of its time, her fiction is significant for its strong female heroines and her conviction that spiritualist beliefs could conform to Christian theological tenets.

ANB; NoAW; Elizabeth Stuart, "Elizabeth Stuart Phelps: A Good Feminist Woman Doing Bad Theology?" in *Feminist Theology* 26 (2001); Elizabeth Stuart Phelps, *Three Spiritualist Novels,* intro. Nina Baym (2000); Carol Farley Kessler, "A Literary Legacy: Elizabeth Stuart Phelps, Mother and Daughter," *Frontiers: A Journal of Women Studies* 5, no. 3 (Autumn 1980).

SANDRA L. BEARDSALL

Ward, Nancy (Nanye'hi) (ca. 1738–1822). Cherokee leader and intercultural mediator. Born into the Wolf Clan of the Cherokee Nation, Nancy Ward distinguished herself as a leader among her people. Following her husband, Kingfisher, to war against the Creek Nation in 1755 she took his place when he fell in battle. This act of courage earned her the name and title Nanye'hi (War Woman), the right to speak and vote in the council of chiefs, and leadership of the women's council. She was married briefly to Bryant Ward, who returned to his European American wife and children after a few years, but who remained on good terms with Nanye'hi. She sided with the revolutionaries during the American Revolution. After the war she served among Cherokee delegates at major treaty conferences and petitioned the Cherokee national council on behalf of all Cherokee women. Ward established a plantation in North Carolina, but as the Cherokee lost more land, she moved to the Ocoee River Valley, Tennessee, and ran an inn for travelers. After her death the new Cherokee constitution barred women from the general council.

ANB; NaAW; NoAW; Karen Kilcup, ed., *Native American Women's Writing* (2000); Theda Perdue, *Cherokee Women* (1998).

LISA J. POIRIER

Warde, Mary Frances Xavier (1810–84). Founder of *Sisters of Mercy in the U.S. Mary Warde was born in County Queens, Ireland. At the age of 16 she moved to Dublin, where in 1828 she met Catherine McAuley, founder of the Sisters of Mercy. Warde joined McAuley in 1831, professed in 1833, and became superior in 1836 at a newly established community in Carlow. After founding three more communities in Ireland, Warde, with six other sisters, was sent to Pittsburgh in 1843. Under her direction, the Pittsburgh community established a convent, orphanage, three schools, and a hospital within four years and expanded to Latrobe. By the time of her death, Warde had overseen the establishment of 25 convents in 11 states, including New York, Nebraska, Illinois, and California. These communities established schools, orphanages, hospitals, and other social service institutions that proved critical in the formation of U.S. Catholicism.

ANB; EACH; NCE; ROWUS; Kathleen A. Healy, *Frances Warde* (1973).

SANDRA YOCUM MIZE

Washington, Margaret Murray (ca. 1861–1925). Educator and social reformer. Born in rural Mississippi to a black mother and a white father, Margaret Murray was raised by Quakers after the death of her father. She graduated from Fisk University in 1886 and began teaching at Tuskegee Institute in 1889. She soon became dean of the girls' institute, a position that she held until her death. She married Booker T. Washington in 1891, becoming his third wife. In 1895 she organized the Tuskegee Woman's Club, an auxiliary to the institute. She advocated the consolidation of local clubs into the *National Association of Colored Women and was its president from 1912 to 1918. She helped organize a pioneering women's conference in 1920 that brought together white and black reformers. An irenic spirit and a commitment to industrial education were themes of her life's work.

ANB; BWA; NBAW.

SCOTT D. SEAY

Wasserman, Dora Goldfarb (1919–2003). Theatre founder, director, and actress. Born in Chernikov, Russia, Dora Goldfarb trained with the Moscow Yiddish Academy. During World War II she toured with the Kiev State Theatre and later staged Yiddish plays in displaced persons' camps. She married Shura Wasserman in 1944, and in 1950 they immigrated to Montreal. Wasserman worked for the Jewish Public Library, the Jewish Peoples' and Peretz schools. In 1958 she produced her first Yiddish play and went on to establish North America's only resident Yiddish theatre company. Wasserman produced 25 plays in Montreal and toured with the company to Israel, the U.S., Austria, and Russia. Recognized as a grande dame of theatre and a cultural protector of Yiddish she was invested as a member of the Order of Canada in 1992 and the Order of Quebec in 2003.

Ariel Zilber, "Dora Wasserman, Yiddish Theater's Grand Dame, Dies," *Jewish Daily Forward* (26 December 2003); Alan Hustak, "Dora Wasserman, the Indefatigable Founding Director of Canada's Only Yiddish Theatre Died at 84," *Jewish Theatre News* (December 2003); Edmond Lipsitz, *Canadian Jewish Women Today* (1983).

TRUDY FLYNN

Waters, Ethel (1896–1977). Performer, dancer, actress, and singer. Racism and poverty marked Ethel Waters's early years. She experienced her first spiritual awakening at the age of 12 at a black Pentecostal church. In 1917 Waters gave her debut singing performance in a Philadelphia saloon. Tall and thin, she was given the stage name Sweet Mama Stringbean. She worked the vaudeville circuit and established a distinctive jazz vocal style. Waters also performed in Broadway musicals and dramatic plays, and in film and television. In 1957, empty and spent, Waters attended the Billy Graham New York Crusade where she rededicated her life to Christ. She devoted increasing amounts of time to church work, Youth for Christ meetings, and Billy Graham crusades.

ANB; BWA; EAWR; EE; NBAW; Sally Plaskin, *American Women in Jazz* (1982); Ethel Waters, *His Eye Is on the Sparrow* (1951).

JUDITH L. GIBBARD

Watteville, Henrietta Benigna Zinzendorf von (1725–89). Founder of Moravian women's education in the U.S. Benigna Zinzendorf was the daughter of Nikolaus (leader of the Moravian Church), and Ermuth Dorothea von Zinzendorf. In 1741 Zinzendorf accompanied her father to Pennsylvania, where they established a school for German settlers in eastern Pennsylvania in 1742 and appointed Zinzendorf as head of staff. After her return to Germany, Zinzendorf became the head of the single sisters for the worldwide Moravian Church. (Refer to *Moravian Women Choirs.) In 1746 she married Johannes von Watteville. The couple visited Pennsylvania in 1748, during which time von Watteville reorganized her school. After her mother's death in 1756 von Watteville became mistress of the family estates in Germany. She was part of the governing council that administered the church after the death of her father in 1760. Her last visit to America in 1783 included a shipwreck off of the island of Barbuda.

Transactions of the Moravian Historical Society 27 (1992); Mabel Haller, *Early Moravian Education in Pennsylvania* (1953).

CRAIG D. ATWOOD

Way, Amanda J. (1828–1914). Reformer and minister. Amanda Way grew up in Winchester, Indiana, and opened a dressmaking and millinery shop to support her widowed mother. Way's interest in abolition, temperance, and women's rights began early. She gave her first antislavery lecture at the age of 20. She was instrumental in founding the Indiana Woman's Rights Society and organized 50 women into a woman's temperance army, which raided local saloons. She gave temperance lectures, helped in the passage of Prohibition laws in Indiana and Kansas, and organized the Kansas chapter of the *Woman's Christian Temperance Union. Although a Quaker, Way was influenced by evangelical Protestantism. In 1871 she became a minister of the Methodist Episcopal Church. When the church voted to discontinue licensing female preachers, Way returned to her Quaker roots. Once again a minister she moved to Whittier, California.

ANB; NoAW; Elizabeth Cady Stanton et al., *History of Woman Suffrage* (1881).

JANET MOORE LINDMAN

Webb, Mary (1779–1861). Baptist churchwoman and organizer of a mission society. From her wheelchair, Mary Webb organized the Boston Female Society for Missionary Purposes in 1800, probably the first women's missionary society in the U.S. She was its treasurer and corresponding secretary for over 50 years. The society initially included Baptist and Congregational women and supported home and foreign missions. It established a regular concert of prayer for women in 1812 and corresponded with at least 120 other societies over the years. It divided along denominational lines in 1829, and Webb served the Baptist society until its demise. Webb also ministered among the poor, was the superintendent of the first Sabbath school established by Boston's Second Baptist Church, and organized or supported other missionary and benevolent societies.

HDB; R. Pierce Beaver, *American Protestant Women in World Mission,* 2nd ed. (1980) [1968]; Albert L. Vail, *Mary Webb and the Mother Society* (1914).

KENDAL P. MOBLEY

Wedel, Cynthia Clark (1908–86). Episcopalian leader and ecumenist. Cynthia Wedel was the first woman to head the U.S. National Council of Churches (1969–72) and to be president of the World Council of Churches (1975–83). She grew up in Evanston, Illinois, and earned her BA and MA at Northwestern University. She entered teaching after her marriage to the Reverend Theodore Wedel in 1939. Wedel used positions on the national board of the Episcopal women's auxiliary and the executive council to increase women's opportunities. She held national leadership roles in the Girl Scouts, Red Cross, Commission on the Status of Women, and *Church Women United. In 1957 she earned her PhD in psychology. Wedel served as one of three women consultants to the 1978 meeting of Anglican bishops at Lambeth.

ANBO; DARB; RLA; Archive collections in the Episcopal Women's History Project (Episcopal Church U.S.A.), World Council of Churches (Geneva), and the National Council of Churches (New York City).

JOAN R. GUNDERSEN

Weilerstein, Sadie Rose (1894–1993). Author of Jewish children's books. Raised and educated in Rochester, New York, Sadie Weilerstein began a career as an English teacher. She was inspired to create her first book for children, *What Danny Did* (1928), to provide her young son a positive reflection of Jewish life from a child's perspective. Her most famous literary character was K'tonton, a thumb-sized boy whose life lessons exemplified both Conservative Jewish and broadly humanistic values. Weilerstein received numerous awards in her lifetime, including the Jewish Book Council of America Award and the Yovel Award, given by the National Women's League of the United Synagogue of America.

JWA; *Something about the Author*, vol. 3 (1972) and vol. 75 (1994); Sadie Rose Weilerstein, *K'tonton in Israel* (1964), *What the Moon Brought* (1942), *The Adventures of K'tonton* (1935).

EMILY ALICE KATZ

Weiss-Rosmarin, Trude (1908–89). Editor, scholar, and Jewish intellectual. Born in Frankfurt-am-Main, Germany, to a wealthy Orthodox Jewish family, Trude Weiss received a secular and religious education generally reserved for boys. In 1931, after earning a doctorate in Semitics, archaeology, and philosophy, Weiss-Rosmarin immigrated to New York City with her husband, Aaron Rosmarin. In 1935 the couple published the first volume of a newsletter, renamed the *Jewish Spectator* in 1936. In 1943 Weiss-Rosmarin became its editor, and under her leadership it emerged as a premiere intellectual journal. Her editorial columns addressed issues such as Zionism, feminism, and Jewish survival. Weiss-Rosmarin authored books in her academic areas and on contemporary Jewish affairs. At a time when few women received higher education, hyphenated their last names, or took on positions of leadership, Weiss-Rosmarin was a pathfinder.

ANB; JWA; NoAWC; Deborah Dash Moore, "Trude Weiss-Rosmarin and the *Jewish Spectator*," in *The "Other" New York Jewish Intellectuals*, ed. Carole Kessner (1994).

LILA CORWIN BERMAN

Wells-Barnett, Ida Bell (1862–1931). Journalist and civil rights leader. Ida B. Wells was born in rural Mississippi to former slaves. She began teaching to support her seven siblings after her parents died in 1878. In 1884 she successfully sued the Chesapeake and Ohio Railroad after she was forced from a train for refusing to sit in a segregated car, a decision later reversed by the Tennessee State Supreme Court. From 1889 to 1892 she edited several church-related newspapers, wrote exposés of racial violence, and encouraged freedmen to emigrate from the South. The Memphis School Board fired her in 1891 because of these publications. Threats against her life forced her to move to the North. She settled in Chicago by 1893. In 1895 she married Ferdinand Barnett, and they raised four children. In the 1910s and 1920s she worked through the National Association for the Advancement of Colored People (NAACP) and her own local initiative, the Negro Fellowship League. By 1916 she affiliated with Marcus Garvey's United Negro Improvement Association. In response to the race riots in St. Louis (1917), Chicago (1919), and Arkansas (1922) she published essays, editorials, and pamphlets that linked oppression and racial violence to white economic self-interest.

ANB; BWA; NBAW; NoAW; WBC; Patricia Schechter, *Ida B. Wells-Barnett and American Reform* (2001); Linda McMurray Edwards, *To Keep the Waters Troubled* (1998); Alfreda Duster, ed., *The Autobiography of Ida B. Wells* (1970); William Greaves, dir., *Ida B. Wells: A Passion for Justice* [VHS/DVD] (1989); Papers, Special Collections Research Center, University of Chicago Library.

SCOTT D. SEAY

Wheatley, Phillis (ca. 1753–84). Poet and evangelical. John and Susannah Wheatley of Boston purchased a newly imported slave who was about eight years old in 1761. Intended as a lady's maid, Phillis became a family favorite and was educated by Susannah Wheatley and her daughter. The Countess of Huntington learned of Phillis Wheatley's poems through evangelical networks in 1770. Three major events marked Wheatley's life in 1773: a trip to England (where she was feted by the countess), her emancipation from slavery, and the English publication of her poems (financed by Huntington). Susannah Wheatley died in 1774, and Phillis Wheatley's support of the American cause estranged her from the rest of the family. In 1778 she married a free black, John Peters. She died in poverty after the birth of her third child and was buried in an unmarked grave.

ANBO; BWA; DARB; NBAW; NoAW; William H. Robinson, *Phillis Wheatley in the Black American Beginnings* (1975).

JOAN R. GUNDERSEN

White, Alma Bridwell (1862–1946). Founder and bishop of the Pillar of Fire. Alma Bridwell grew up with 11 siblings in rural Kentucky. Converted as a teenager she earned a teacher training certificate, taught in a local school, and then moved to Montana at age 19 with relatives. In 1887 she married Kent White, a Methodist minister. The Whites set up an independent mission in Denver that evolved, despite her husband's protests, into the Pillar of Fire denomination. Their marriage disintegrated, and they were never reconciled. The Pillar of Fire spread across the U.S. and Great Britain. Its headquarters was in the self-sufficient town founded by White in Zarephath, New Jersey. Alma White's commitment to Christian education prompted the establishment of schools in Cincinnati, Baltimore, Los Angeles, Jacksonville, and Denver. In 1918 she became the first woman bishop in the U.S. She supported the platform of the National Women's Rights Party, including the Equal Rights Amendment, and published her feminist teachings in her periodical, *Woman's Chains*.

ANB; DARB; EAWR; EE; NoAW; RLA; Susie Cunningham Stanley, *Feminist Pillar of Fire* (1993); Alma White, *Looking Back from Beulah* (1902), *The Story of My Life*, 5 vols. (1919–1930).

PRISCILLA POPE-LEVISON

White, Anna (1831–1910). Foremost advocate for progressive Shakerism. Drawing upon Shaker notions of spiritual equality, Anna White argued for the expansion of women's leadership roles in Shaker communities. She held leadership positions as junior and senior eldress of the New Lebanon North Family and as coeditor of *Shaker and Shakeress*, a monthly publication. Her interests in reform led her to form close ties with reformers outside the Shaker community. She was a member of the National American Woman Suffrage Association, served as vice president of the U.S. National Council of Women, and became vice president of the New York chapter of the Women's International League of Peace and Arbitration. Through her reform work, both inside and outside the Shaker community, she helped to transform Shakerism into a significant agent of political and social reform in the U.S. and around the world.

EAWR; NoAW; Edward Andrews, *The People Called Shakers* (1963).

ELIZABETH HINSON-HASTY

White, Ellen Gould Harmon (1827–1915). Visionary, writer, and cofounder of the Seventh-day Adventist Church (SDA). Ellen Harmon grew up near Portland, Maine, in a devout Methodist family that embraced the premillennialist views of William Miller. When Christ did not return in 1844 (as predicted by Miller), Harmon experienced visions suggesting solutions to the religious dilemma. In relating them she also found a religious vocation for herself, even as a woman with frequent illness and without formal education or seminary training. Supported by her new husband James White, with whom she had four sons, she wrote out her visions and published them. She eventually wrote 40 books and over 4,000 articles. White stressed the necessity of moral and spiritual preparation for the imminent return of Christ, and also incorporated popular reforms such as health, education, temperance, and women's concerns. Her central theological theme was the "great controversy" between Christ and Satan manifested in history. Her best-known work was *Desire of Ages* (1898), a life of Christ. Although she attracted criticism for her literary practices White claimed the "fruits" of her visions and writings as validation. By 2000 the SDA Church had over 12 million adult members and operated more than 6,000 schools and 700 medical facilities around the world.

ANB; DARB; EAWR; EE; NoAW; RLA; Ronald L. Numbers, ed., *Prophetess of Health: A Study of Ellen G. White*, 2nd ed. (1992) [1976]; Arthur L. White, *Ellen G. White*, 6 vols. (1982–85); Ellen G. White, *Life Sketches of Ellen G. White* (1881).

GRAEME SHARROCK

Whitman, Narcissa Prentiss (1808–47). Presbyterian missionary. Born in Prattsburg, New York, into a devoutly Presbyterian family, Narcissa Prentice pledged her life to mission work at the age of 16. After attending school and teaching in Prattsburg she married medical missionary Marcus Whitman in 1836. The Whitmans headed to Oregon with another missionary couple, Henry and *Eliza Spalding; the two wives were the first white women to cross the Continental Divide. They settled in Walla Walla Valley and founded a mission among the Cayuse Indians at Waiilatpu. After an encouraging beginning to their work the Whitmans' only child, a two-year-old daughter, drowned. Whitman struggled with depression and failing eyesight, and dissension broke out among the Oregon missionaries. Angered at the growing number of white settlers and their introduction of a measles epidemic to the community, the Cayuse attacked the mission in 1847 and killed 14 people, including Whitman.

ANB; DARB; EAWR; EE; NoAW; Julie Roy Jeffrey, *Converting the West* (1991).

BEVERLY ZINK-SAWYER

Whittelsey, Abigail Goodrich (1788–1858). Journalist and editor. Abigail Goodrich, the daughter of a Congregational minister, was born in Ridgefield, Connecticut. She married Congregational minister Samuel Whittelsey in 1808, and they had seven children. In 1833, while living in Utica, New York, she began editing *Mother's Magazine*, a periodical of the Maternal Association. Whittelsey took the magazine with her to New York City in 1834, and by 1837 its circulation soared to 10,000. She continued editing the magazine until a disagreement with the new owner in 1848 prompted her to leave. Whittelsey began publishing *Mrs. Whittelsey's Magazine for Mothers and Daughters* in 1850, which circulated for about two years. (It is archived at the New-York Historical Society). One of the few women writers and editors of the 1830s, Whittelsey promoted the importance of marriage and motherhood.

ANB; NoAW; Charles B. Whittelsey, *Genealogy of the Whittelsey-Whittlesey Family*, 2nd ed. (1941) [1898].

MANDY E. MCMICHAEL

Wilcox, Ella Wheeler (1850–1919). Writer. Ella Wheeler wrote her first novel when she was nine years old, and at age 14 she quit school to support her family by writing religious and sentimental poems. Her 1883 *Poems of Passion* sold 60,000 copies in two years. In 1887 Wilcox enrolled in a class offered by New

Thought leader *Emma Curtis Hopkins; Wilcox wrote several books on this theme and women's rights. After her husband died Wilcox wrote about her attempts to reach his spirit. In 1916 the flamboyant author toured Allied camps in Europe, where she exhorted men to sexual cleanliness and read lines from her poetry, such as "Laugh and the world laughs with you; Weep and you weep alone."

ANB; EAWR; NoAW; RLA; Ella Wheeler Wilcox and Ella Giles Ruddy, *Story of a Literary Career* (2003) [1905]; Jenny Ballou, *Period Piece: Ella Wheeler Wilcox and Her Times* (1940).

GRAEME SHARROCK

Wilkes, Eliza Tupper (1844–1917). Unitarian minister. Born in Houlton, Maine, into a Baptist family, Eliza Tupper was a graduate of Iowa Central University. She converted to universal salvation and began to preach in Neenah and Menasha, Wisconsin. She married in 1869 and was ordained in 1871. Wilkes ministered in Rochester (Minnesota), Colorado Springs, Sioux Falls (Dakota, now North Dakota), Luverne (Minnesota), and Rock Rapids (Iowa). She directed the Iowa Unitarian Conference in 1887 and was Post Office Missions secretary. She sustained societies in Huron, Madison, and Miner (South Dakota), and founded the Adrian (Minnesota) church. Her sister, Cornell student Mila Tupper, assisted at Luverne from 1887 to 1890. Wilkes moved to California for health reasons, but continued to serve congregations, was president of the Woman's Pacific Unitarian Conference, and helped organize Unity Society in Palo Alto.

DUUB; UUWM; Cynthia Grant Tucker, *Prophetic Sisterhood* (1990); E. R. Hanson, *Our Woman Workers* (1882).

IRENE BAROS-JOHNSON

Wilkinson, Jemima (1752–1819). Religious dissenter and visionary. Jemima Wilkinson was born into a prosperous Quaker Rhode Island family. After reading the sermons of George Whitefield in 1768 she affiliated with Newport's New Light Baptists and then left the Quakers altogether. Recovering from typhus fever in 1776 she claimed that she had died and God had replaced her spirit with the Spirit of God. She adopted the title "Publick Universal Friend" and proclaimed a faith that blended evangelical theology with Quaker social activism. Although her androgynous manner of dress, her claim to have powers of healing and clairvoyance, and her insistence on celibacy drew sharp criticism from some people, she gathered a following from among the elite of southern New England. Her Jerusalem Community in western New York, a utopian settlement that grew to include 260 inhabitants, disbanded after her death.

ANB; DARB; EAWR; NoAW; Herbert Wisbey, *Pioneer Prophetess* (1964).

SCOTT D. SEAY

Willard, Frances Elizabeth (1839–98). International temperance leader and reformer. Raised in a Methodist family that understood civic and social responsibility as an integral aspect of religious faith, Frances Willard early espoused temperance and women's suffrage. After a decade of elementary and secondary teaching and a two-year educational sojourn in Europe and the Middle East, Willard became president of the Evanston College for Ladies (an affiliate of Northwestern University) in 1871. In the wake of the women's temperance crusade of 1873–74, Willard became corresponding secretary in the national *Woman's Christian Temperance Union (WCTU). Elected its second president in 1879 Willard convinced the organization to espouse women's suffrage in the struggle for the nation's sobriety and to widen its agenda to include an array of women's rights reforms. By the late 1880s she had persuaded the WCTU to endorse many of the aims of the burgeoning labor movement and throw its support behind the Prohibition Party. Willard's legendary speaking ability was influential in enlisting a large number of Americans into reform work. She founded the World's WCTU in the mid-1880s to address temperance and women's rights issues globally, and became president of the National Council of Women in 1888. By the early 1890s she had become a Christian socialist who believed that the capitalist economic system was fundamentally unjust and needed to be replaced by cooperative ownership of public utilities, corporations, and transportation systems. During the 1890s she spent half her time in England working with the British Woman's Temperance Association. Willard envisioned a global network of women reformers tackling a wide variety of injustices.

ANB; DARB; EAWR; EE; NoAW; RLA; WBC; Carolyn De Swarte Gifford, ed., *"Writing Out My Heart": Selections from the Journal of Frances E. Willard* (1995); Ruth Bordin, *Frances Willard* (1986); Mary Earhart, *Frances Willard* (1944).

CAROLYN DESWARTE GIFFORD

Williams, Delores Seneva (b. 1930s?). Womanist theologian. A native of Louisville, Kentucky, Delores Williams earned a bachelor's degree (1955) from the University of Louisville, a master's degree from Columbia University, and a doctoral degree from Union Theological Seminary in New York City, where she is the Paul Tillich Professor of Theology and Culture Emerita. The author of *Sisters in the Wilderness: The Challenge of Womanist God-talk* (1993), Williams called attention to the theological truths that are contained in the lives of black women who seek creative ways to foster hope in order to counter the effects associated with the social constructions of race, gender, class, and other fragmentations. A member of several professional guilds, her work focuses on womanist theology, theological doctrines, and the critique of American culture and the African American church. She is a member of the Presbyterian Church (U.S.A.) and the mother of four children. (Editor's note: Williams does not disclose her age.)

NBAW; "Festschrift for Delores S. Williams," *Union Seminary Quarterly Review* 58, nos. 3–4 (2004); Delores S. Williams, in *Transforming the Faith of Our Fathers*, ed. Ann Braude (2004).

ANGELA D. SIMS

Willing, Jennifer Fowler (1834–1916). Church leader and social reformer. Largely self-educated due to ill health, Jennie Fowler married William Crossgrove Willing, a Methodist Episcopal clergyman, in 1853. Not only was Willing a prolific author, but her leadership also contributed to the formation of several key women's organizations. One of the first secretaries of the Woman's Foreign Missionary Society, formed in 1869, she wrote regularly for its periodical, *The Heathen Woman's Friend*. Willing was appointed professor of English at Illinois Wesleyan University in 1874. Although she declined national office in the *Woman's Christian Temperance Union, she edited the first year of its periodical. She helped organize the Woman's Home Missionary Society in 1884. After her husband's death she opened the New York Training School and Settlement House in Hell's Kitchen in 1895, where she combined church work and social reform (until its closing in 1910), and also taught, wrote, and edited a magazine called *The Open Door*.

ANB; NoAW; Joanne Carlson Brown, "Shared Fire: The Flame Ignited by Jennie Fowler Willing," in *Spirituality and Social Responsibility*, ed. Rosemary Skinner Keller (1993).

LACEYE C. WARNER

Wilson, Lois Miriam Freeman (1927–). Church leader, writer, and advocate for social justice. An ordained minister of the United Church of Canada, Lois Wilson was its first woman moderator (1980–82) and the first woman president of the Canadian Council of Churches (1976–79). She was also the first Canadian president of the World Council of Churches (1983–91), where she was instrumental in founding the Ecumenical Decade of Churches in Solidarity with Women. Wilson was appointed to the Canadian Senate (as an Independent) and served from 1998 to 2002. Raised in a social gospel milieu and active in the Student Christian Movement, in ecumenical and interfaith organizations both nationally and internationally, she is recognized as an ambassador for peace, justice, women, and Canada. With spirit, keen wit, and indomitable courage Wilson has championed a spectrum of causes ranging from social, economic, and ecological issues in Canada to global peace, human rights, and religious freedom. She has written several books, including *Telling Her Story: Theology Out of Women's Struggles* (1992), *Miriam, Mary and Me* (1996)—a collection of biblical stories retold for children from a feminist theological perspective—and *Nuclear Waste* (2000).

Lois Wilson, *Turning the World Upside Down: A Memoir* (1989).

JANET SILMAN

Winchester, Olive Mary (1879–1947). Professor and academic dean. An heiress of the Winchester rifle estate, Olive Winchester studied Semitic languages at Harvard before her 1902 graduation from Radcliffe College. In 1912 she became the first woman to earn the bachelor of divinity degree from the University of Glasgow and the first woman ordained to the ministry in Scotland. She facilitated the Pentecostal Church of Scotland's merger in 1915 with the Church of the Nazarene. Winchester earned other degrees at Pacific School of Religion (STM) and Drew University (ThD). She headed the theology department at Eastern Nazarene College, was professor of biblical literature at Northwest Nazarene College, and dean of the Graduate School of Religion at Pasadena College. At Northwest Nazarene she also served simultaneously as vice president and academic dean (1922–35), greatly influencing the school's internal structure. She published three books on the Bible. Never married, she made Pasadena College her heir.

Jean Whiteford, "Olive Mary Winchester," *Trinity College Bulletin* (University of Glasgow), n.s., no. 14 (1997); Rebecca Laird, *Nazarene Women in Ordained Ministry* (1993); Ross Price, "Data about Miss Olive M. Winchester, ThD," Olive Winchester Collection, Nazarene Archives; *Who's Who in American Education*, vol. 12 (1945–46).

STAN INGERSOL

Winthrop, Margaret Tyndal (ca. 1591–1647). Puritan wife and leader. Born into a prominent family in Essex, England, Margaret Tyndal married John Winthrop in 1618 and eventually raised eight children with him. Her husband went to New England in 1630, but she remained behind for almost a year until preparations could be made for her arrival. Winthrop had no official role in either the governmental or religious life of the Bay Colony, but she supported her husband in his multiple leadership roles until her death.

ANB; NoAW; Edmund S. Morgan, *The Puritan Dilemma*, 2nd ed. (1998) [1958].

SCOTT D. SEAY

Wise, Louise Waterman (1874–1947). Community activist and philanthropist. Louise Waterman was born in

New York City and raised in a wealthy, nonreligious Jewish household. Despite parental disapproval she married Stephen S. Wise, who became one of America's most renowned rabbis. Louise Wise became renowned in her own right, particularly for her influential advocacy, and her volunteer and philanthropic work on behalf of Jewish orphans, schoolchildren, and refugees. Wise founded the Women's Division of the American Jewish Congress (AJC) in 1931 and led it until her death. She created AJC's Congress House, which fed, housed, and served 3,000 refugees between 1933 and 1939. Wise became an unflinching supporter of the Zionist cause, and in 1946 she even refused honorary membership in the Order of the British Empire based on what she considered Britain's unjust treatment of Jewish settlers in Palestine.

JWA; James Wise, *Legend of Louise* (1949); Obituary, *New York Times* (11 December 1947).

DEBORAH SKOLNICK EINHORN

Wittenmyer, Sarah Anne ("Annie") Turner (1827–1900). Methodist churchwoman, relief organizer, editor, and temperance leader. An Ohio native who moved with her husband to Iowa in 1850 Annie Wittenmyer organized women's relief efforts during and after the Civil War. In 1868 she established the Ladies' and Pastors' Christian Union, recruiting laywomen to aid clergy in caring for sick and poor parishioners. After moving to Philadelphia she edited a periodical, *The Christian Woman,* for 11 years and wrote books on her war experiences and women's role in Christianity. In 1874 she was elected president of the newly organized national *Woman's Christian Temperance Union (WCTU). Under her leadership the organization grew significantly, but her conservative stance and opposition to women's suffrage led to her unseating in 1879 by *Frances Willard.

ANB; EAWR; NoAW; Virginia L. Beattie, *Annie Wittenmyer: Mentor to Millions* (2002); Tom Sillanpa, *Annie Wittenmyer: God's Angel* (1972); Annie T. Wittenmyer, *Woman's Work for Jesus* (1871).

CAROLYN DESWARTE GIFFORD

Wolfe, Catharine Lorillard (1828–87). Philanthropist. Catharine Wolfe inherited a massive fortune when her father died in 1872 and spent the rest of her life dispensing that fortune. Influenced by Henry Codman Potter, the rector of Grace Episcopal Church, where she was a member, Wolfe gave major gifts to the church and to its outreach ministries in New York City and abroad. She provided funding for a diocesan office and St. Luke's and St. Johnland hospitals. Wolfe supported the archaeological expedition of William Hayes Ward that led to the excavation of the biblical city of Nippur. At her death she bequeathed her extensive collection of paintings to New York's Metropolitan Museum of Art, along with an endowment to support the bequest.

ANB; NoAW; "Catharine L. Wolfe," *Churchwork* 2 (1887); William R. Huntington, "The Religious Use of Wealth: A Sermon Commemorative of Catharine Lorillard Wolfe," Grace Church, New York (10 April 1887).

MARY SUDMAN DONOVAN

Wolff, Madeleva (Mary Evaline) (1887–1964). Catholic educator and college administrator. The daughter of Wisconsin German immigrants, Mary Evaline Wolff entered the novitiate of the *Sisters of the Holy Cross (CSC) while a student at St. Mary's College in Notre Dame, Indiana. After graduation Sister Madeleva taught at the college with little preparation on the assigned subjects. This experience informed her later work in training women religious teachers. She served as a college president at her alma mater from 1934 to 1961, where in

1943 she created the first Catholic graduate program in theology open to women. Her work with the National Catholic Education Association convention resulted in a book, *The Education of Sister Lucy*, which initiated teacher-training reform for women religious in the 1950s. The annual Madeleva Lectures, which feature leading Catholic women scholars, honor her memory.

ANB; EACH; NoAWMP; Gail Porter Mandell, *Madeleva* (1997); Madeleva Wolff, *My First Seventy Years* (1959).

ANNIE RUSSELL

Woman's Christian Temperance Union (WCTU) (1874–). Nonsectarian reform organization. The WCTU was founded as a response to the women's temperance crusade of 1873–74. President *Annie Wittenmyer guided the organization for its first five years. It developed state and local branches and enlisted its membership against the liquor industry under the banner "For God and Home and Native Land." President *Frances Willard encouraged the WCTU to espouse women's suffrage, using "The Ballot for Home Protection" as a rallying cry. During Willard's presidency (1879–98), the "Do Everything" policy broadened its reform efforts to encompass a range of women's rights and support of the aims of the rising labor movement. The WCTU became an effective pressure group. It lobbied for local, state, and national reforms and participated in coalitions to improve living conditions. It promoted scientific temperance instruction in public and Sunday schools and raised the age of consent in nearly every state. The WCTU pushed for passage of the 18th (National Prohibition) Amendment. By 1900 the WCTU claimed nearly 200,000 members; it was the largest women's organization of the time. During the mid-1920s, with *Anna Gordon's presidency, the WCTU reached its peak membership of 500,000. The World's WCTU was founded in the mid-1880s, and by the 1920s it had 766,000 members with branches in 40 nations. With the repeal of the U.S. Prohibition Amendment in 1933 the WCTU began to lose members and prestige. By 1997 the U.S. membership had dwindled to 7,000. Education for abstinence became its main goal. Although the WCTU no longer commands the influence it once wielded, its concern for the dangers of substance abuse remains relevant in the 21st century.

BWA; EAWR; Elizabeth Putnam Gordon, *Women Torch-bearers* (2005) [1924]; Ian Tyrell, *Woman's World, Woman's Empire* (1991); Ruth Bordin, *Woman and Temperance* (1981).

CAROLYN DESWARTE GIFFORD

Women of Reform Judaism (WRJ) [National Federation of Temple Sisterhoods (NFTS)] (1913–). Organization of affiliated sisterhoods. In 1993 NFTS was renamed Women of Reform Judaism—The Federation of Temple Sisterhoods. NFTS encouraged weekly synagogue attendance, enhanced festival celebrations, improved the quality of children's religious education through better textbooks and teacher training, and provided financial support to the Hebrew Union College. Later it fostered expanded programming for high school and college youth. NFTS cooperated with the Red Cross during the two world wars, espoused disarmament in the 1920s, and actively opposed encroachments of religion into the public schools from the 1920s onward. In 1933 NFTS acquired a full-time executive director, *Jane Evans, who strengthened the organization and broadened its mission to include political and social issues. In the postwar decades NFTS expanded its involvement with Jewish life in Israel and supported women's rabbinic ordination. On the American scene it aligned itself with many feminist and liberal causes, such as reproductive rights, civil rights, deescalation in Vietnam, eliminating capital punishment, and passage of the Equal Rights Amendment. The overall purpose of NFTS/WRJ is to further the religious spirit of Reform Judaism in the synagogue, the religious school, and the community.

JWA.

JOAN S. FRIEDMAN

Women-Church (1983–). Feminist liturgical groups rooted in Catholicism. In the early 1980s, when the church was increasingly hostile toward feminism, American Catholic feminists were searching for new ways to fight sexism and live their faith. Fourteen hundred feminists gathered for a Woman-Church Speaks conference in 1983; in their recognition of common experiences of disappointment and marginalization a new movement was born. Participants in Women-Church gathered in small groups across the U.S. The groups enabled women to retain a connection to Catholicism (if they chose), explore feminist spirituality, and work toward feminist goals. Women-Church hoped to model an inclusive experience of church that was neither completely within the bounds of the institutional church nor separatist. Beginning in 1987 many of these groups affiliated as Women-Church Convergence.

Mary E. Hunt, "Women-Church," in *Encyclopedia of Women and Religion in North America*, vol. 3, ed. Rosemary Skinner Keller et al. (2006); Rosemary Radford Ruether, *Women-Church* (1985).

MARY J. HENOLD

Women's League for Conservative Judaism (WLCJ) (1918–). Synagogue-based organization. Organized by *Mathilde Roth Schechter in New York WLCJ began as a women's counterpart to the newly formed United Synagogues of America, a consortium of synagogues dedicated to the Conservative movement of Judaism. The league dedicated itself to the dispersal of Jewish knowledge and, in its early years, offered an introduction to Americanization for new Jewish immigrants. Its education branch, through its *Outlook* magazine, provided literature to women that promoted living a Jewish life and offered venues for doing so, which included keeping dietary laws and observing holidays. Social action was another of its platforms. Through membership and fund-raising activities, the league collected materials to ship overseas to assist the Red Cross during and after World War II, and raised awareness for women's issues by supporting the Equal Rights Amendment and legislation supporting abortion rights and battered women. It remains actively involved with Israel and assists in providing the country with funds, and has recently called for support for and recognition of the Conservative movement by the Israeli government. WLCJ presently boasts hundreds of chapters with more than 120,000 members.

EAWR; JWA; Shuly Rubin Schwartz, *The Rabbi's Wife* (2006); "Tradition and Change—Finding the Right Balance: Conservative and Reconstructionist Judaism," in *Encyclopedia of Women and Religion in North America*, vol. 2, ed. Rosemary Skinner Keller et al. (2006).

SHIRA M. KOHN

Women's Lodges of the Filipino Federation of America (1925–). A spiritual community for Filipina immigrant women. The women's lodges were part of a mutual aid society for Filipinos founded by Hilario Camino Moncado in 1925 in Los Angeles. The lodges each comprised 12 women who were dedicated to practicing prayer, fasting, and meditation from the tradition of Filipino folk Catholicism. Women leaders were highly valued by the founder, Dr. Moncado, who wrote *Divinity of Woman* in 1925.

Steffi San Buenaventura, "Filipino Folk Spirituality and Immigration: From Mutual Aid to Religion," in *New Spiritual Homes: Religion and Asian Americans*, ed. David K. Yoo (1999).

BARBARA E. REED

Women's Ministerial Conference (Universalist) (1873–1914). Organization dedicated to fellowship among women in ministry. One of many organizations founded and presided over by *Julia Ward Howe, this group first convened in 1873 when Howe issued a call for a Woman Preachers' Convention in Boston. The group that formed was originally called the Woman's Church; in 1892 it became the Woman's Ministerial Conference (WMC). (The name was later changed to the Women's Ministerial Conference.) Howe claimed that she formed the group to fulfill her dream of "a church of true womanhood." She believed that men's domination had left the church bereft of its "womanly side" and that women ministers would be "less sectarian" than men. In offering women ministers the opportunity to encourage one another in their work, the WMC was an effort to restore the gendered wholeness of the church universal.

ANBO; UUWM; Laura E. Richards and Maud Howe Elliott, *Julia Ward Howe* (1915); Records, Andover-Harvard Theological Library, Harvard University.

ROBYNNE ROGERS HEALEY

Women's Ordination Conference (WOC) (1975–). Catholic feminist organization. WOC began when 1,200 Catholics gathered in Detroit to discuss women's ordination in the Roman Catholic Church. As the first of its kind, the conference was a milestone in the history of the American Catholic feminist movement. Combining scholarship, liturgy, and protest, the conference inspired feminists to rally around the issue of women's ordination; as a result the WOC became a permanent organization in 1976. Its activist strategies have included dialogue with—and lobbying of—the church hierarchy, the fostering of separate female communities, periodic conferences, and public protest. The WOC has sought to balance women's rights activism, the support of women in their vocations, the creation of a renewed priestly ministry, and an inclusive Catholic Church.

New Women, New Church [serial] (1978–); Anne Marie Gardiner, ed., *Women and Catholic Priesthood: An Expanded Vision, Proceedings of the Detroit Ordination Conference* (1976).

MARY J. HENOLD

Women's Tefilla Network (1980s–). Orthodox Jewish women's organization. The network was formed in the mid-1980s following the 1985 "teshuva: responsa," in which five prominent rabbis from Yeshiva University in New York City explicitly prohibited Orthodox women's tefilla (prayer) groups from organizing. Objectors to the groups generally situate their critiques in relationship to specific activities associated with them (e.g., women reading from a Torah) or the idea of the groups in their entirety. Tefilla groups began, most notably in Manhattan in the late 1960s, as locations for women wishing to remain within Orthodox halakic (Jewish legal) traditions to read and study the Torah. (These activities traditionally were prohibited to Orthodox women during Shabbat and holiday services). The network now provides resources, guidance, newsletters, and prayer books for women's tefilla groups across Canada, the U.S., Israel, Australia, and England.

JWA; Bat Sheva Marcus, "Walk Humbly with Your God," *Sh'ma* 27 (1997).

KAREN-MARIE WOODS

Women's Union Missionary Society (WUMS) (1861–). Missionary organization. Despite protests from American male mission authorities, *Sarah Doremus founded the first American mission society to be run by women for the evangelization and service of women overseas. The UMS bucked the trends of other Protestant mission boards by sending single women. In 1862 its first missionary sailed for India. Their early efforts began in creating schools and biblical literacy, but took on a medical mandate as well. In 1971 their name changed to the United Fellowship for Christian Service, reflecting the new reality of men and married couples among their ranks. In 1976 they merged with their British sister organization, Bible and Medical Missionary Fellowship International. The new union, later renamed International Service Fellowship, contains branches in 19 countries, focused on northern Africa, the Middle East, and Asia.

Judith MacLeod, *Women's Union Missionary Society: The Story of a Continuing Mission* (1999); Dana Robert, *American Women in Mission* (1996); Interserve USA, www.interserveusa.org.

CATHERINE BOWLER

Wood, Julie Amanda Sargent (Minnie Mary Lee) (1825–1903). Novelist. Born in New Hampshire, Julie Sargent married in 1849 and moved with her husband, W. H. Wood, to Sauk Rapids, Minnesota, in 1851. Wood and her husband ran the *New Era*, a weekly Sauk Rapids newspaper. Wood wrote frequently for the *New Era* and other publications under the pseudonym Minnie Mary Lee. A convert to Roman Catholicism, Wood wrote frequently of her newfound and passionately held faith. The *St. Cloud Daily Times* described her novels as "controversial," but Wood was a popular figure in Minnesota during her lifetime.

Minnie Mary Lee, *Strayed from the Fold* (1878), *The Brown House of Duffield* (1876), *The Heart of Myrrha Lake, Or, Into the Light of Catholicity* (1872); St. John's University Archives, Collegeville, Minnesota.

COLLEEN CARPENTER CULLINAN

Wood, Mary Elizabeth (1861–1931). Missionary librarian. A native of Elba, New York, and a librarian, Mary Wood visited her missionary brother in Wuch'ang, China, in 1899 and stayed to teach elementary English at the Boone School. Appointed a missionary by the Protestant Episcopal Church in 1904 Wood collected donations to build a library for the school's collegiate department. The library opened in 1910. Wood established several library branches and traveling collections of Chinese and English books. She sent Chinese students to the U.S. for library training, and in 1920 opened the Boone Library School that trained librarians until 1949. Wood organized a petition in 1923 to allocate funds from the U.S. Boxer Rebellion indemnity to develop public libraries in China and lobbied senators and congressmen personally for these funds; the result was nearly $12 million for the establishment of a national library school in Peking.

ANB; NoAW; Hwa-Wei Lee, *American Contributions to Modern Library Development in China* (1996); John H. Winkleman, "Mary Elizabeth Wood (1861–1931)," *Journal of Library and Information Science* [Taiwan] 9 (April 1982).

MARY SUDMAN DONOVAN

Woods, Katharine Pearson (1853–1923). Author and teacher. Katharine Woods's interest in social justice found its greatest expression in her novels. Through her acquaintance with the Christian Socialist and fellow Episcopalian Richard T. Ely, her first novel, *Metzerott: Shoemaker*, became a literary sensation in 1889. The novel reflected her experiences as a teacher and social worker with the working-class German immigrants of Wheeling, West Virginia. It also reflected her advocacy for just relations between capital and labor through Christian cooperation. Woods also worked in settlement houses and conducted studies of factory conditions under the auspices of the College Settlements Association. In her later years she lived primarily in Philadelphia and was active in philanthropic efforts associated with the Episcopal Church.

ANB; NoAW; Susan Hill Lindley, "Gender and the Social Gospel Novel," in *Gender and the Social Gospel*, ed. Wendy J. Deichmann Edwards and Carolyn DeSwarte Gifford (2003).

ANNIE RUSSELL

Woodsmall, Ruth Frances (1883–1963). *YWCA (Young Women's Christian Association) executive, teacher, and author. Ruth Woodsmall earned a BA from the University of Nebraska (1905) and an MA from Wellesley College (1906), and continued her studies at Columbia University and Heidelberg University. In 1917, following 11 years as a high school teacher in Colorado and Nevada, Woodsmall became the director of the YWCA Hostess House in Little Rock, Arkansas. In 1920 she became executive secretary of the YWCA in the Near East. Based in Istanbul she supervised YWCAs in Turkey, Syria, and Lebanon. In 1935 she became the general secretary of the World YWCA. From 1949 to 1954 she served as chief of the women's affairs section of the U.S. High Commission of Occupied Germany. Her books include *Eastern Women Today and Tomorrow* (1933), *Moslem Women Enter a New World* (1936), and *Women and the New East* (1960).

ANB; NoAW; Papers in the Sophia Smith Collection, Women's History Manuscripts at Smith College.

PAMELA R. DURSO

Woodworth-Etter, Maria B. Underwood (1844–1924). Faith-healing Pentecostal evangelist. Maria Underwood was born in rural Ohio and experienced a religious conversion at age 13 and a call to evangelism. A difficult marriage to Philo H. Woodworth and the death of five of their six children catapulted her into severe illnesses. Woodworth claimed her recovery was due to her promise that she would become an evangelist at age 35. When she began to preach, the phenomenon of trances occurred during her meetings. She also believed that she had the gift of healing. Crowds overflowed her tent (which held 8,000 people), and many new churches resulted from her meetings. In 1902 she married Samuel Etter. By 1912 she joined the Pentecostal movement and was a featured evangelist across the country, meeting with success and controversy.

ANB; DARB; EAWR; EE; Wayne Warner, *The Woman Evangelist* (1986); Maria Woodworth-Etter, *The Life and Experiences of Maria B. Woodworth* (1885).

PRISCILLA POPE-LEVISON

Woolley, Celia Parker (1848–1918). Unitarian minister and reformer. Born in Toledo, Ohio, Celia Parker attended Coldwater Female Seminary (Michigan) and married in 1868. As president of the Chicago Woman's Club (1888–90) she opened membership to blacks. She was on the editorial staff of the Unitarian publication *Unity* from 1884 to 1918, and also wrote for the *Christian Register* and lectured for women's groups. Ordained a Unitarian minister in 1894 she later ministered on Chicago's North Side. As a member of the Chicago's All Souls Church she often conducted services for Jenkin Lloyd Jones in his absence. She stirred controversy when she and her husband moved to the Frederick Douglass Center, located in a black section of the city. She encouraged racial integration and equal opportunity among blacks and whites.

UUWM; WBC; Koby Lee-Forman, "Simple Love of Truth: The Racial Justice Activism of Celia Parker Woolley" (PhD diss., Northwestern University, 1995); Cynthia Grant Tucker, *Prophetic Sisterhood* (1990).

IRENE BAROS-JOHNSON

Woolley, Mary Emma (1863–1947). Educator, feminist, and peace activist. Born and raised in New England, Mary Woolley was deeply religious, with a strong commitment to peace and social justice. She taught at Wheaton Seminary from 1885 to 1891. In 1894 she became the first woman to receive a BA from Brown University. After completing an MA in 1895 she taught at Wellesley College, where she moved quickly through the academic ranks. In 1901 Woolley became president of Mount Holyoke College. In her 36-year presidency Woolley implemented reforms that transformed it into one of the finest colleges in the U.S. Woolley was an active pacifist; she was the only woman delegate to the 1932 Geneva Conference on Reduction and Limitation of Armaments. Woolley was one of the most influential women of her time.

ANBO; Anna Mary Wells, *Miss Marks and Miss Woolley* (1978); Jeannette Marks, *Life and Letters of Mary Emma Woolley* (1955); Arthur C. Cole, *A Hundred Years of Mount Holyoke College* (1940).

ROBYNNE ROGERS HEALEY

Woosley, Louisa Mariah Layman (1862–1952). First woman ordained in the Cumberland Presbyterian (CP) Church. Born in central Kentucky, Louisa Layman felt a call to preach from the moment of her conversion at age 12. After she married in 1879 and gave birth to two children she accepted an invitation to preach in her home congregation. She continued to preach as an evangelist and was licensed by Nolin Presbytery (Kentucky) and then ordained as a minister on 5 November 1889. Her ordination was challenged by the synod and remained in question until she was recognized as a member of Leitchfield Presbytery in 1911 and added to the General Assembly's roll of ministers in 1913. She served three churches in Kentucky, was stated clerk of Leitchfield Presbytery for 25 years, and moderator of the Kentucky Synod in 1938.

Mary Lin Hudson, "'Shall Women Preach?' Louisa Woosley and the Cumberland Presbyterian Church," *American Presbyterians* 68 (Summer 1990); Louisa M. Woosley, *Shall Women Preach?* (1891).

BEVERLY ZINK-SAWYER

Workman, Mary Julia (1871–1964). Roman Catholic reformer and settlement house founder. Born into a politically prominent Los Angeles family, Mary Workman founded the Brownson House Settlement Association in 1901 and led it for 19 years. She became the first woman to join the Municipal League, a civic watchdog group. A Roman Catholic who built cooperative relationships with church leaders she founded the diocesan chapter of the *National Council of Catholic Women in 1924. She led the Los Angeles Civil Service Commission from 1927 to 1928 and helped establish local chapters of the League of Women Voters and the National Conference of Christians and Jews. Throughout her life Workman was active in numerous social and religious efforts in her native city.

EACH; Michael E. Engh, SJ, "Mary Julia Workman: The Catholic Conscience of Los Angeles," *California History* 72, no. 1 (Spring 1993); Workman Family Papers, Von Der Ahe Library, CSLA Research Collection, Loyola Marymount University.

ANNIE RUSSELL

Wright, Frances ("Fanny") (Madame D'Arusmont) (1795–1852). Reformer, author, and freethinker. Born in Scotland and raised in England, Fanny Wright sailed to the U.S. in 1818 and wrote *Views of Society and Manners in America* in 1821. Wright was influenced by Robert Owen and by antislavery views, and in 1825 she founded the utopian Nashoba community in Tennessee. She purchased several slaves and expected them soon to earn their freedom, thereby attempting to prove the institution unprofitable. Nashoba, however, eventually floundered on allegations of impropriety. Wright coedited a newspaper; spoke to mixed audiences; promoted women's equality, "free love," and birth control; and advocated public education. She also attacked religion and the clergy as obstacles to human rights and rational thought. Her controversial lectures often incited mob violence. She led the Free Thought movement in New York and supported the Workingman's Party. She married a Frenchman in 1831, lost custody of their child after divorcing, and experienced disillusionment in her last decade of life.

ANB; EAWR; NoAW; Celia Morris Eckhardt, *Fanny Wright* (2002) [1984]; Frances Wright, *Address on the State of the Public Mind* (1829); Letters at Duke University, University Archives; University of Chicago Archives; and the Working Men's Institute (New Harmony, Indiana).

AMY BLACK VOORHEES

Wright, Laura Maria Sheldon (1809–86). Missionary to the Seneca Indians. Born in Vermont as a descendant of pioneer settlers Laura Sheldon was the 10th of 12 children. She became acquainted with Indians at an early age, and at the age of 10 she held prayer meetings for her playmates. After teaching school for several years she married the Reverend Asher Wright, a missionary to the Senecas. Under the auspices of the American Board of Commissioners for Foreign Missions they moved to Buffalo to begin what would become for Wright a 53-year sojourn. The Wrights reduced Seneca to a written and printed language and became accomplished speakers. Along with creating schoolbooks and hymnals, some of which are still in use, Wright also founded the Iroquois Temperance League. "Auntie Wright" became legendary among the Seneca people.

NoAW; Harriet S. Caswell, *Our Life among the Iroquois Indians* (1892).

BETH SPAULDING

Wright, Lucy (1760–1821). Shaker leader. Lucy Wright was appointed in 1787 by Joseph Meacham as the first eldress to lead the "female line" of the Shakers. When Meacham became ill, he named Wright as elder so that she could lead the Shakers after his death. Wright's appointment as elder was not well received by the entire community. Although Shakers promoted equality between the sexes, patterns of leadership in the community did not always portray this ideal. Some male members of the community refused to accept Wright as a female head. She also faced other problems, such as community debt and the attrition of members. Wright, however, accomplished much during the 25 years she led the Shakers; she enlivened Shaker worship and approved *The Testimony of Christ's Second Appearing* (1808), the first authoritative statement of Shaker beliefs and practices.

NoAW; Edward Andrews, *The People Called Shakers* (1963).

ELIZABETH HINSON-HASTY

Wynkoop, Mildred Bangs (1905–97). Theologian and missionary. Born in Seattle, Wynkoop was at Pasadena College a student of H. Orton Wiley, a noted Wesleyan-Arminian theologian. She was ordained in 1934 and was a copastor and evangelist with her husband, Ralph. A deep yearning led her to earn advanced degrees in theology. Subsequently, she taught systematic theology at Western Evangelical Seminary (1956–61); Japan Nazarene Theological Seminary (1963–66), of which she was the founding president; Trevecca Nazarene College (1966–76); and Nazarene Theological Seminary (1976–79). Nazarene theology continued the apologetic models of 19th-century Methodist theology, but Wynkoop broke from this pattern, establishing her own agenda in *A Theology of Love* (1972), which reinterpreted the Wesleyan doctrine of sanctification. Other works include *Foundations of Wesleyan-Arminian Theology* (1967); *John Wesley: Christian Revolutionary* (1970); a college history, *The Trevecca Story* (1976); and numerous articles. In 1973 she became the first woman to serve as president of the Wesleyan Theological Society.

Linda K. Alexander, "A Rebel in the Ranks: A Biography of Mildred Bangs Wynkoop" (PhD diss., University of Kansas, 2003); Obituary, *Herald of Holiness* (July 1997); Carl Bangs, "Ralph and Mildred Wynkoop on Their 65th Wedding Anniversary, a Life Synopsis," Mildred Bangs Wynkoop Collection, Nazarene Archives.

STAN INGERSOL

Yelin, Shulamis (1913–2002). Writer and educator. Shulamis Yelin was born in Montreal. She graduated from Macdonald College (1932) and went on to study at Columbia Union Teachers College in New York City. She completed her MA at the University of Montreal in 1961. Yelin was a versatile and accomplished teacher who taught every age from nursery to university. She established the first day school kindergarten for the J. Peretz School in 1941 and was assistant principal of the Young Israel Day School from 1953 to 1954. She was a founding member of Montreal's Reconstructionist synagogue. Yelin was an award-winning writer whose work reflected her love of *yiddishkeit* and the Jewish community in Montreal. She published a collection of poetry entitled *Seeded in Sinai* (1975), as well as *Shulamis: Stories from a Montreal Childhood* (1983) and *Au Soleil De Me Nuit* (1985).

Edmond Lipsitz, *Who's Who of Canadian Women* (1983); Tamara Cohen, *Recollections of Shulamis Yelin*, Jewish Women's Archive, www.jwa.org; Jewish Public Library Archive (Montreal).

TRUDY FLYNN

Yezierska, Anzia (ca. 1883–1970). Jewish fiction writer. Born in Plinsk, a shtetl on the Russian-Polish border, Anzia Yezierska immigrated to the U.S. with her family in 1892. She graduated from Columbia University Teachers College in 1904 and decided that her future career involved writing. She married Arnold Levitas in 1911 and had one child, Louise, before divorcing Levitas in 1915. By 1918 she was writing fiction. She formed a close relationship with the philosopher John Dewey, who encouraged her to use her own life experiences when writing stories. Her story *Fat of the Land* (1919), was widely acclaimed and named best short story of the year. Other works soon followed, such as a collection of short stories, *Hungry Hearts* (1920), and books such as *Salome of the Tenements* (1923) and *Bread Givers* (1925). Most of her stories dealt with the complexities of immigrant women's lives in America. She focused on issues such as family struggles, economic difficulties, and spiritual crises. After the Great Depression began she found it difficult to get published, and the last of her major works, *Red Ribbon on White Horse*, did not appear until 1950.

ANB; JWA; NoAWMP; Louise Levitas Henriksen, *Anzia Yezierska* (1988); Carol Schoen, *Anzia Yezierska* (1982).

SHIRA M. KOHN

Yifa, Bhiksuni (Venerable Yifa) (1951–). Buddhist scholar and leader of Chinese Buddhism in the U.S. Bhiksuni Yifa has served as a faculty member and provost at His Lai (Xilai) University (now University of the West) in California and as abbess of the Greater Boston Buddhist Cultural Center. She was born in Beigang, Taiwan, and attended Taiwan National University. In 1979 she was ordained as a Buddhist nun at Foguang Shan Monastery (Taiwan). She earned her PhD in religious studies at Yale University (1996) with the sponsorship of Foguang Shan. She was the first Chinese Buddhist nun to receive a PhD in the U.S. She has been an international leader in advocating for Buddhist laywomen and ordained women.

Venerable Yifa, *Sisters of the Buddha* (2005), *Safeguarding the Heart* (2002).

BARBARA E. REED

Youmans, Letitia Creighton (1827–96). Teacher and temperance reformer. Born and educated in Ontario, Letitia Creighton was a faculty member at Burlington Ladies' Academy and at Picton Ladies' Academy before marrying Arthur Youmans in 1850. After the couple moved to Picton, Ontario, she became interested in temperance and Sunday school work in the Methodist church they attended, and she organized a Band of Hope to educate the children in temperance. In 1874 she attended a meeting in Chautauqua, New York, the first since the founding of the *Woman's Christian Temperance Union (WCTU) in the U.S. Inspired by her experience, Youmans returned home to found the second woman's temperance group in Canada. She became Canada's leading temperance organizer and was the author of the slogan "home protection," later adopted so effectively by *Frances Willard. Youmans became the first president of the Ontario WCTU in 1877 and of the Dominion WCTU in 1885.

DCB; Letitia Youmans, *Campaign Echoes* (1893).

MARILYN FÄRDIG WHITELEY

Young, Ann Eliza Webb (1844–ca. 1908). Anti-Mormon propagandist. Born in Nauvoo, Illinois, to Mormon parents, Ann Eliza Webb migrated to Salt Lake City in 1848 with her father and his two wives. Her opposition to polygamy seethed as her father took three more wives in 1856. When Brigham Young developed an interest in her in 1860, she vowed not to marry him. She married another man in 1863 and divorced him after two years. According to her account she reluctantly became Young's 27th wife in 1868 because he threatened to bankrupt her family. (Editor's note: Some sources name her as Young's 19th wife.) She filed for divorce four years later. After converting to Methodism she lectured against polygamy. Her efforts aided the passage of the Edmunds Bill (1882), outlawing polygamy in the U.S. She spent her later life in relative obscurity.

ANB; NoAW; Irving Wallace, *The Twenty-Seventh Wife* (1961); Ann Eliza Young, *Life in Mormon Bondage* (1908).

SCOTT D. SEAY

Younger, Ruth Elaine ("Mother Ruth") (1897–1986). Religious and founder of the Community of the Holy Spirit. Baptized in a Presbyterian church, Younger was confirmed in the Episcopal Church and experienced a call to religious life while in her teens. Refused admission to American orders because of her biracial background, she was admitted to the Sisterhood of St. John the Divine in Toronto. A graduate of St. Hilda's College at the University of Toronto and the Ontario College of Education, Sister Ruth taught in schools and missions in Canada until 1949. Believing she could work more effectively in the American church she was granted a leave of absence and established a preschool with Sister Edith Margaret. In 1952 Sister Ruth founded the Community of the Holy Spirit (CHS) in New York City. She was named superior and served in that capacity until 1976. Mother Ruth earned a doctorate in education from Columbia University and founded St. Hilda's and St. Hugh's School in New York City. She was the head of the school until her retirement in 1985.

Sheryl A. Kujawa-Holbrook, *Freedom Is a Dream: A Documentary History of Women in the Episcopal Church* (2002); Obituary, *New York Times* (17 January 1987).

SHERYL A. KUJAWA-HOLBROOK

Youville, Marie-Marguérite DuFrost de Lajemmerais d' (1701–71). First Canadian-born saint and founder of the Sisters of Charity of Montreal (SGM) (Soeurs Grises de Montreal or "Grey Nuns"). After some schooling by the *Ursulines, Marie-Marguérite DuFrost de Lajemmerais married in 1722 and was widowed eight years later. To support her children she eked out an impoverished existence. After 1738 she joined with three other women in an informal society dedicated to religious devotion and care of the poor. The Grey Nuns grew from this group. When the local hospital failed she and a few like-minded women were entrusted with its resurrection. In spite of constraints by the Roman Catholic hierarchy, Mother d'Youville and her sisters persisted in caring for the city's needy, abandoned children, and wounded soldiers. D'Youville was beatified in 1959 and canonized in 1990.

NCE; Mary Pauline Fitts, *Hands to the Needy* (2000) [1949]; Rita McGuire, *Marguérite d'Youville* (1982).

OSCAR COLE-ARNAL

YWCA (Young Women's Christian Association) (1855–). An ecumenical lay movement working to empower women. The YWCA is rooted in the Christian tradition but is open to women of all faiths. The movement began in England in 1855 and spread to the U.S., where residence facilities for women were first opened in Boston and New York City in 1858. Its early focus was on the spiritual nurture of college students and young working women. Bible classes were begun as well as services such as typing classes and an employment bureau. Boardinghouses and facilities for physical education were also established. The World YWCA was organized in 1894 (with representation from the U.S.) and is headquartered in Geneva, Switzerland; it represents 122 countries with 25 million members. A national organization in the U.S. was formed in 1906 when independent city and student associations united. The present organization, YWCA USA, comprises approximately 300 local associations with 2.6 million members. The YWCA has been at the forefront of social causes throughout its history. It has worked to establish fair labor laws, supported racial integration and the elimination of racism, worked for economic empowerment and on behalf of women's health concerns. While identified as a Christian organization the YWCA has sought to avoid sectarianism, choosing to focus its mission primarily on social goals. That work has taken members around the world working as teachers, administrators, and social workers. Current goals include advocacy work, the elimination of racism, and the development of young leaders worldwide.

BWAZ; EARH; EE; Janine M. Denomme, "Abundant Life for All: The Young Women's Christian Association," in *Encyclopedia of Women and Religion in North America*, ed. Rosemary Skinner Keller et al. (2006); Nancy Boyd, *Emissaries: The Overseas Work of the American YWCA* (1986); Frances Hyelen Mains and Grace Loucks Elliott, *From Deep Roots: The Story of the YWCA's Religious Dimensions* (1974).

VALERIE REMPEL

Zeisberger, Susanna Lecron (1744–1824). Missionary. Susanna Lecron was born in Lancaster, Pennsylvania, and moved into the single sisters' house (see *Moravian Women Choirs) in Lititz when she was 16 years old. In 1781 she married veteran Moravian missionary David Zeisberger, and was ordained a deacon the following year. She was a coworker with her husband in the mission to Native Americans in the Ohio Valley in the difficult years following the massacre of 96 Moravian Indians at Gnadenhutten by an American militia. The Zeisbergers were kidnapped by Indians shortly after arriving in Schönbrunn; they survived only through the kindness of Christian natives who shared their food with them. The Zeisbergers were among the most effective evangelists to the eastern tribes, especially the Lenape, in part because of their appreciation for tribal culture. After being widowed in 1808 Zeisberger retired to the widows' house in Bethlehem.

Hermann Wellenreuther and Carola Wessel, eds., *The Moravian Mission Diaries of David Zeisberger* (2005); Earl P. Olmstead, *David Zeisberger* (1997); Bethlehem Digital History Project, Personal Papers, Memoirs, "Zeisberger, Susanna," bdhp .moravian.edu.

CRAIG D. ATWOOD

Zikmund, Barbara Brown (1939–). Historian and theological educator. Known as "BBZ" to many people, Barbara Brown Zikmund is a scholar of American religious history, a leader in theological education, and active in interfaith relations. Brown married Joseph Zikmund in 1961, and they have one son. Ordained as a minister in the United Church of Christ (UCC) in 1964, Zikmund received her PhD from Duke University in 1969. Her research has focused on women in ordained ministry in the U.S. and on the history of the UCC. She coauthored an influential study on clergywomen (*Clergy Women*, 1998) and was series editor for a seven-volume history of the UCC (*The Living Theological Heritage of the United Church of Christ*, 1995–2005). From 1991 to 2007 she served on the Interfaith Relations Committee of the National Council of Churches, including seven years as committee chair. Zikmund was academic dean at the Pacific School of Religion (1981–90) and president of Hartford Seminary (1990–2000). From 1986 to 1988 she was the first female president of the Association of Theological Schools in the United States and Canada (ATS). She served on the World Council of Churches Programme for Theological Education (1984–92). After leaving Hartford Seminary, Zikmund has taught in Japan and been a visiting scholar at the Catholic University of America and Wesley Theological Seminary.

Barbara Brown Zikmund, "Reflections on My Twenty-Five Years in Theological Education," *Theological Education* 36, no. 2 (Spring 2000); Papers, Archives of Women in Theological Scholarship, Burke Library, Union Theological Seminary.

ANNIE RUSSELL